STOP!

This is the back of the book!
Start from the other side.

NATIVE MANGA readers read manga from *right to left*.

1
2
1
3
2
3
5
4
4
6
5
8
7
6

*If you run into our **Native Manga** logo on any of our books... you'll know that this manga is published in it's true original native Japanese right to left reading format, as it was intended. Turn to the other side of the book and start reading from right to left, top to bottom.*

Follow the diagram to see how its done.
Surf's Up!

NATIVE MANGA
READ RIGHT TO LEFT

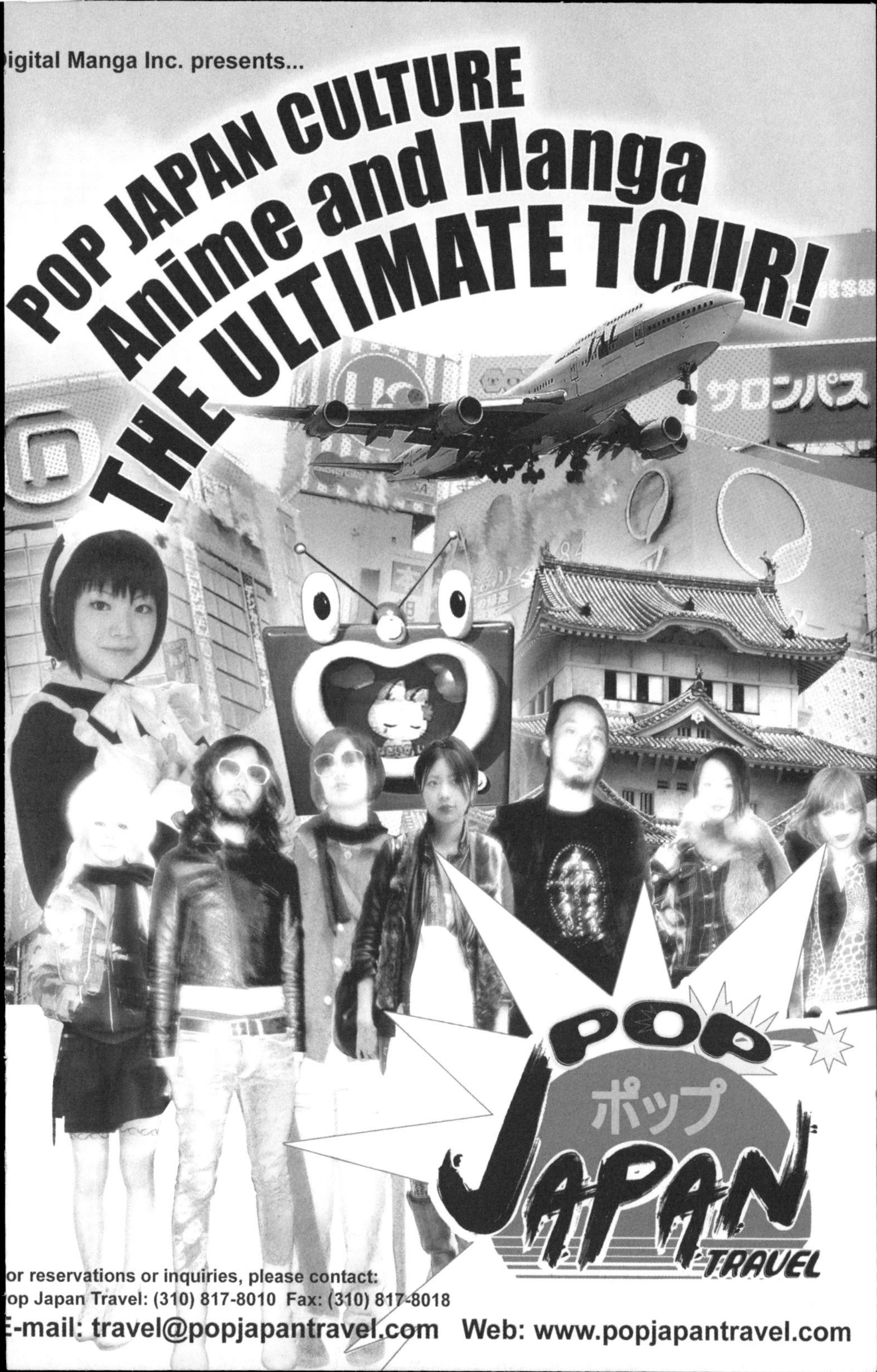
igital Manga Inc. presents...
POP JAPAN CULTURE
Anime and Manga
THE ULTIMATE TOUR!
サロンパス
POP
ポップ
JAPAN
TRAVEL
or reservations or inquiries, please contact:
op Japan Travel: (310) 817-8010 Fax: (310) 817-8018
-mail: travel@popjapantravel.com Web: www.popjapantravel.com

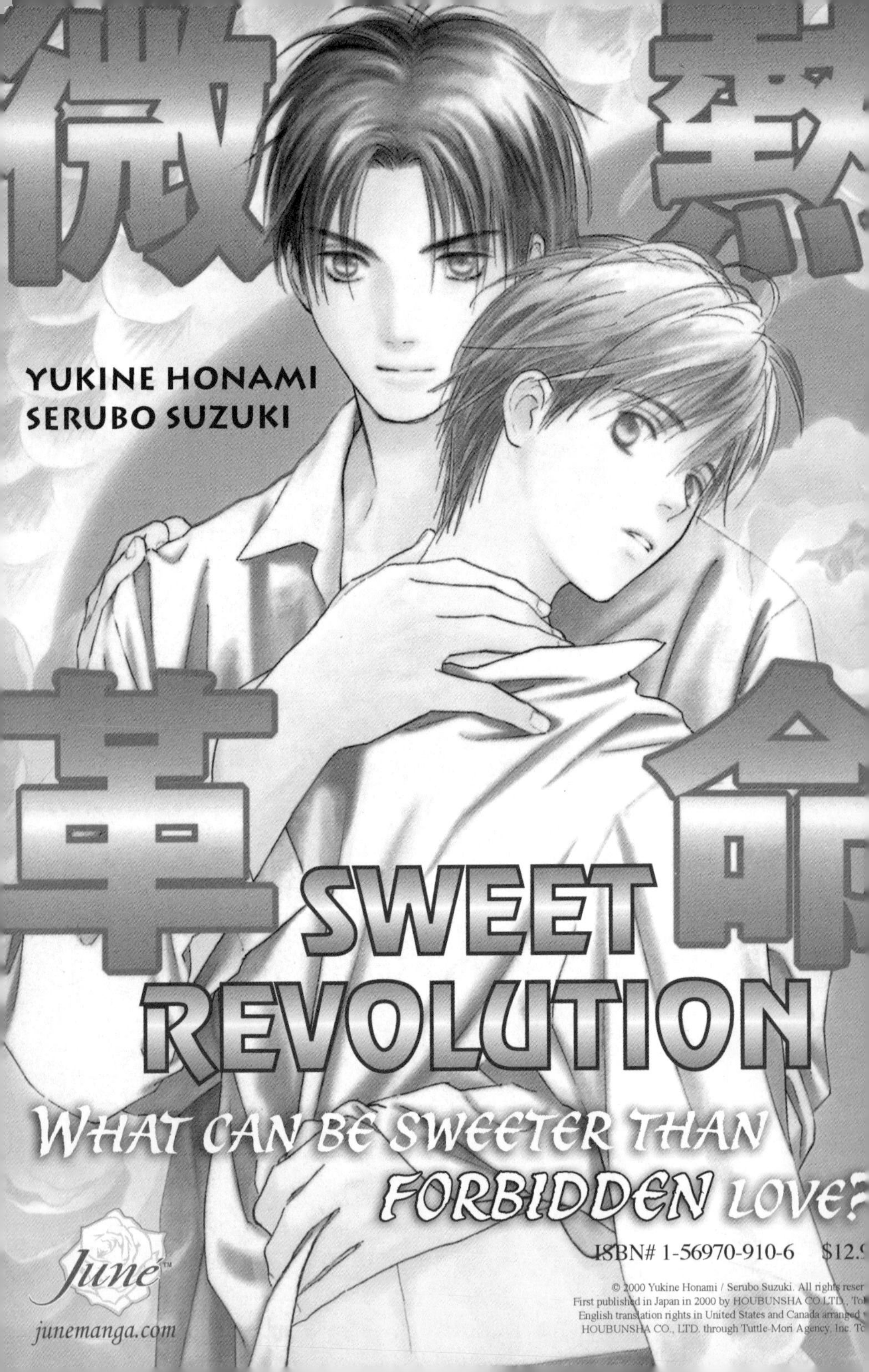

微熱革命
YUKINE HONAMI
SERUBO SUZUKI
SWEET REVOLUTION
WHAT CAN BE SWEETER THAN FORBIDDEN LOVE?
ISBN# 1-56970-910-6 $12.
June™
junemanga.com
© 2000 Yukine Honami / Serubo Suzuki. All rights reser
First published in Japan in 2000 by HOUBUNSHA CO.LTD., To
English translation rights in United States and Canada arranged
HOUBUNSHA CO., LTD. through Tuttle-Mori Agency, Inc. To

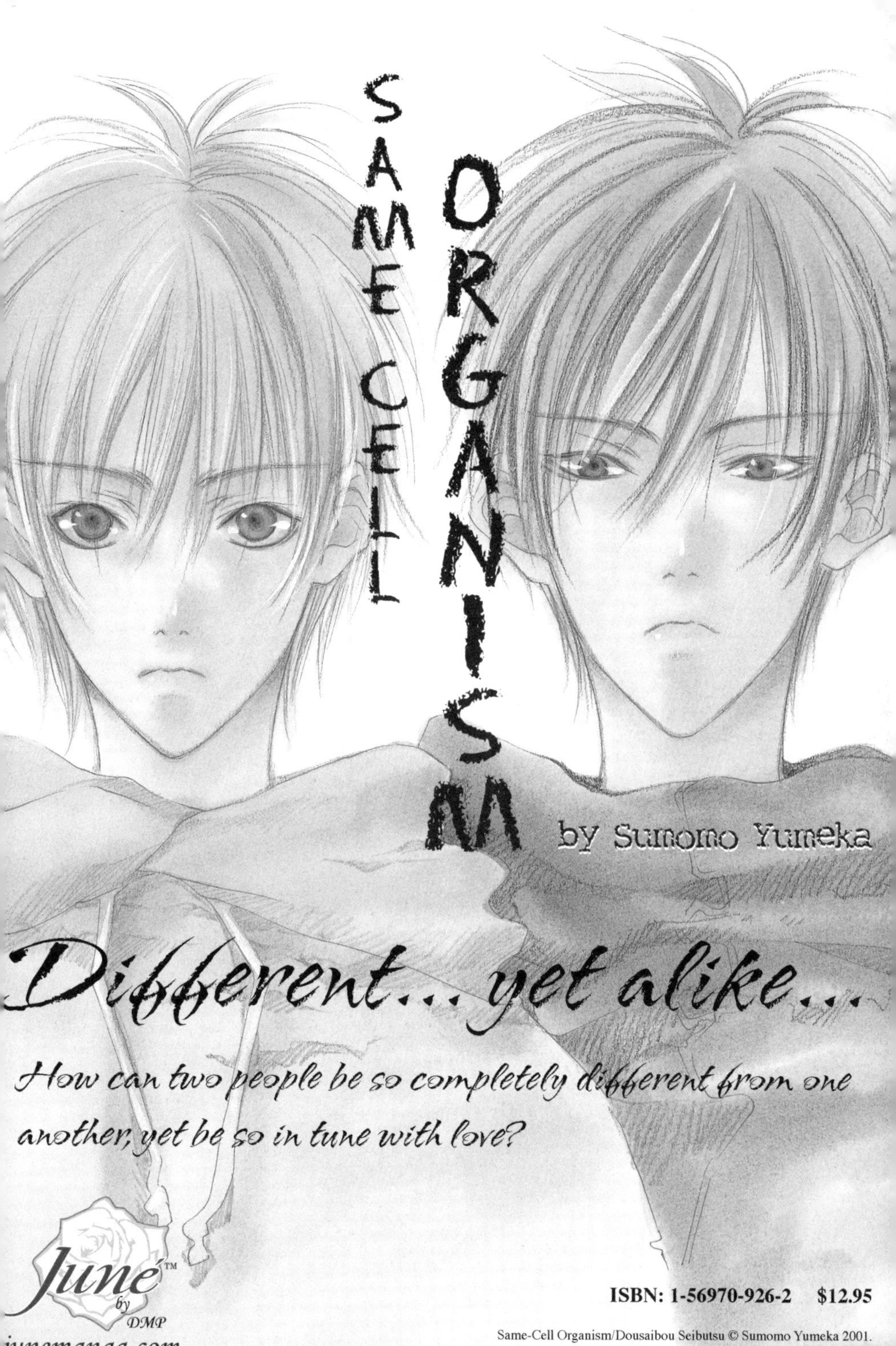
SAME CELL ORGANISM
by Sumomo Yumeka
Different... yet alike...
How can two people be so completely different from one another, yet be so in tune with love?
June™ by DMP
junemanga.com

ISBN: 1-56970-926-2 $12.95

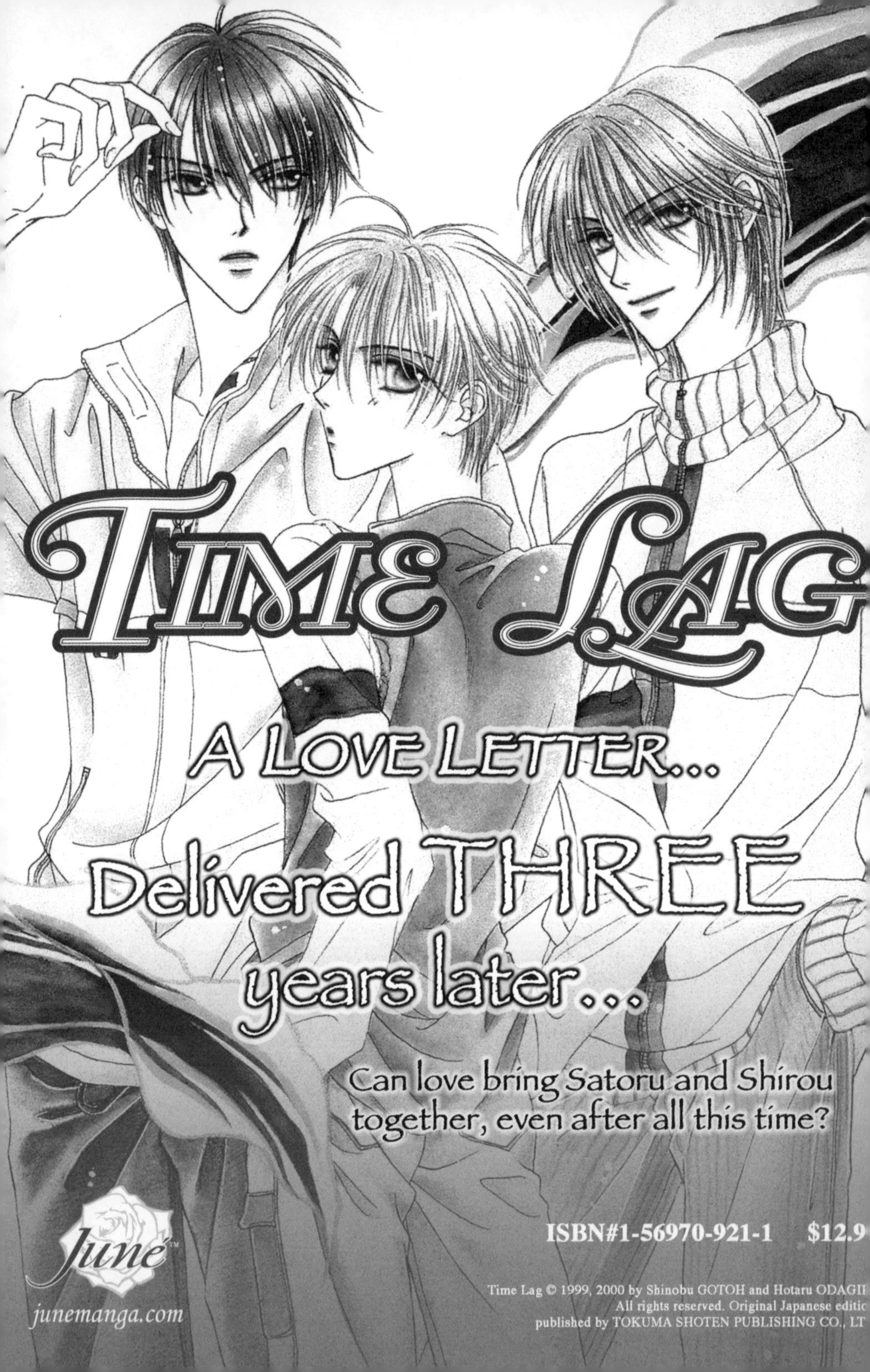
TIME LAG
A LOVE LETTER...
Delivered THREE
years later...
Can love bring Satoru and Shirou
together, even after all this time?
ISBN#1-56970-921-1 $12.9
June™
junemanga.com
Time Lag © 1999, 2000 by Shinobu GOTOH and Hotaru ODAGII
All rights reserved. Original Japanese editic
published by TOKUMA SHOTEN PUBLISHING CO., LT

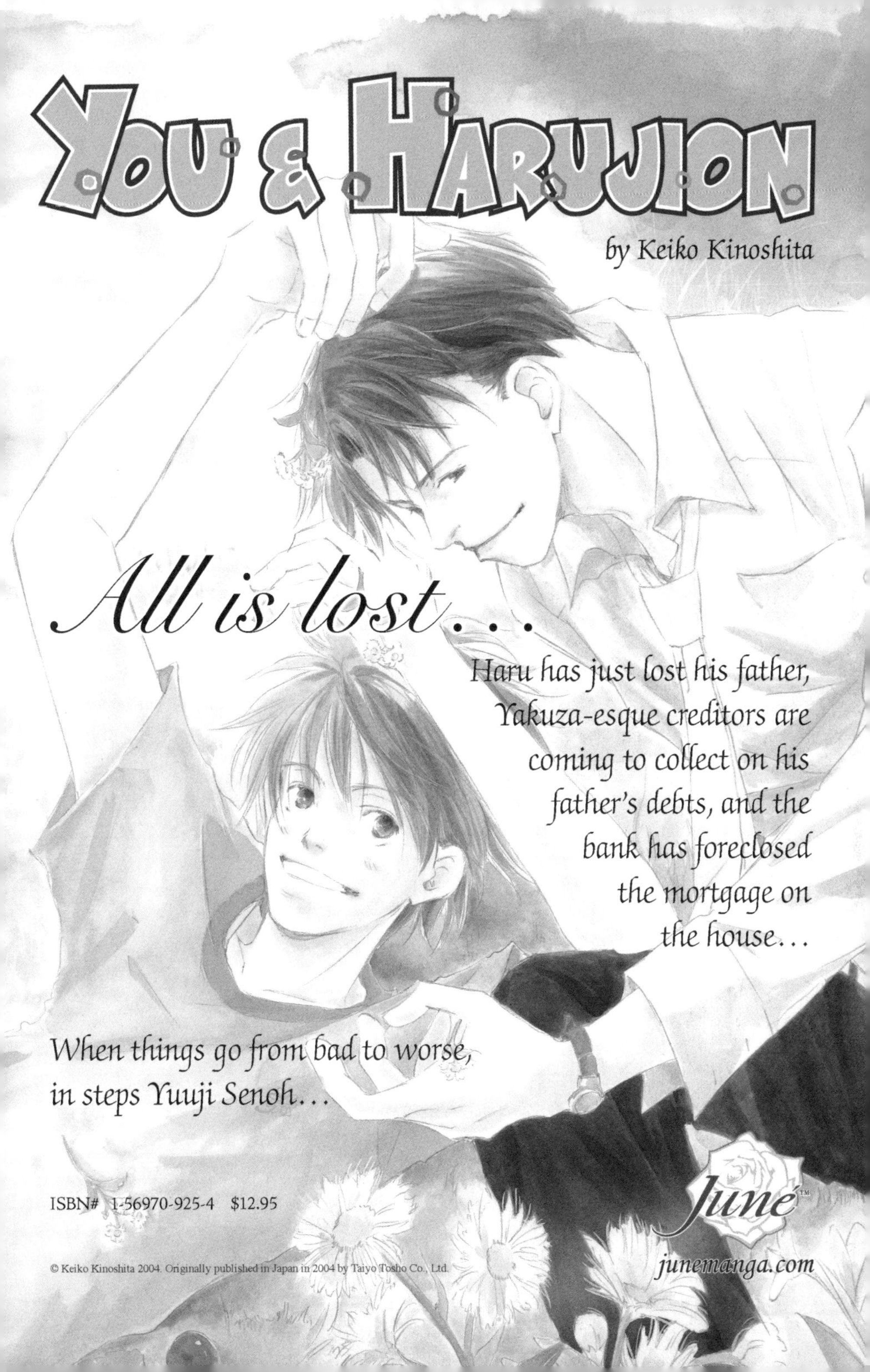
YOU & HARUJION
by Keiko Kinoshita
All is lost . . .
Haru has just lost his father, Yakuza-esque creditors are coming to collect on his father's debts, and the bank has foreclosed the mortgage on the house…
When things go from bad to worse, in steps Yuuji Senoh…
ISBN# 1-56970-925-4 $12.95
June™
junemanga.com
© Keiko Kinoshita 2004. Originally published in Japan in 2004 by Taiyo Tosho Co., Ltd.

Kissing

Written by TEIKO SASAKI
Illustrated by SHOKO TAKAKU

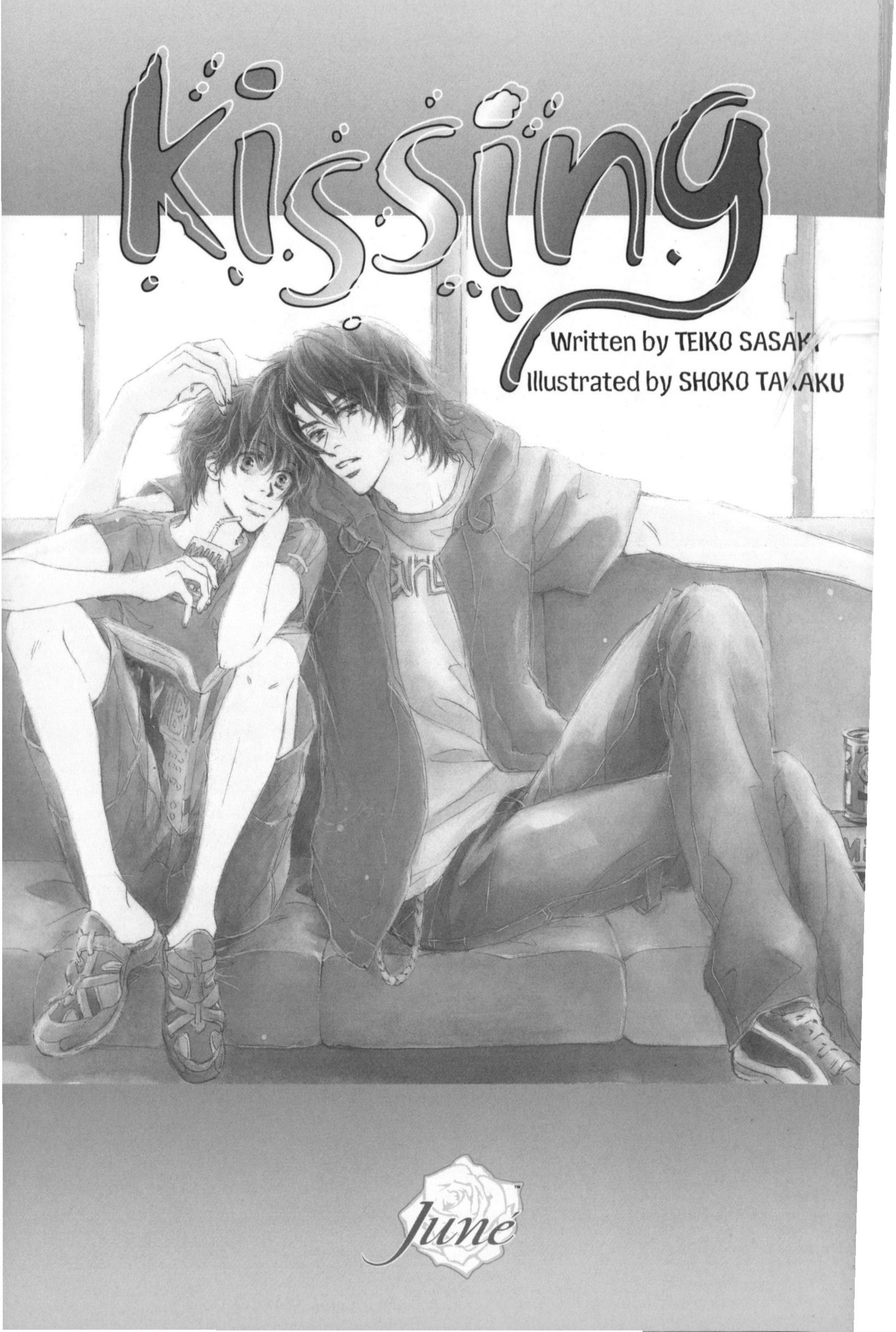

June

Translation	Bruce Dorsey
Lettering	Replibooks
Graphic Design	Wendy Lee / Fred Lui
Editing	Daryl Kuxhouse
Editor in Chief	Fred Lui
Publisher	Hikaru Sasahara

English Edition Published by
DIGITAL MANGA PUBLISHING
A division of DIGITAL MANGA, Inc.
1487 W 178th Street, Suite 300
Gardena, CA 90248

www.dmpbooks.com

First Edition: November 2006
ISBN-10: 1-56970-922-X
ISBN-13: 978-1-56970-922-1

1 3 5 7 9 10 8 6 4 2

Printed in China

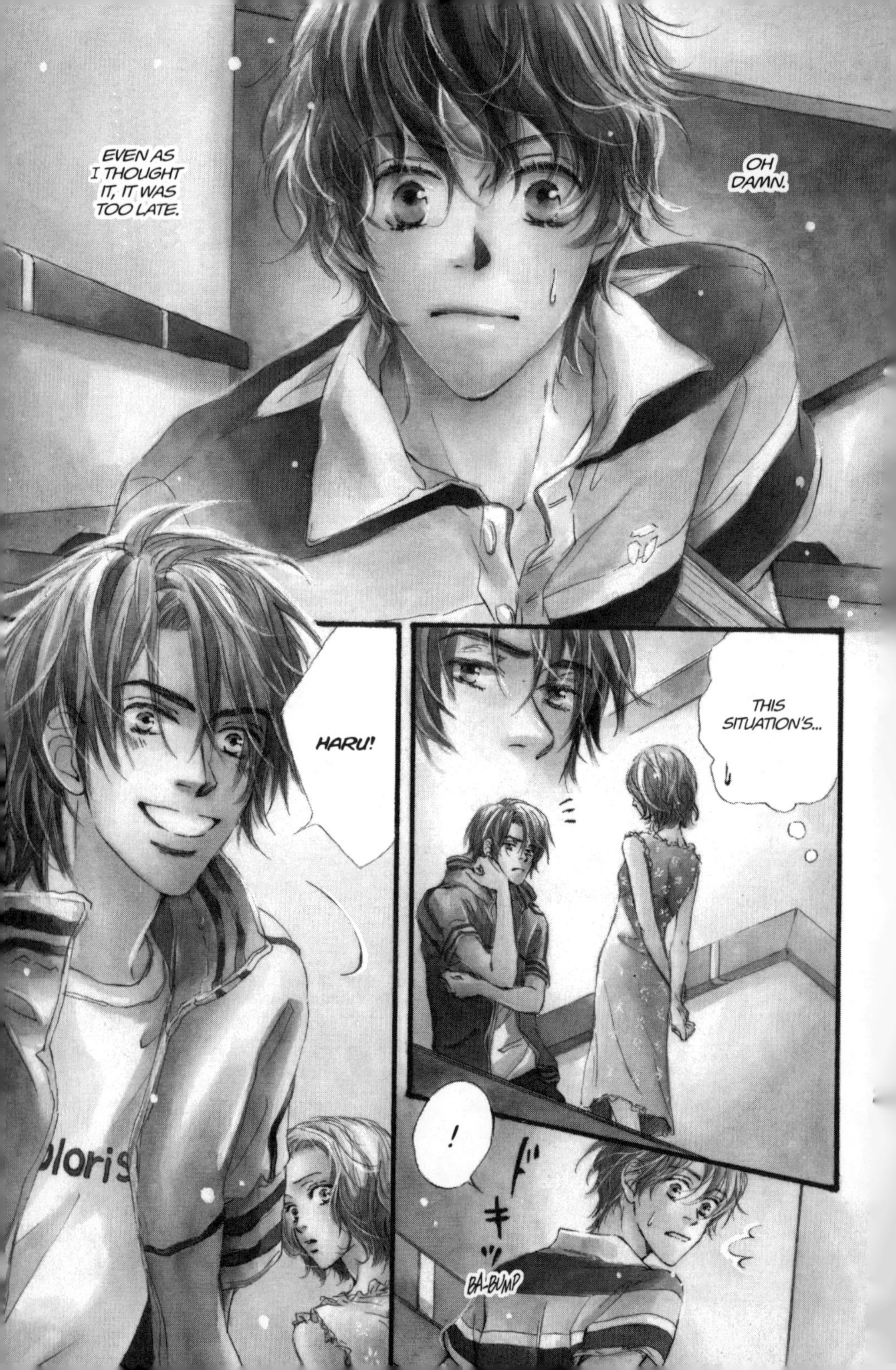
OH DAMN.
EVEN AS I THOUGHT IT, IT WAS TOO LATE.
THIS SITUATION'S...
!
ドキッ
BA-BUMP
HARU!

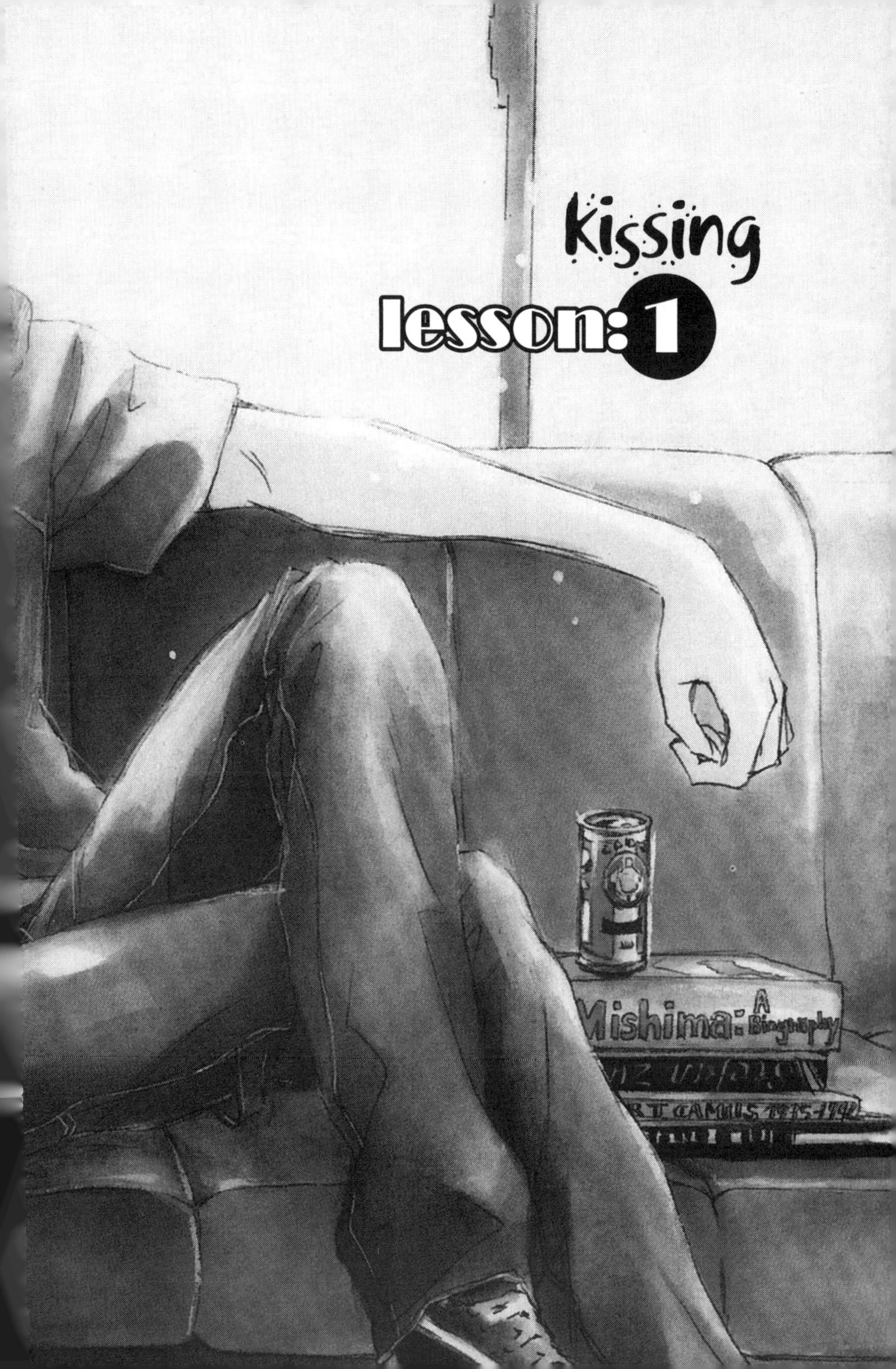
Kissing
lesson: 1
Mishima: A Biography

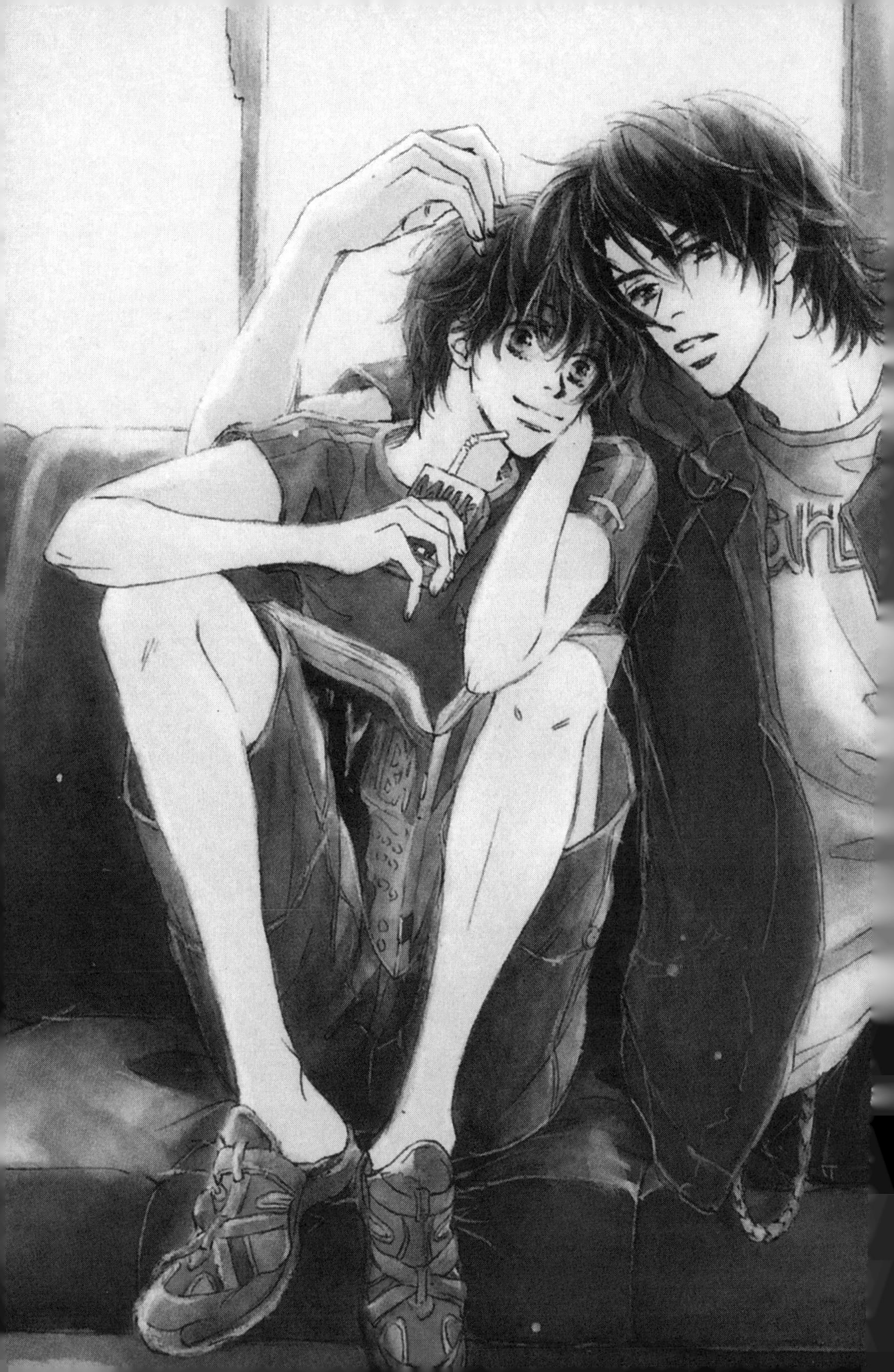

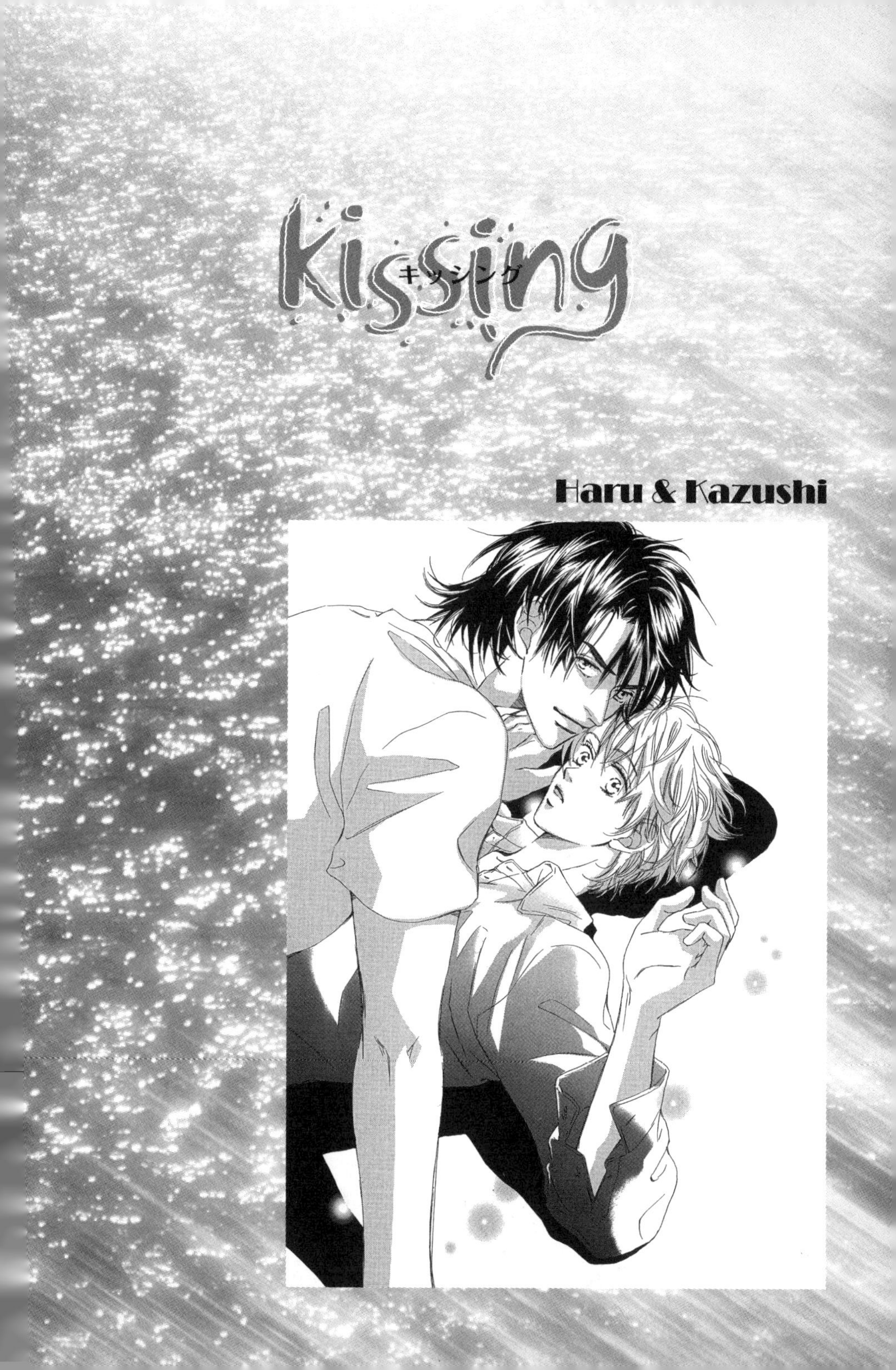
kissing
キッシング
Haru & Kazushi

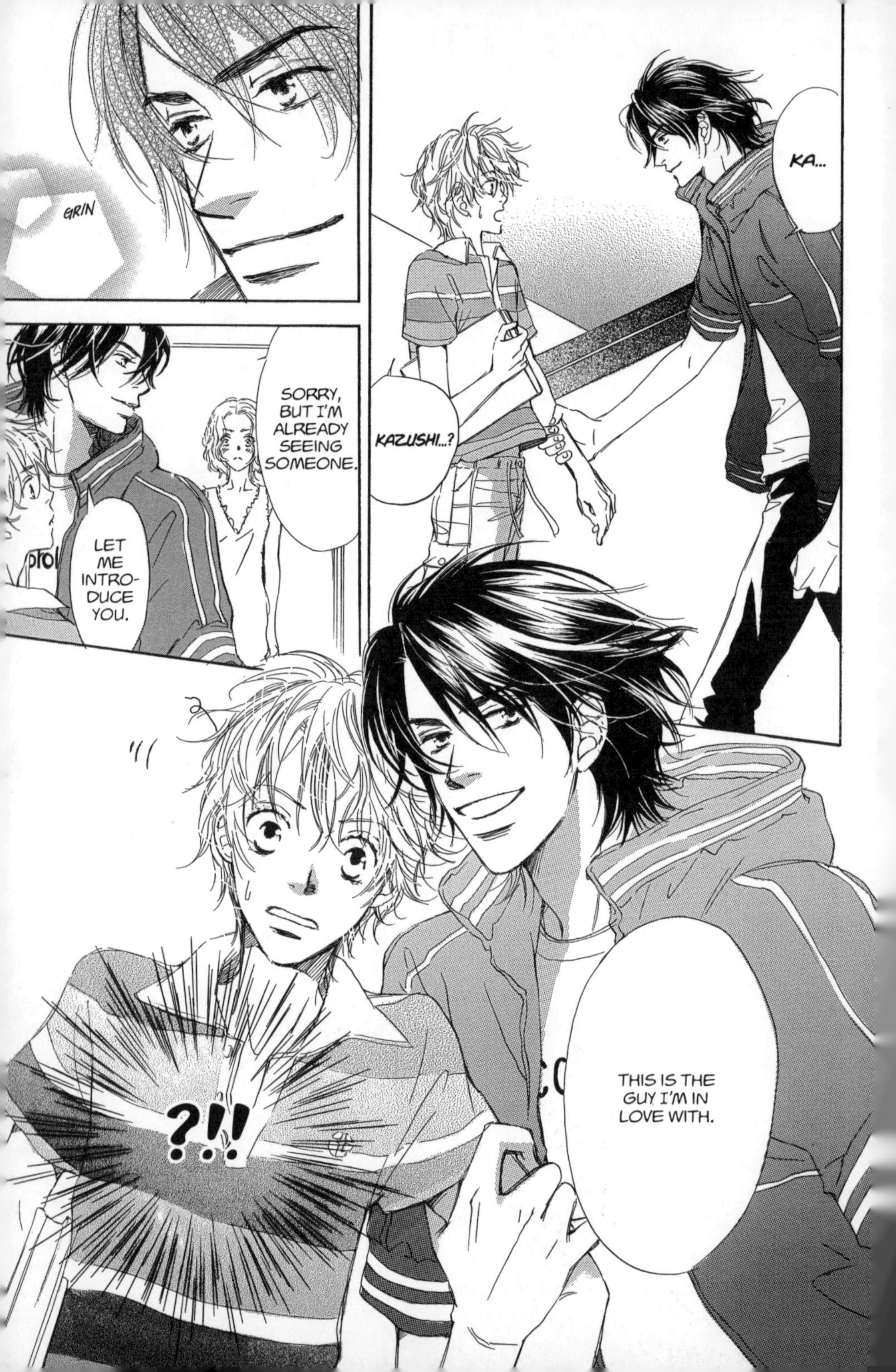
KA...
KAZUSHI...?
GRIN
SORRY, BUT I'M ALREADY SEEING SOMEONE.
LET ME INTRODUCE YOU.
THIS IS THE GUY I'M IN LOVE WITH.
?!!

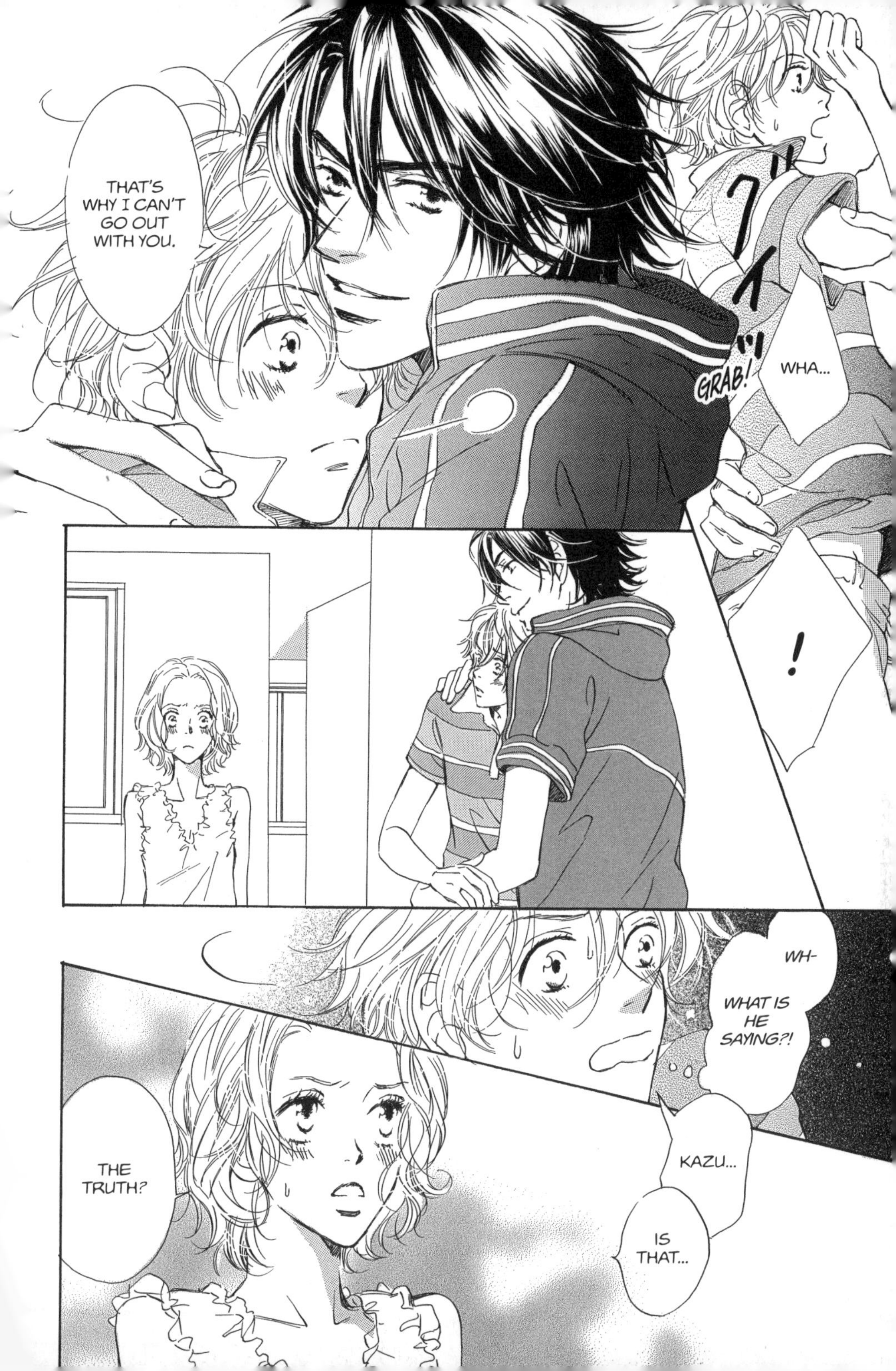
GRAB!
WHA...
THAT'S WHY I CAN'T GO OUT WITH YOU.
!
WH-
WHAT IS HE SAYING?!
KAZU...
IS THAT...
THE TRUTH?

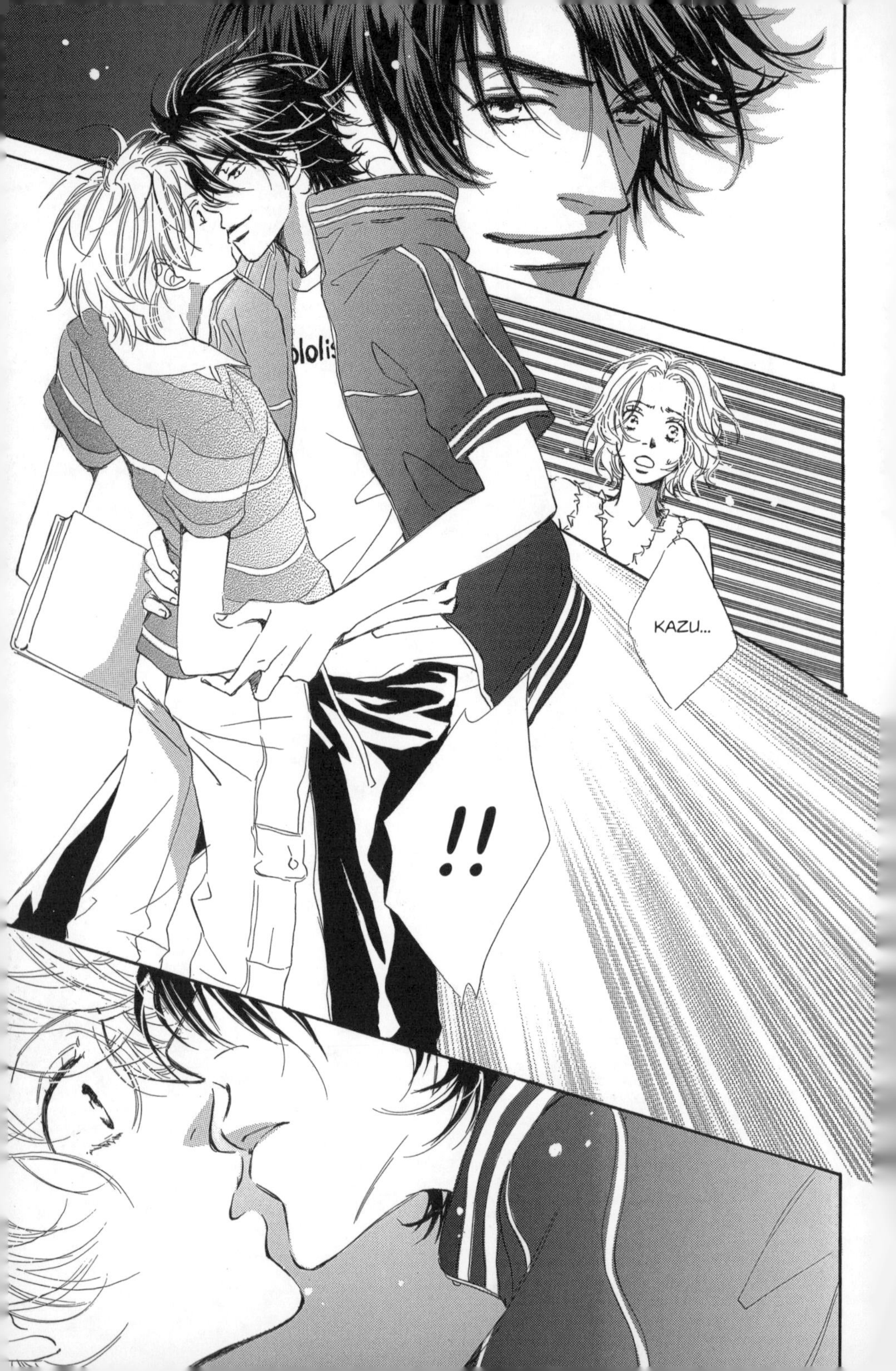
Kazu...
!!

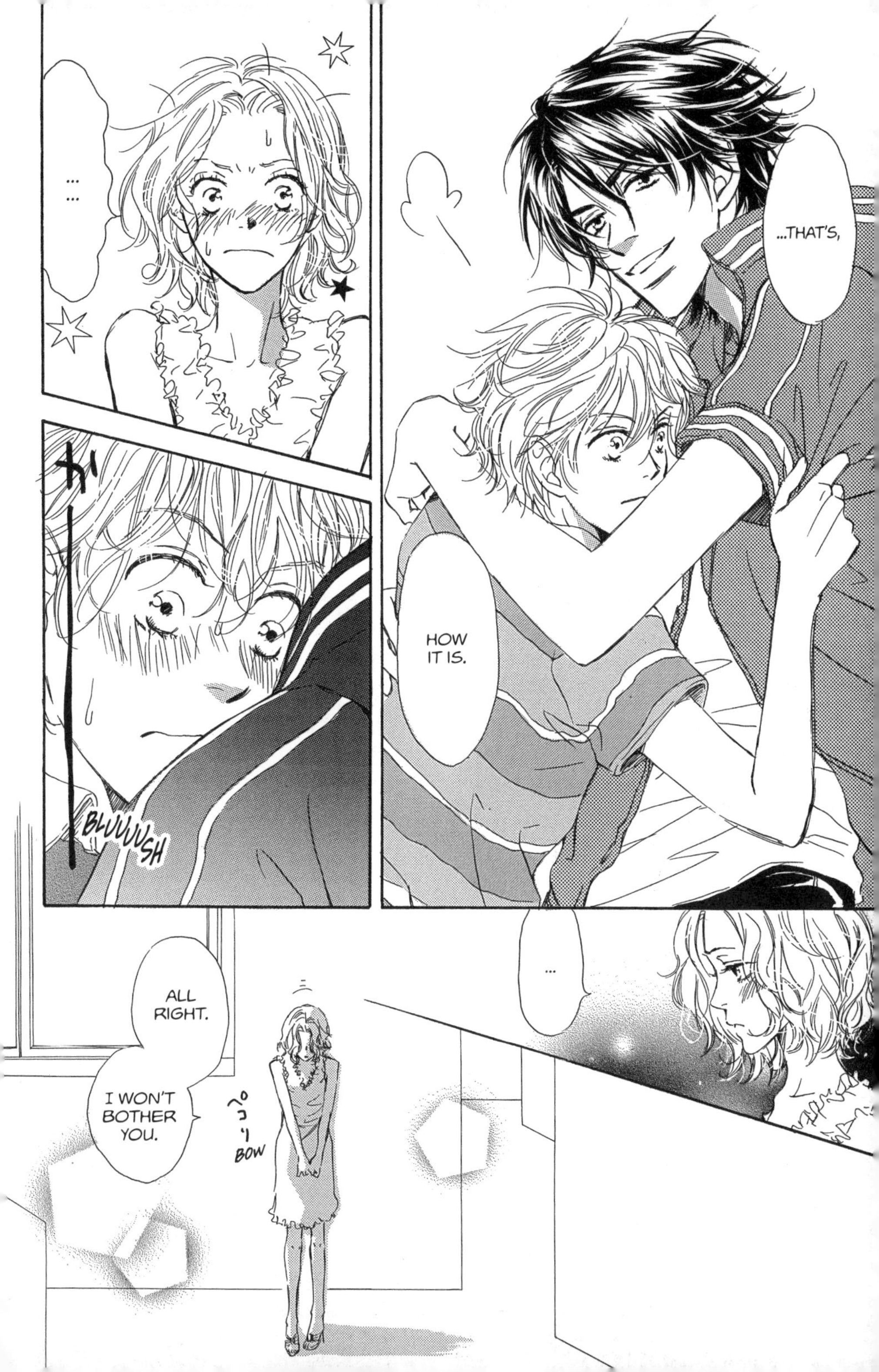

...THAT'S,
HOW IT IS.
... ...
BLUUUUSH
...
ALL RIGHT.
I WON'T BOTHER YOU.
BOW

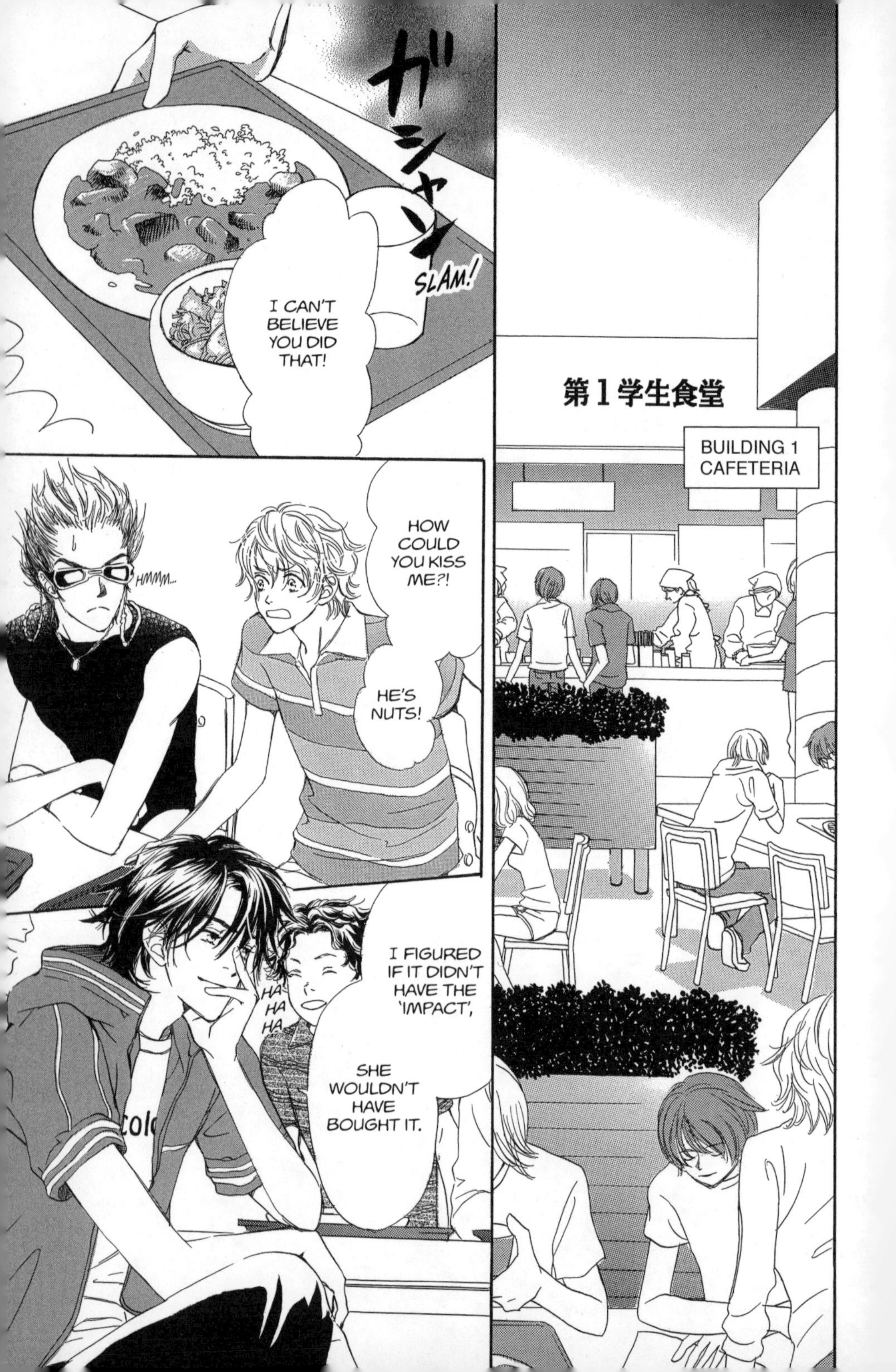
第1学生食堂
BUILDING 1 CAFETERIA
ガシャン
SLAM!
I CAN'T BELIEVE YOU DID THAT!
HMMM...
HOW COULD YOU KISS ME?!
HE'S NUTS!
HA HA HA
I FIGURED IF IT DIDN'T HAVE THE 'IMPACT',
SHE WOULDN'T HAVE BOUGHT IT.

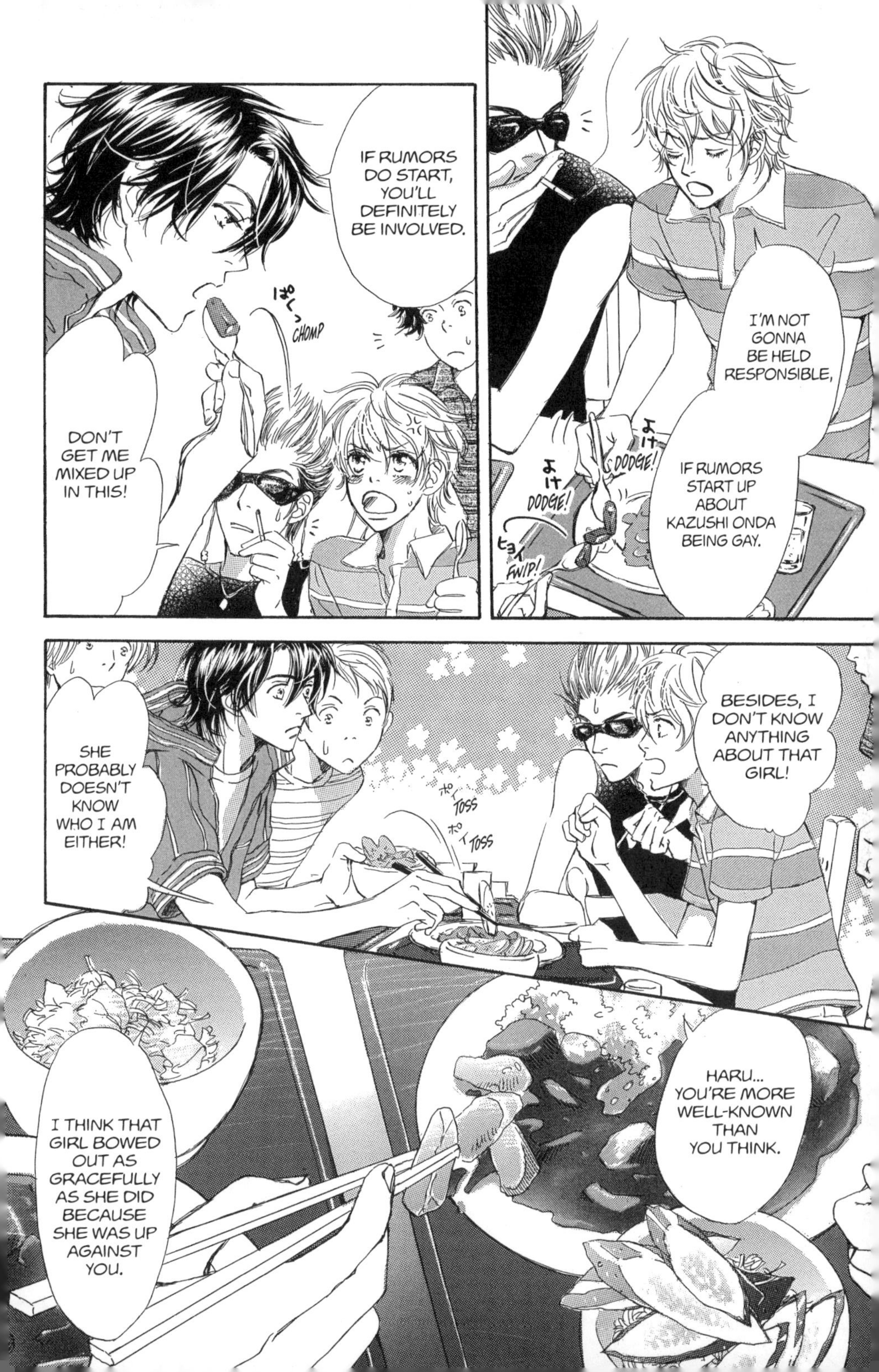
I'M NOT GONNA BE HELD RESPONSIBLE,
IF RUMORS START UP ABOUT KAZUSHI ONDA BEING GAY.
よけ DODGE!
よけ DODGE!
ヒョイ FWIP!
IF RUMORS DO START, YOU'LL DEFINITELY BE INVOLVED.
ぱくっ CHOMP
DON'T GET ME MIXED UP IN THIS!
BESIDES, I DON'T KNOW ANYTHING ABOUT THAT GIRL!
ポイ TOSS
ポイ TOSS
SHE PROBABLY DOESN'T KNOW WHO I AM EITHER!
HARU... YOU'RE MORE WELL-KNOWN THAN YOU THINK.
I THINK THAT GIRL BOWED OUT AS GRACEFULLY AS SHE DID BECAUSE SHE WAS UP AGAINST YOU.

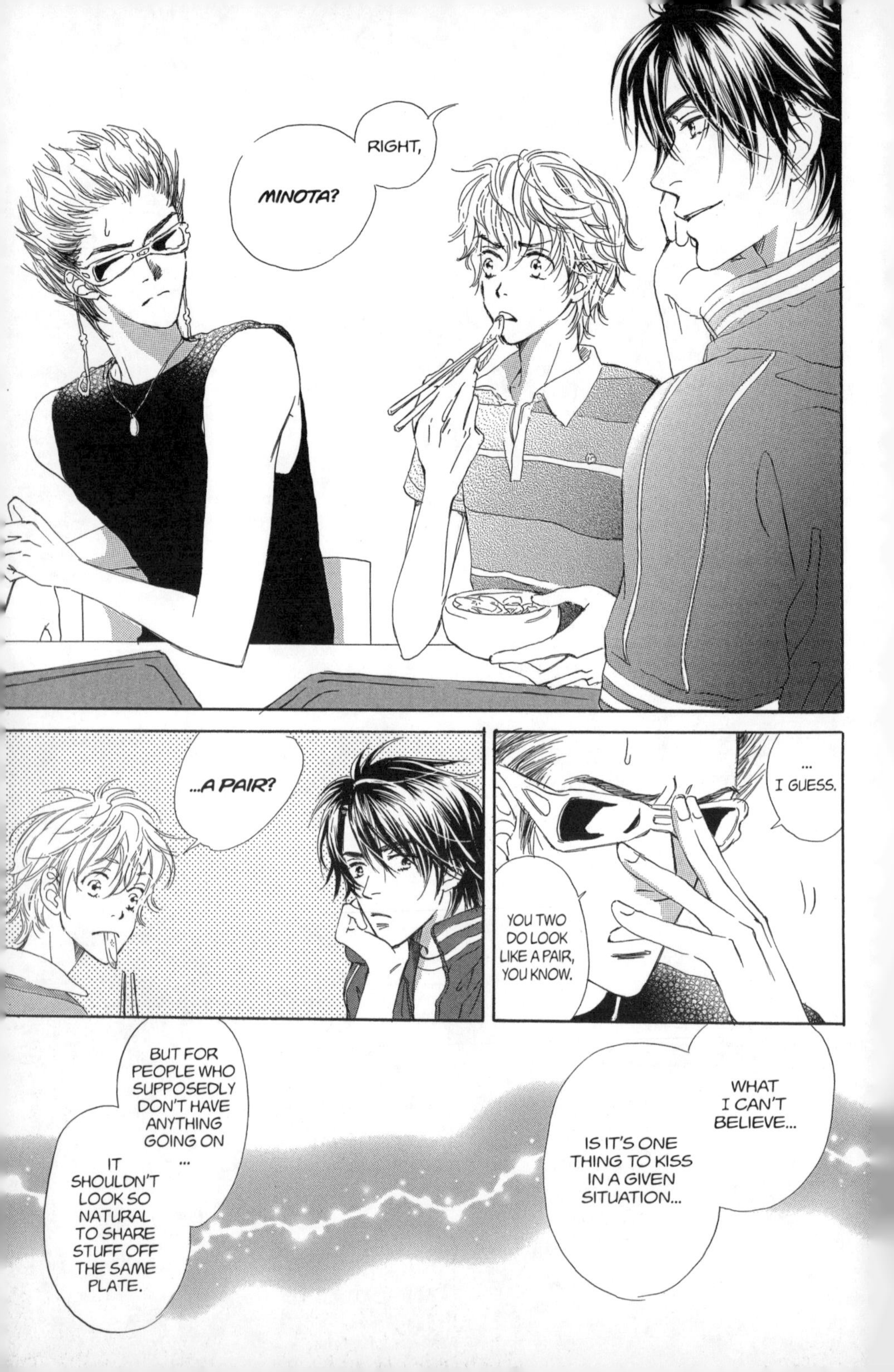
RIGHT, MINOTA?
... I GUESS.
YOU TWO DO LOOK LIKE A PAIR, YOU KNOW.
...A PAIR?
WHAT I CAN'T BELIEVE...
IS IT'S ONE THING TO KISS IN A GIVEN SITUATION...
BUT FOR PEOPLE WHO SUPPOSEDLY DON'T HAVE ANYTHING GOING ON ...
IT SHOULDN'T LOOK SO NATURAL TO SHARE STUFF OFF THE SAME PLATE.

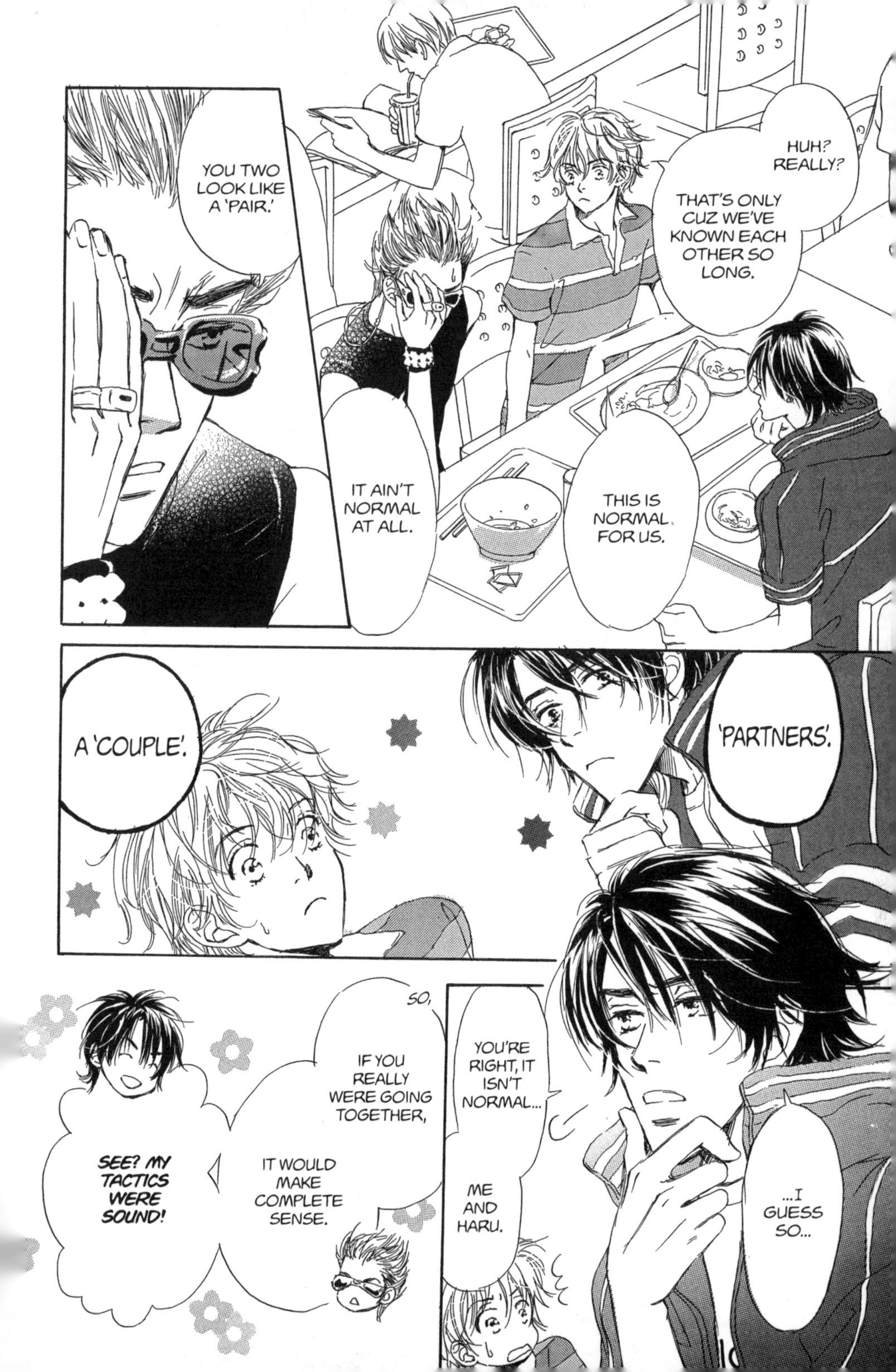
HUH? REALLY?
THAT'S ONLY CUZ WE'VE KNOWN EACH OTHER SO LONG.
THIS IS NORMAL FOR US.
IT AIN'T NORMAL AT ALL.
YOU TWO LOOK LIKE A 'PAIR.'
'PARTNERS'.
A 'COUPLE'.
...I GUESS SO...
YOU'RE RIGHT, IT ISN'T NORMAL...
ME AND HARU.
SO,
IF YOU REALLY WERE GOING TOGETHER,
IT WOULD MAKE COMPLETE SENSE.
SEE? MY TACTICS WERE SOUND!

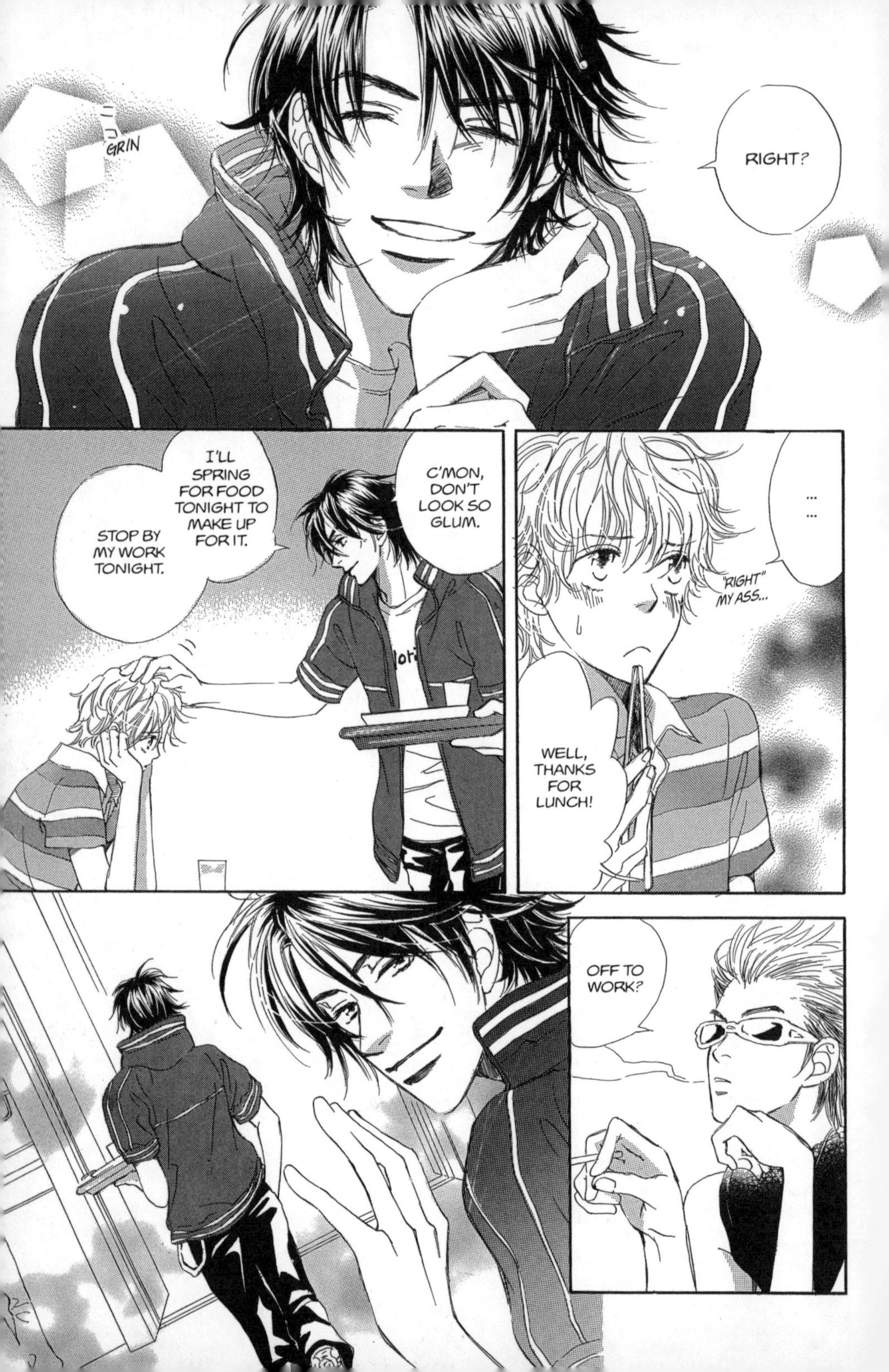
RIGHT?
GRIN
……
"RIGHT" MY ASS...
WELL, THANKS FOR LUNCH!
C'MON, DON'T LOOK SO GLUM.
I'LL SPRING FOR FOOD TONIGHT TO MAKE UP FOR IT.
STOP BY MY WORK TONIGHT.
OFF TO WORK?

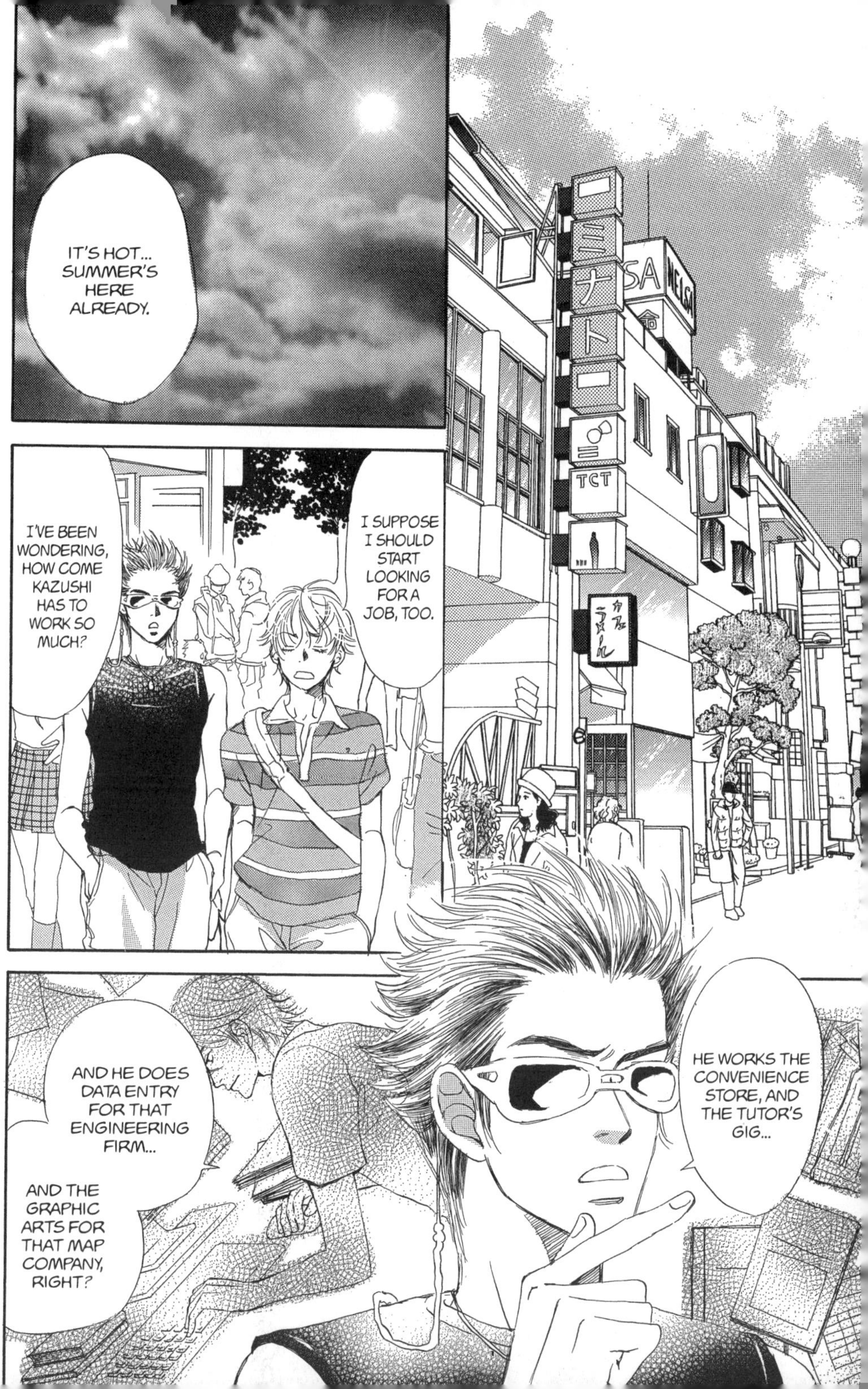
IT'S HOT... SUMMER'S HERE ALREADY.
I SUPPOSE I SHOULD START LOOKING FOR A JOB, TOO.
I'VE BEEN WONDERING, HOW COME KAZUSHI HAS TO WORK SO MUCH?
HE WORKS THE CONVENIENCE STORE, AND THE TUTOR'S GIG...
AND HE DOES DATA ENTRY FOR THAT ENGINEERING FIRM...
AND THE GRAPHIC ARTS FOR THAT MAP COMPANY, RIGHT?

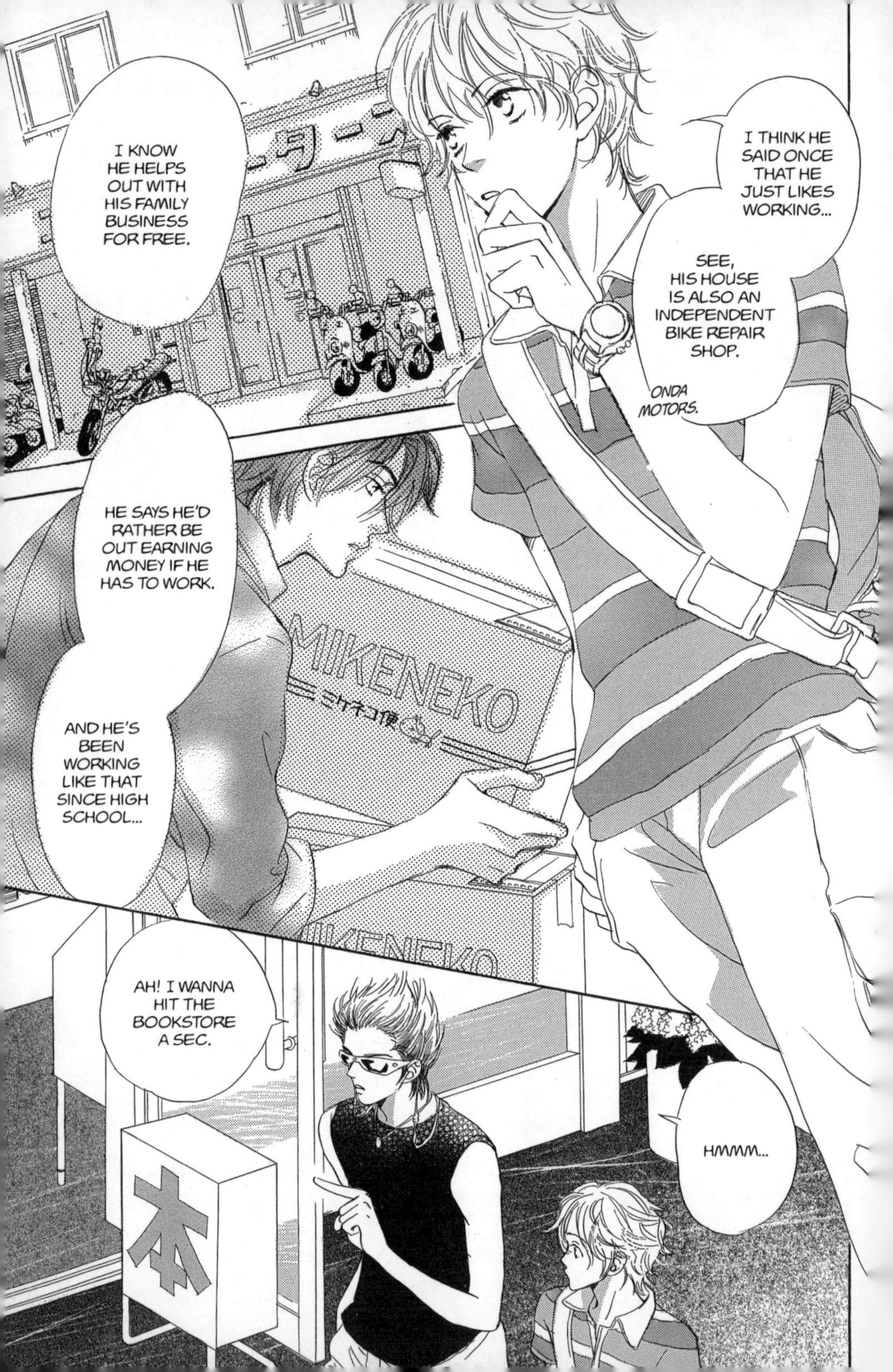
I THINK HE SAID ONCE THAT HE JUST LIKES WORKING...
SEE, HIS HOUSE IS ALSO AN INDEPENDENT BIKE REPAIR SHOP.
ONDA MOTORS.
I KNOW HE HELPS OUT WITH HIS FAMILY BUSINESS FOR FREE.
HE SAYS HE'D RATHER BE OUT EARNING MONEY IF HE HAS TO WORK.
MIKENEKO
ミケネコ便
AND HE'S BEEN WORKING LIKE THAT SINCE HIGH SCHOOL...
HMMM...
AH! I WANNA HIT THE BOOKSTORE A SEC.
本

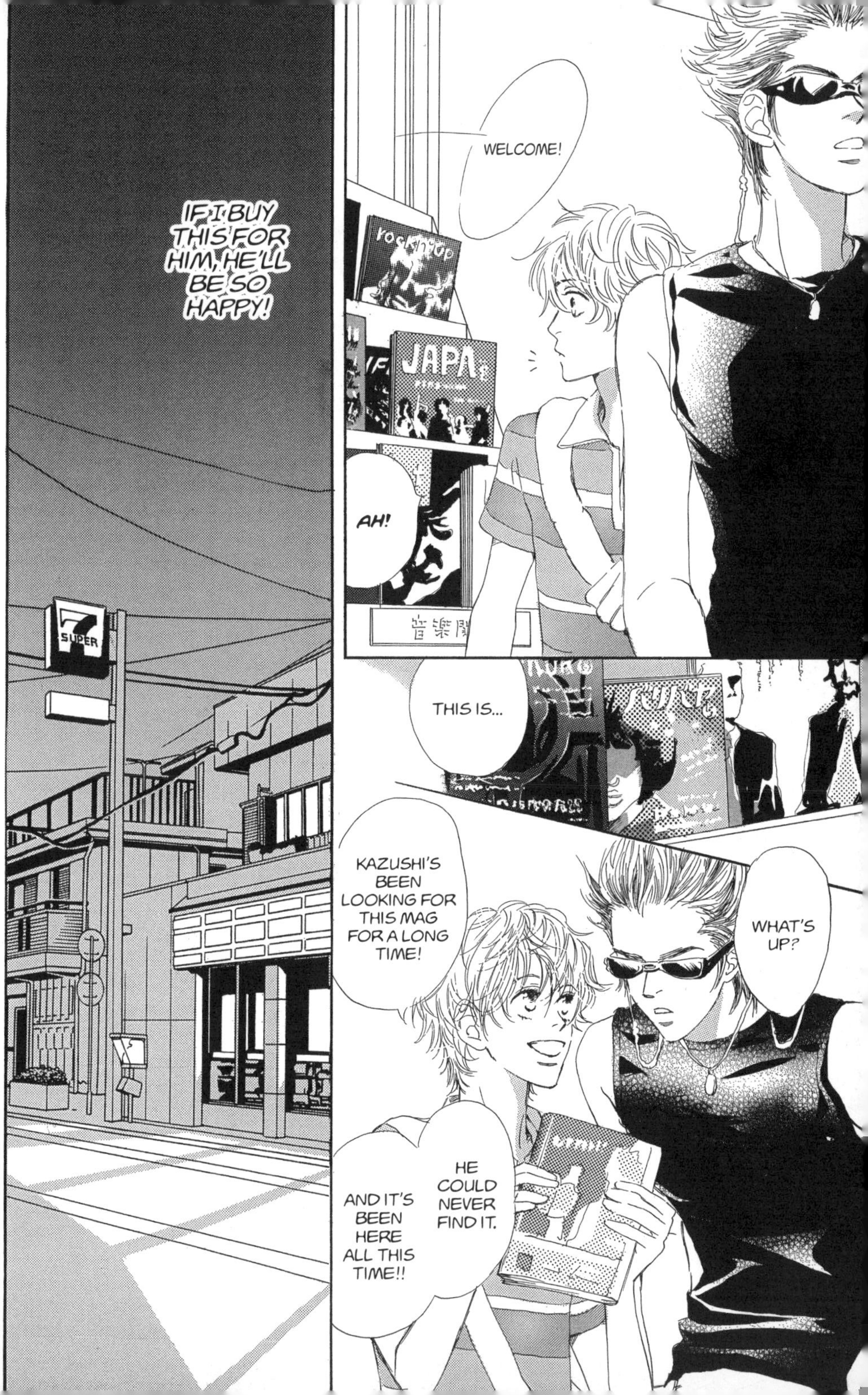
WELCOME!
AH!
THIS IS...
WHAT'S UP?
KAZUSHI'S BEEN LOOKING FOR THIS MAG FOR A LONG TIME!
HE COULD NEVER FIND IT.
AND IT'S BEEN HERE ALL THIS TIME!!
IF I BUY THIS FOR HIM, HE'LL BE SO HAPPY!

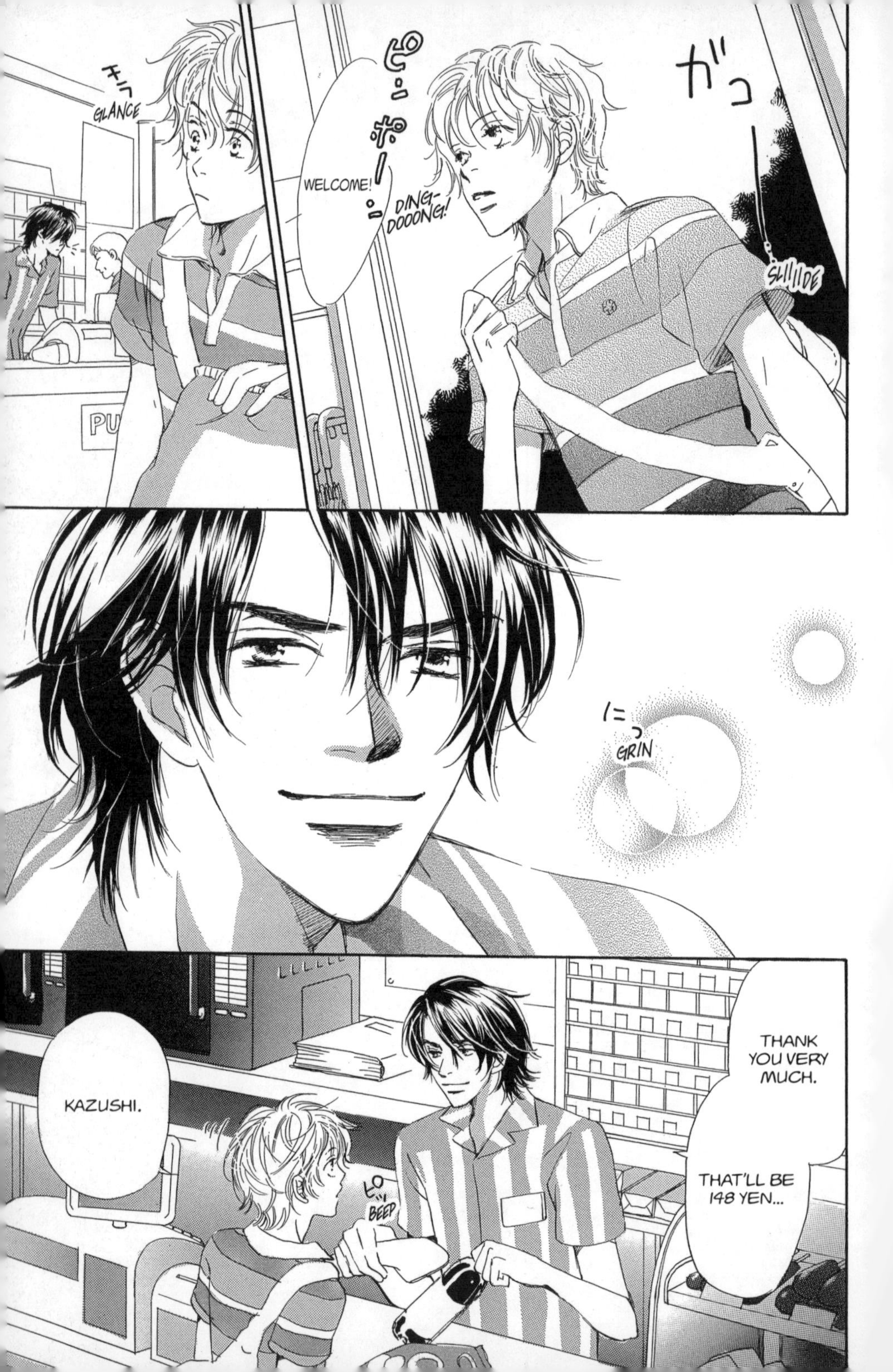
SLIIIDE
DING-DOOOONG!
WELCOME!
GLANCE
PU
にっ
GRIN
THANK YOU VERY MUCH.
THAT'LL BE 148 YEN...
ピッ
BEEP
KAZUSHI.

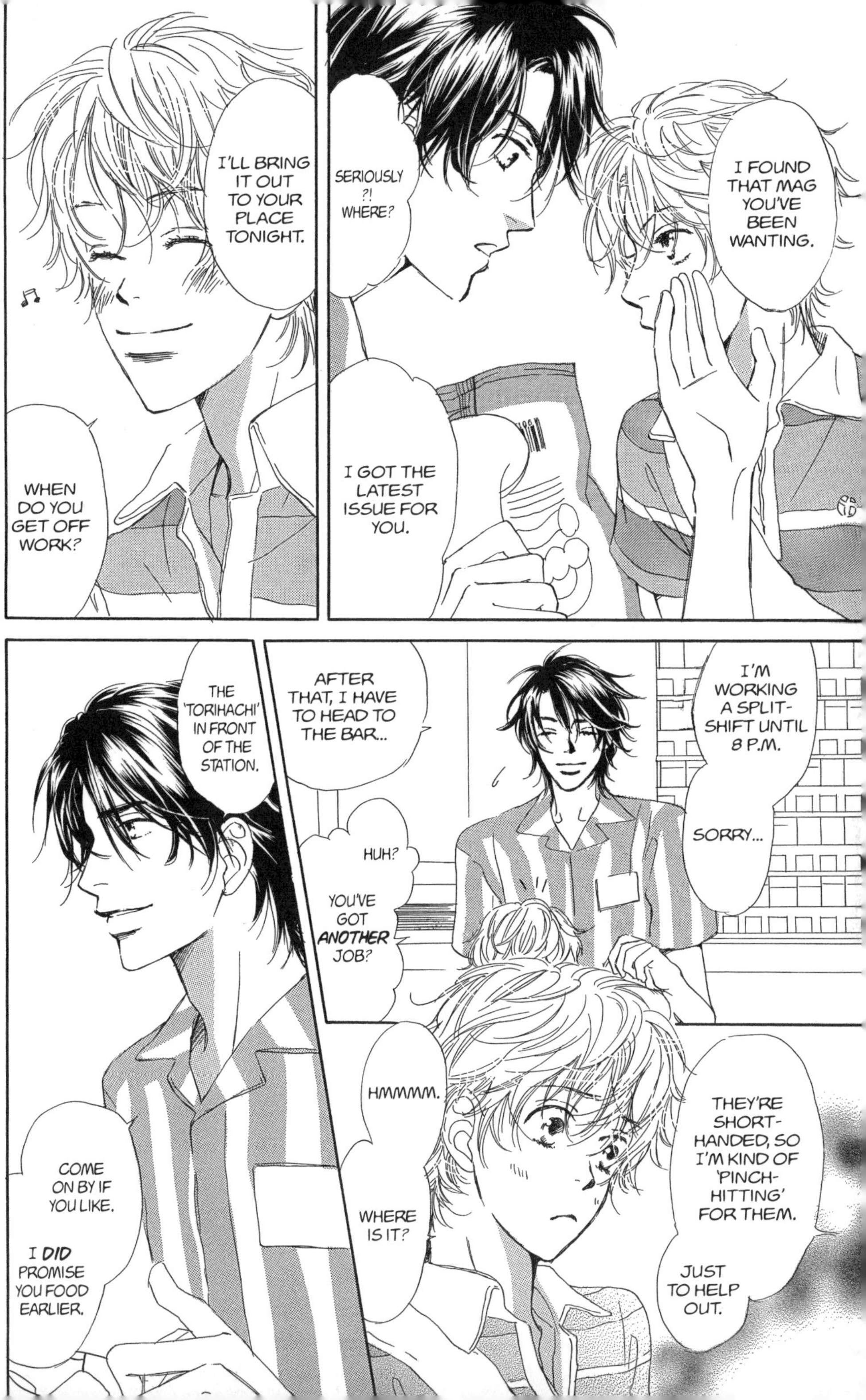
I FOUND THAT MAG YOU'VE BEEN WANTING.
SERIOUSLY?! WHERE?
I GOT THE LATEST ISSUE FOR YOU.
I'LL BRING IT OUT TO YOUR PLACE TONIGHT.
WHEN DO YOU GET OFF WORK?
I'M WORKING A SPLIT-SHIFT UNTIL 8 P.M.
SORRY...
AFTER THAT, I HAVE TO HEAD TO THE BAR...
HUH?
YOU'VE GOT **ANOTHER** JOB?
THEY'RE SHORT-HANDED, SO I'M KIND OF 'PINCH-HITTING' FOR THEM.
JUST TO HELP OUT.
HMMMM.
WHERE IS IT?
THE 'TORIHACHI' IN FRONT OF THE STATION.
COME ON BY IF YOU LIKE.
I **DID** PROMISE YOU FOOD EARLIER.

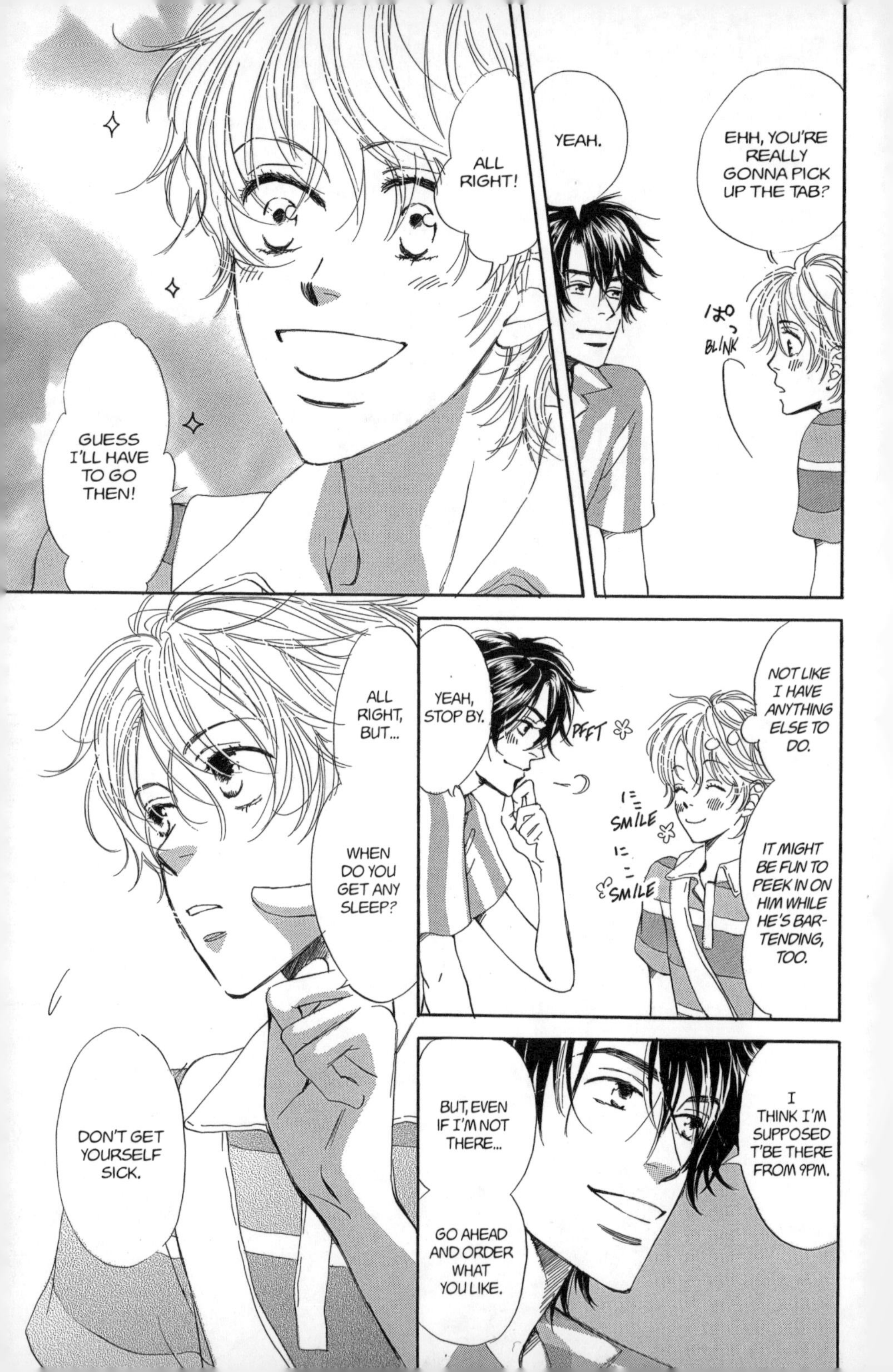
EHH, YOU'RE REALLY GONNA PICK UP THE TAB?
ぱっ
BLINK
YEAH.
ALL RIGHT!
GUESS I'LL HAVE TO GO THEN!
NOT LIKE I HAVE ANYTHING ELSE TO DO.
IT MIGHT BE FUN TO PEEK IN ON HIM WHILE HE'S BAR-TENDING, TOO.
にこ
SMILE
にこ
SMILE
PFFT
YEAH, STOP BY.
I THINK I'M SUPPOSED T'BE THERE FROM 9PM.
BUT, EVEN IF I'M NOT THERE...
GO AHEAD AND ORDER WHAT YOU LIKE.
ALL RIGHT, BUT...
WHEN DO YOU GET ANY SLEEP?
DON'T GET YOURSELF SICK.

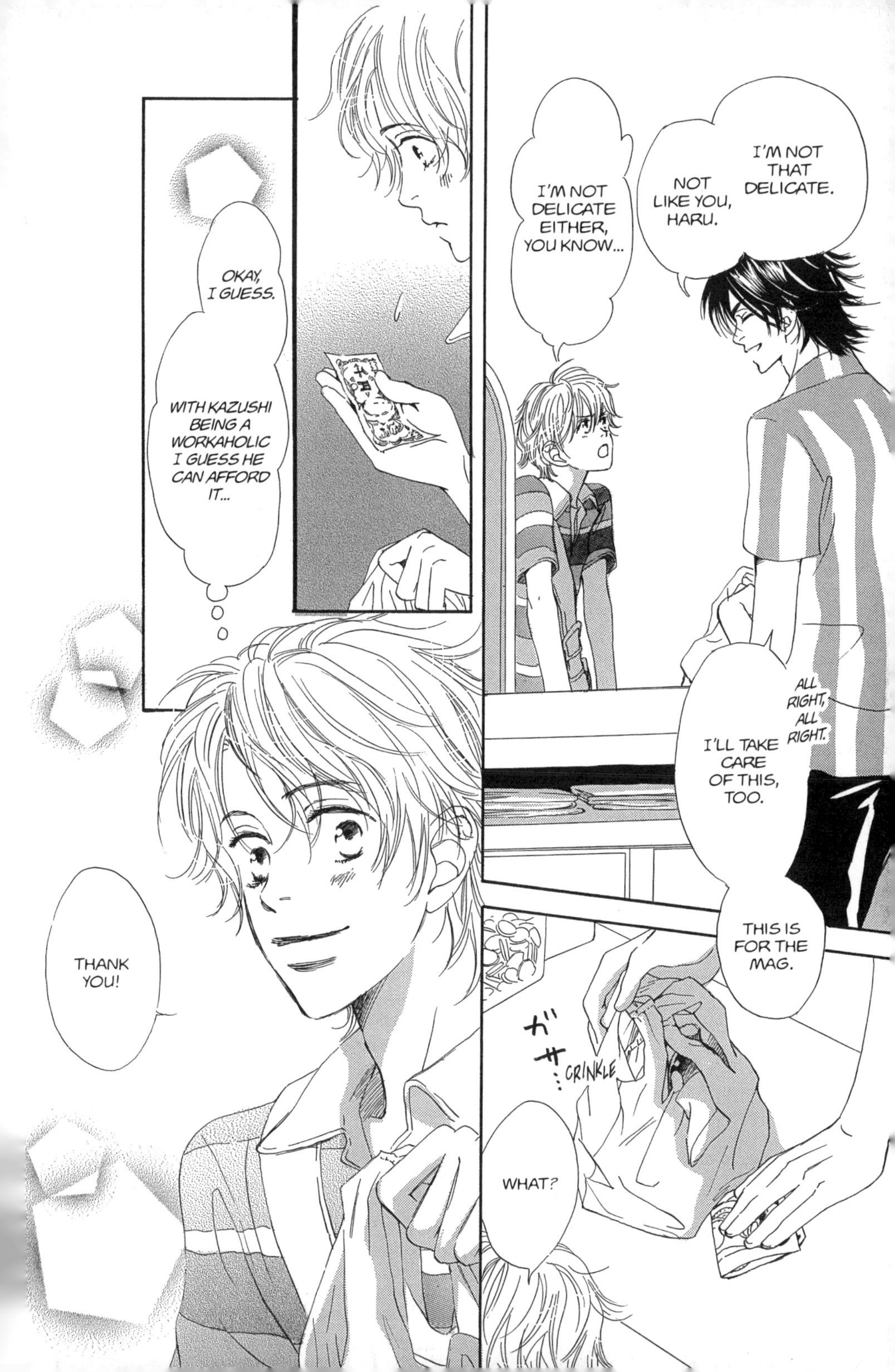
I'M NOT THAT DELICATE.
NOT LIKE YOU, HARU.
I'M NOT DELICATE EITHER, YOU KNOW...
ALL RIGHT, ALL RIGHT.
I'LL TAKE CARE OF THIS, TOO.
THIS IS FOR THE MAG.
ガサ... CRINKLE
WHAT?
OKAY, I GUESS.
WITH KAZUSHI BEING A WORKAHOLIC I GUESS HE CAN AFFORD IT...
THANK YOU!

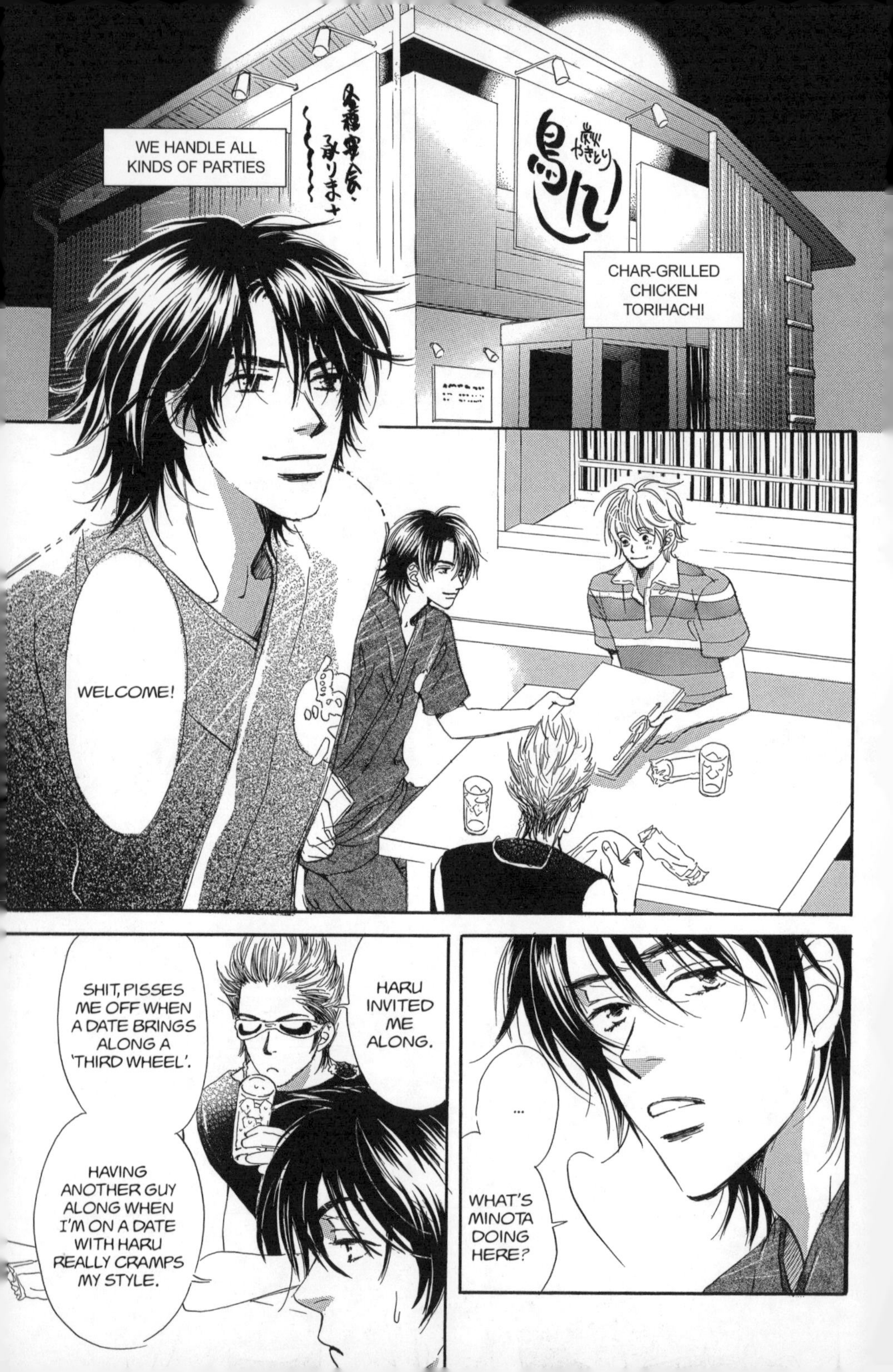
CHAR-GRILLED CHICKEN TORIHACHI
WE HANDLE ALL KINDS OF PARTIES
WELCOME!
...
WHAT'S MINOTA DOING HERE?
HARU INVITED ME ALONG.
SHIT, PISSES ME OFF WHEN A DATE BRINGS ALONG A 'THIRD WHEEL'.
HAVING ANOTHER GUY ALONG WHEN I'M ON A DATE WITH HARU REALLY CRAMPS MY STYLE.

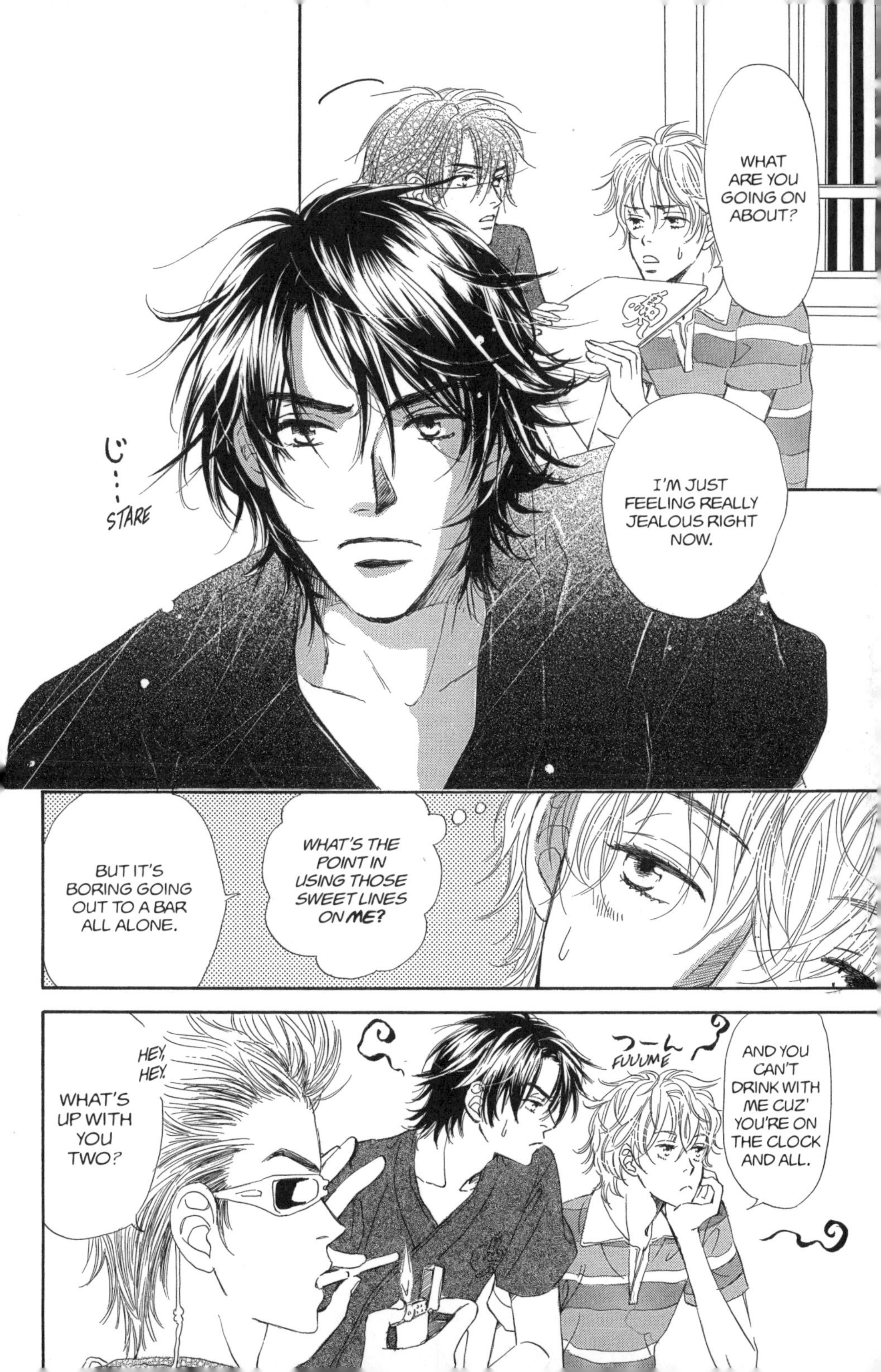
WHAT ARE YOU GOING ON ABOUT?
I'M JUST FEELING REALLY JEALOUS RIGHT NOW.
じ・・・
STARE
WHAT'S THE POINT IN USING THOSE SWEET LINES ON ME?
BUT IT'S BORING GOING OUT TO A BAR ALL ALONE.
AND YOU CAN'T DRINK WITH ME CUZ' YOU'RE ON THE CLOCK AND ALL.
つーん
FUUUME
HEY, HEY.
WHAT'S UP WITH YOU TWO?

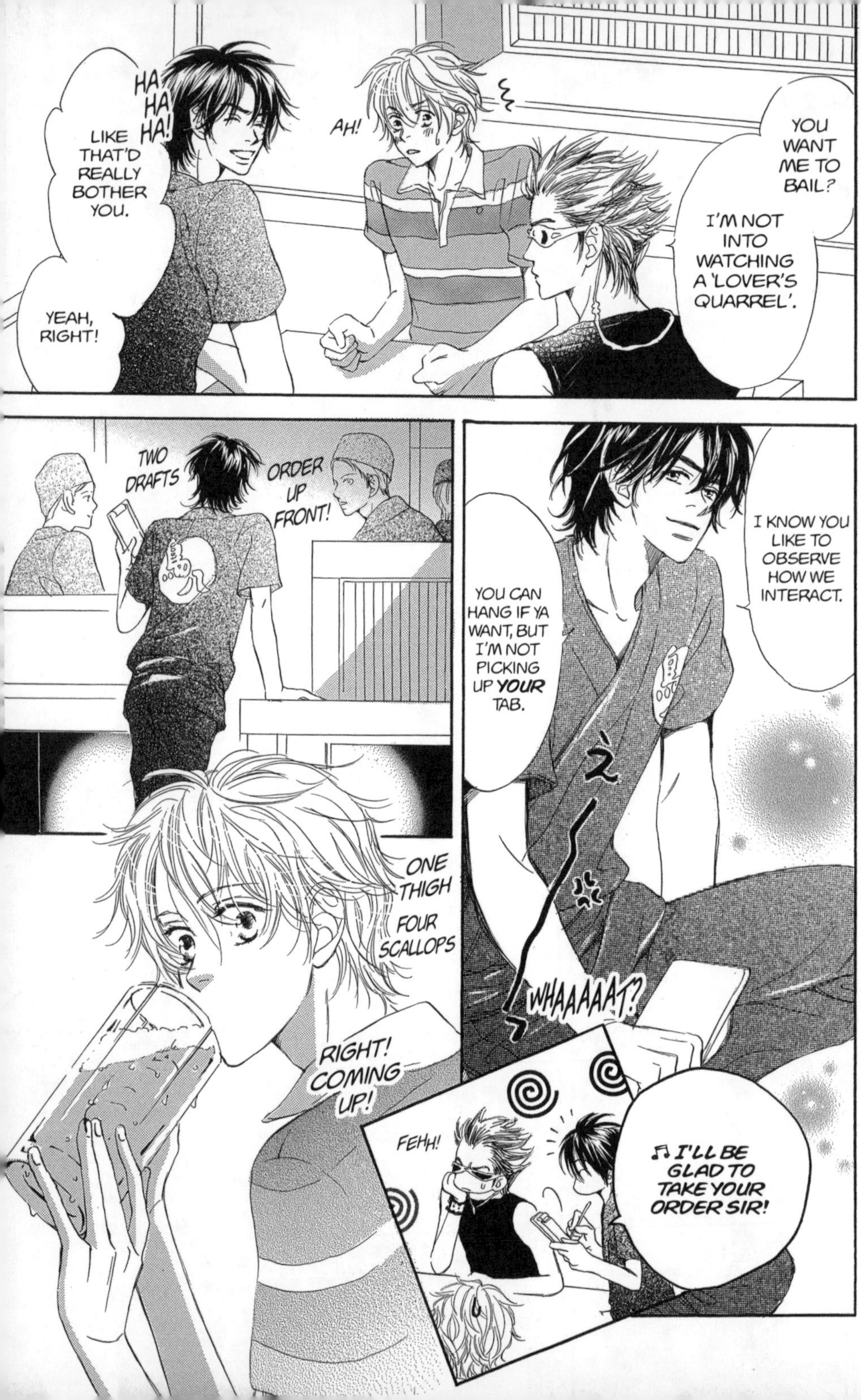

YOU WANT ME TO BAIL?
I'M NOT INTO WATCHING A 'LOVER'S QUARREL'.
AH!
HA HA HA!
LIKE THAT'D REALLY BOTHER YOU.
YEAH, RIGHT!
I KNOW YOU LIKE TO OBSERVE HOW WE INTERACT.
YOU CAN HANG IF YA WANT, BUT I'M NOT PICKING UP **YOUR** TAB.
WHAAAAAT?
♫ I'LL BE GLAD TO TAKE YOUR ORDER SIR!
FEHH!
ORDER UP FRONT!
TWO DRAFTS
ONE THIGH
FOUR SCALLOPS
RIGHT! COMING UP!

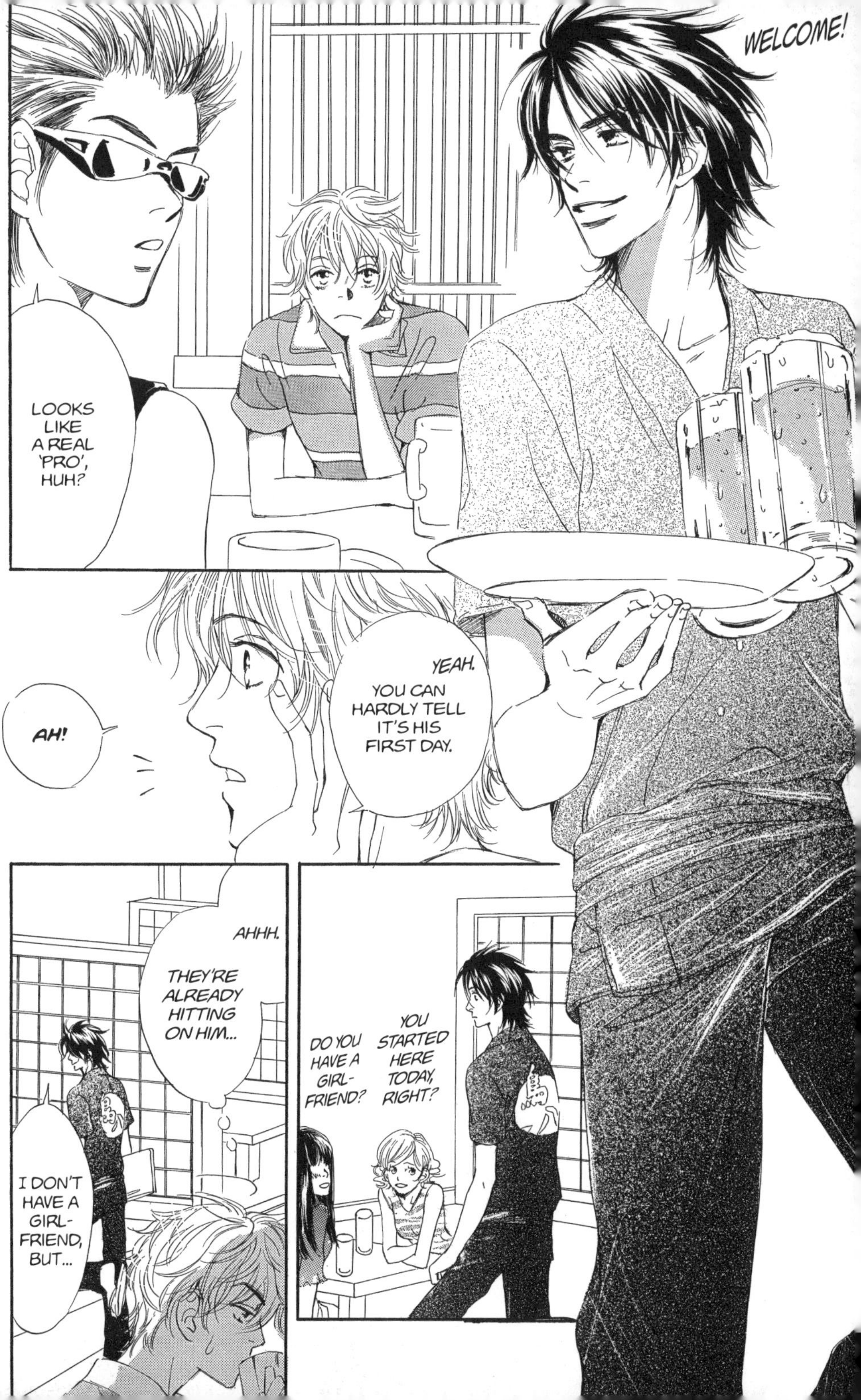
WELCOME!
LOOKS LIKE A REAL 'PRO', HUH?
YEAH. YOU CAN HARDLY TELL IT'S HIS FIRST DAY.
AH!
YOU STARTED HERE TODAY, RIGHT?
DO YOU HAVE A GIRLFRIEND?
AHHH. THEY'RE ALREADY HITTING ON HIM...
I DON'T HAVE A GIRLFRIEND, BUT...

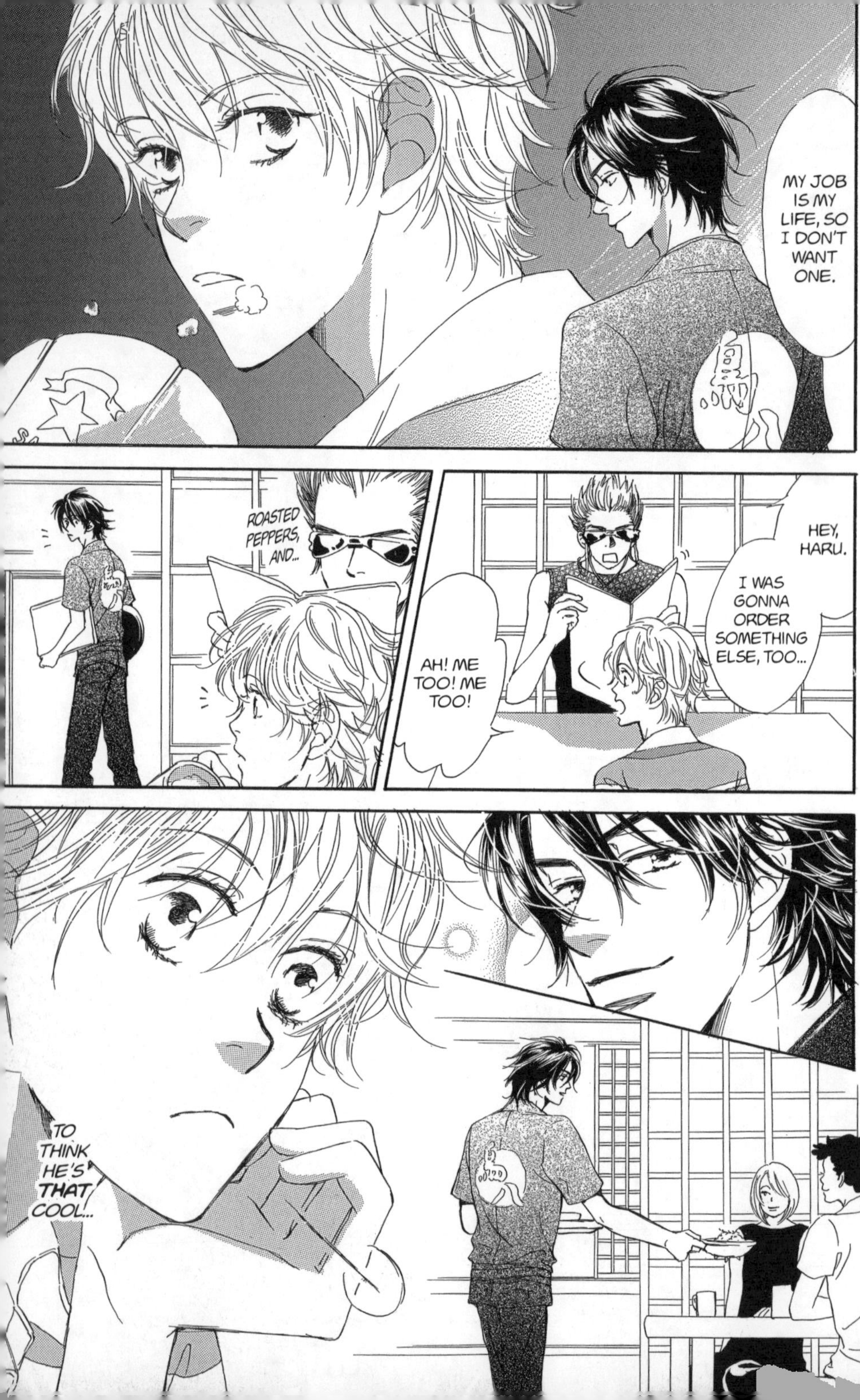
MY JOB IS MY LIFE, SO I DON'T WANT ONE.
HEY, HARU.
I WAS GONNA ORDER SOMETHING ELSE, TOO...
AH! ME TOO! ME TOO!
ROASTED PEPPERS, AND...
TO THINK HE'S THAT COOL...

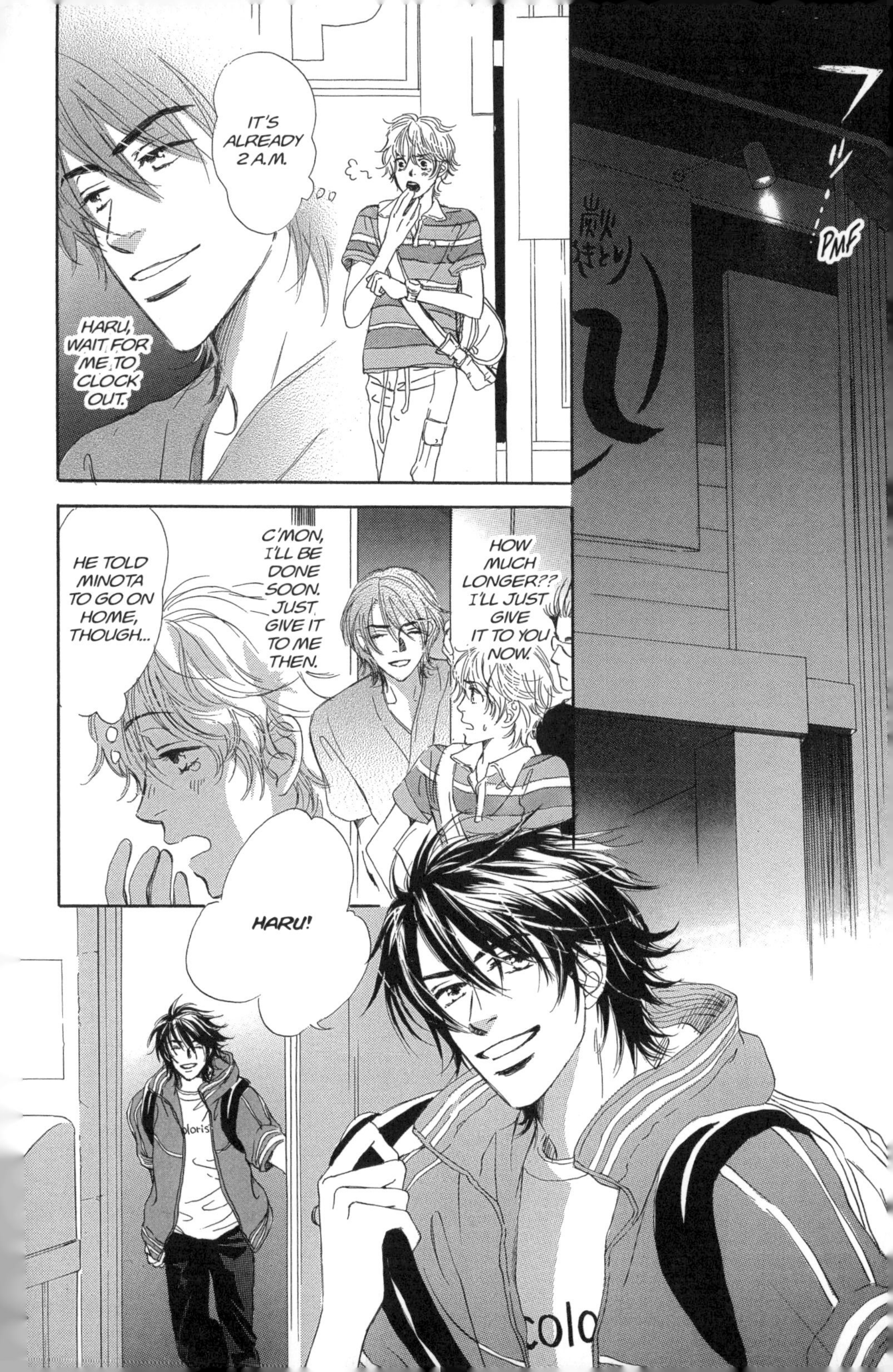
PMF
IT'S ALREADY 2 A.M.
HARU, WAIT FOR ME TO CLOCK OUT.
HOW MUCH LONGER?? I'LL JUST GIVE IT TO YOU NOW.
C'MON, I'LL BE DONE SOON. JUST GIVE IT TO ME THEN.
HE TOLD MINOTA TO GO ON HOME, THOUGH...
HARU!

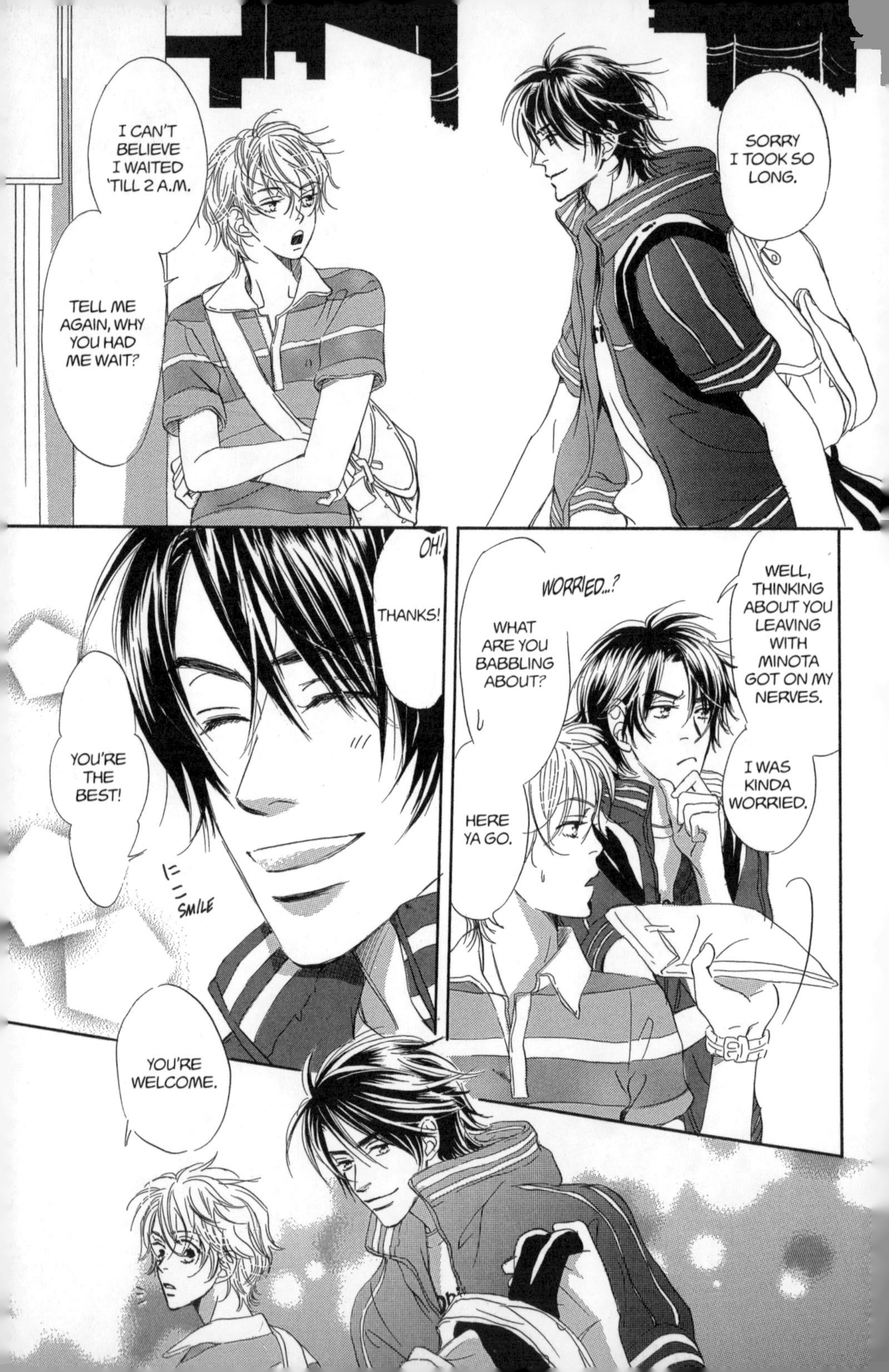
SORRY I TOOK SO LONG.
I CAN'T BELIEVE I WAITED 'TILL 2 A.M.
TELL ME AGAIN, WHY YOU HAD ME WAIT?
WELL, THINKING ABOUT YOU LEAVING WITH MINOTA GOT ON MY NERVES.
I WAS KINDA WORRIED.
WORRIED...?
WHAT ARE YOU BABBLING ABOUT?
HERE YA GO.
OH!
THANKS!
YOU'RE THE BEST!
SMILE
YOU'RE WELCOME.

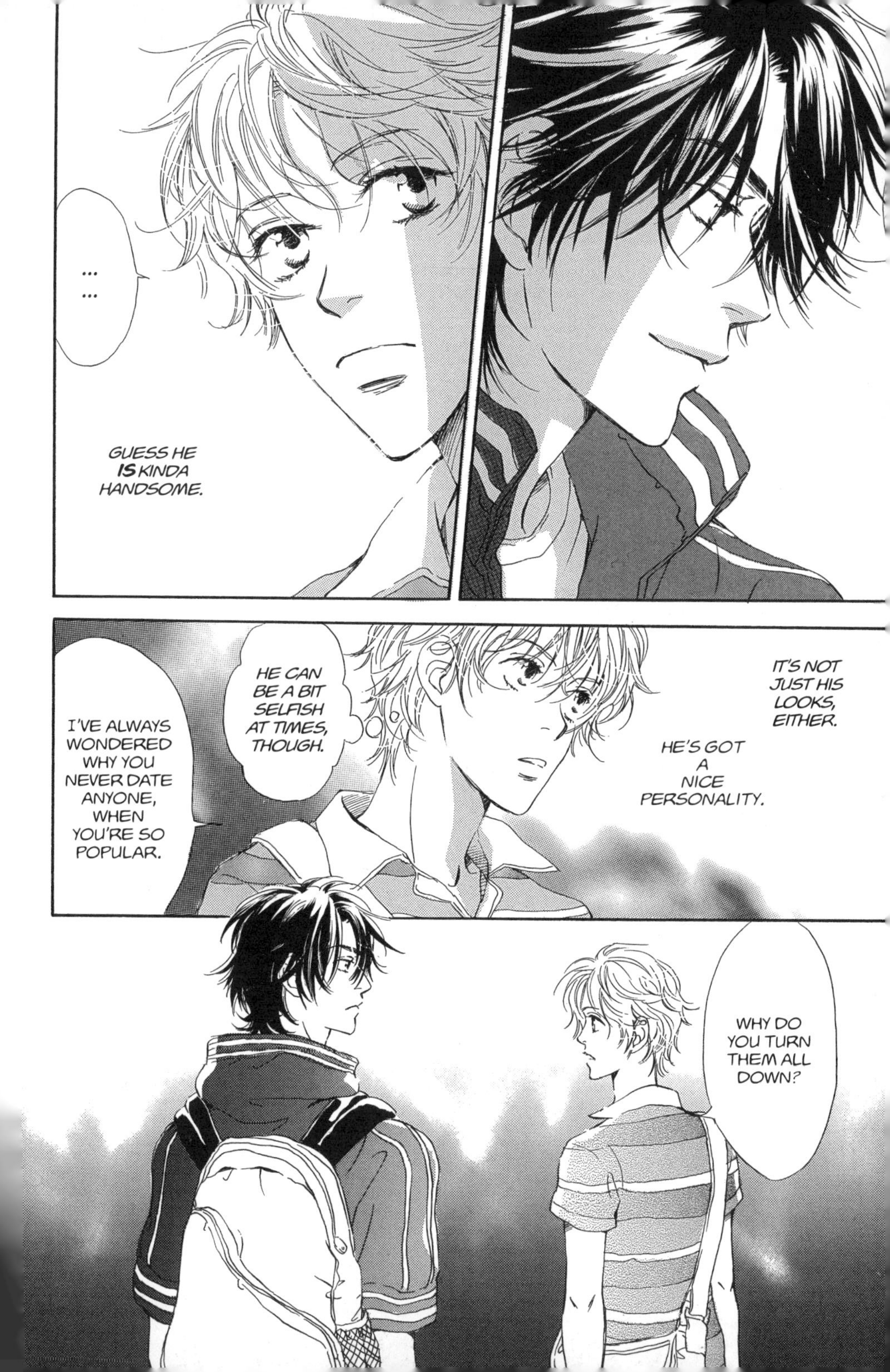
……
GUESS HE IS KINDA HANDSOME.
IT'S NOT JUST HIS LOOKS, EITHER.
HE'S GOT A NICE PERSONALITY.
HE CAN BE A BIT SELFISH AT TIMES, THOUGH.
I'VE ALWAYS WONDERED WHY YOU NEVER DATE ANYONE, WHEN YOU'RE SO POPULAR.
WHY DO YOU TURN THEM ALL DOWN?

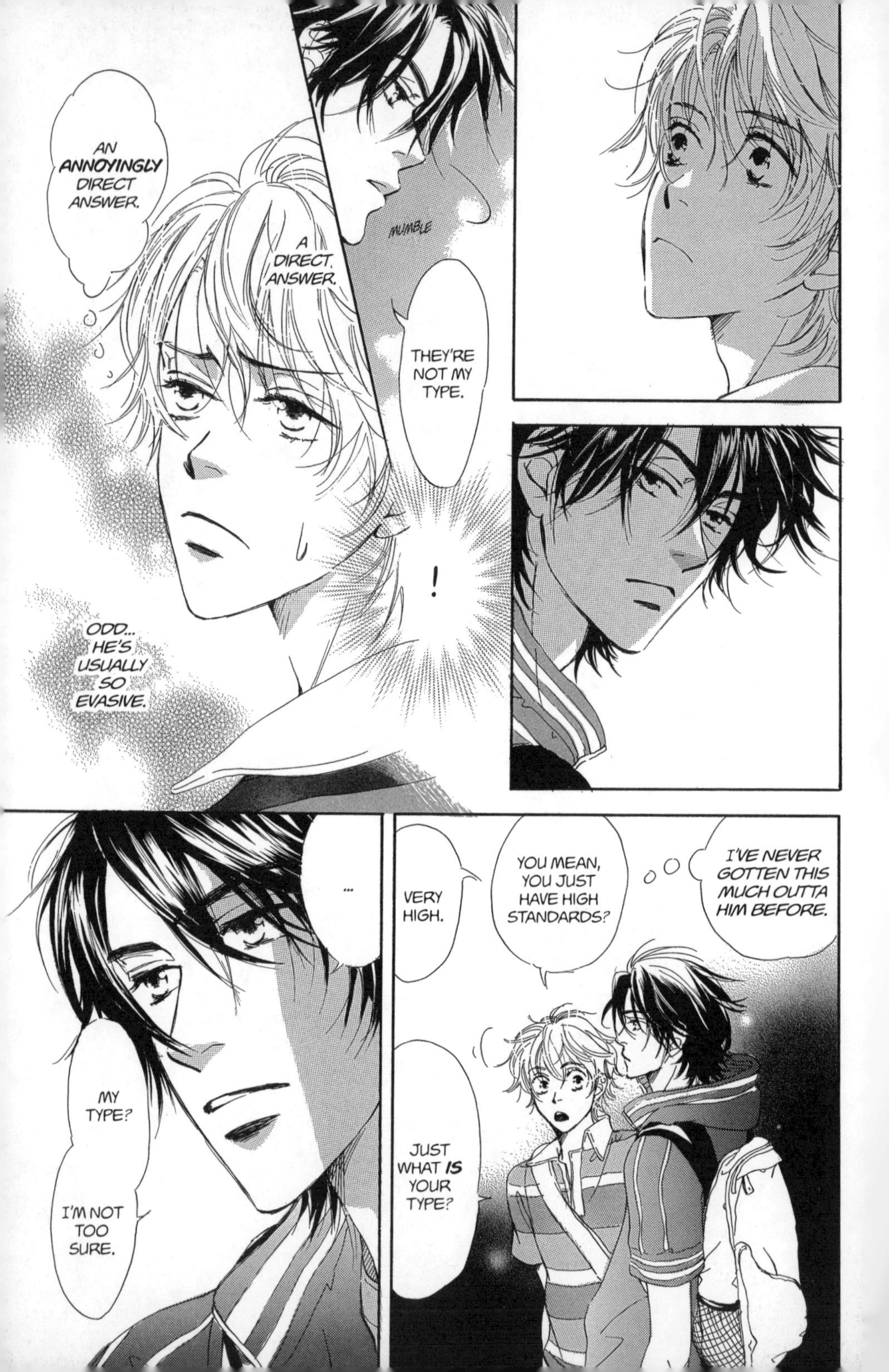
MUMBLE
THEY'RE NOT MY TYPE.
A DIRECT. ANSWER.
AN **ANNOYINGLY** DIRECT ANSWER.
!
ODD... HE'S USUALLY SO EVASIVE.
I'VE NEVER GOTTEN THIS MUCH OUTTA HIM BEFORE.
YOU MEAN, YOU JUST HAVE HIGH STANDARDS?
VERY HIGH.
JUST WHAT ***IS*** YOUR TYPE?
...
MY TYPE?
I'M NOT TOO SURE.

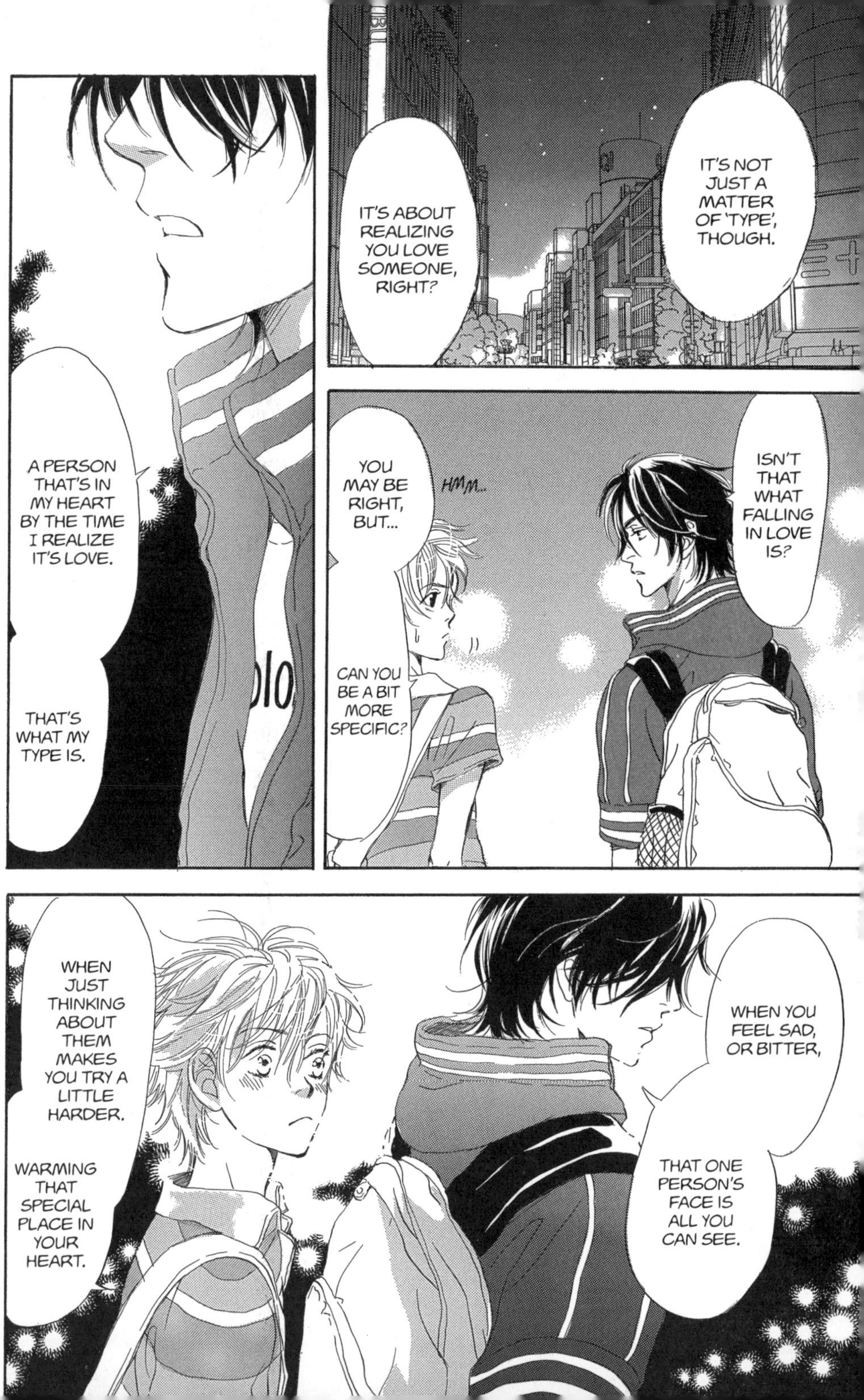
IT'S NOT JUST A MATTER OF 'TYPE', THOUGH.
IT'S ABOUT REALIZING YOU LOVE SOMEONE, RIGHT?
ISN'T THAT WHAT FALLING IN LOVE IS?
HMM...
YOU MAY BE RIGHT, BUT...
CAN YOU BE A BIT MORE SPECIFIC?
A PERSON THAT'S IN MY HEART BY THE TIME I REALIZE IT'S LOVE.
THAT'S WHAT MY TYPE IS.
WHEN YOU FEEL SAD, OR BITTER,
THAT ONE PERSON'S FACE IS ALL YOU CAN SEE.
WHEN JUST THINKING ABOUT THEM MAKES YOU TRY A LITTLE HARDER.
WARMING THAT SPECIAL PLACE IN YOUR HEART.

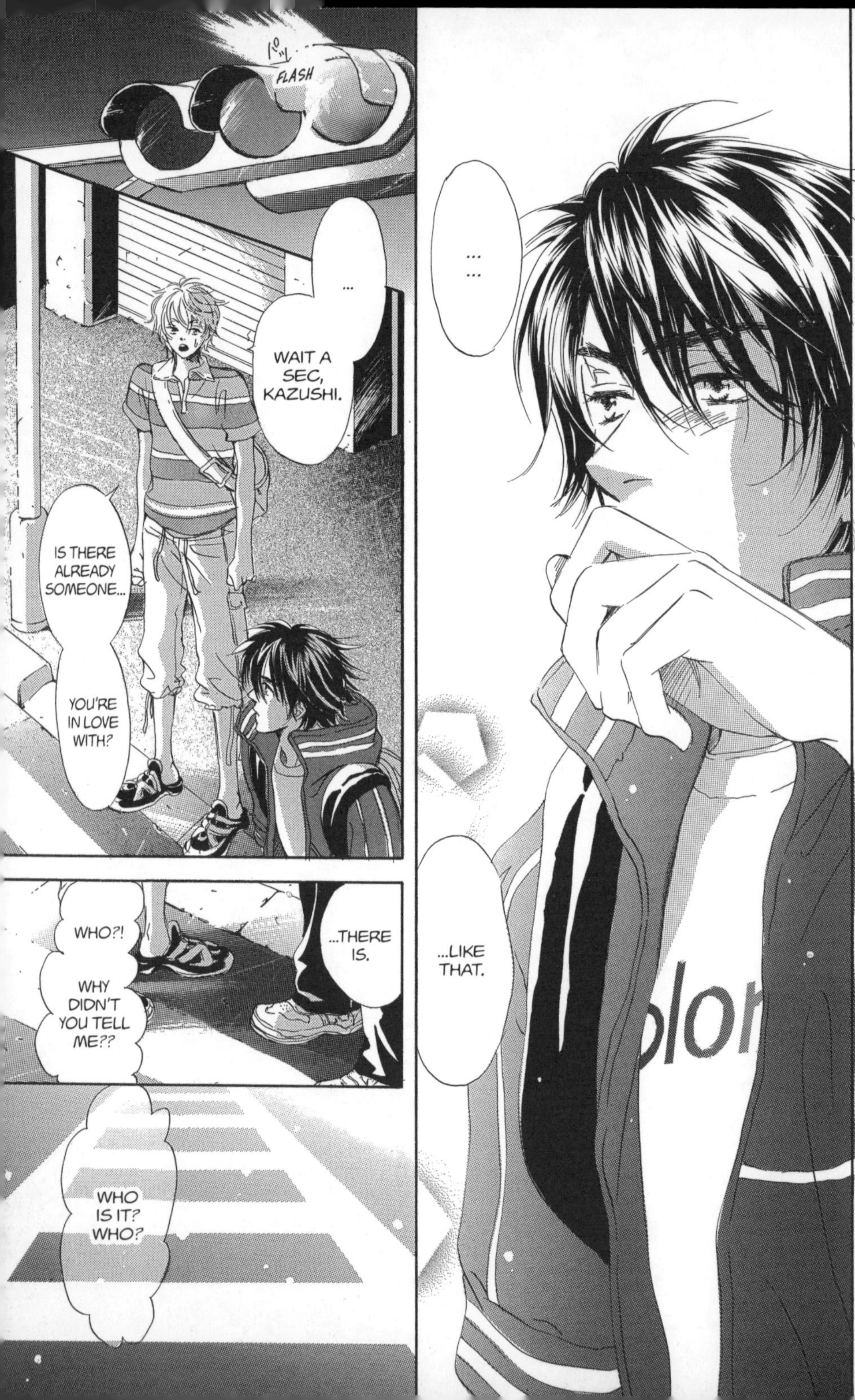

……
...LIKE THAT.
パッ
FLASH
...
WAIT A SEC, KAZUSHI.
IS THERE ALREADY SOMEONE...
YOU'RE IN LOVE WITH?
...THERE IS.
WHO?!
WHY DIDN'T YOU TELL ME??
WHO IS IT? WHO?

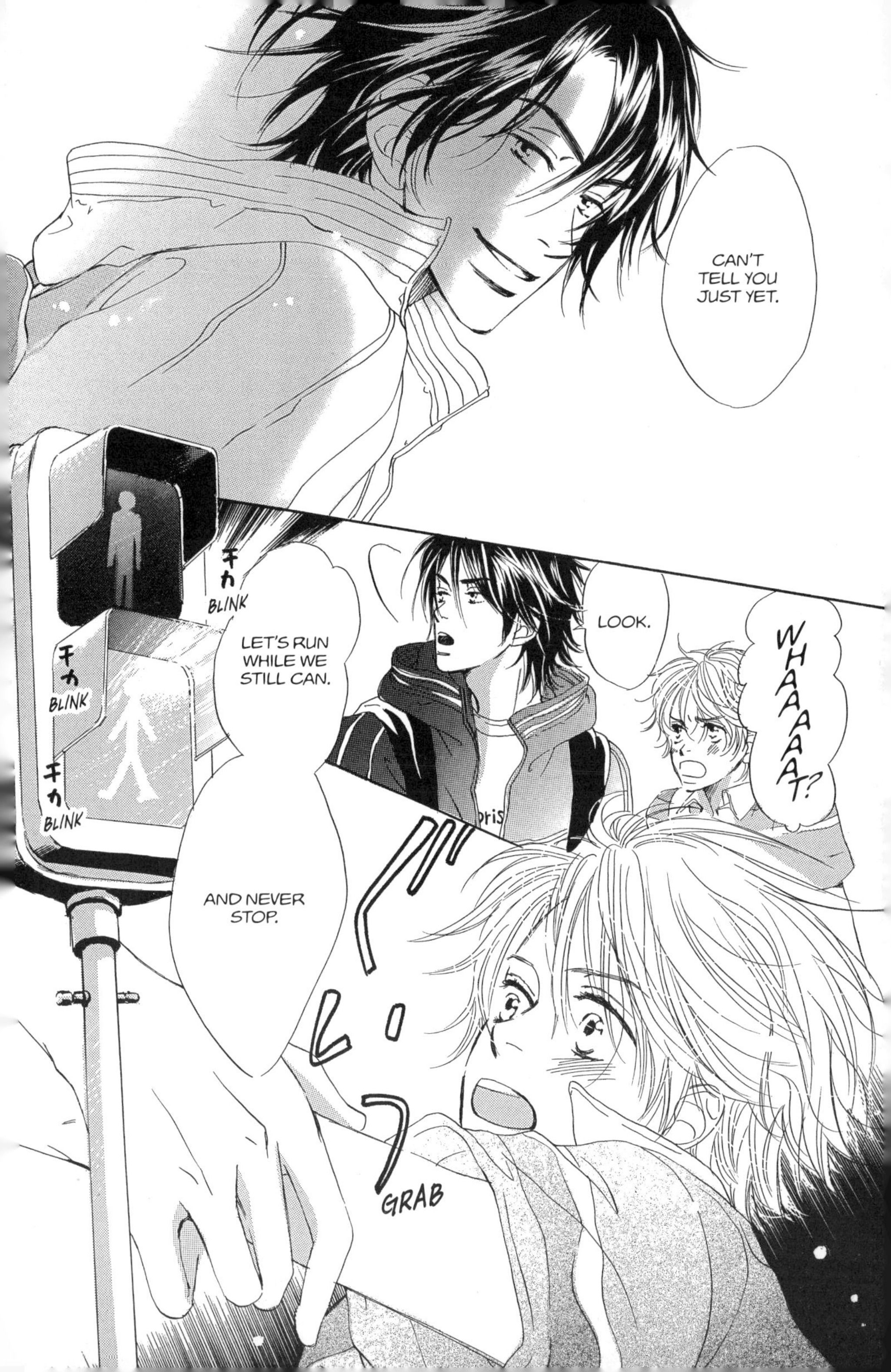
CAN'T TELL YOU JUST YET.
WHAAAAAT?
LOOK.
LET'S RUN WHILE WE STILL CAN.
チカ BLINK
チカ BLINK
チカ BLINK
AND NEVER STOP.
GRAB

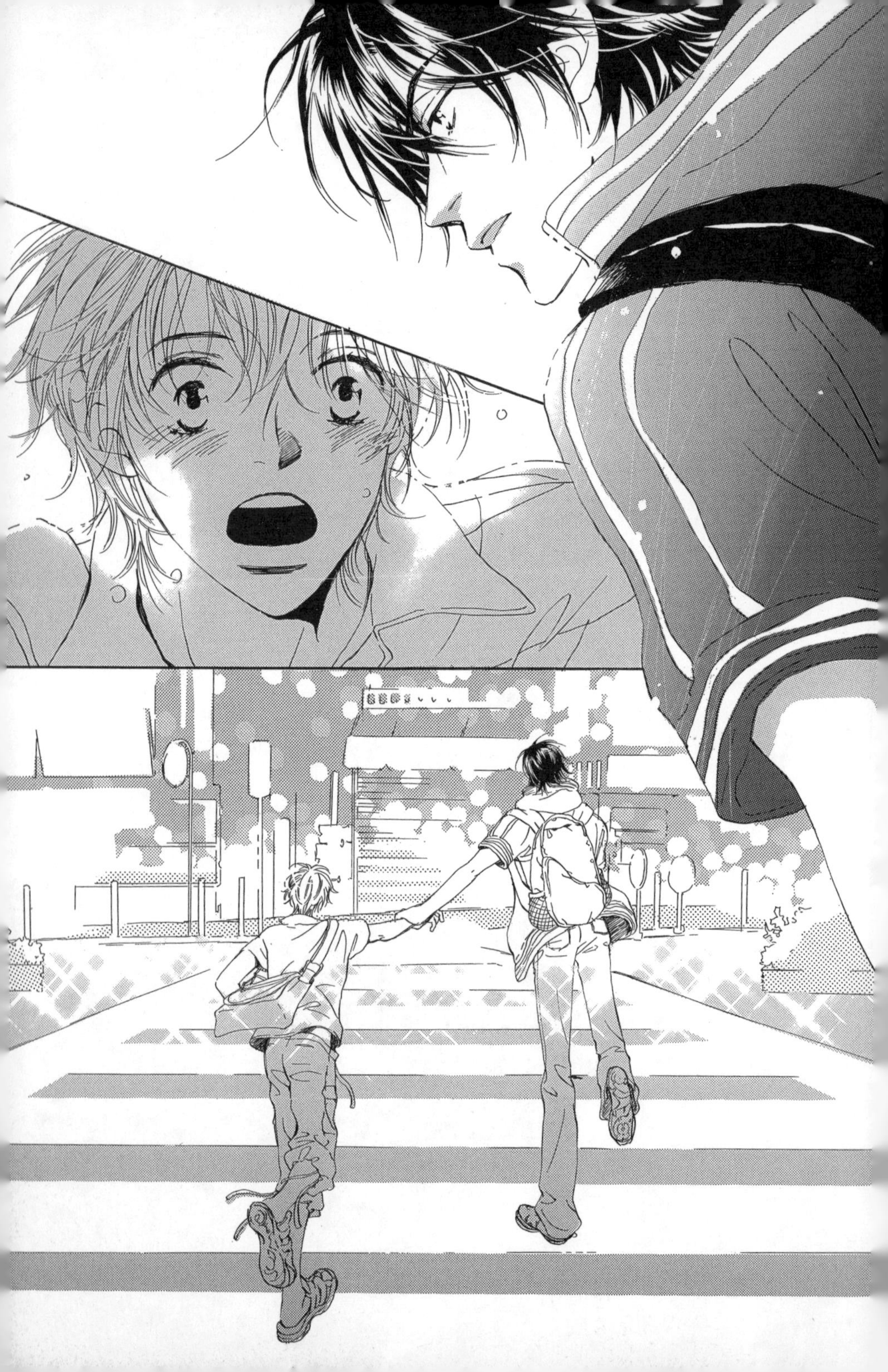

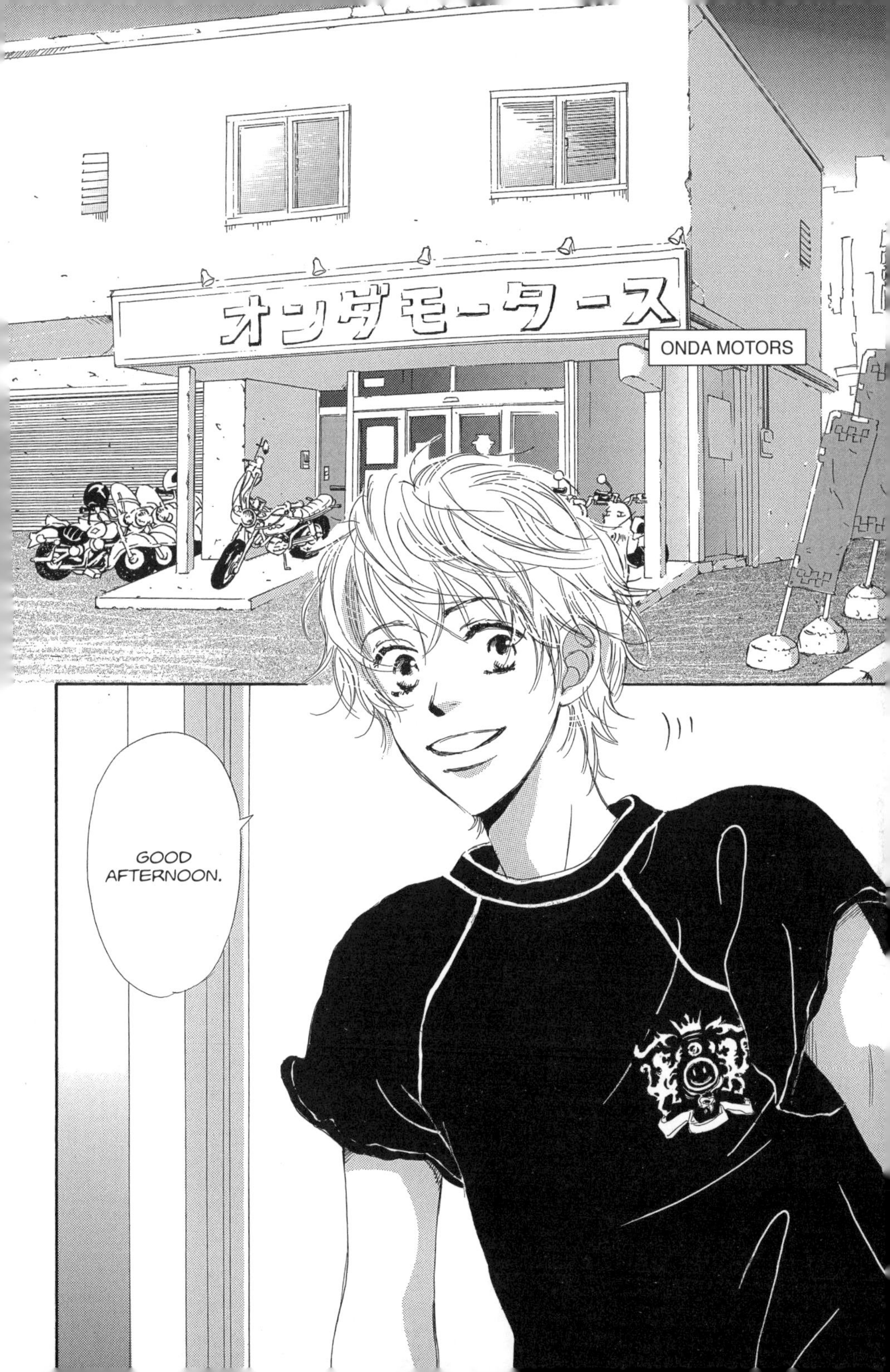
オンダモータース
ONDA MOTORS
GOOD AFTERNOON.

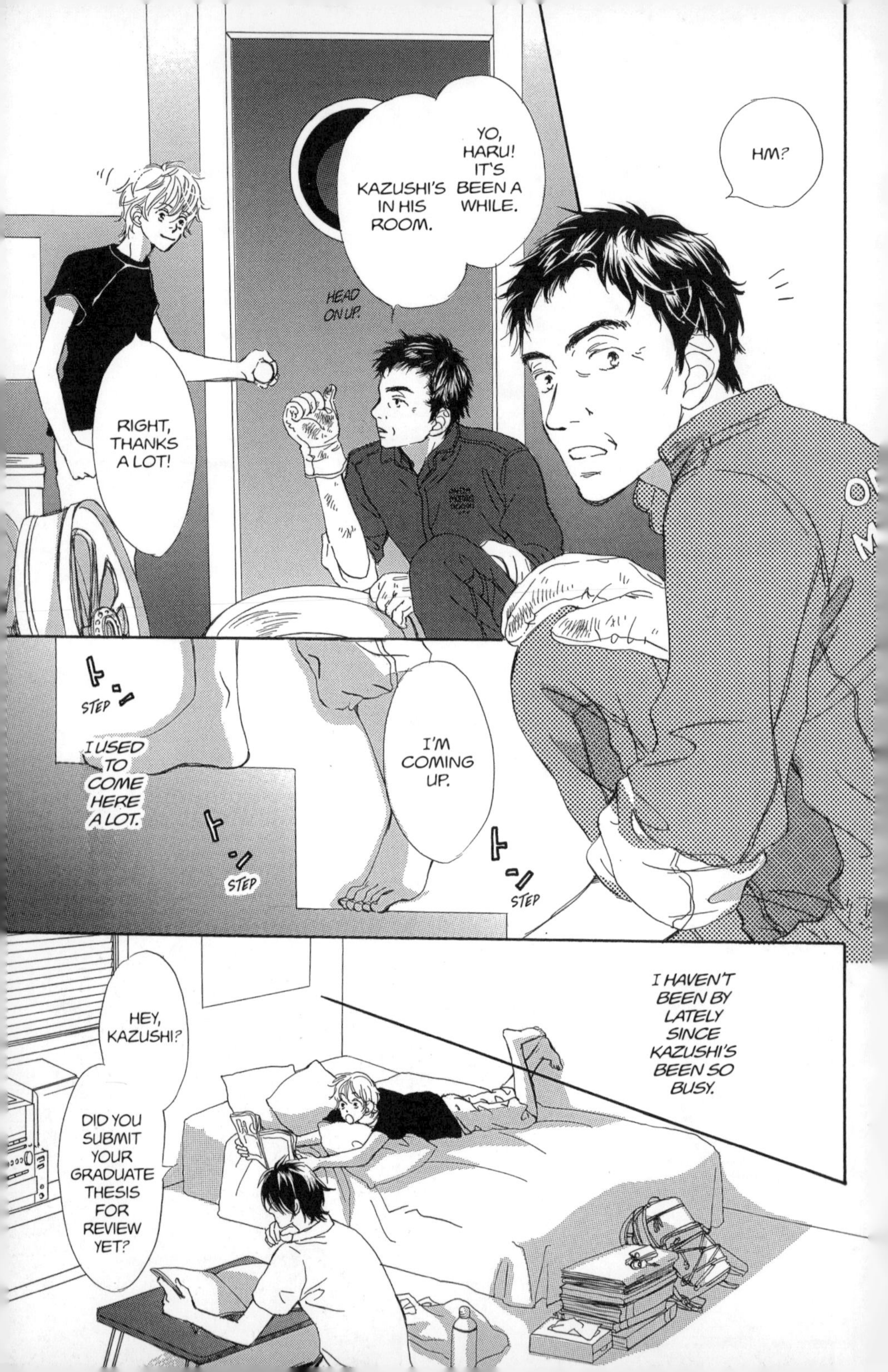
HM?
YO, HARU! IT'S BEEN A WHILE.
KAZUSHI'S IN HIS ROOM.
HEAD ON UP.
RIGHT, THANKS A LOT!
STEP
I'M COMING UP.
STEP
STEP
I USED TO COME HERE A LOT.
I HAVEN'T BEEN BY LATELY SINCE KAZUSHI'S BEEN SO BUSY.
HEY, KAZUSHI?
DID YOU SUBMIT YOUR GRADUATE THESIS FOR REVIEW YET?

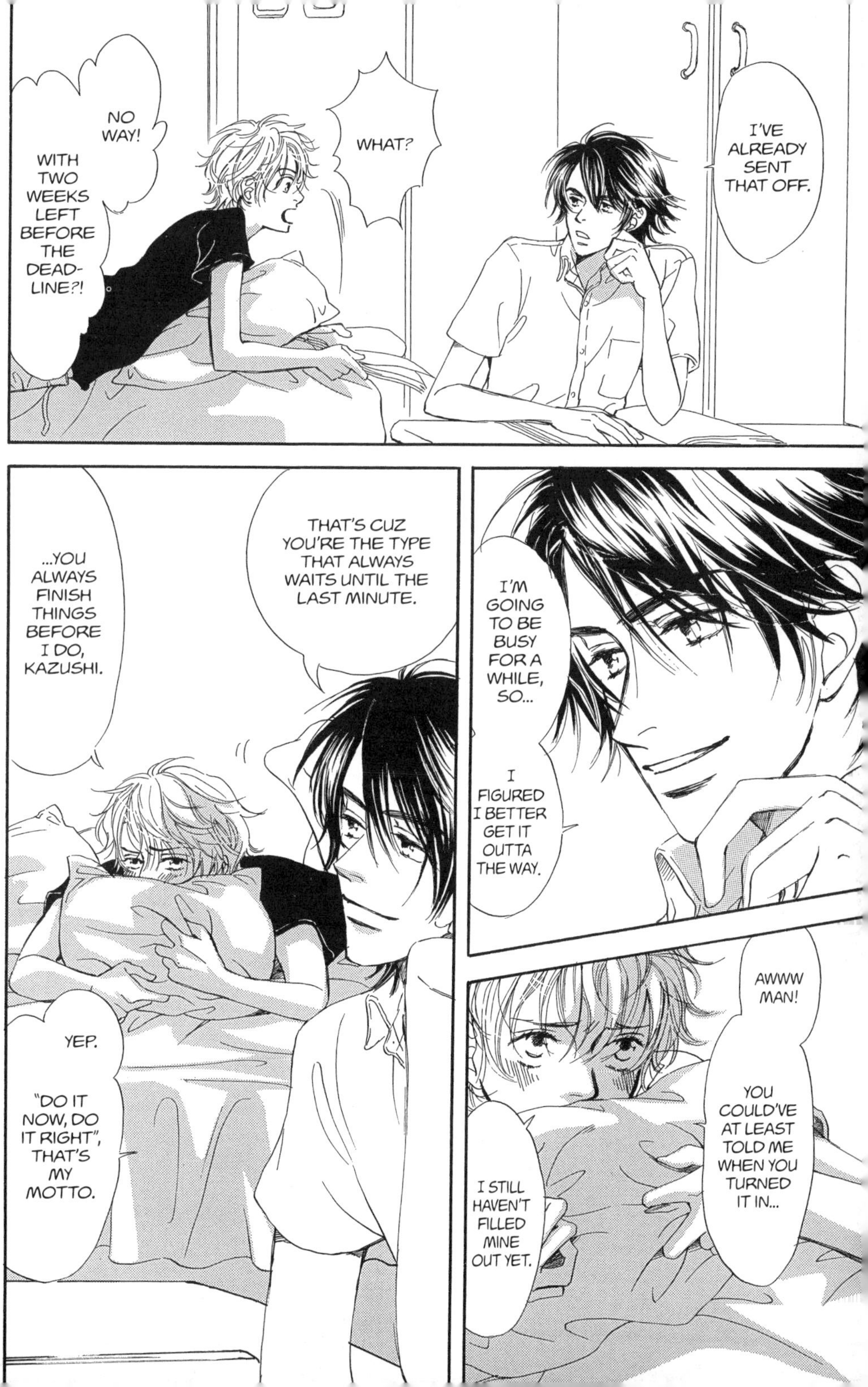
I'VE ALREADY SENT THAT OFF.
WHAT?
NO WAY!
WITH TWO WEEKS LEFT BEFORE THE DEAD-LINE?!
I'M GOING TO BE BUSY FOR A WHILE, SO...
I FIGURED I BETTER GET IT OUTTA THE WAY.
AWWW MAN!
YOU COULD'VE AT LEAST TOLD ME WHEN YOU TURNED IT IN...
I STILL HAVEN'T FILLED MINE OUT YET.
...YOU ALWAYS FINISH THINGS BEFORE I DO, KAZUSHI.
THAT'S CUZ YOU'RE THE TYPE THAT ALWAYS WAITS UNTIL THE LAST MINUTE.
YEP.
"DO IT NOW, DO IT RIGHT", THAT'S MY MOTTO.

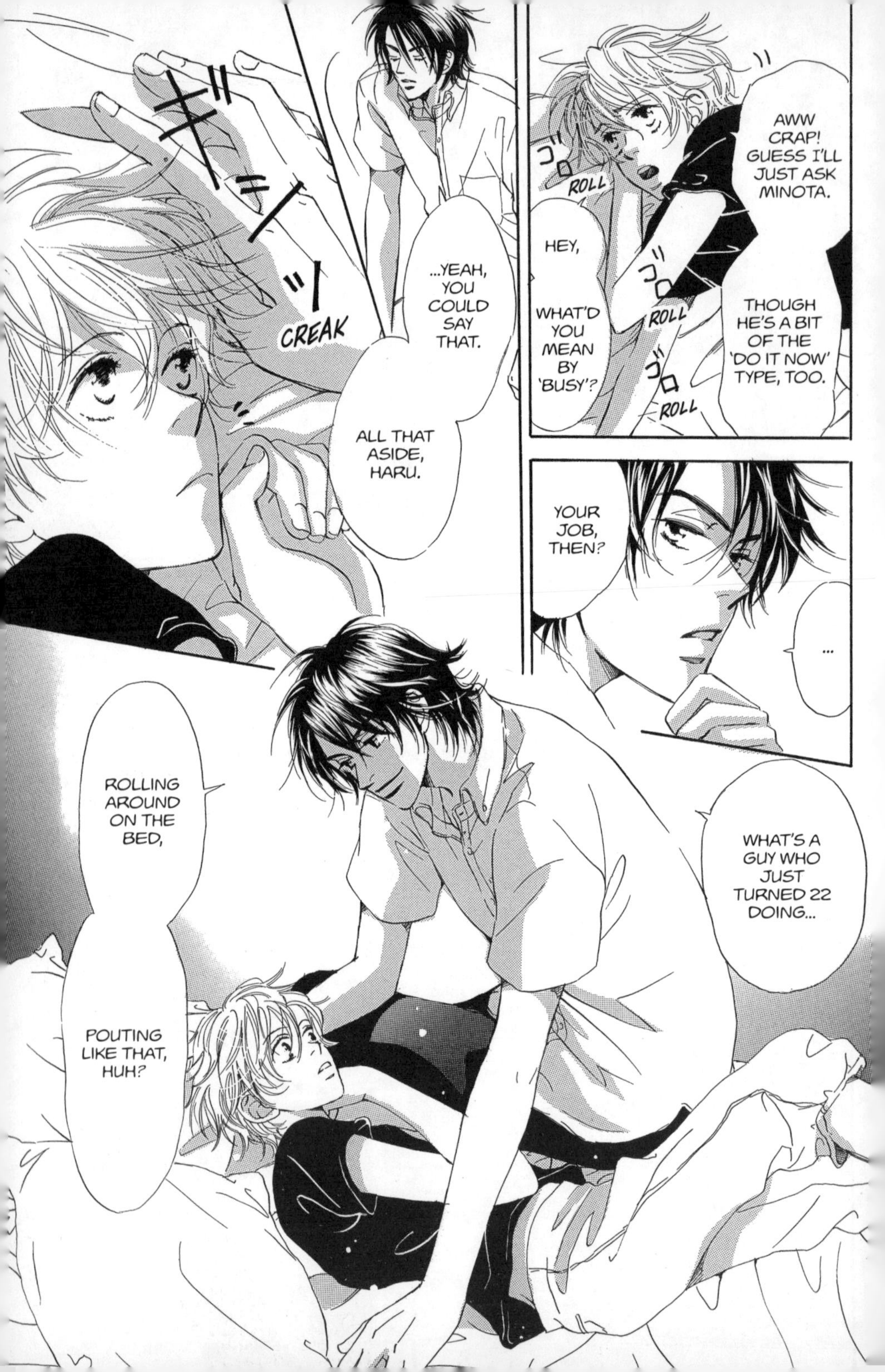
AWW CRAP! GUESS I'LL JUST ASK MINOTA.
ROLL
ROLL
ROLL
THOUGH HE'S A BIT OF THE 'DO IT NOW' TYPE, TOO.
HEY,
WHAT'D YOU MEAN BY 'BUSY'?
YOUR JOB, THEN?
...
...YEAH, YOU COULD SAY THAT.
CREAK
ALL THAT ASIDE, HARU.
WHAT'S A GUY WHO JUST TURNED 22 DOING...
ROLLING AROUND ON THE BED,
POUTING LIKE THAT, HUH?

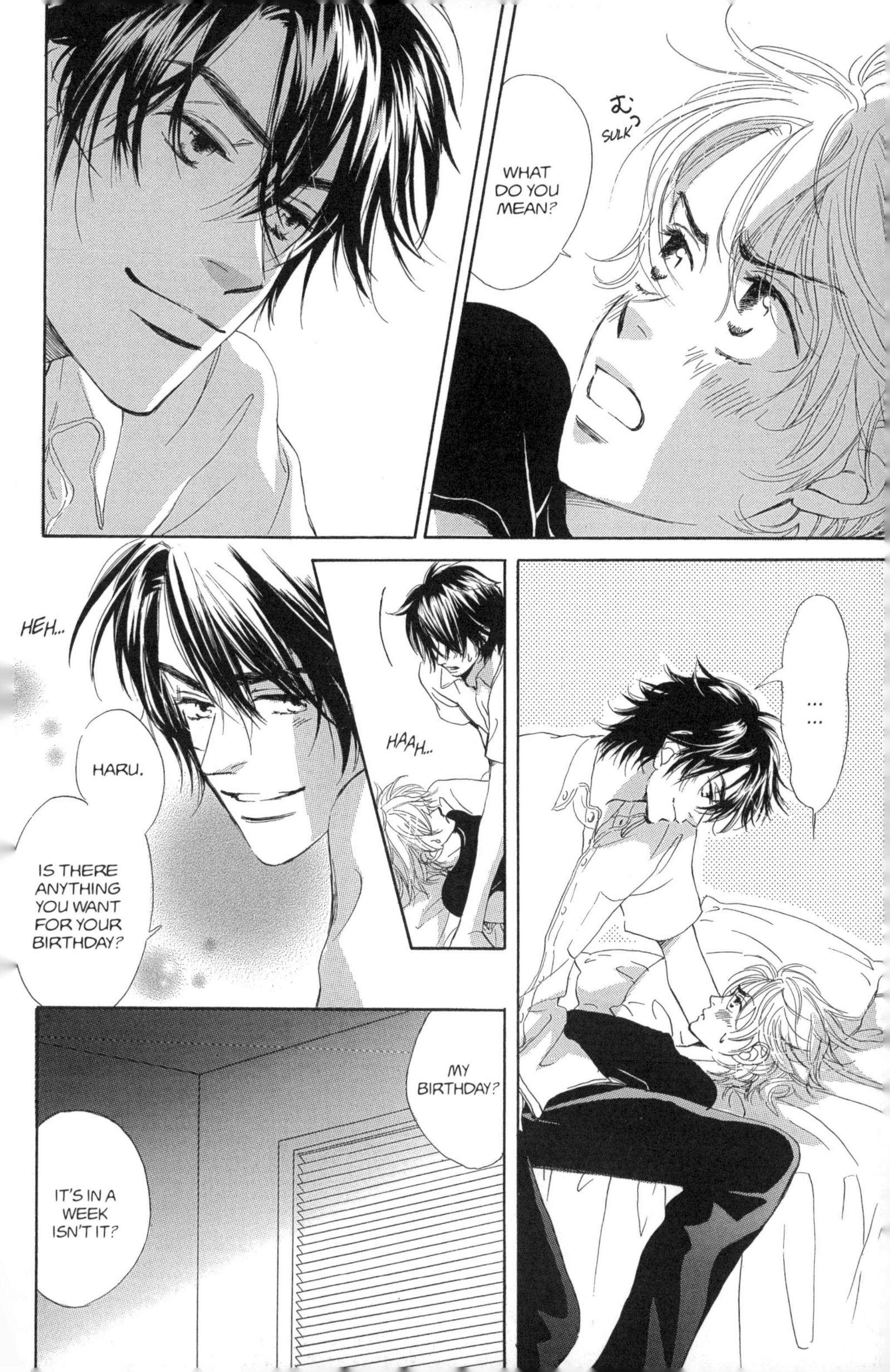
むっ
SULK
WHAT DO YOU MEAN?
......
HAAH...
HEH...
HARU.
IS THERE ANYTHING YOU WANT FOR YOUR BIRTHDAY?
MY BIRTHDAY?
IT'S IN A WEEK ISN'T IT?

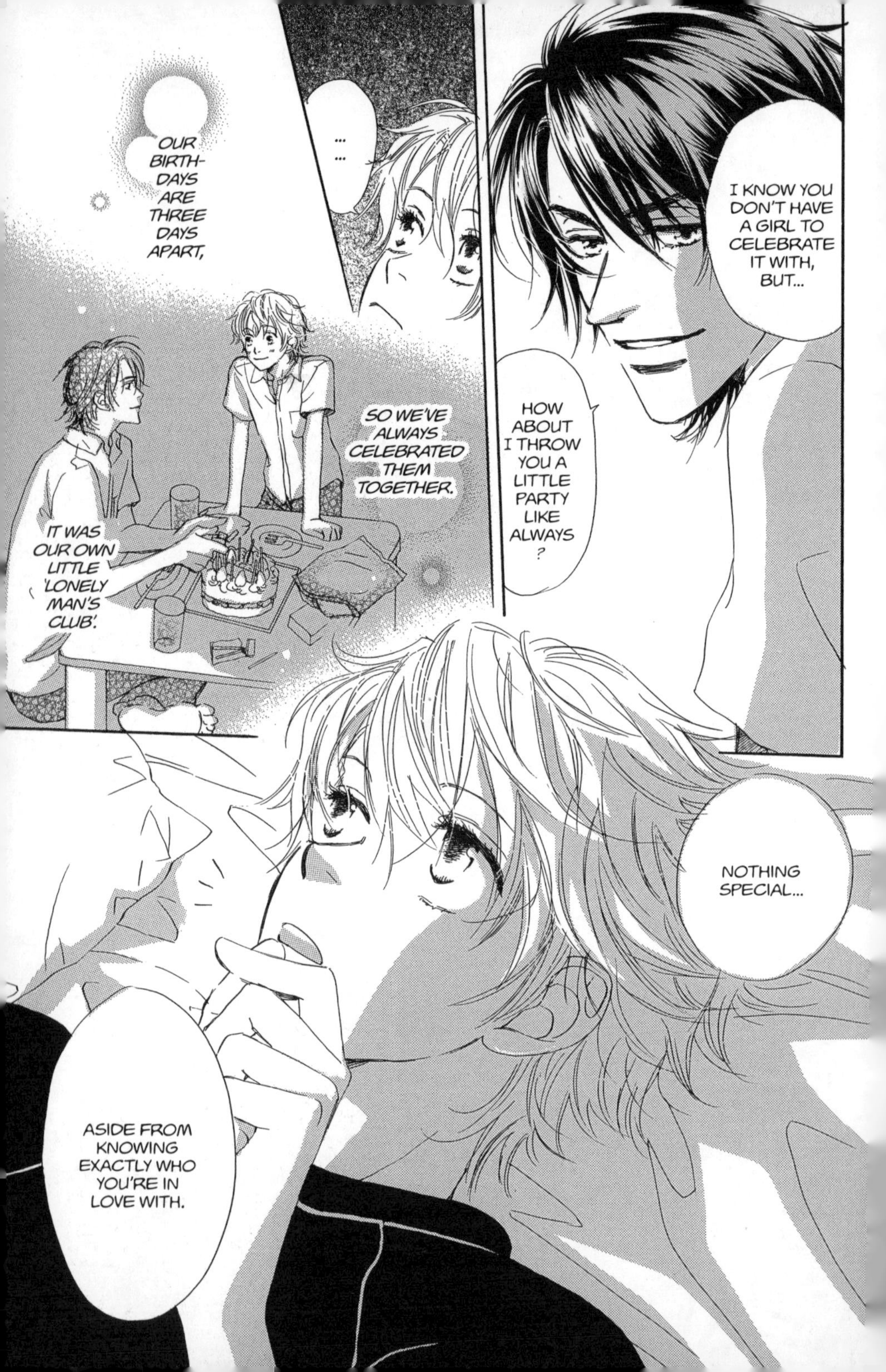
I KNOW YOU DON'T HAVE A GIRL TO CELEBRATE IT WITH, BUT...
HOW ABOUT I THROW YOU A LITTLE PARTY LIKE ALWAYS?
... ...
OUR BIRTH-DAYS ARE THREE DAYS APART,
SO WE'VE ALWAYS CELEBRATED THEM TOGETHER.
IT WAS OUR OWN LITTLE 'LONELY MAN'S CLUB'.
NOTHING SPECIAL...
ASIDE FROM KNOWING EXACTLY WHO YOU'RE IN LOVE WITH.

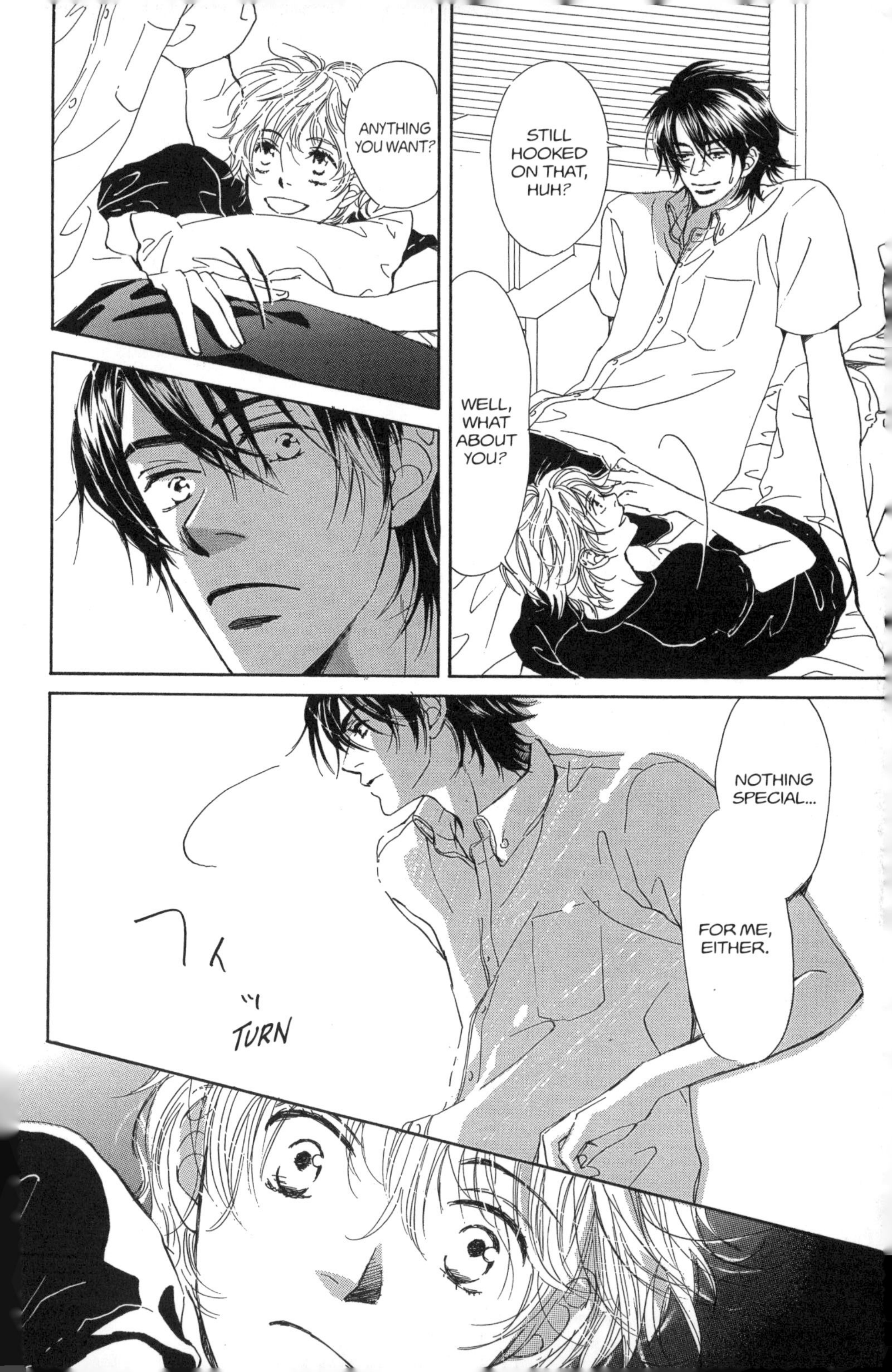
STILL HOOKED ON THAT, HUH?
WELL, WHAT ABOUT YOU?
ANYTHING YOU WANT?
NOTHING SPECIAL...
FOR ME, EITHER.
TURN

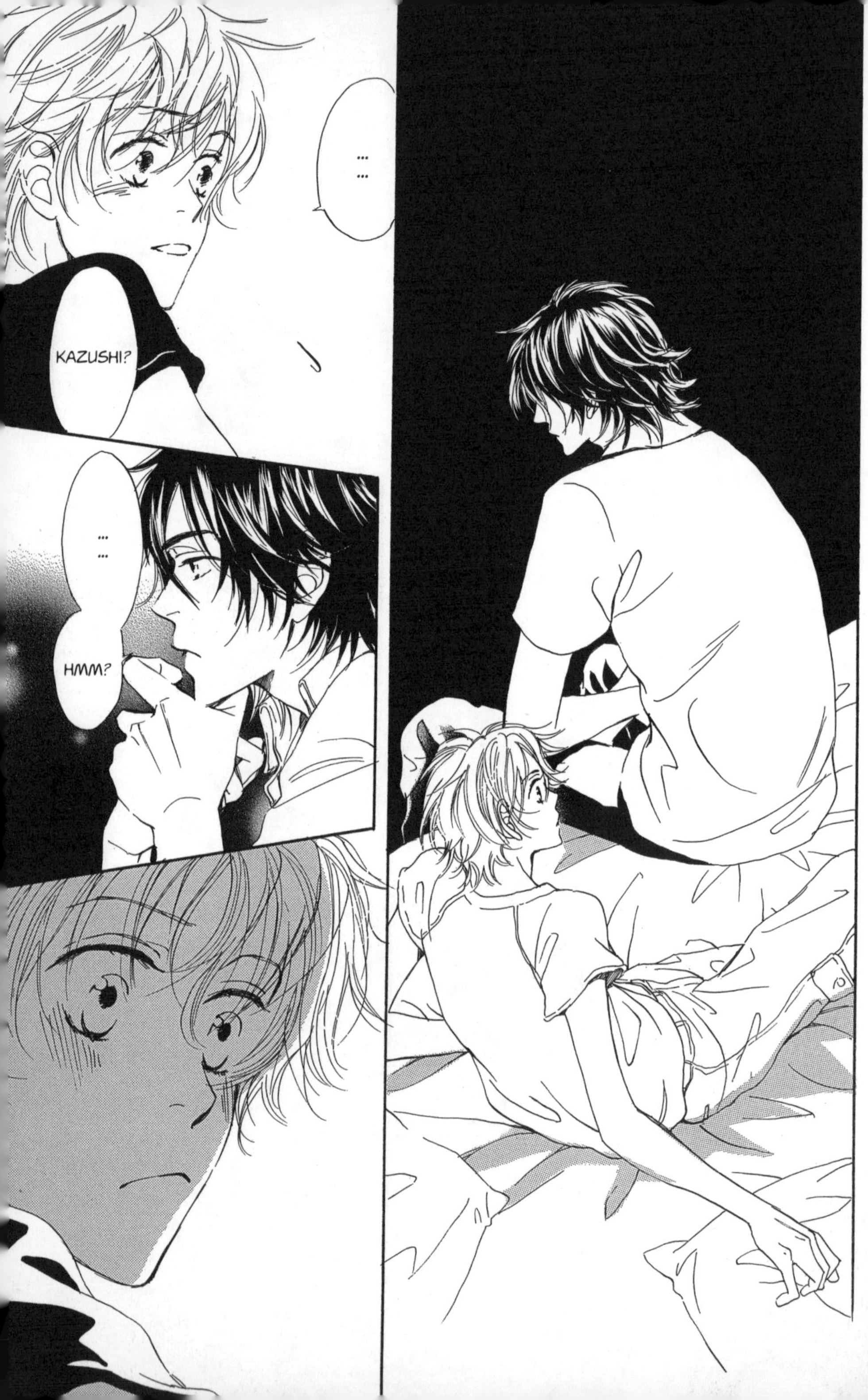
……
KAZUSHI?
……
HMM?

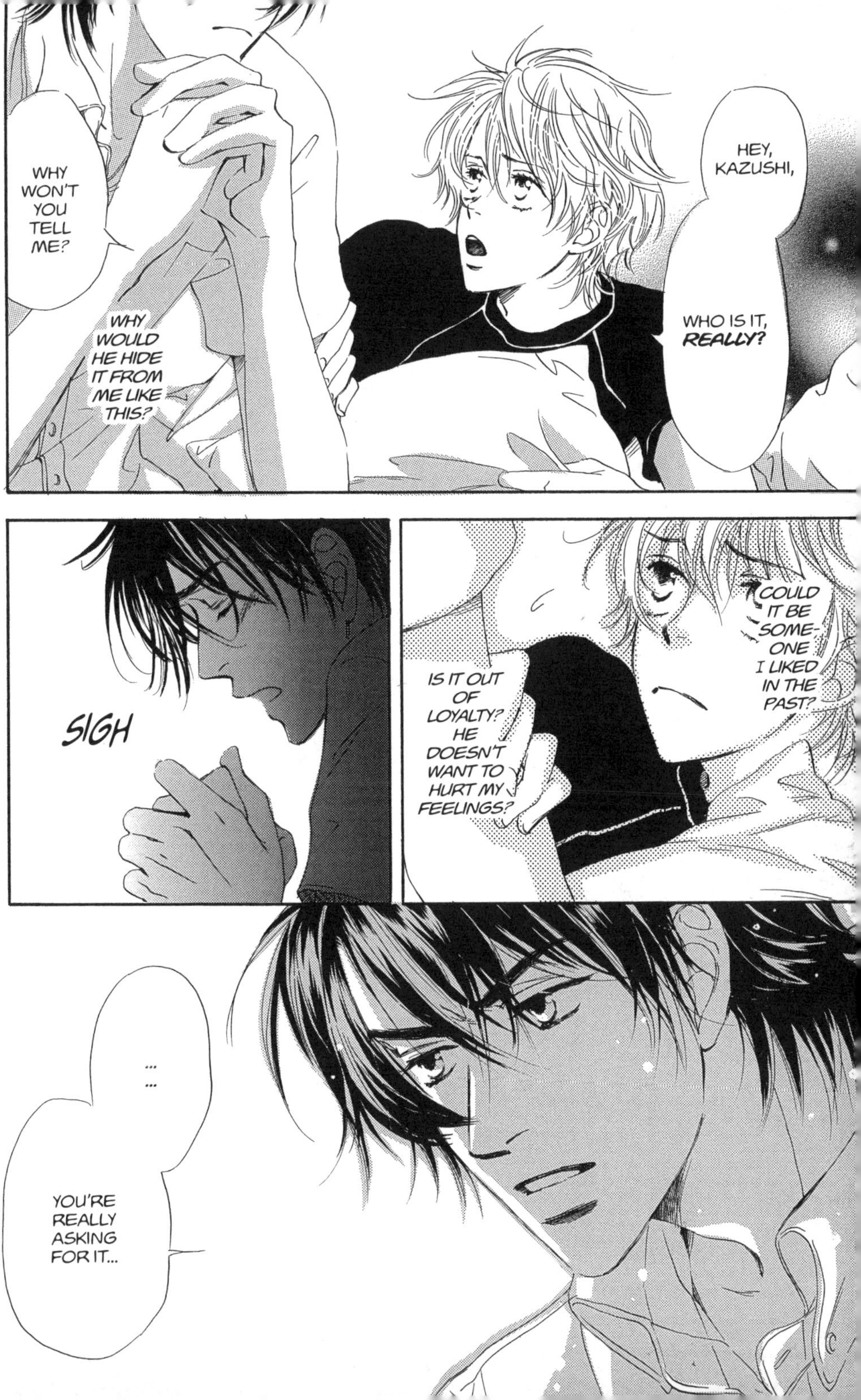
HEY, KAZUSHI,
WHO IS IT, ***REALLY?***
WHY WON'T YOU TELL ME?
WHY WOULD HE HIDE IT FROM ME LIKE THIS?
COULD IT BE SOME-ONE I LIKED IN THE PAST?
IS IT OUT OF LOYALTY? HE DOESN'T WANT TO HURT MY FEELINGS?
SIGH
... ...
YOU'RE REALLY ASKING FOR IT...

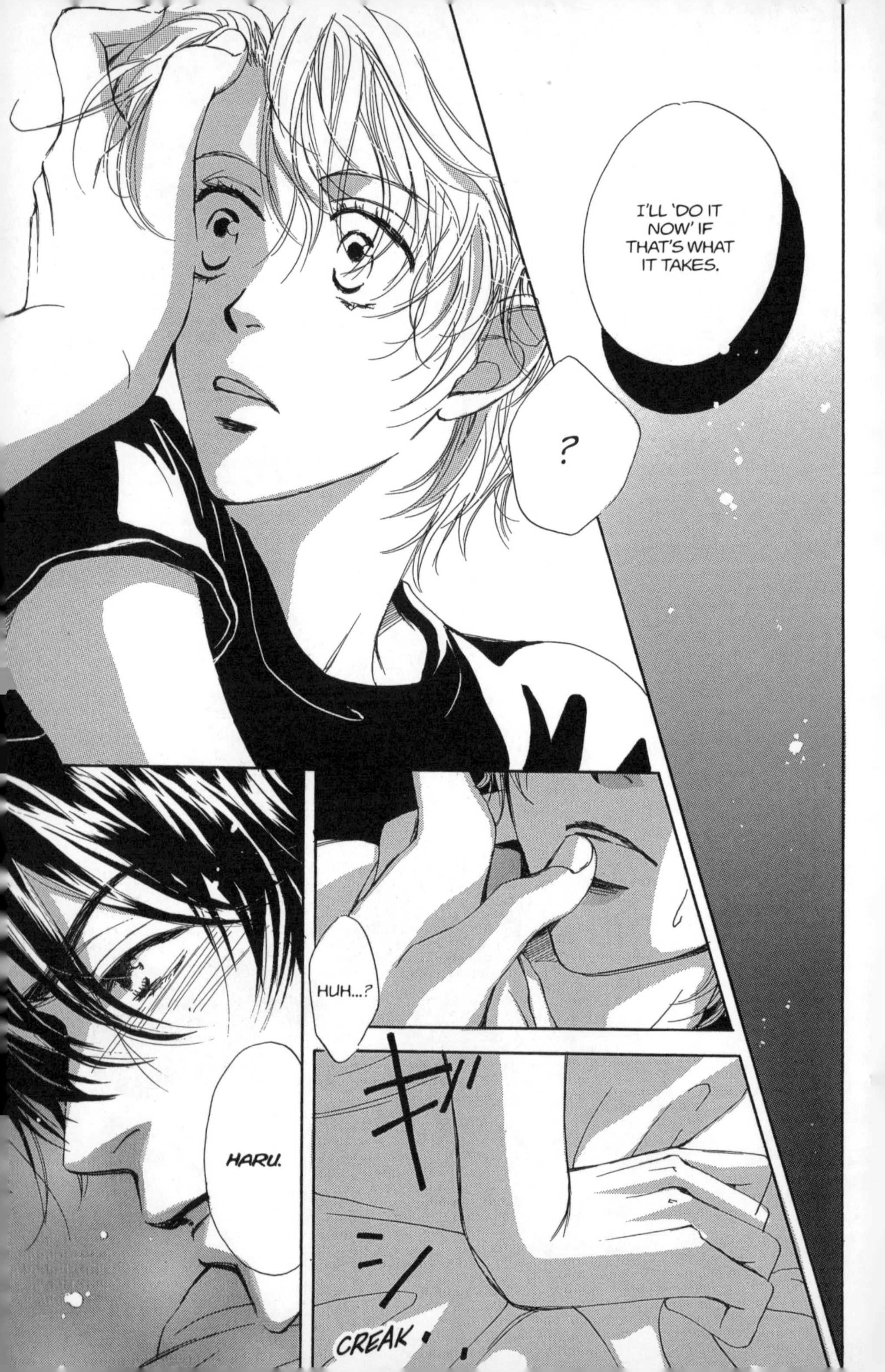
I'LL 'DO IT NOW' IF THAT'S WHAT IT TAKES.
?
HUH...?
CREAK
HARU.

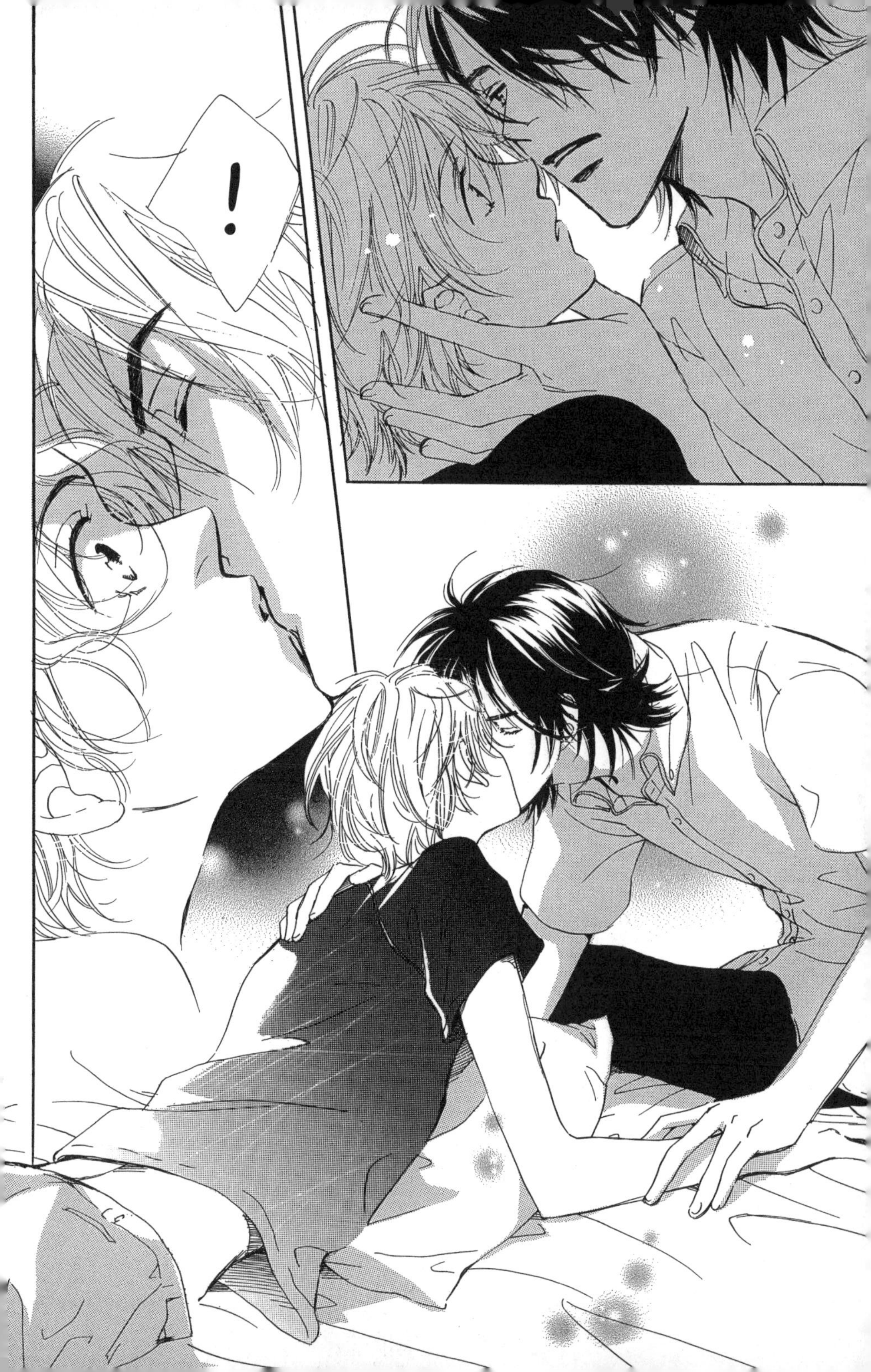
!

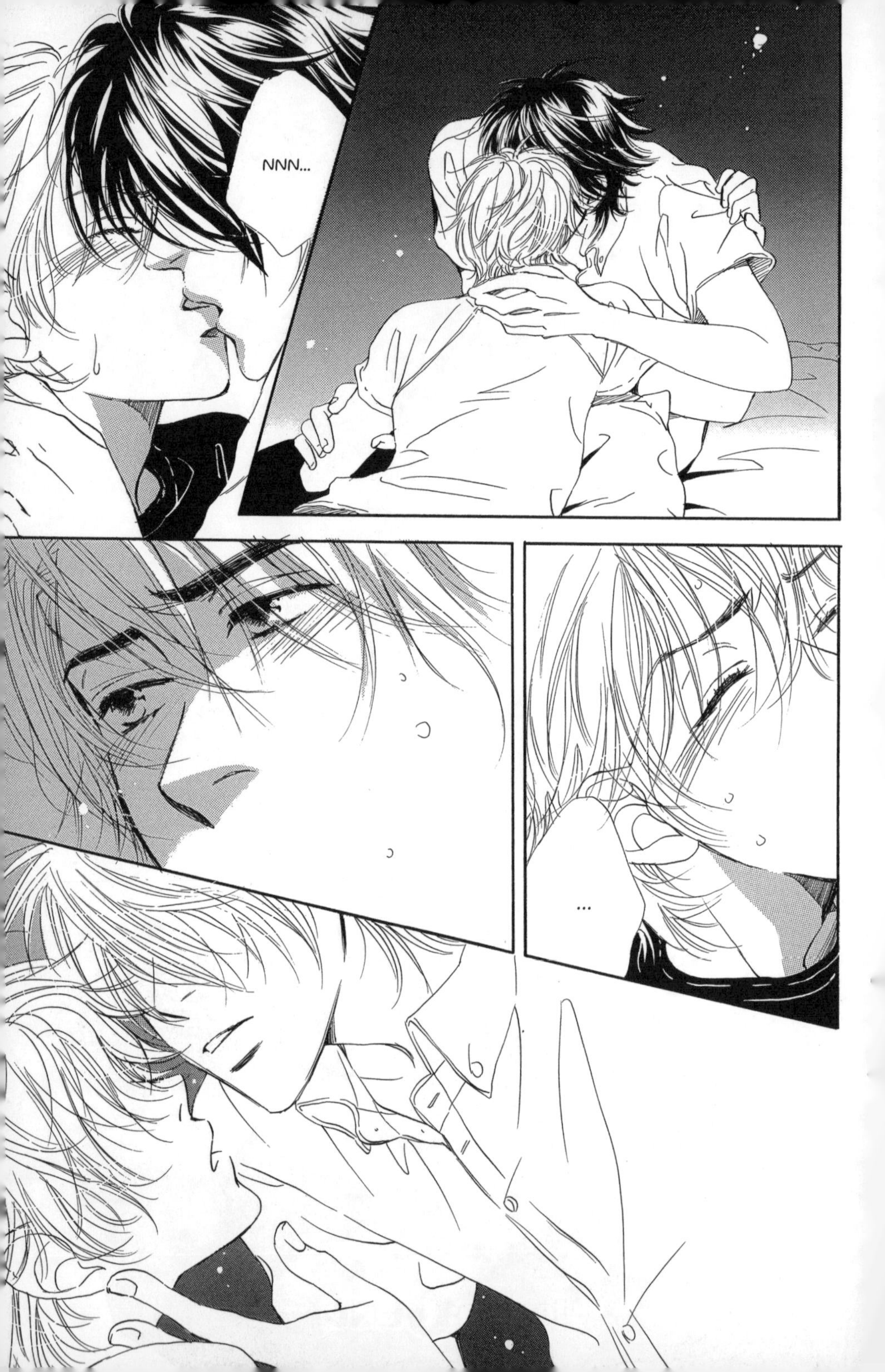
NNN...
...

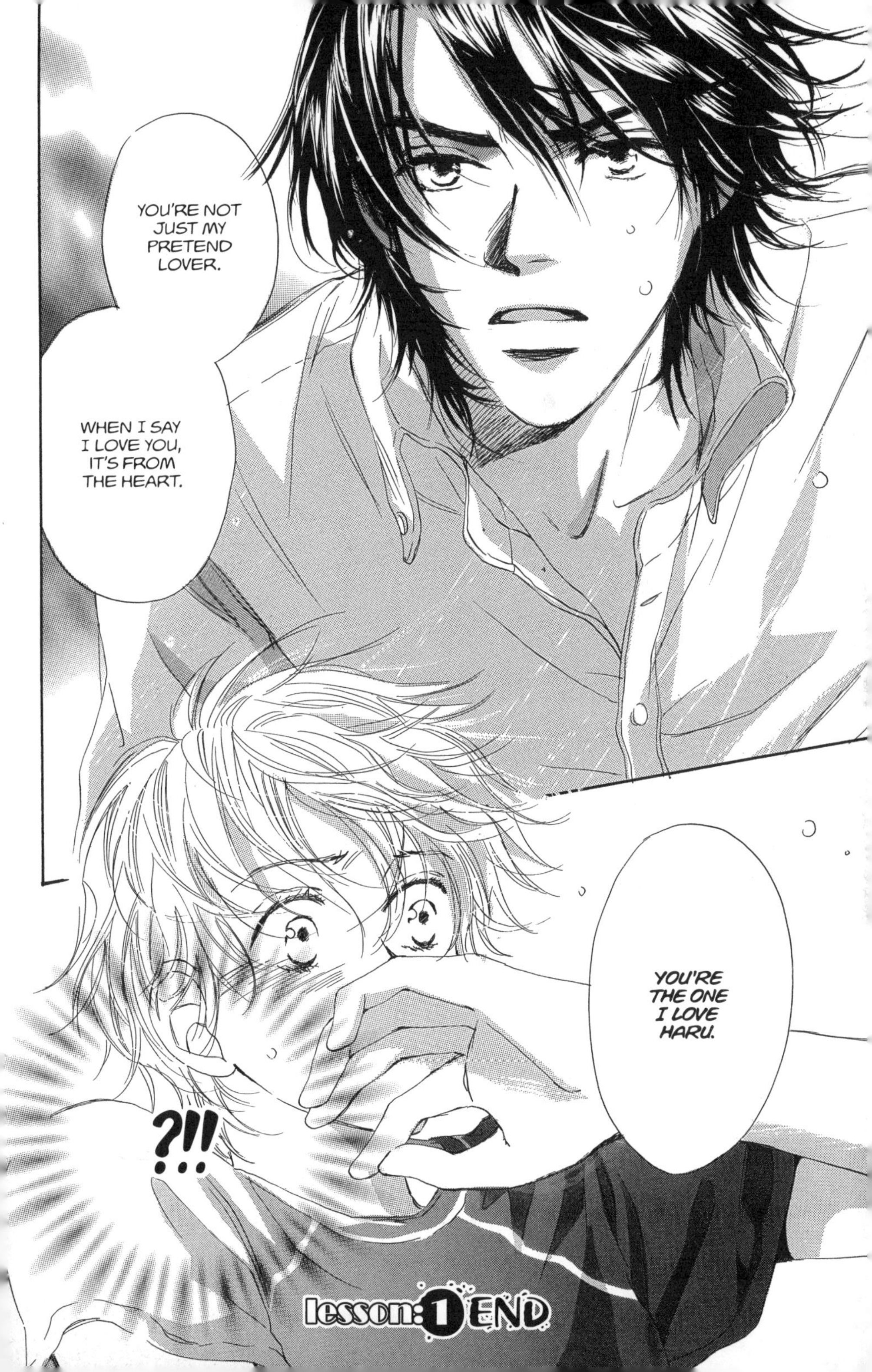
YOU'RE NOT JUST MY PRETEND LOVER.
WHEN I SAY I LOVE YOU, IT'S FROM THE HEART.
YOU'RE THE ONE I LOVE HARU.
?!!
lesson:1 END

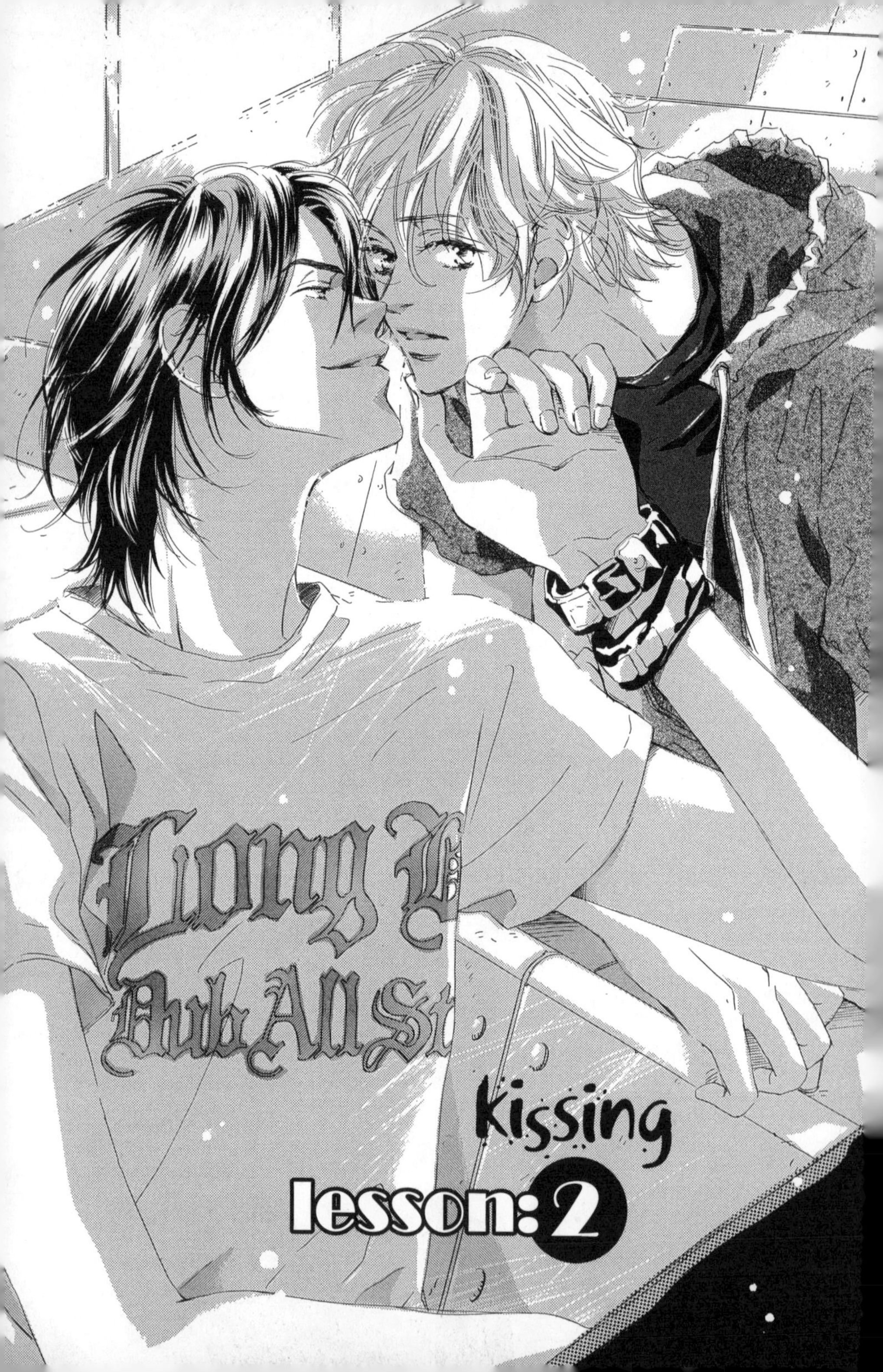
Kissing
lesson: 2

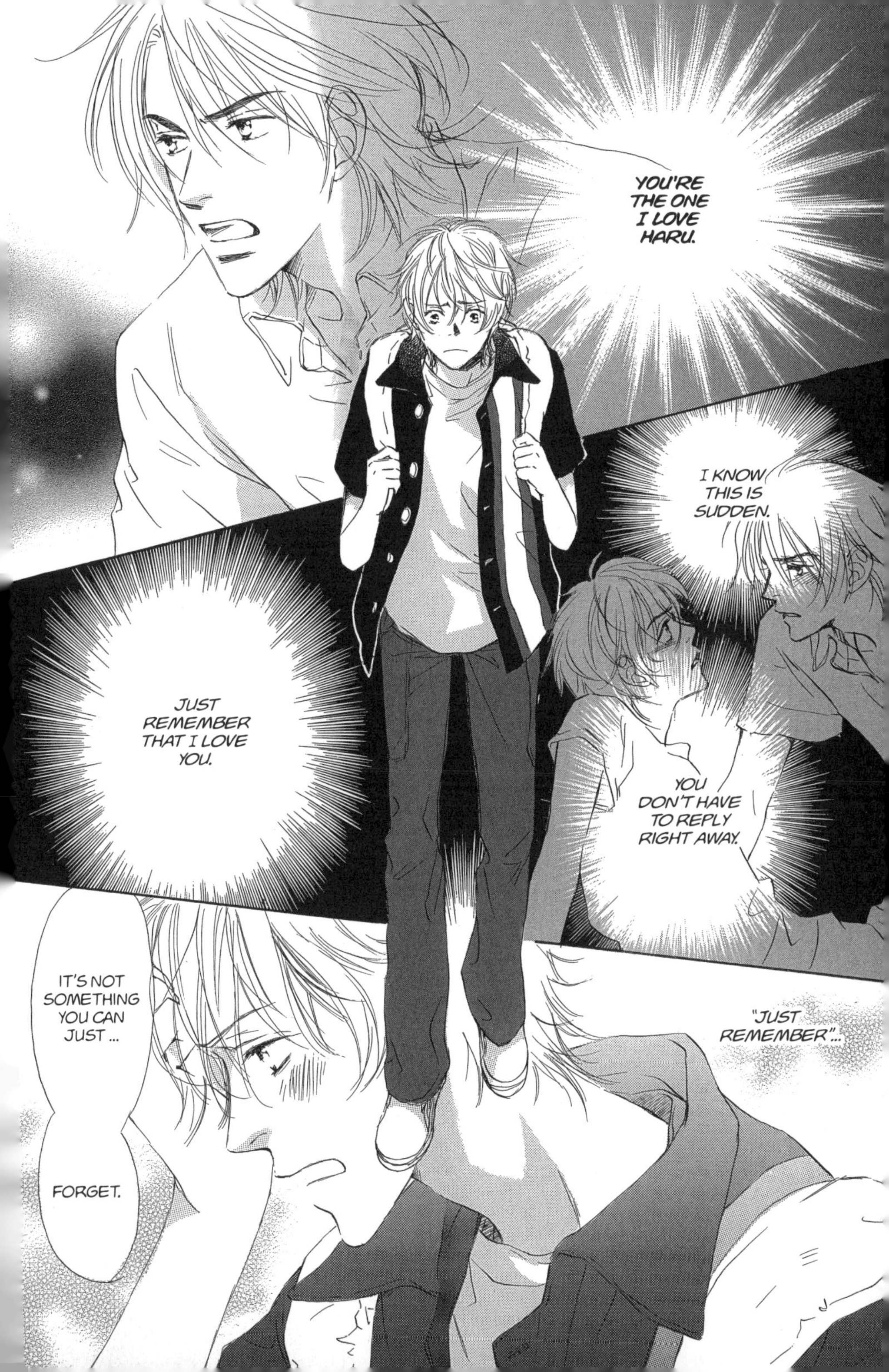
YOU'RE THE ONE I LOVE HARU.
I KNOW THIS IS SUDDEN.
YOU DON'T HAVE TO REPLY RIGHT AWAY.
JUST REMEMBER THAT I LOVE YOU.
"JUST REMEMBER"...
IT'S NOT SOMETHING YOU CAN JUST ...
FORGET.

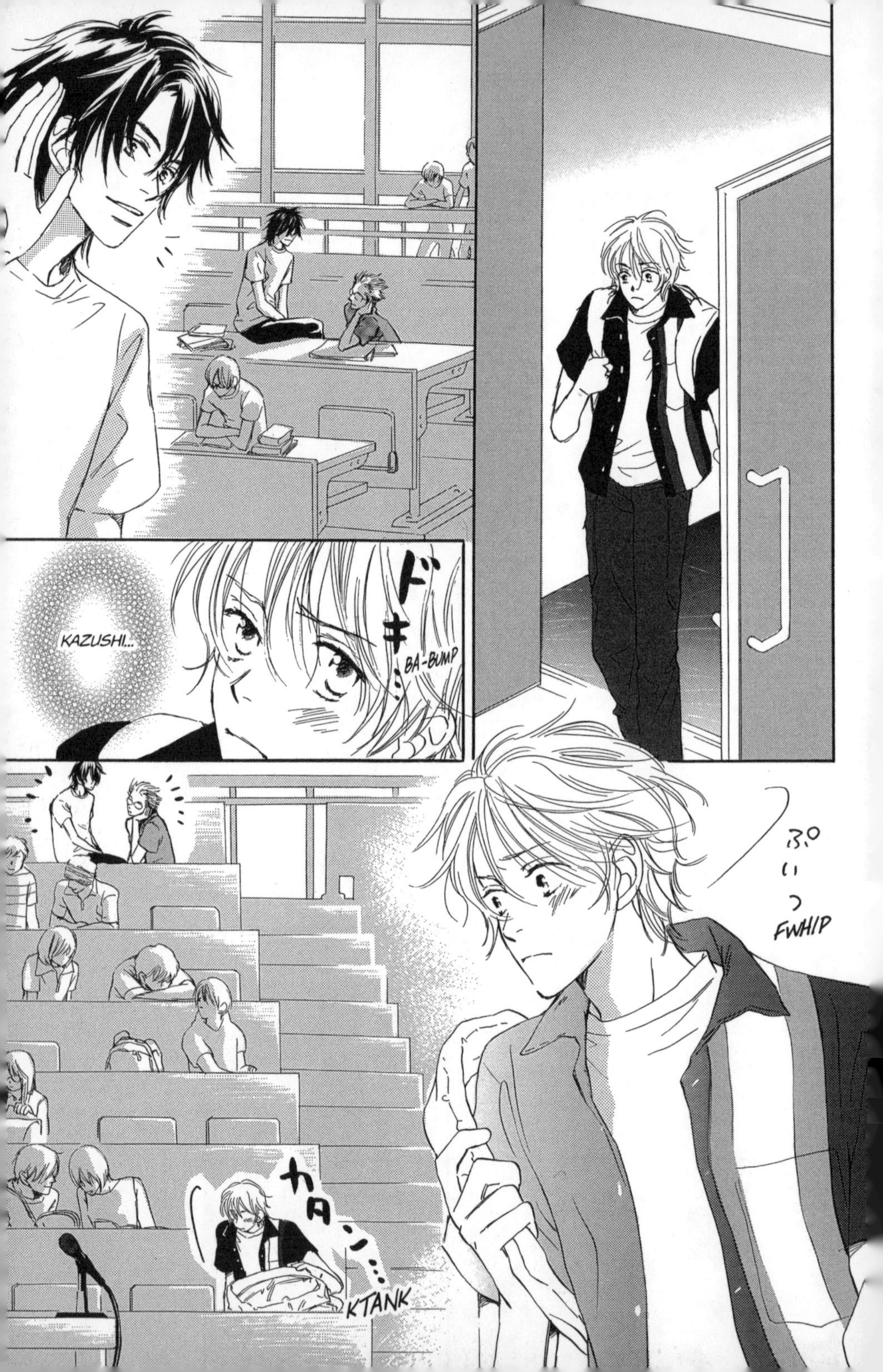
ドキ
BA-BUMP
KAZUSHI...
ぷいっ
FWHIP
カタン...
KTANK

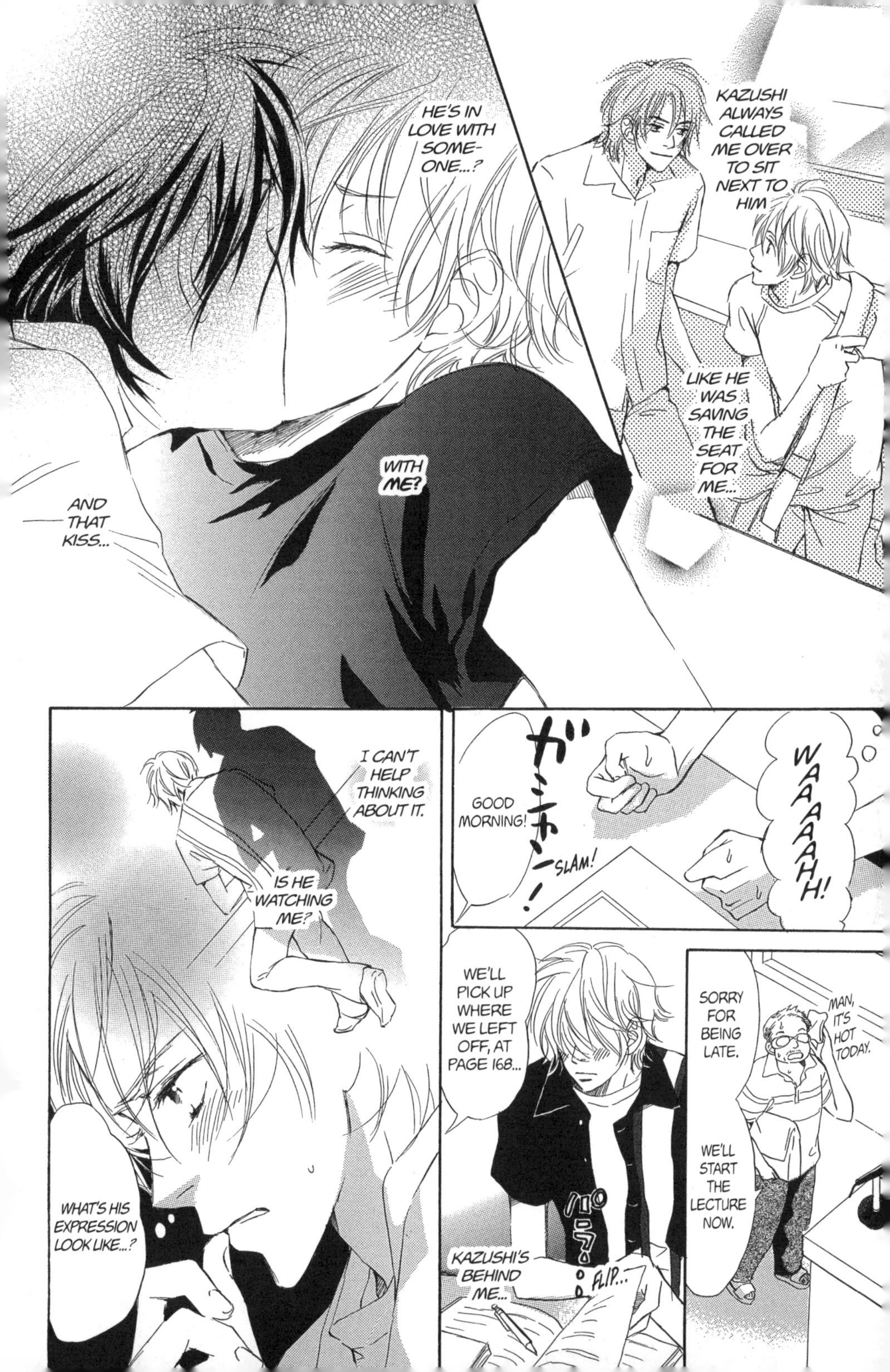
KAZUSHI ALWAYS CALLED ME OVER TO SIT NEXT TO HIM
LIKE HE WAS SAVING THE SEAT FOR ME...
HE'S IN LOVE WITH SOME-ONE...?
WITH ME?
AND THAT KISS...
WAAAAAAH!
GOOD MORNING!
SLAM!
SORRY FOR BEING LATE.
MAN, IT'S HOT TODAY.
WE'LL START THE LECTURE NOW.
WE'LL PICK UP WHERE WE LEFT OFF, AT PAGE 168...
KAZUSHI'S BEHIND ME...
FLIP...
I CAN'T HELP THINKING ABOUT IT.
IS HE WATCHING ME?
WHAT'S HIS EXPRESSION LOOK LIKE...?

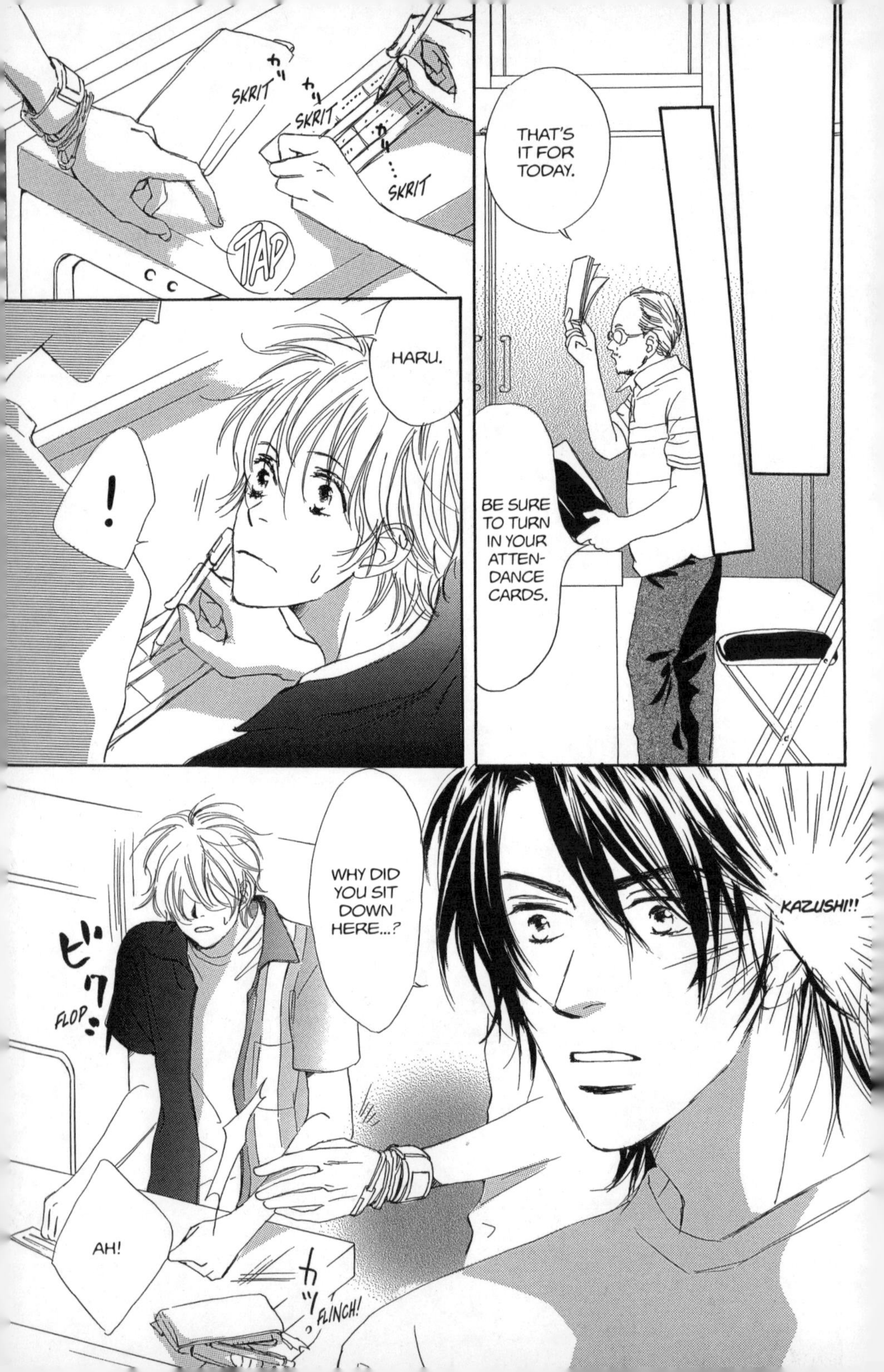
THAT'S IT FOR TODAY.
BE SURE TO TURN IN YOUR ATTEN-DANCE CARDS.
SKRIT
SKRIT
SKRIT
TAP
HARU.
!
KAZUSHI!!
WHY DID YOU SIT DOWN HERE...?
ビク
FLOP
AH!
カッ
FLINCH!

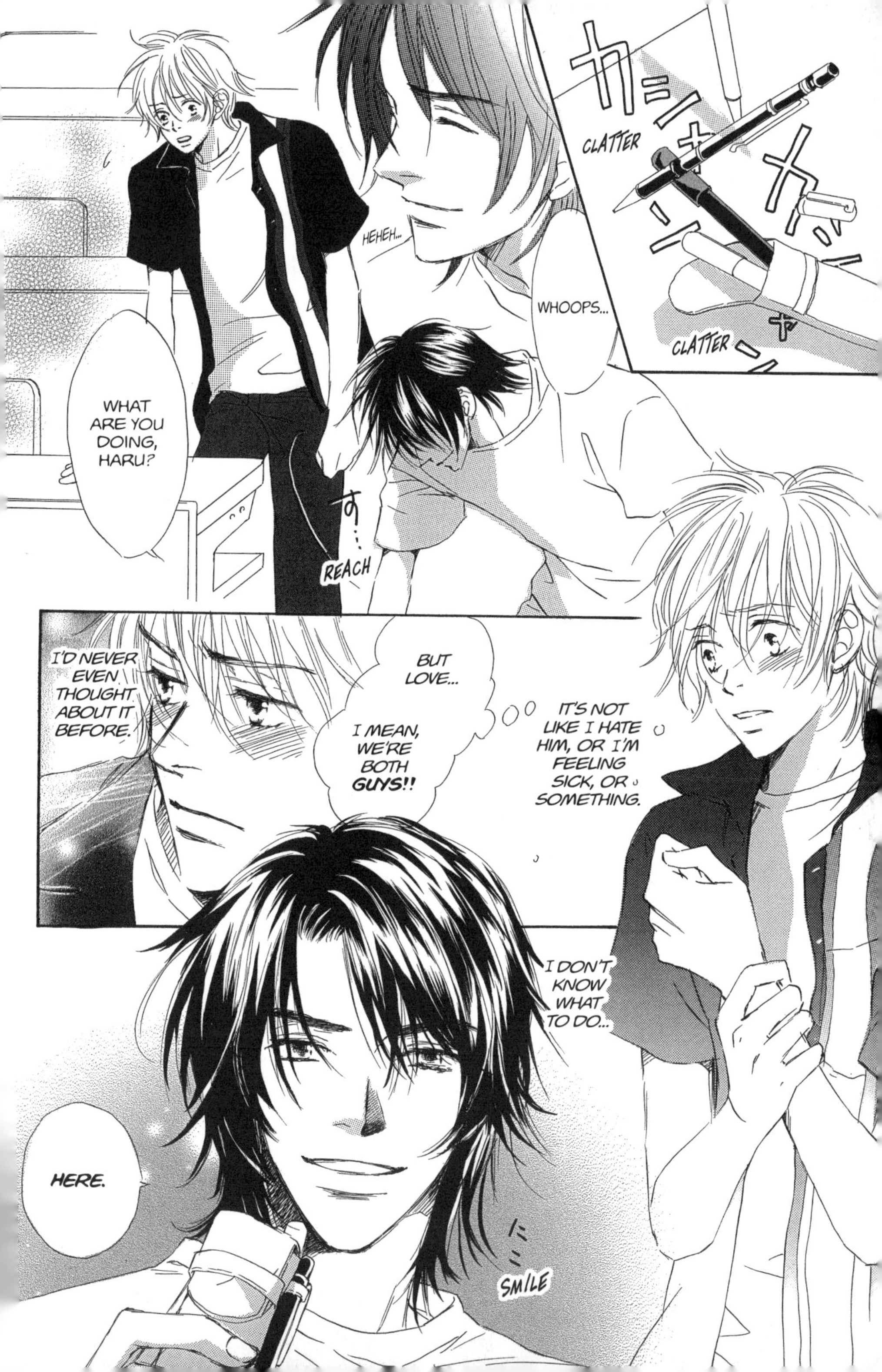
CLATTER
CLATTER
WHOOPS...
HEHEH...
REACH
WHAT ARE YOU DOING, HARU?
IT'S NOT LIKE I HATE HIM, OR I'M FEELING SICK, OR SOMETHING.
I DON'T KNOW WHAT TO DO...
BUT LOVE...
I MEAN, WE'RE BOTH GUYS!!
I'D NEVER EVEN THOUGHT ABOUT IT BEFORE.
SMILE
HERE.

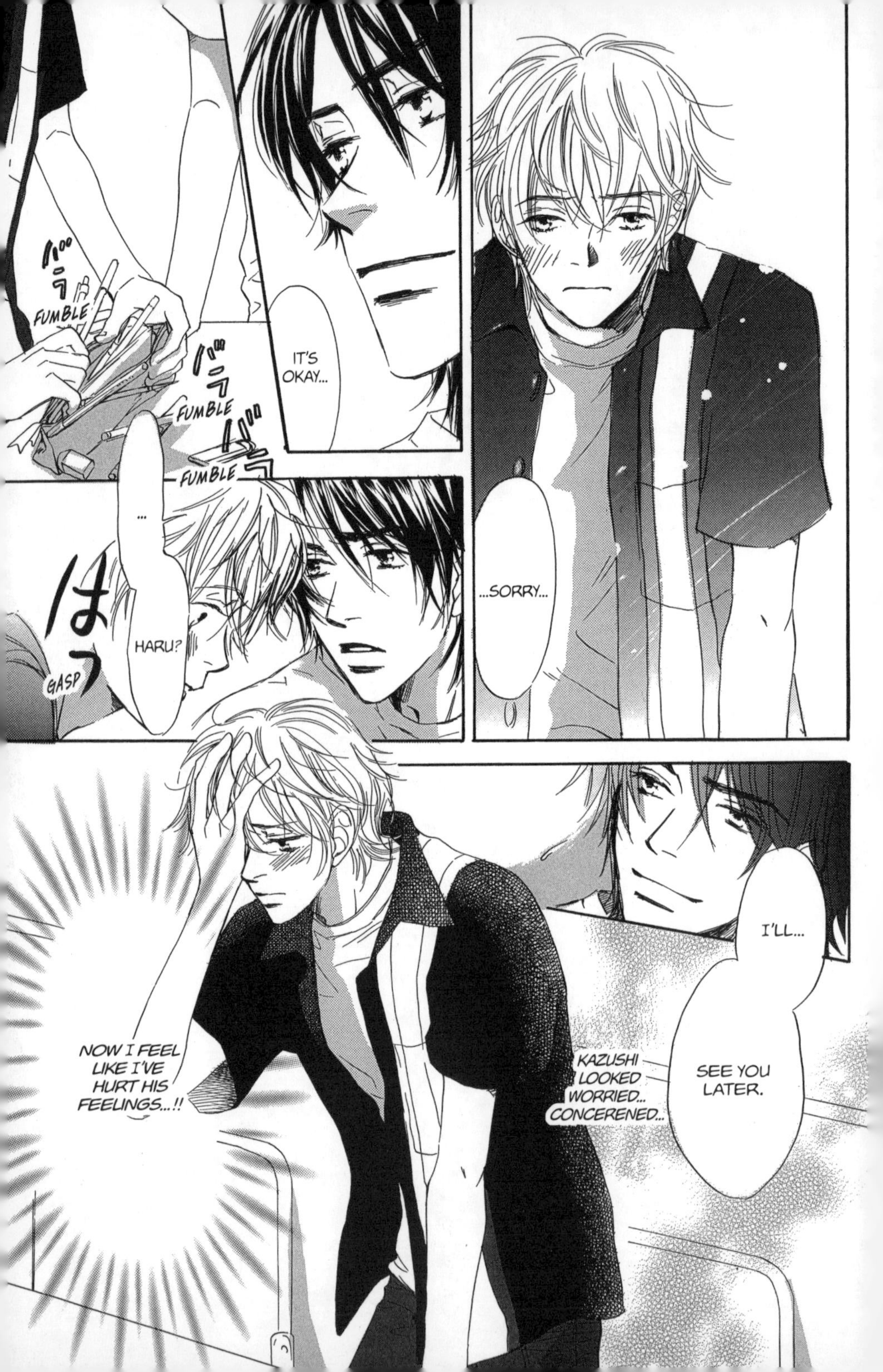

...SORRY...
IT'S OKAY...
FUMBLE
FUMBLE
FUMBLE
...
HARU?
GASP
I'LL...
SEE YOU LATER.
KAZUSHI LOOKED WORRIED... CONCERNED...
NOW I FEEL LIKE I'VE HURT HIS FEELINGS...!!

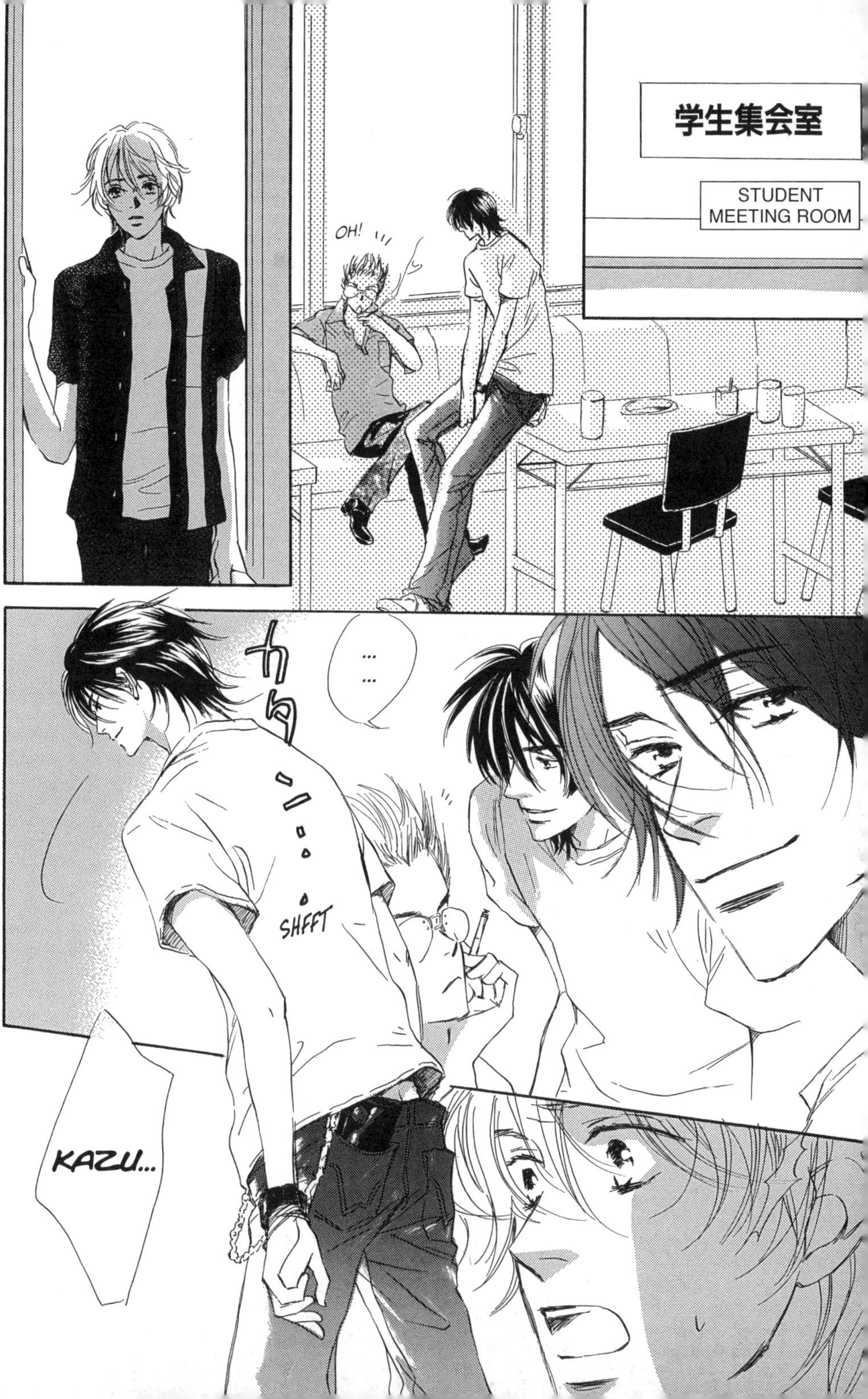
学生集会室
STUDENT MEETING ROOM
OH!
...
...
SHFFT
KAZU...

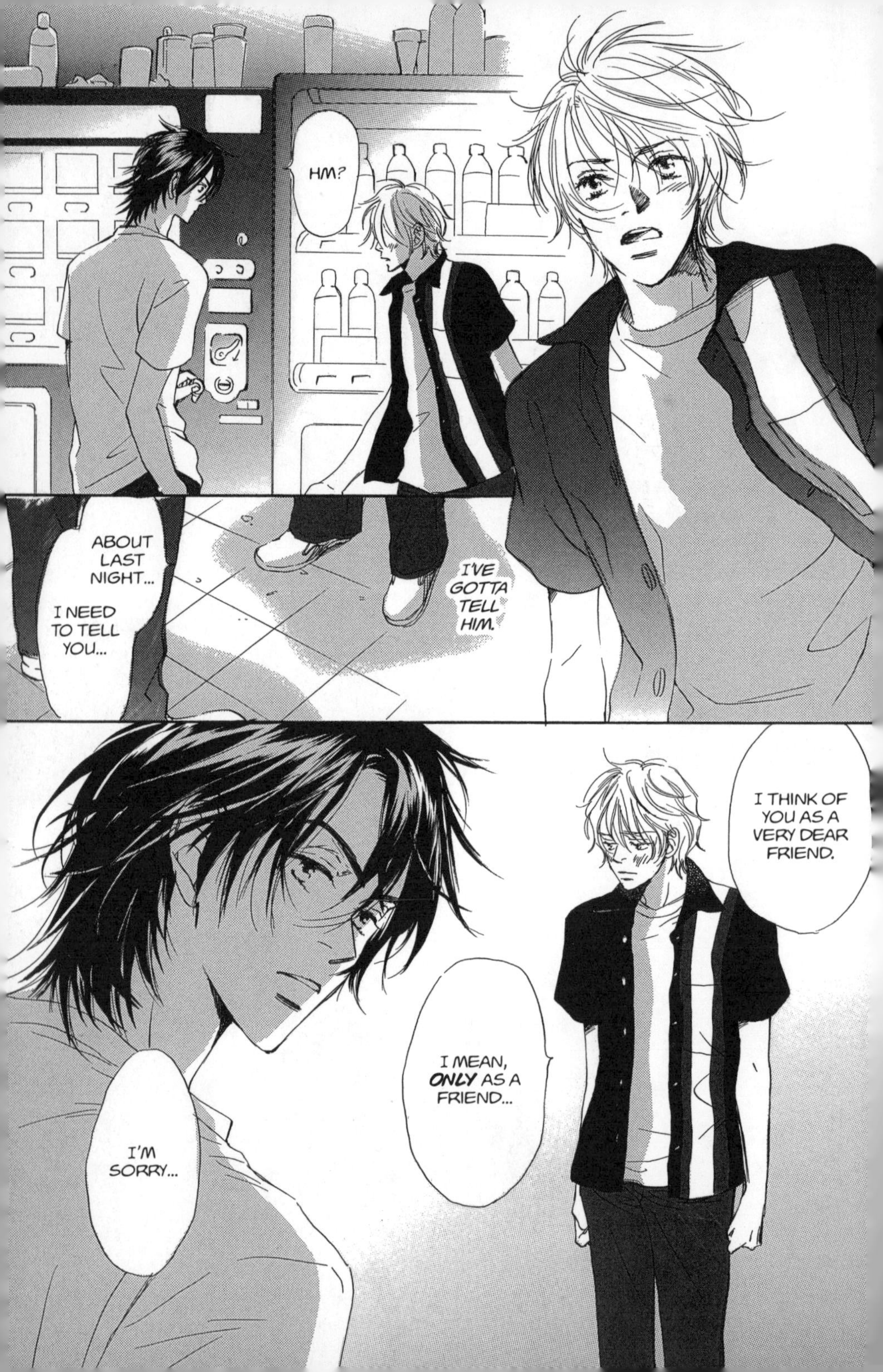
HM?
I'VE GOTTA TELL HIM.
ABOUT LAST NIGHT...
I NEED TO TELL YOU...
I THINK OF YOU AS A VERY DEAR FRIEND.
I MEAN, ONLY AS A FRIEND...
I'M SORRY...

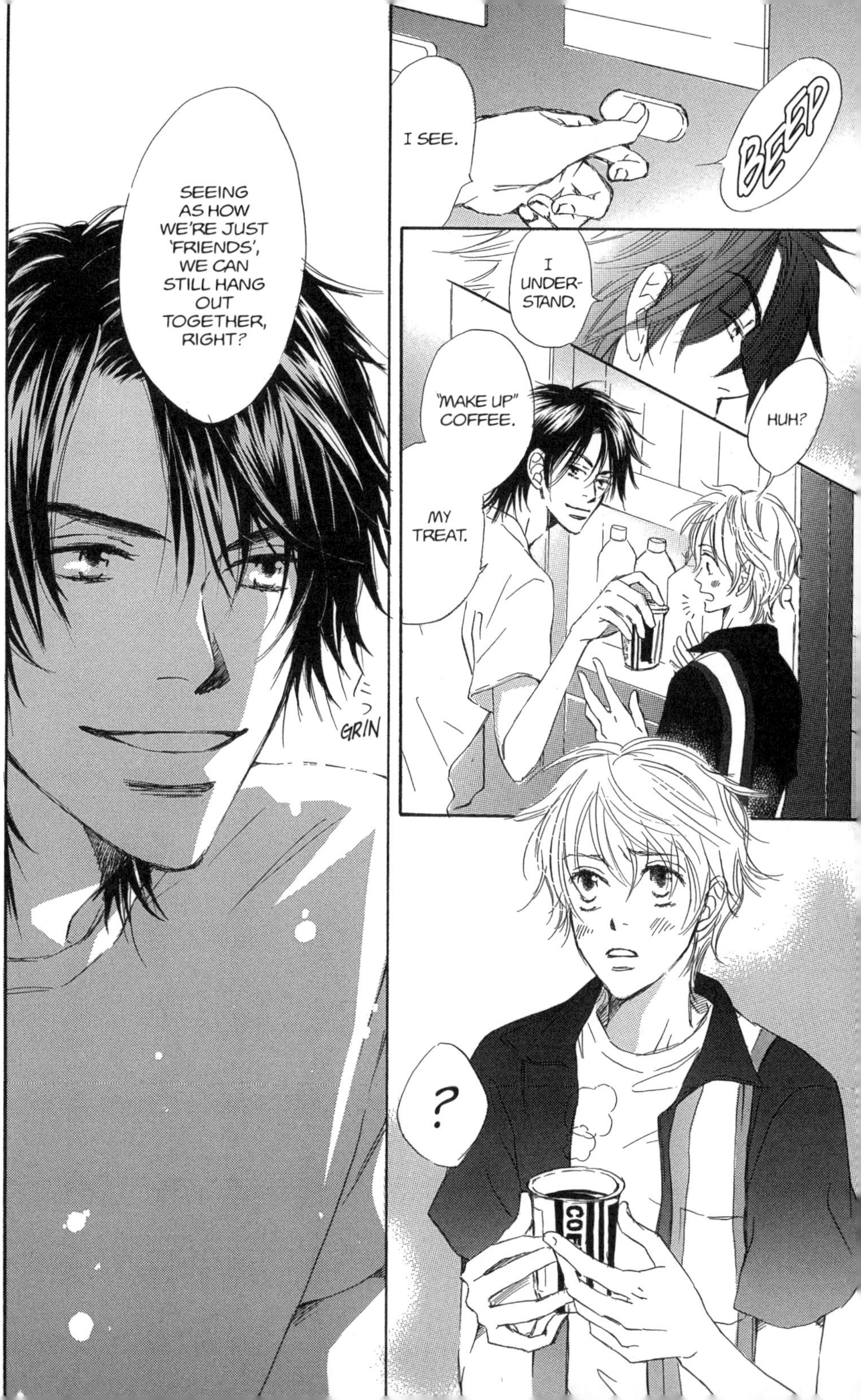
BEEP
I SEE.
I UNDER-STAND.
HUH?
"MAKE UP" COFFEE.
MY TREAT.
?
COF
SEEING AS HOW WE'RE JUST 'FRIENDS', WE CAN STILL HANG OUT TOGETHER, RIGHT?
GRIN

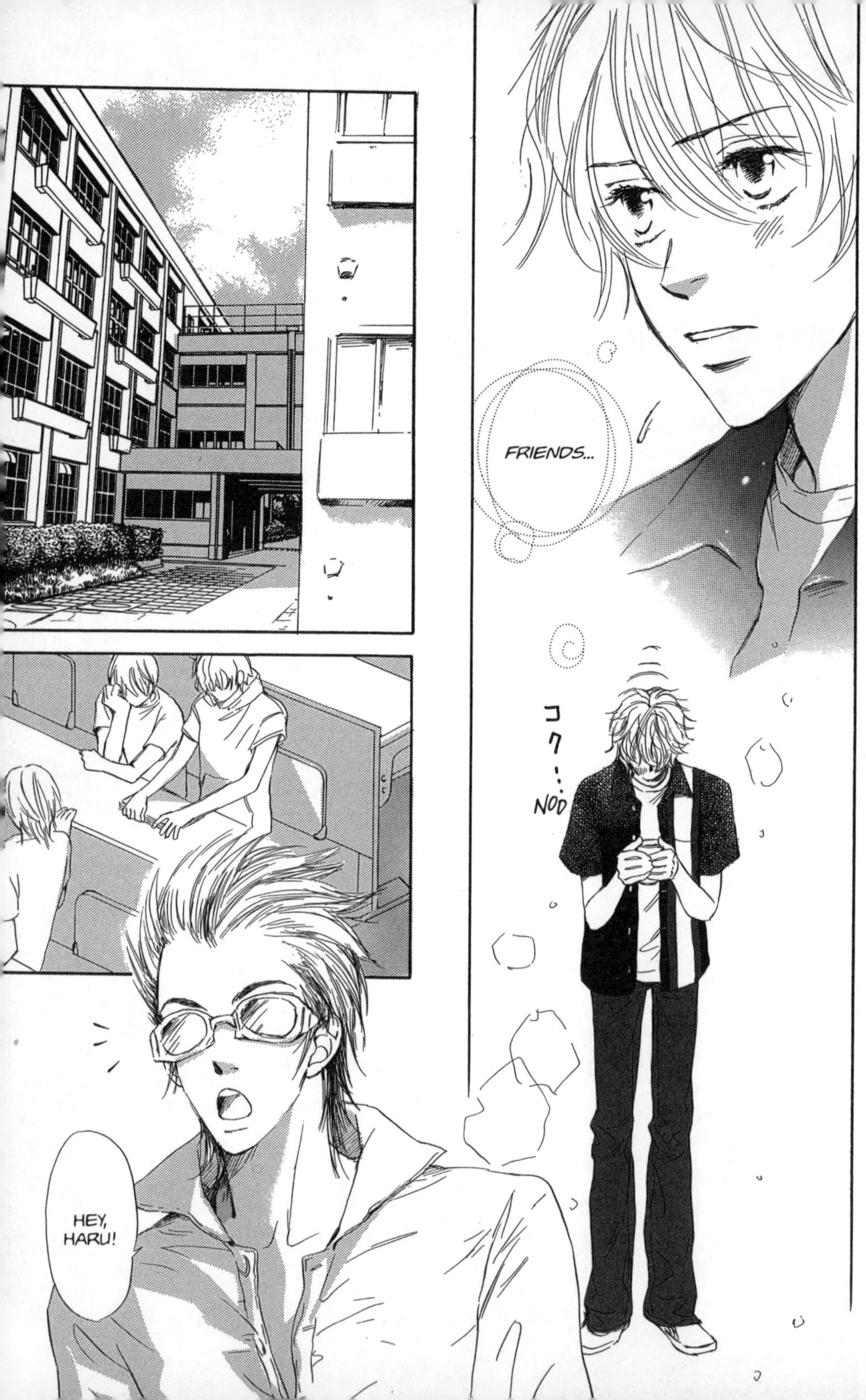
FRIENDS...
コク...
NOD
HEY, HARU!

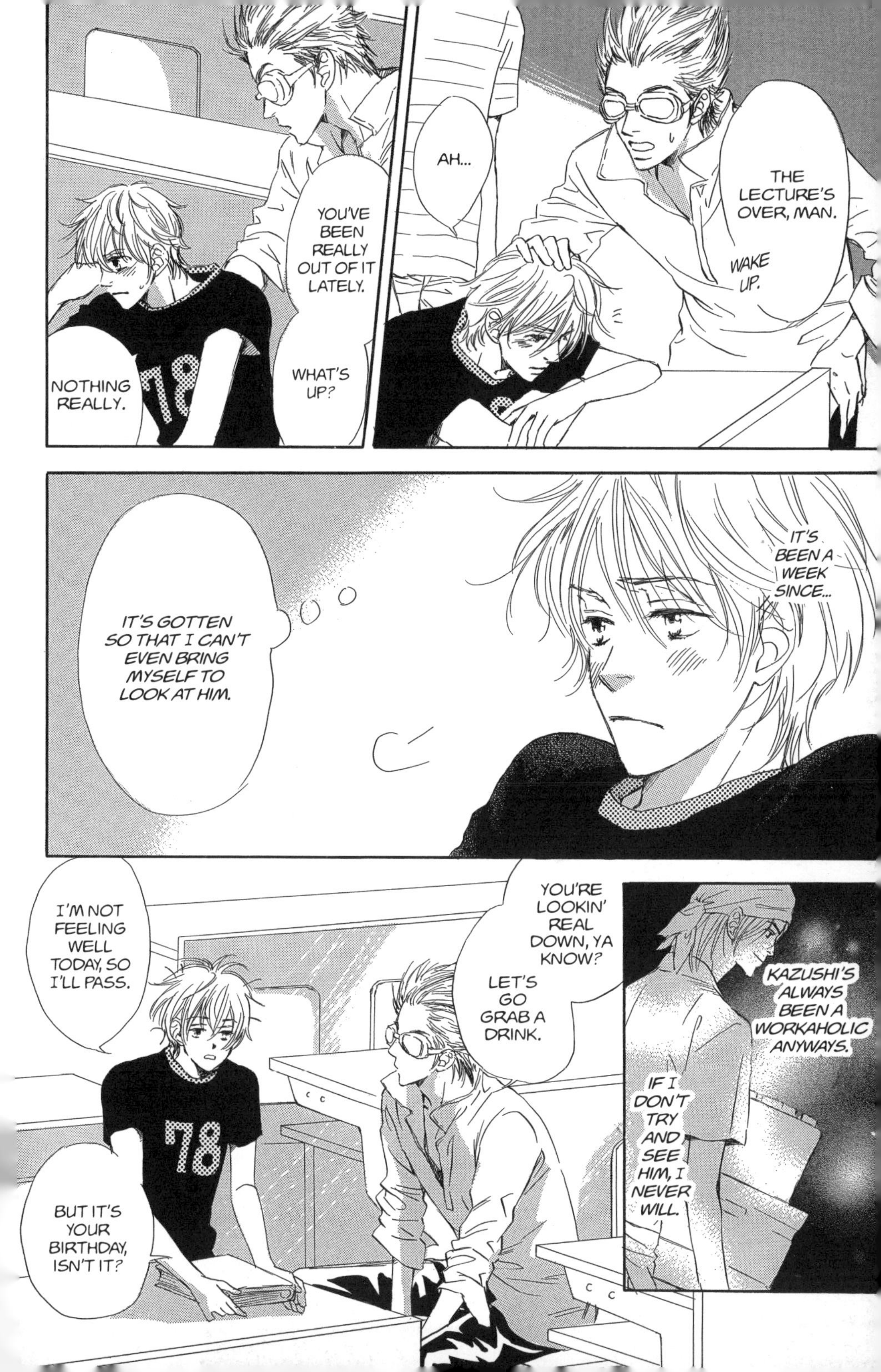
THE LECTURE'S OVER, MAN.
WAKE UP.
AH...
YOU'VE BEEN REALLY OUT OF IT LATELY.
WHAT'S UP?
NOTHING REALLY.
IT'S BEEN A WEEK SINCE...
IT'S GOTTEN SO THAT I CAN'T EVEN BRING MYSELF TO LOOK AT HIM.
KAZUSHI'S ALWAYS BEEN A WORKAHOLIC ANYWAYS.
IF I DON'T TRY AND SEE HIM, I NEVER WILL.
YOU'RE LOOKIN' REAL DOWN, YA KNOW?
LET'S GO GRAB A DRINK.
I'M NOT FEELING WELL TODAY, SO I'LL PASS.
BUT IT'S YOUR BIRTHDAY, ISN'T IT?

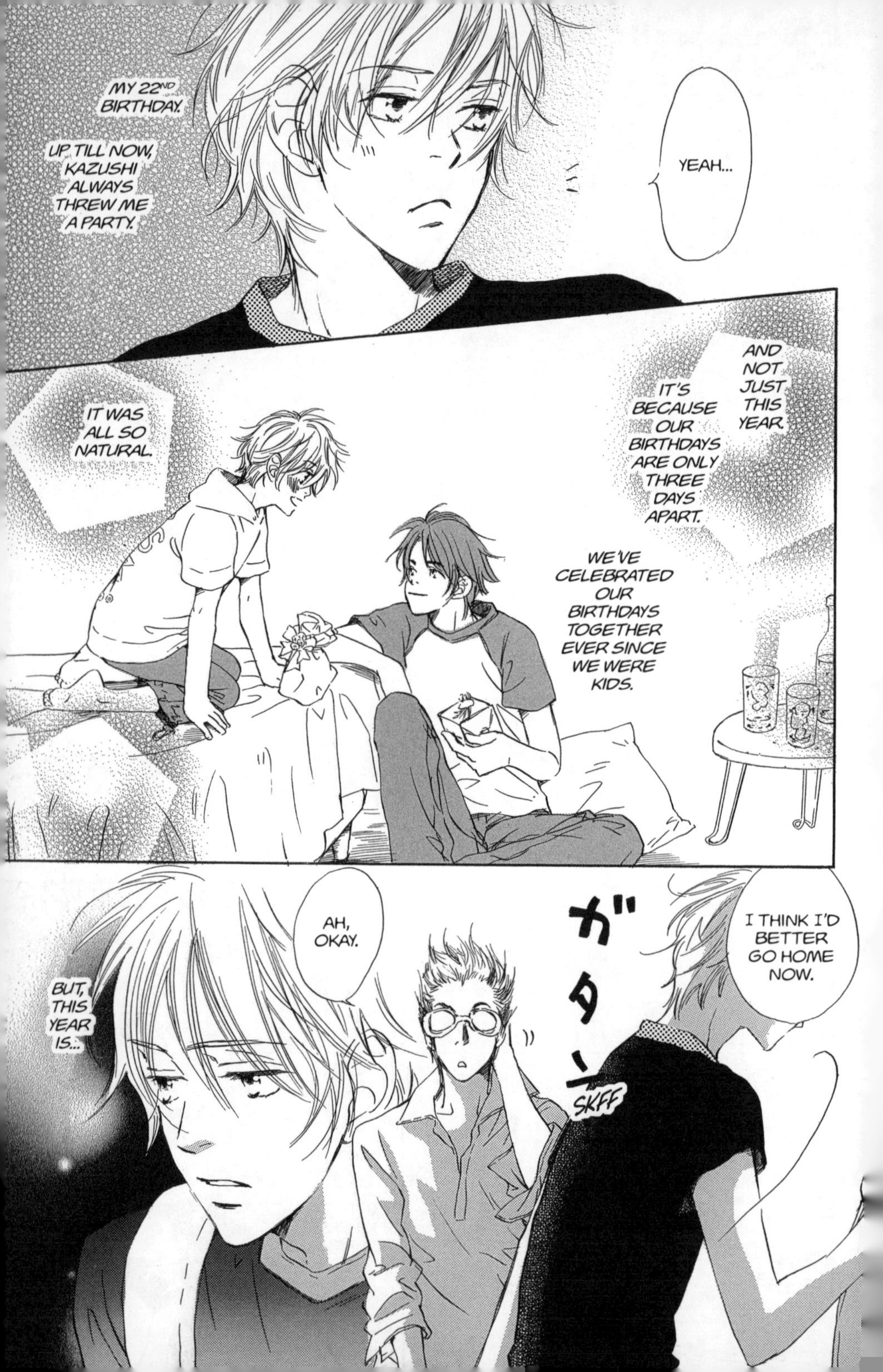
YEAH...
MY 22ND BIRTHDAY.
UP TILL NOW, KAZUSHI ALWAYS THREW ME A PARTY.
AND NOT JUST THIS YEAR.
IT'S BECAUSE OUR BIRTHDAYS ARE ONLY THREE DAYS APART.
WE'VE CELEBRATED OUR BIRTHDAYS TOGETHER EVER SINCE WE WERE KIDS.
IT WAS ALL SO NATURAL.
I THINK I'D BETTER GO HOME NOW.
ガタン
SKFF
AH, OKAY.
BUT, THIS YEAR IS...

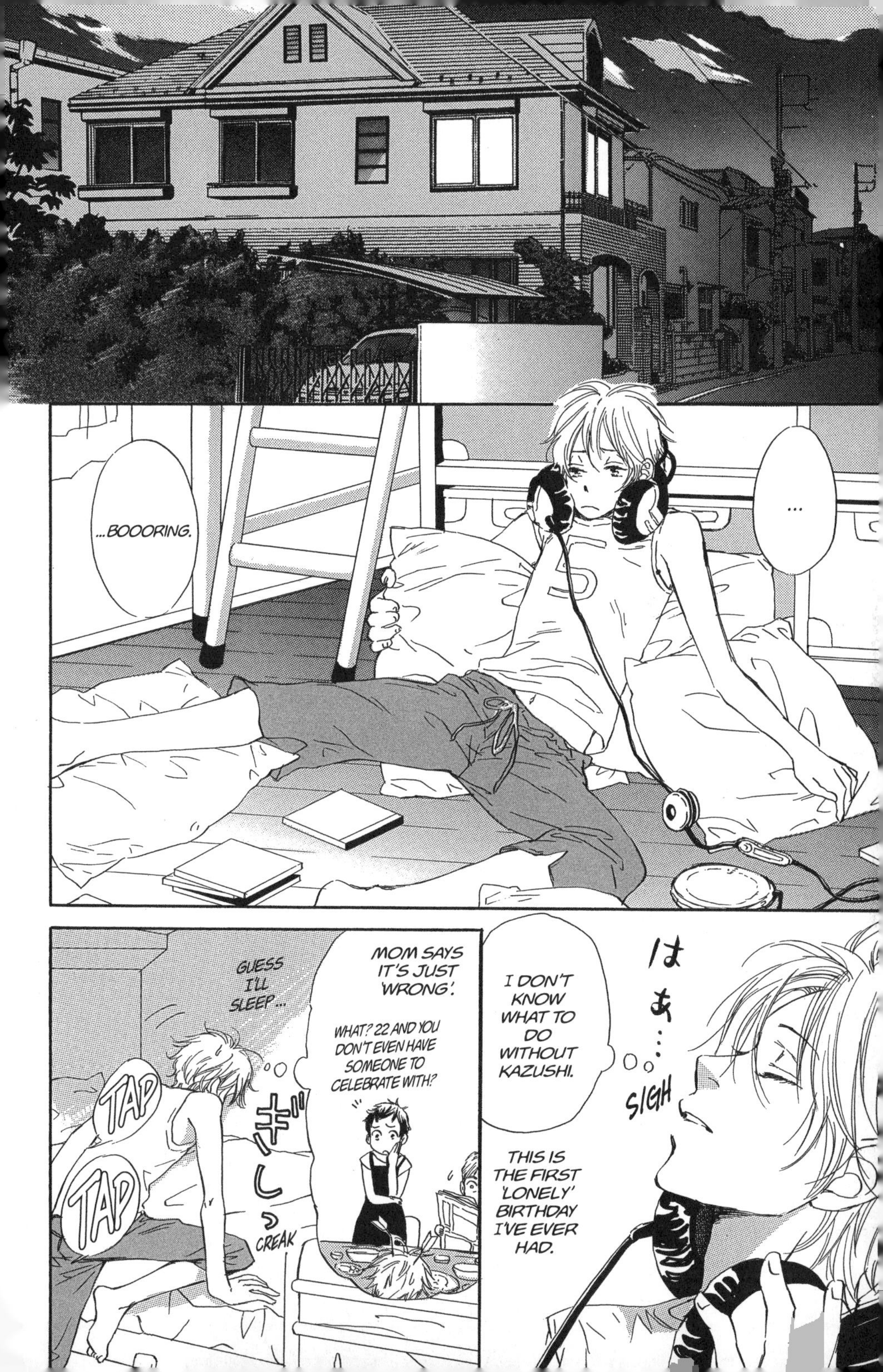
...
...BOOORING.
はぁ…
SIGH
I DON'T KNOW WHAT TO DO WITHOUT KAZUSHI.
THIS IS THE FIRST 'LONELY' BIRTHDAY I'VE EVER HAD.
MOM SAYS IT'S JUST 'WRONG'.
WHAT? 22 AND YOU DON'T EVEN HAVE SOMEONE TO CELEBRATE WITH?
ギシっ
CREAK
GUESS I'LL SLEEP...
TAP
TAP

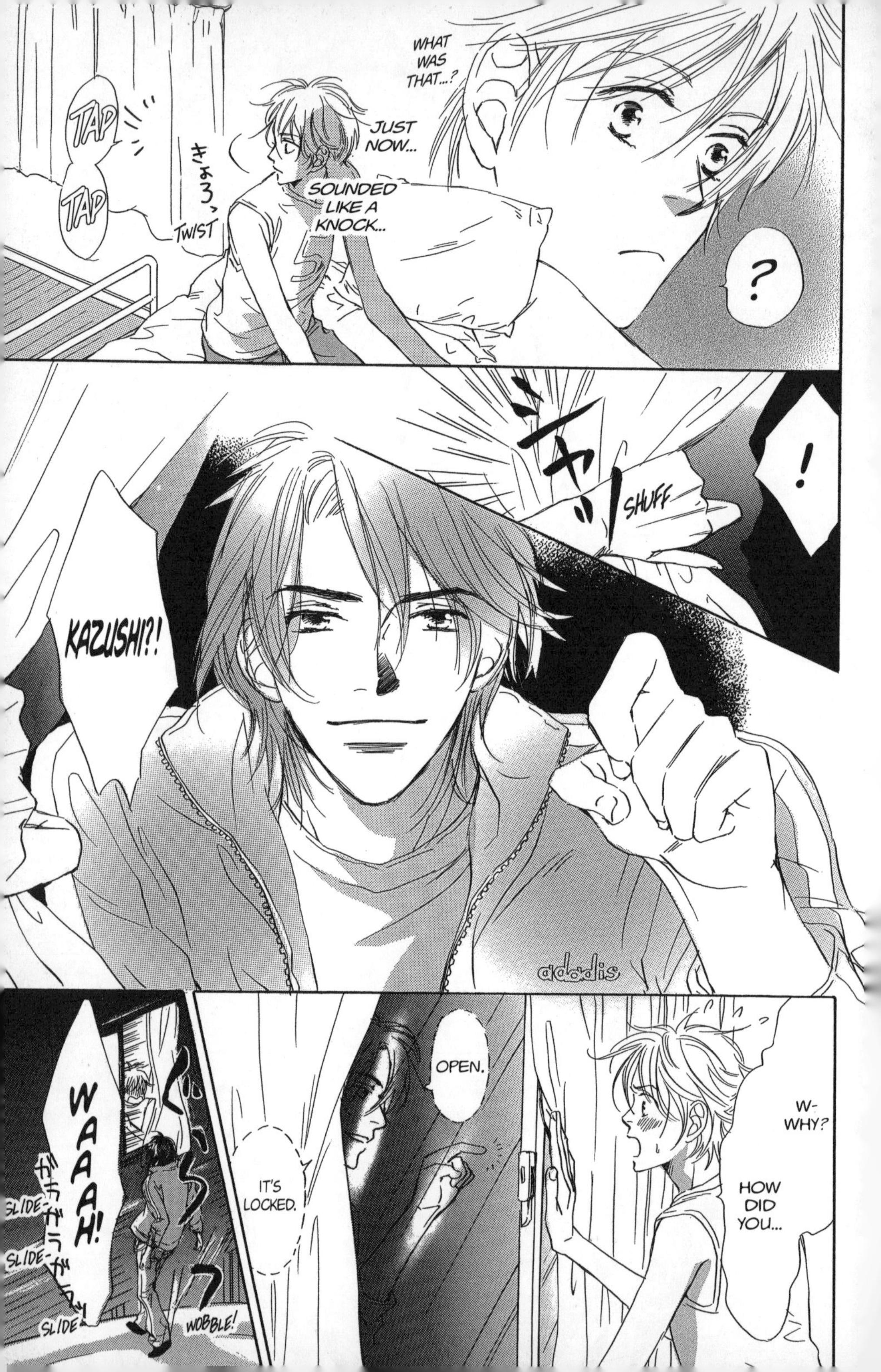
?
WHAT WAS THAT...?
JUST NOW...
SOUNDED LIKE A KNOCK...
きょろっ
TWIST
TAP
TAP
!
SHUFF
KAZUSHI?!
adadis
W-WHY?
HOW DID YOU...
OPEN.
IT'S LOCKED.
WAAAH!
SLIDE-
SLIDE-
SLIDE
WOBBLE!

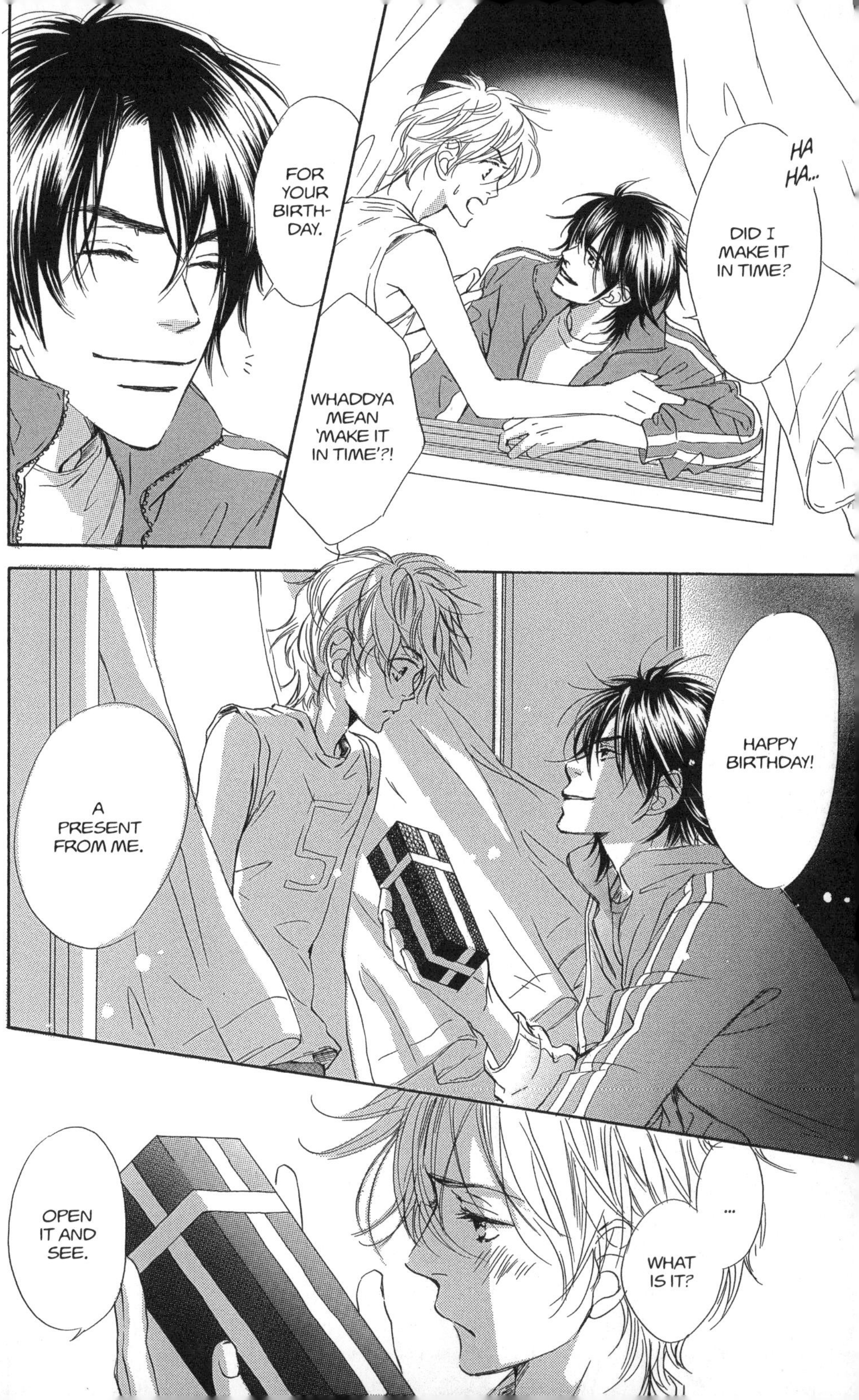
HA HA...
DID I MAKE IT IN TIME?
WHADDYA MEAN 'MAKE IT IN TIME'?!
FOR YOUR BIRTH-DAY.
HAPPY BIRTHDAY!
A PRESENT FROM ME.
... WHAT IS IT?
OPEN IT AND SEE.

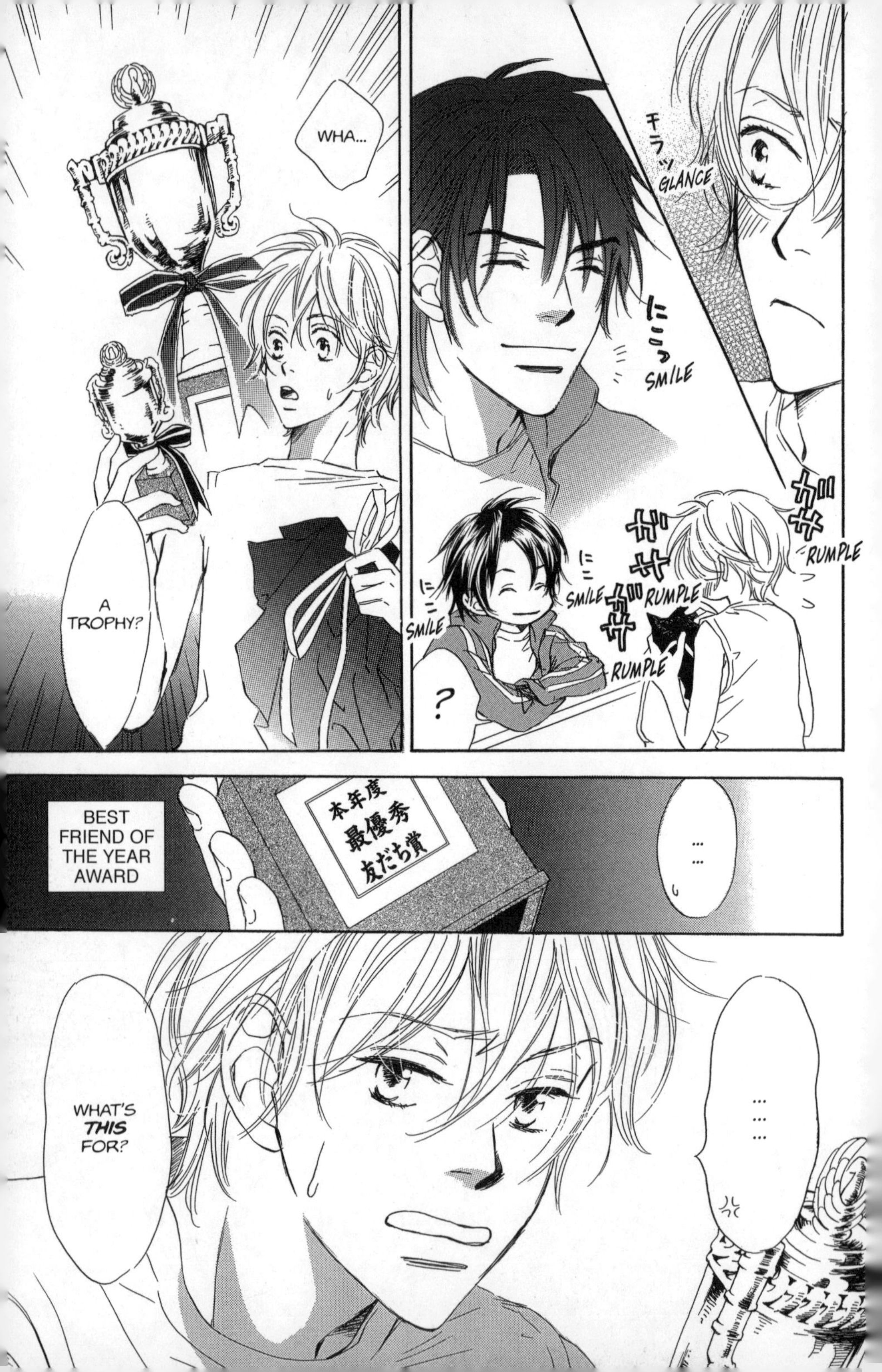

チラッ
GLANCE
にこっ
SMILE
ガサ
RUMPLE
ガサ
RUMPLE
にこ
SMILE
にこ
SMILE
ガサ
RUMPLE
?
WHA...
A TROPHY?
......
BEST FRIEND OF THE YEAR AWARD
本年度 最優秀 友だち賞
....
WHAT'S **THIS** FOR?

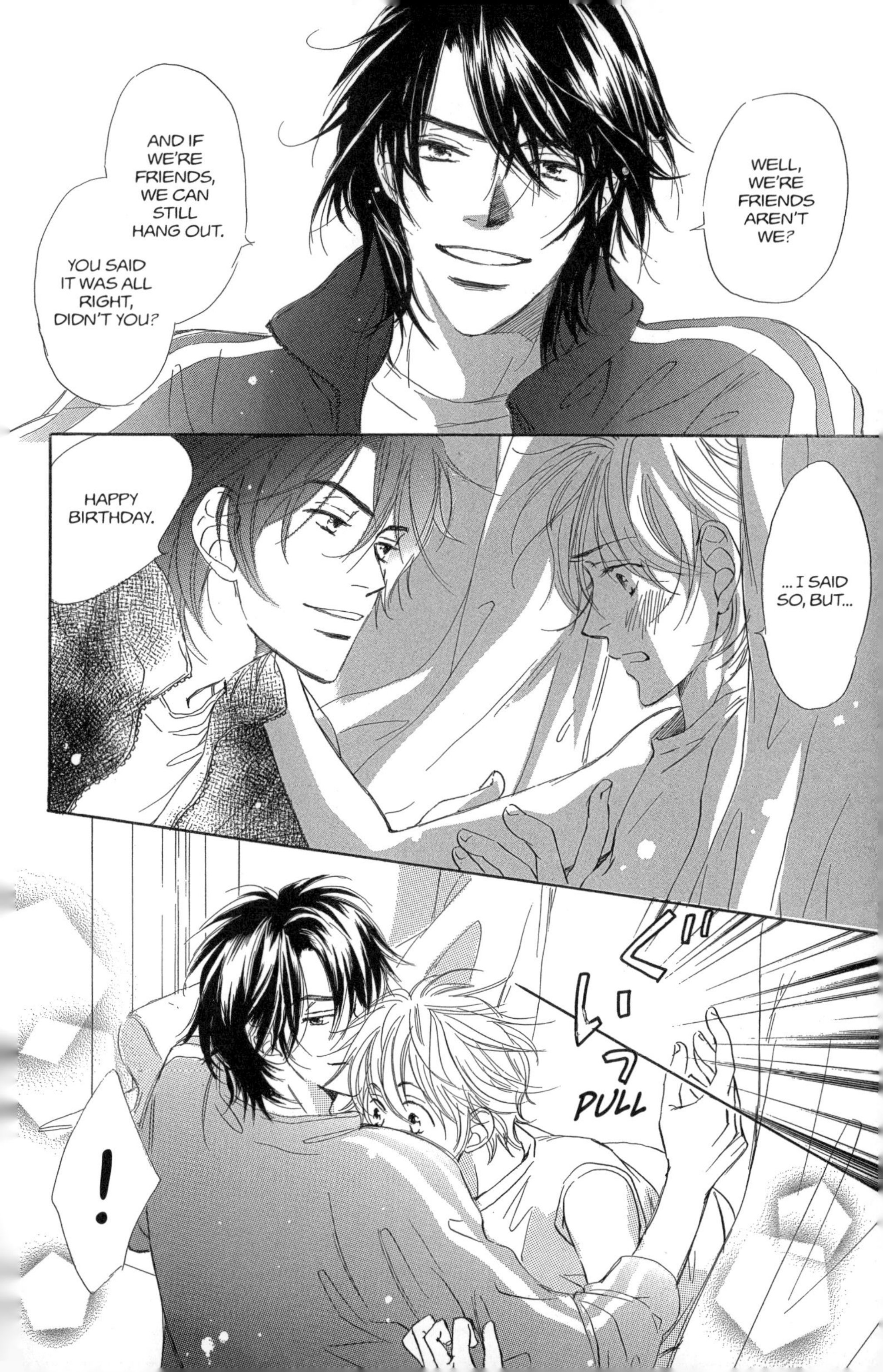
WELL, WE'RE FRIENDS AREN'T WE?
AND IF WE'RE FRIENDS, WE CAN STILL HANG OUT.
YOU SAID IT WAS ALL RIGHT, DIDN'T YOU?
...I SAID SO, BUT...
HAPPY BIRTHDAY.
PULL
!

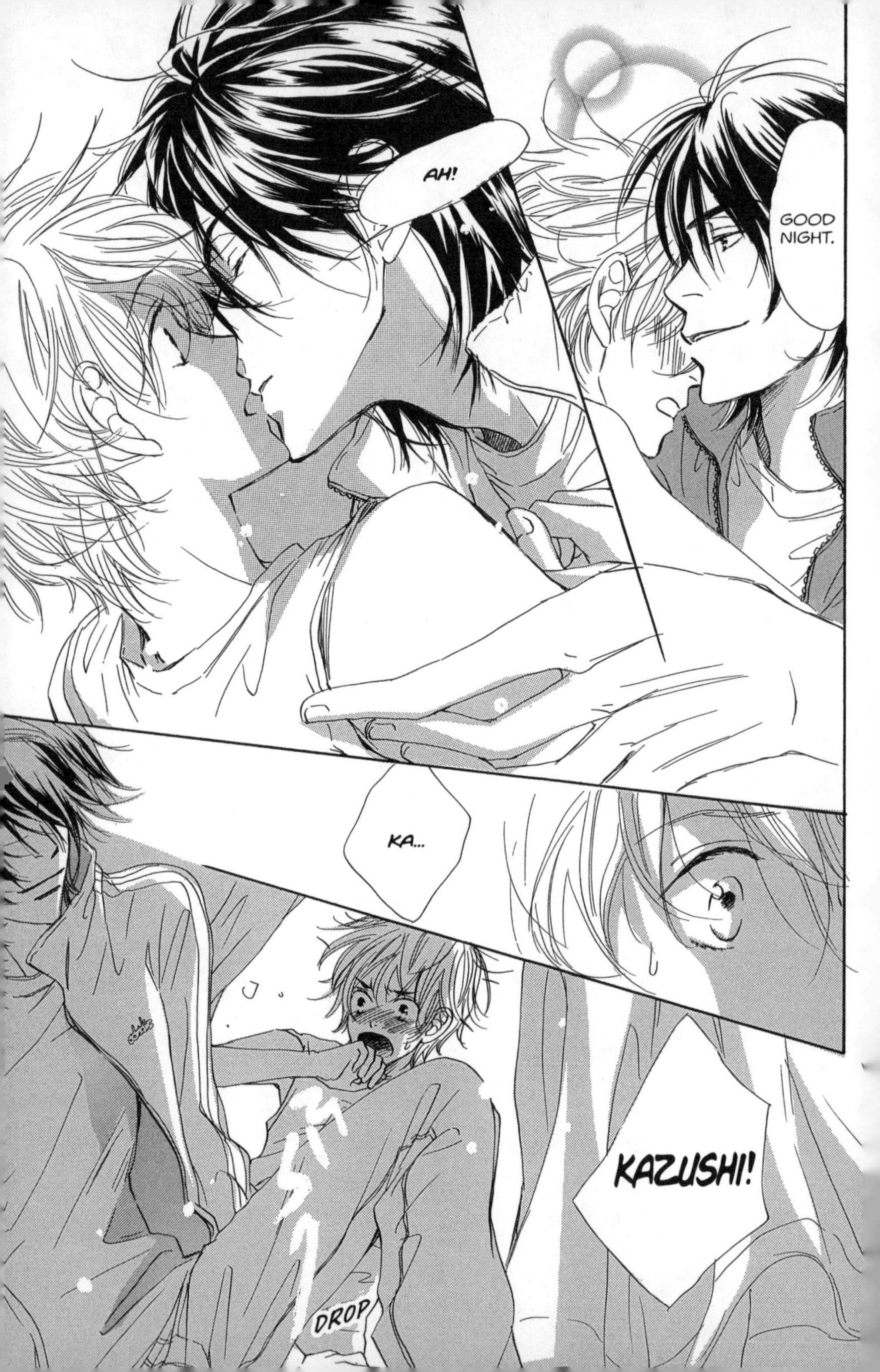

GOOD NIGHT.
AH!
KA...
KAZUSHI!
DROP

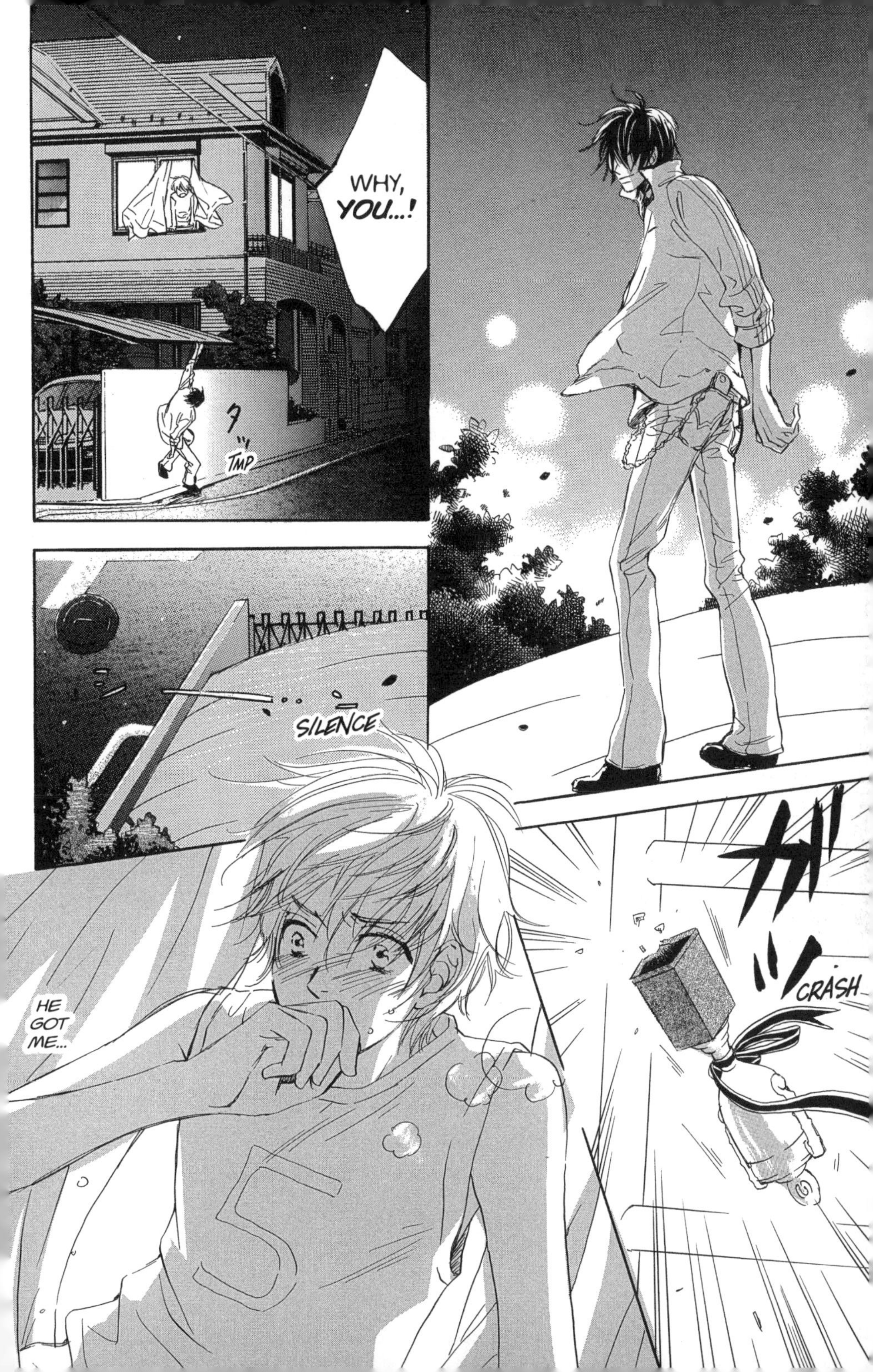

WHY, YOU...!
タッ
TMP
SILENCE
ガッ
CRASH
HE GOT ME...

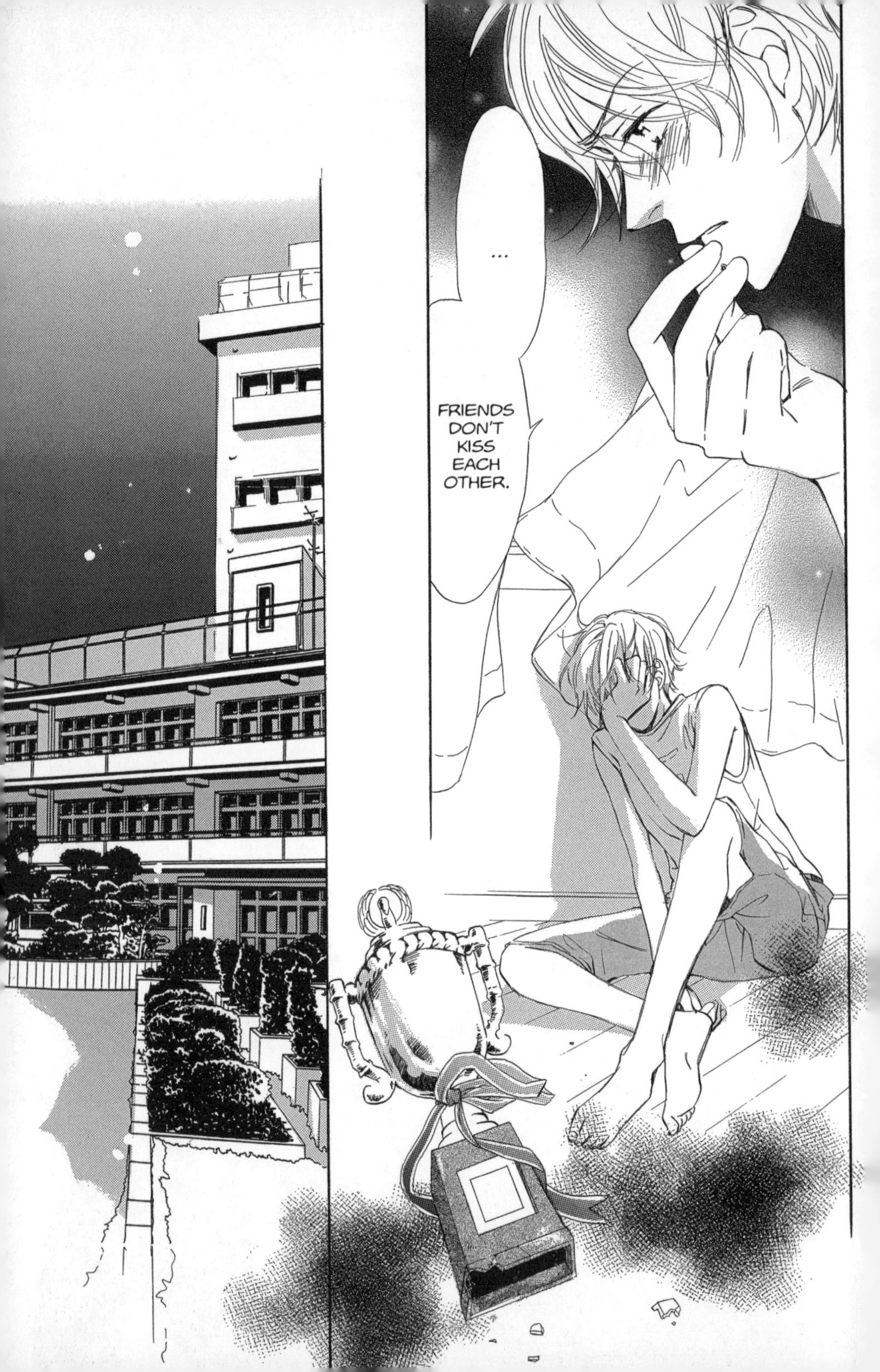
...
FRIENDS DON'T KISS EACH OTHER.

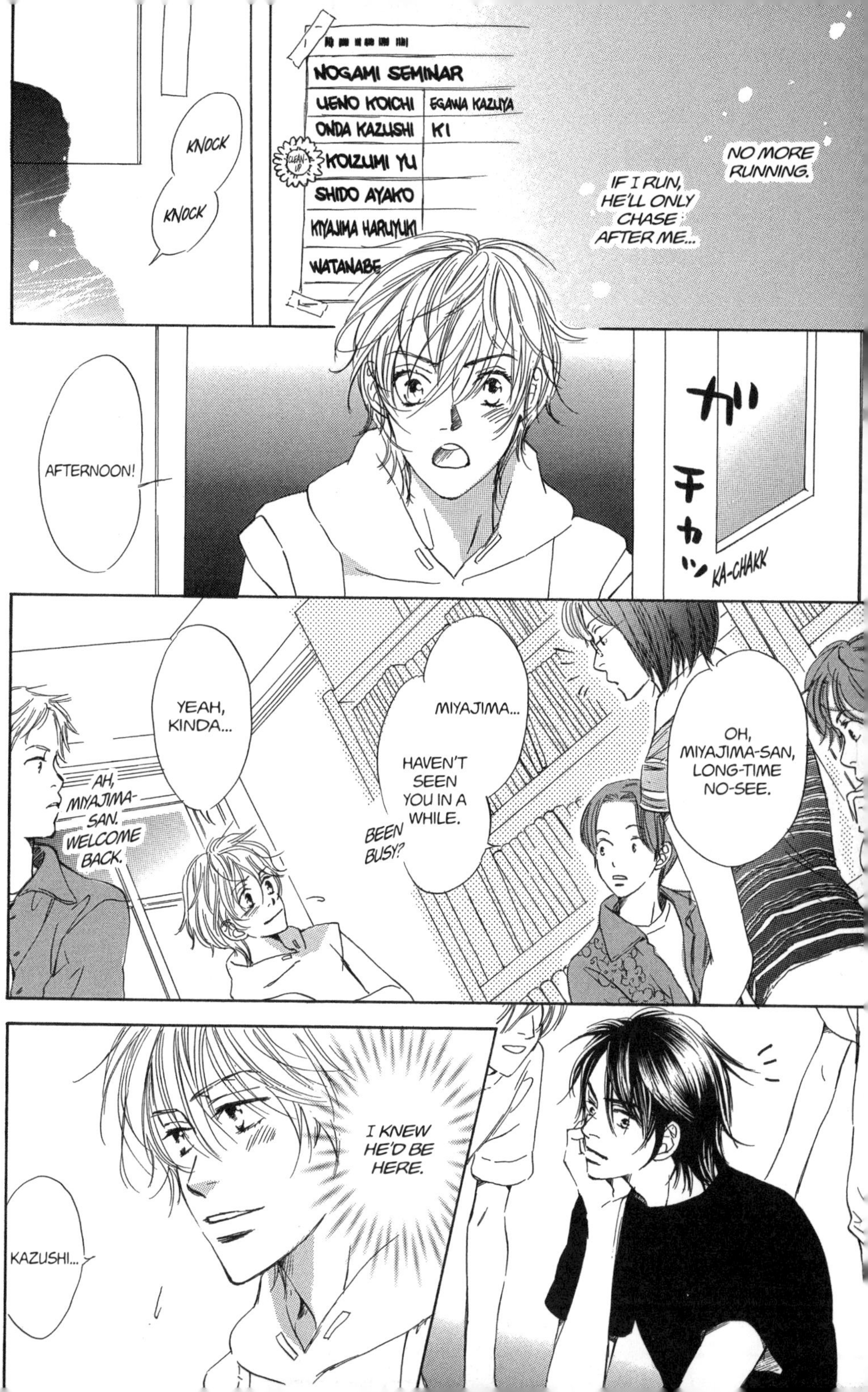
NO MORE RUNNING.
IF I RUN, HE'LL ONLY CHASE AFTER ME...
NOGAMI SEMINAR
UENO KOICHI
EGAWA KAZUYA
ONDA KAZUSHI
KI
CLEAN-UP
KOIZUMI YU
SHIDO AYAKO
KIYAJIMA HARUYUKI
WATANABE
KNOCK
KNOCK
ガチャッ
KA-CHAKK
AFTERNOON!
OH, MIYAJIMA-SAN, LONG-TIME NO-SEE.
MIYAJIMA...
HAVEN'T SEEN YOU IN A WHILE.
BEEN BUSY?
YEAH, KINDA...
AH, MIYAJIMA-SAN. WELCOME BACK.
I KNEW HE'D BE HERE.
KAZUSHI...

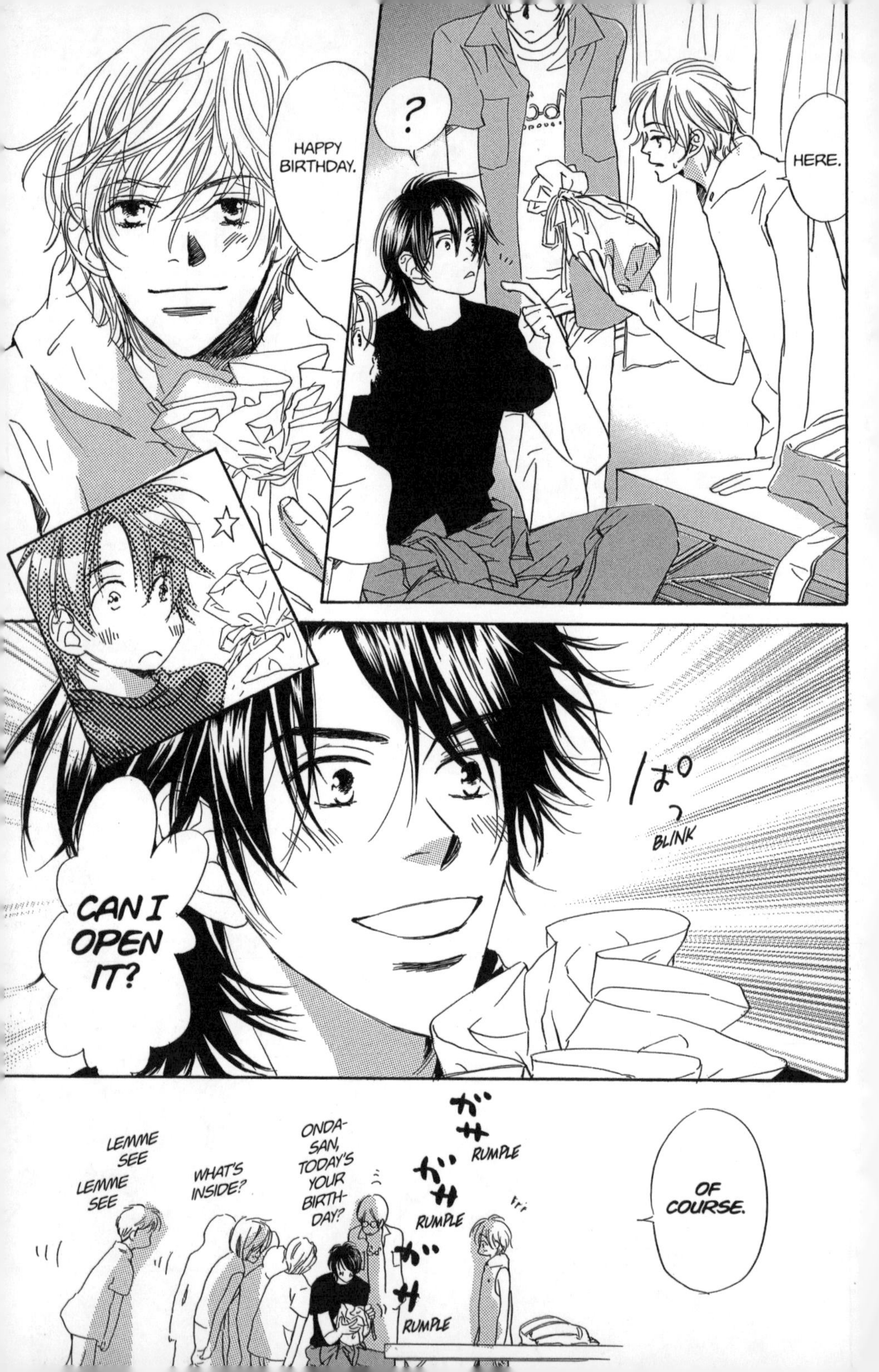
HERE.
?
HAPPY BIRTHDAY.
ぱっ
BLINK
CAN I OPEN IT?
OF COURSE.
ガサ
RUMPLE
ガサ
RUMPLE
ガサ
RUMPLE
ONDA-SAN, TODAY'S YOUR BIRTHDAY?
WHAT'S INSIDE?
LEMME SEE
LEMME SEE

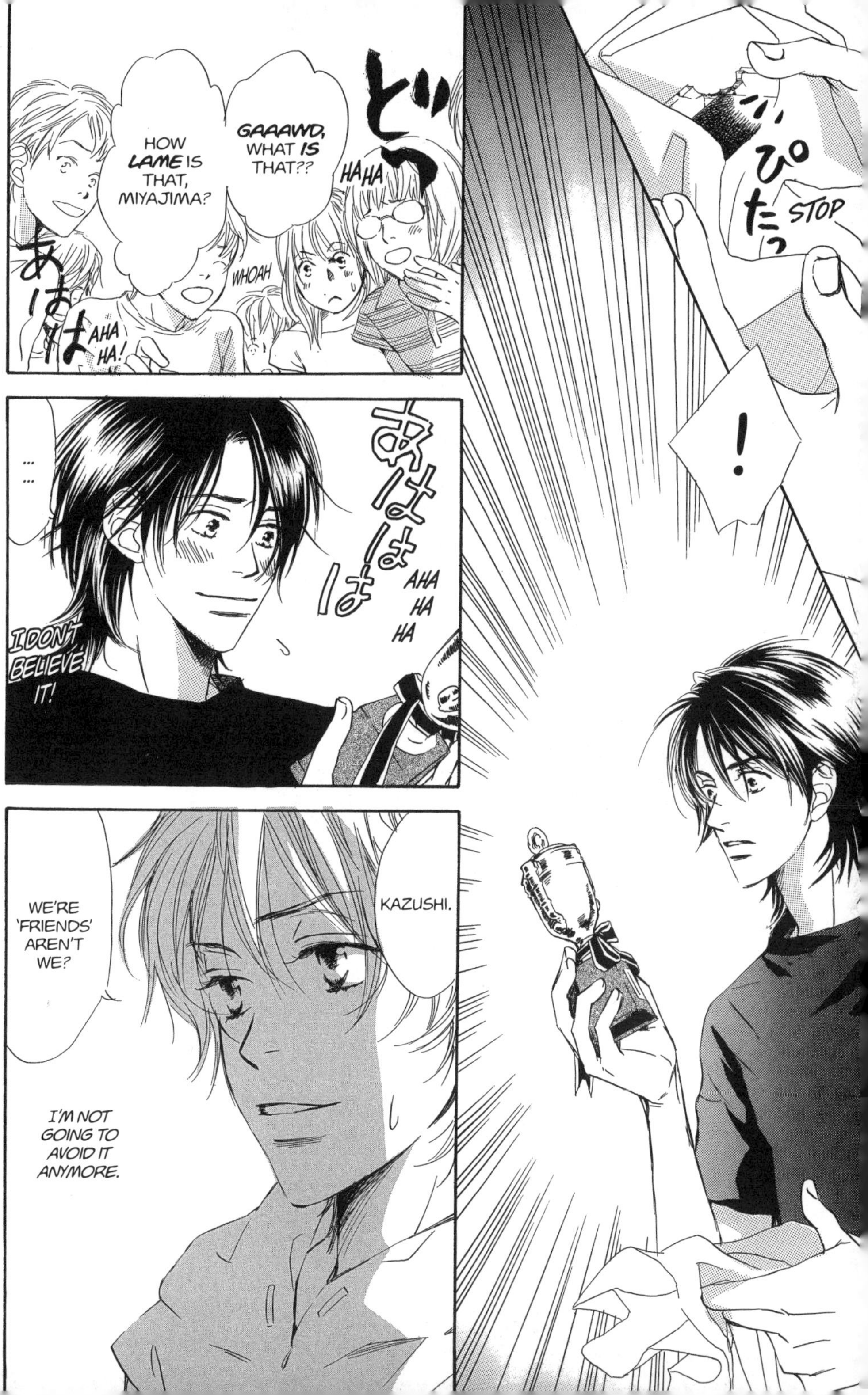
STOP
!
HOW LAME IS THAT, MIYAJIMA?
GAAAWD, WHAT IS THAT??
HA HA
WHOAH
AHA HA!
......
AHA HA HA
I DON'T BELIEVE IT!
KAZUSHI.
WE'RE 'FRIENDS' AREN'T WE?
I'M NOT GOING TO AVOID IT ANYMORE.

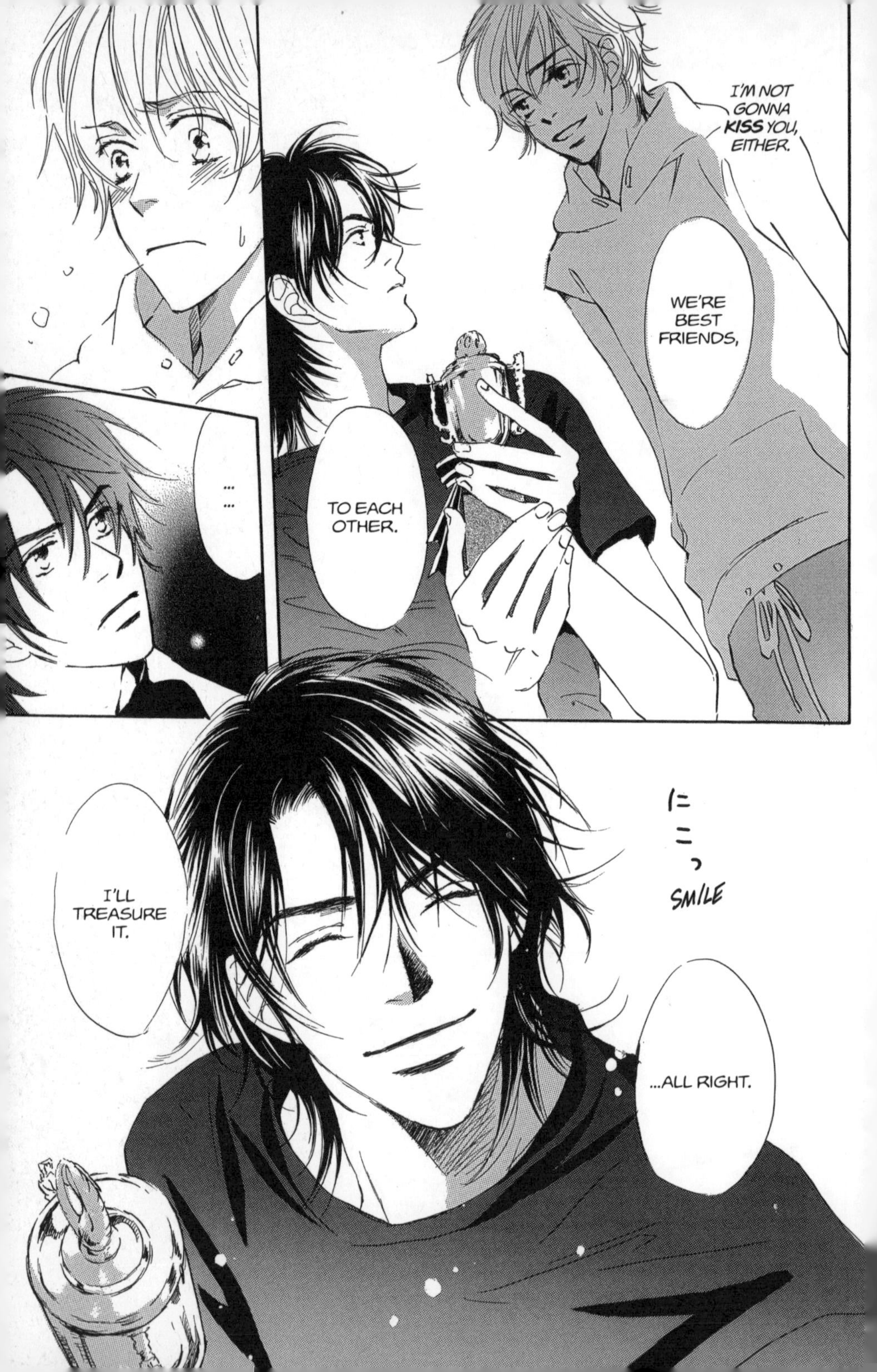
I'M NOT GONNA KISS YOU, EITHER.
WE'RE BEST FRIENDS,
TO EACH OTHER.
……
にこっ
SMILE
...ALL RIGHT.
I'LL TREASURE IT.

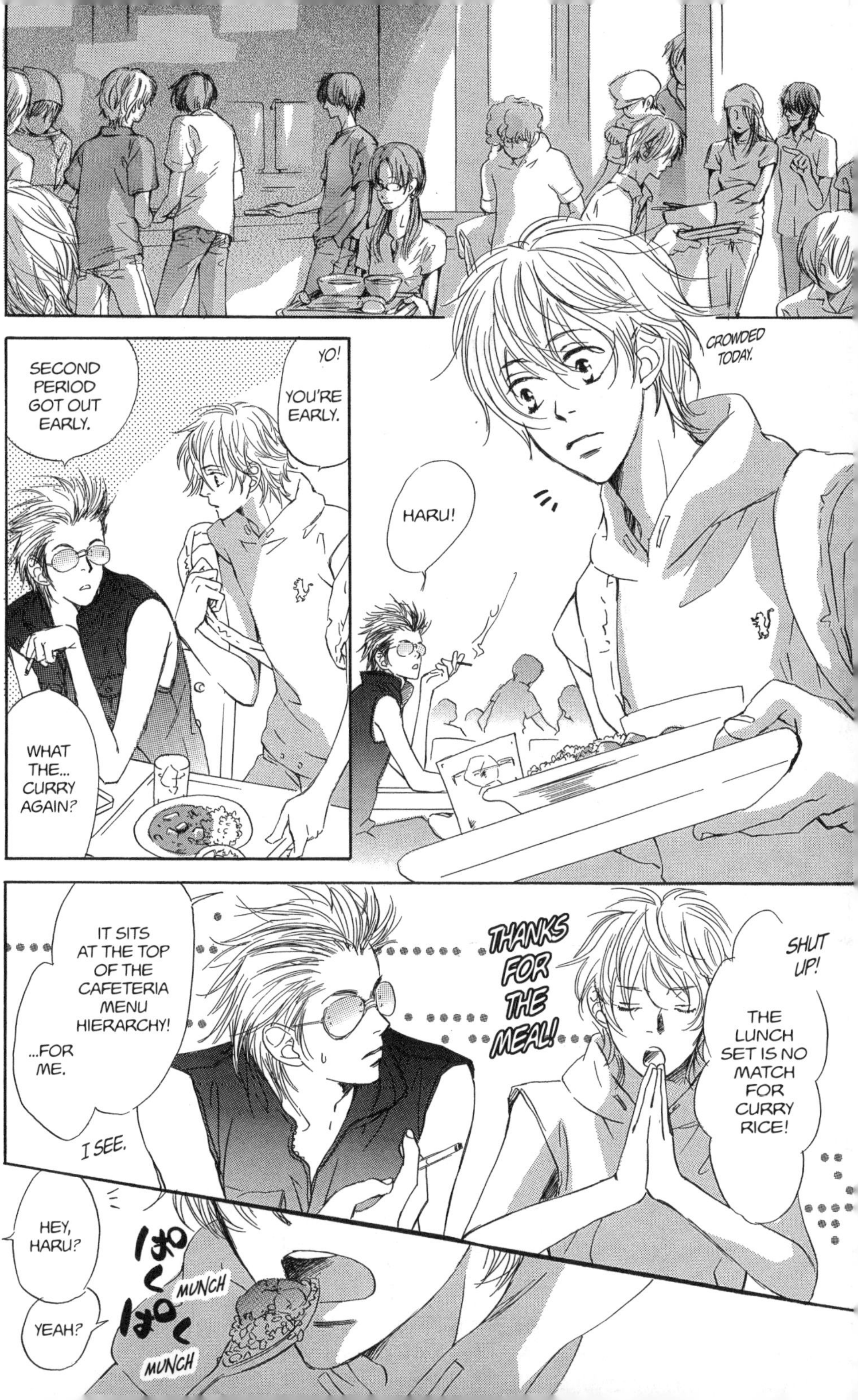
CROWDED TODAY.
HARU!
YO!
YOU'RE EARLY.
SECOND PERIOD GOT OUT EARLY.
WHAT THE... CURRY AGAIN?
SHUT UP!
THE LUNCH SET IS NO MATCH FOR CURRY RICE!
THANKS FOR THE MEAL!
IT SITS AT THE TOP OF THE CAFETERIA MENU HIERARCHY!
...FOR ME.
I SEE.
ぱくぱく
MUNCH
MUNCH
HEY, HARU?
YEAH?

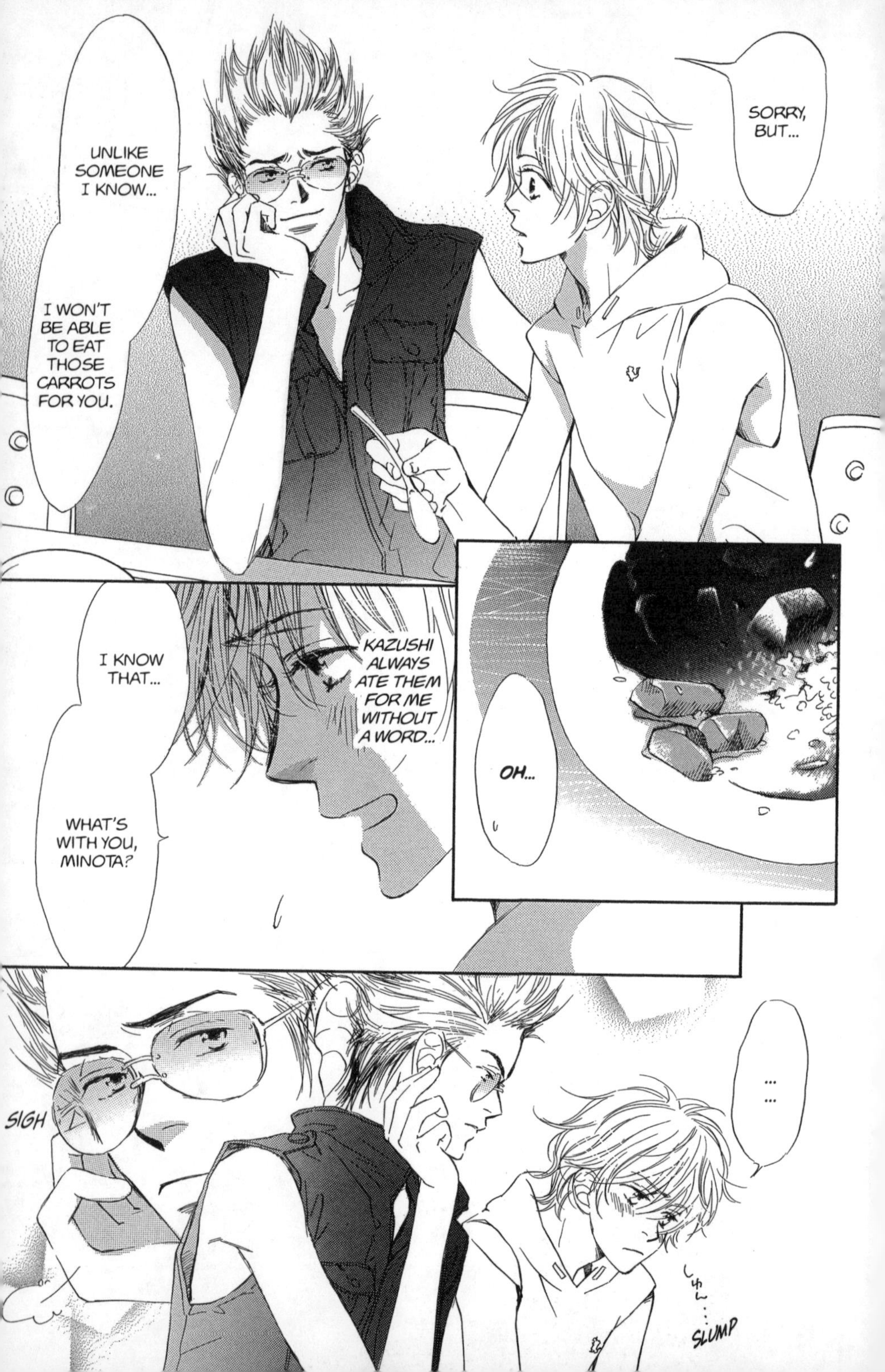
SORRY, BUT...
UNLIKE SOMEONE I KNOW...
I WON'T BE ABLE TO EAT THOSE CARROTS FOR YOU.
OH...
KAZUSHI ALWAYS ATE THEM FOR ME WITHOUT A WORD...
I KNOW THAT...
WHAT'S WITH YOU, MINOTA?
......
しゅん...
SLUMP
SIGH

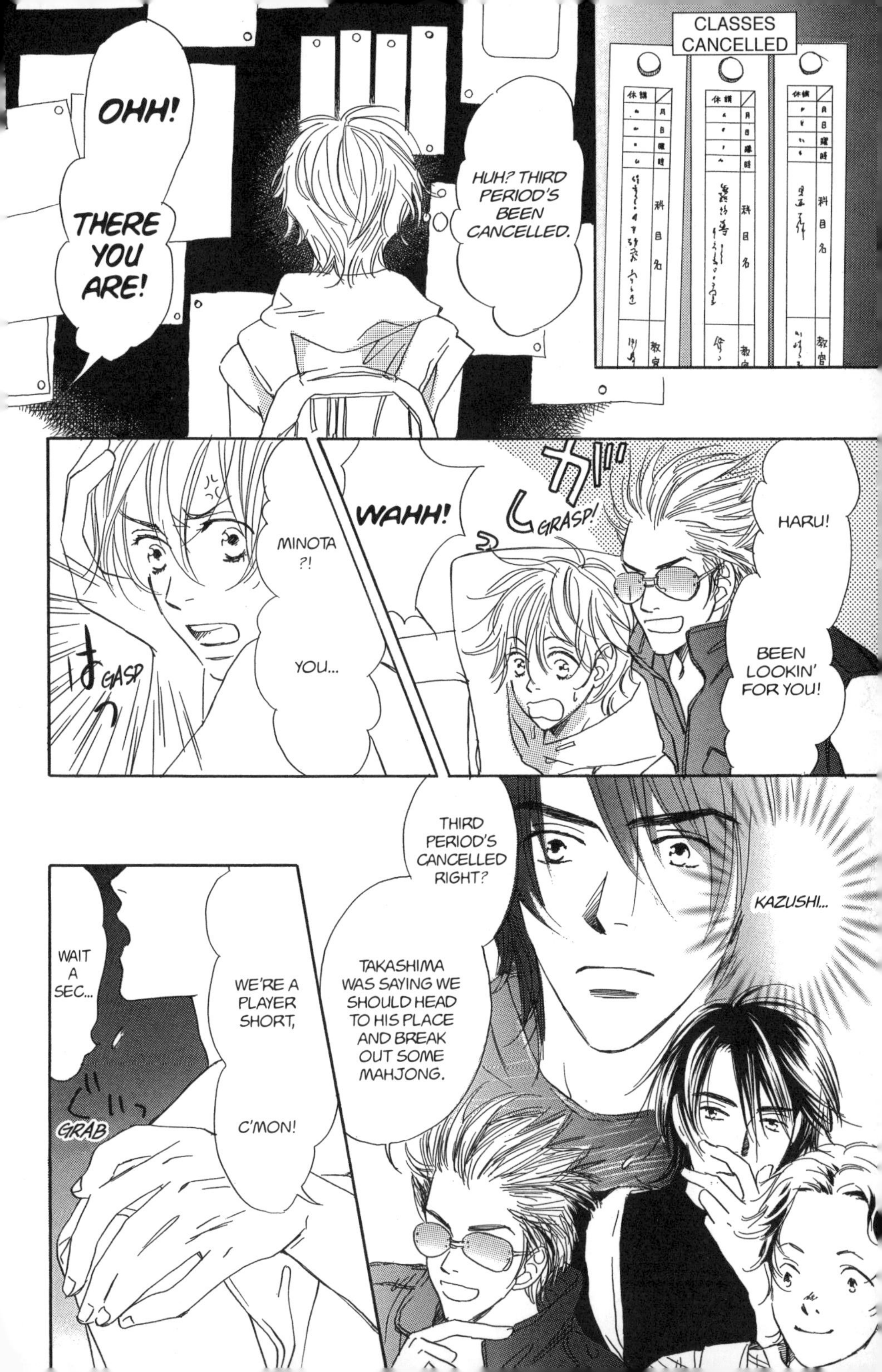
CLASSES CANCELLED
HUH? THIRD PERIOD'S BEEN CANCELLED.
OHH! THERE YOU ARE!
HARU! BEEN LOOKIN' FOR YOU!
GRASP!
WAHH!
MINOTA ?! YOU...
GASP
KAZUSHI...
THIRD PERIOD'S CANCELLED RIGHT?
TAKASHIMA WAS SAYING WE SHOULD HEAD TO HIS PLACE AND BREAK OUT SOME MAHJONG.
WE'RE A PLAYER SHORT, C'MON!
WAIT A SEC...
GRAB

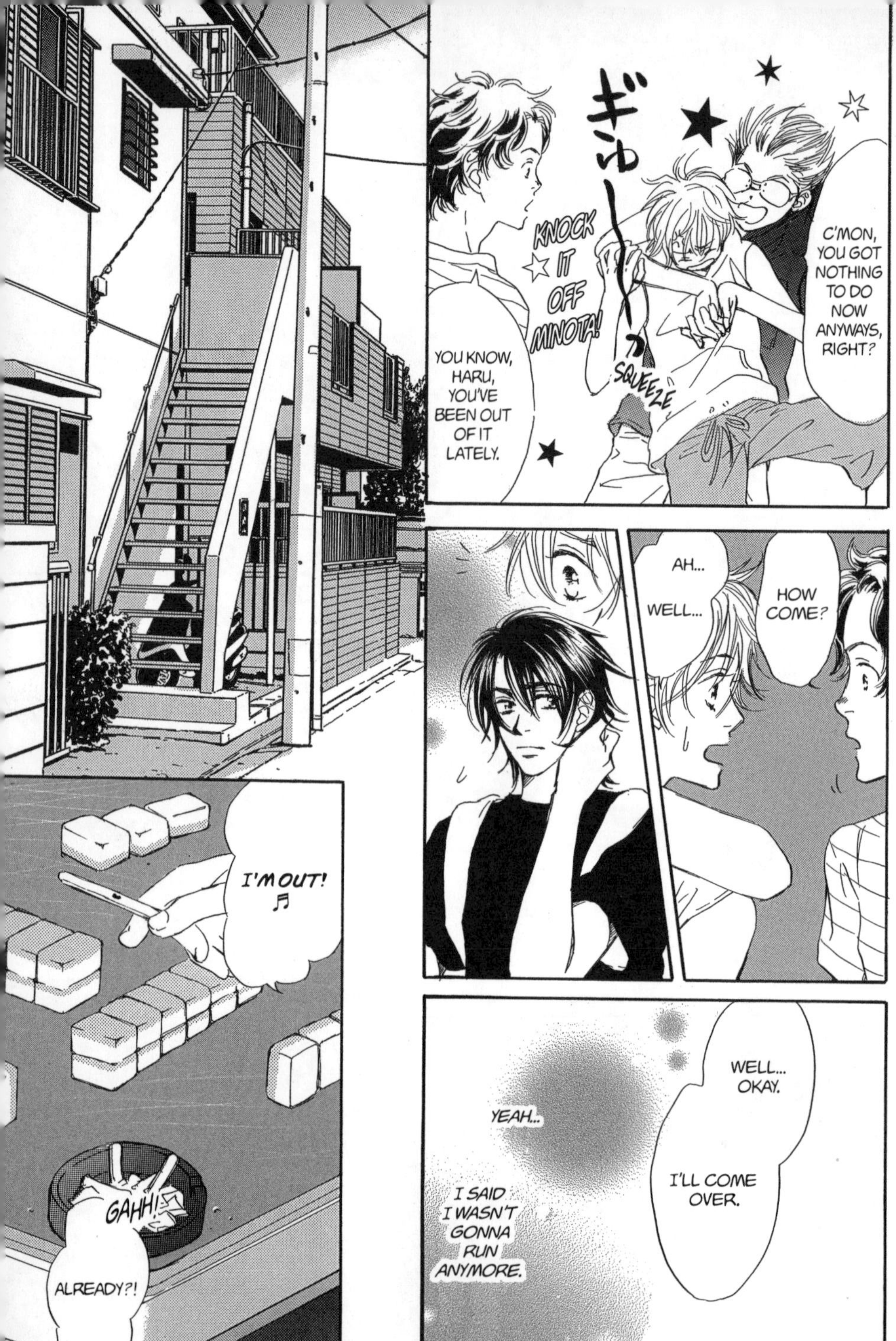
ぎゅーっ
C'MON, YOU GOT NOTHING TO DO NOW ANYWAYS, RIGHT?
KNOCK IT OFF MINOTA!
SQUEEZE
YOU KNOW, HARU, YOU'VE BEEN OUT OF IT LATELY.
HOW COME?
AH... WELL...
WELL... OKAY.
I'LL COME OVER.
YEAH...
I SAID I WASN'T GONNA RUN ANYMORE.
I'M OUT! ♬
GAHH!
ALREADY?!

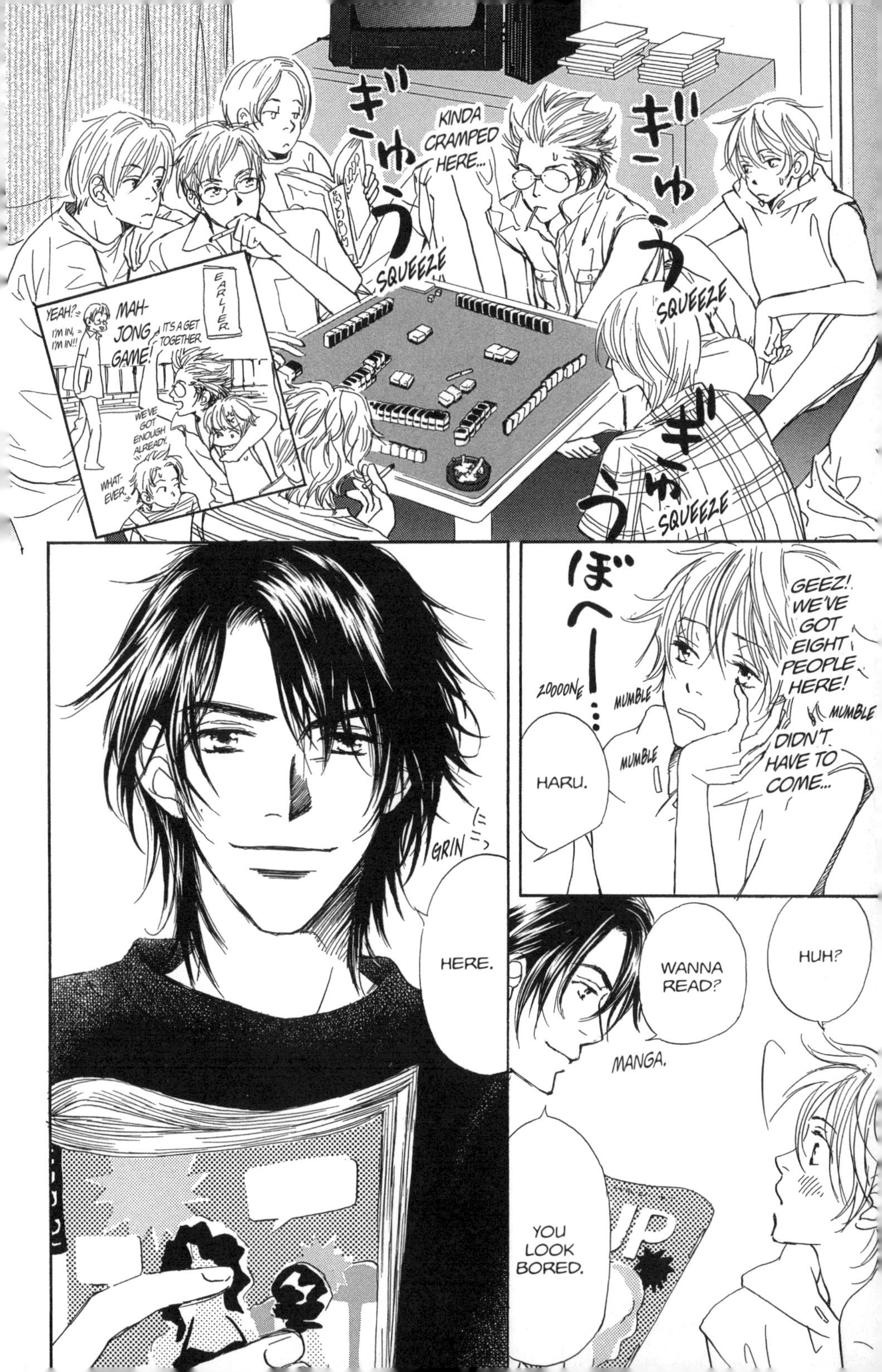
ぎゅう
SQUEEZE
KINDA CRAMPED HERE...
ぎゅう
SQUEEZE
ぎゅう
SQUEEZE
EARLIER.
IT'S A GET TOGETHER.
MAH-JONG GAME!
YEAH!? I'M IN, I'M IN!!
WE'VE GOT ENOUGH ALREADY.
WHATEVER.
GEEZ! WE'VE GOT EIGHT PEOPLE HERE!
MUMBLE
DIDN'T HAVE TO COME...
MUMBLE
MUMBLE
ぼへー...
ZOOOONE
HARU.
HUH?
WANNA READ?
MANGA.
YOU LOOK BORED.
GRIN
HERE.

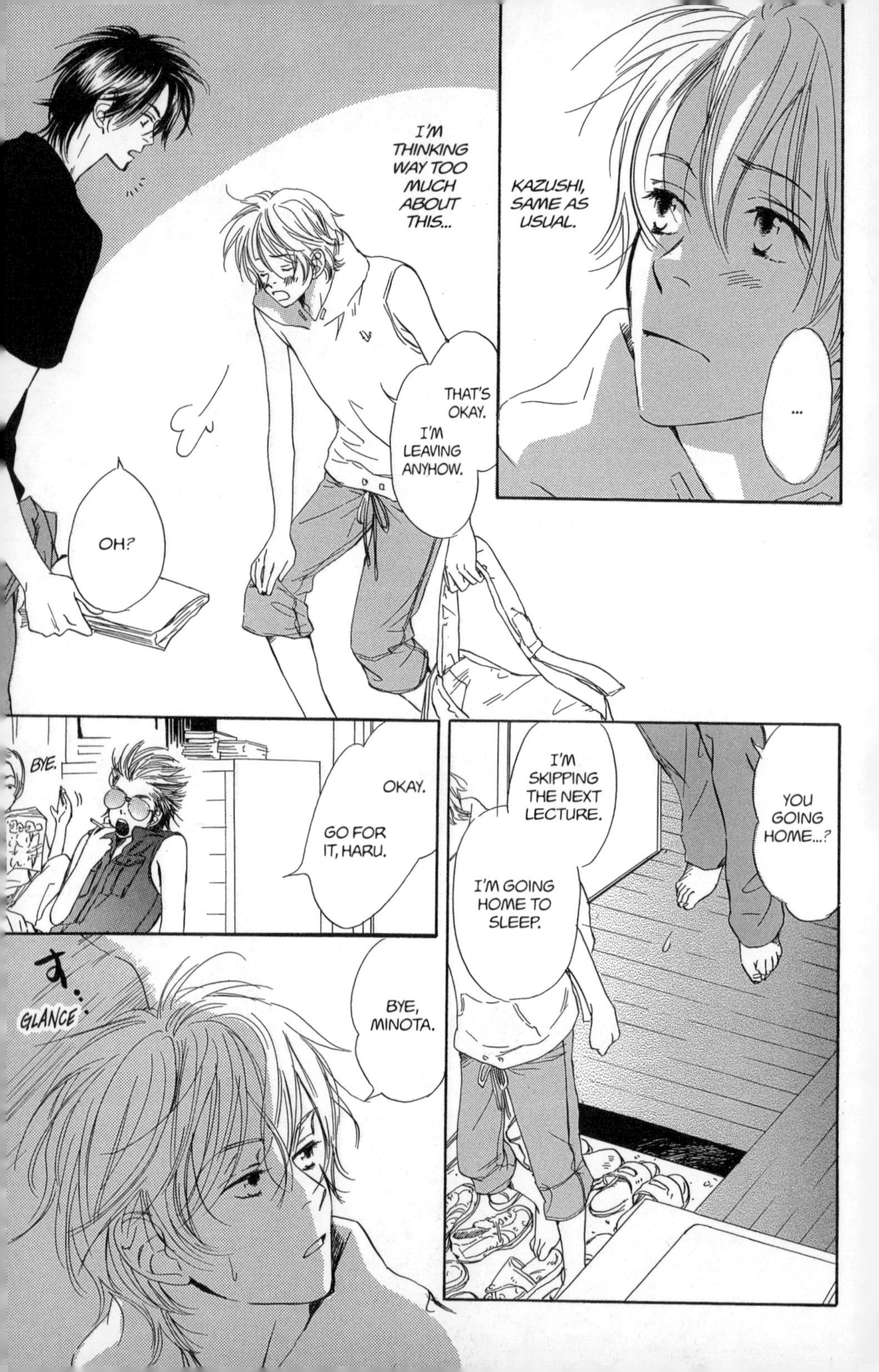
KAZUSHI, SAME AS USUAL.
...
I'M THINKING WAY TOO MUCH ABOUT THIS...
THAT'S OKAY. I'M LEAVING ANYHOW.
OH?
YOU GOING HOME...?
I'M SKIPPING THE NEXT LECTURE.
I'M GOING HOME TO SLEEP.
OKAY.
GO FOR IT, HARU.
BYE.
BYE, MINOTA.
す…
GLANCE

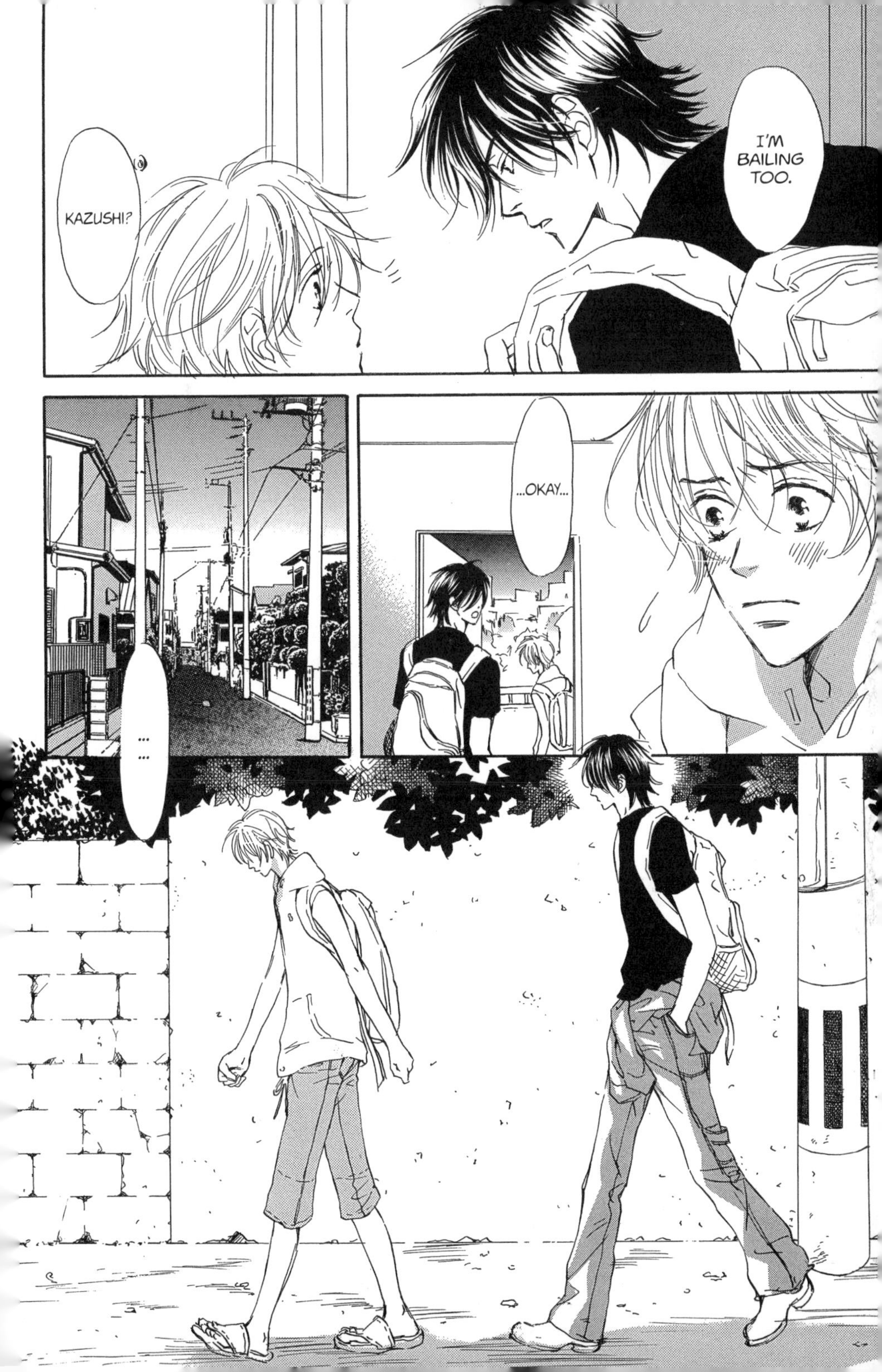
I'M BAILING TOO.
KAZUSHI?
...OKAY...
......

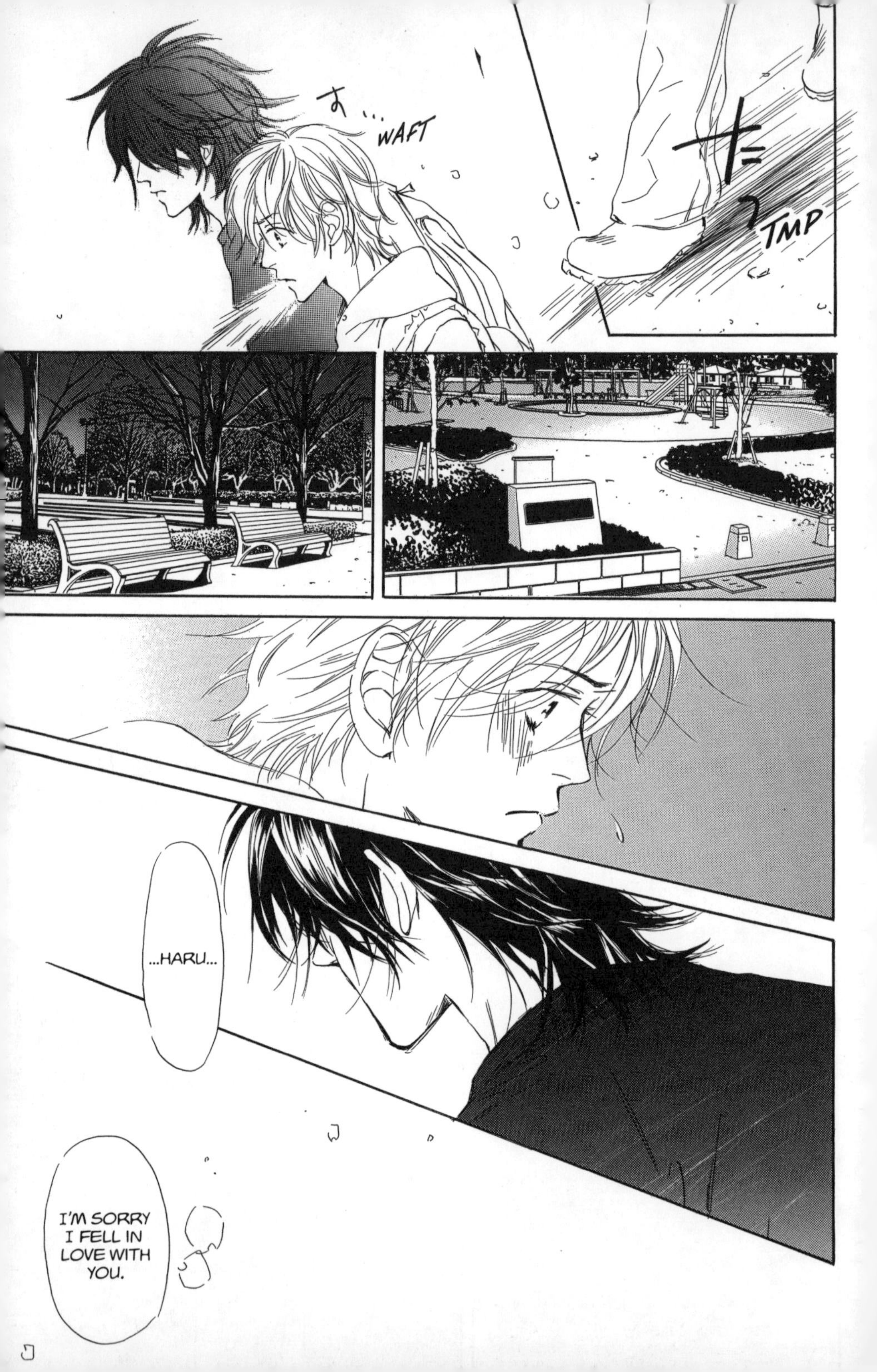
TMP
WAFT
...HARU...
I'M SORRY I FELL IN LOVE WITH YOU.

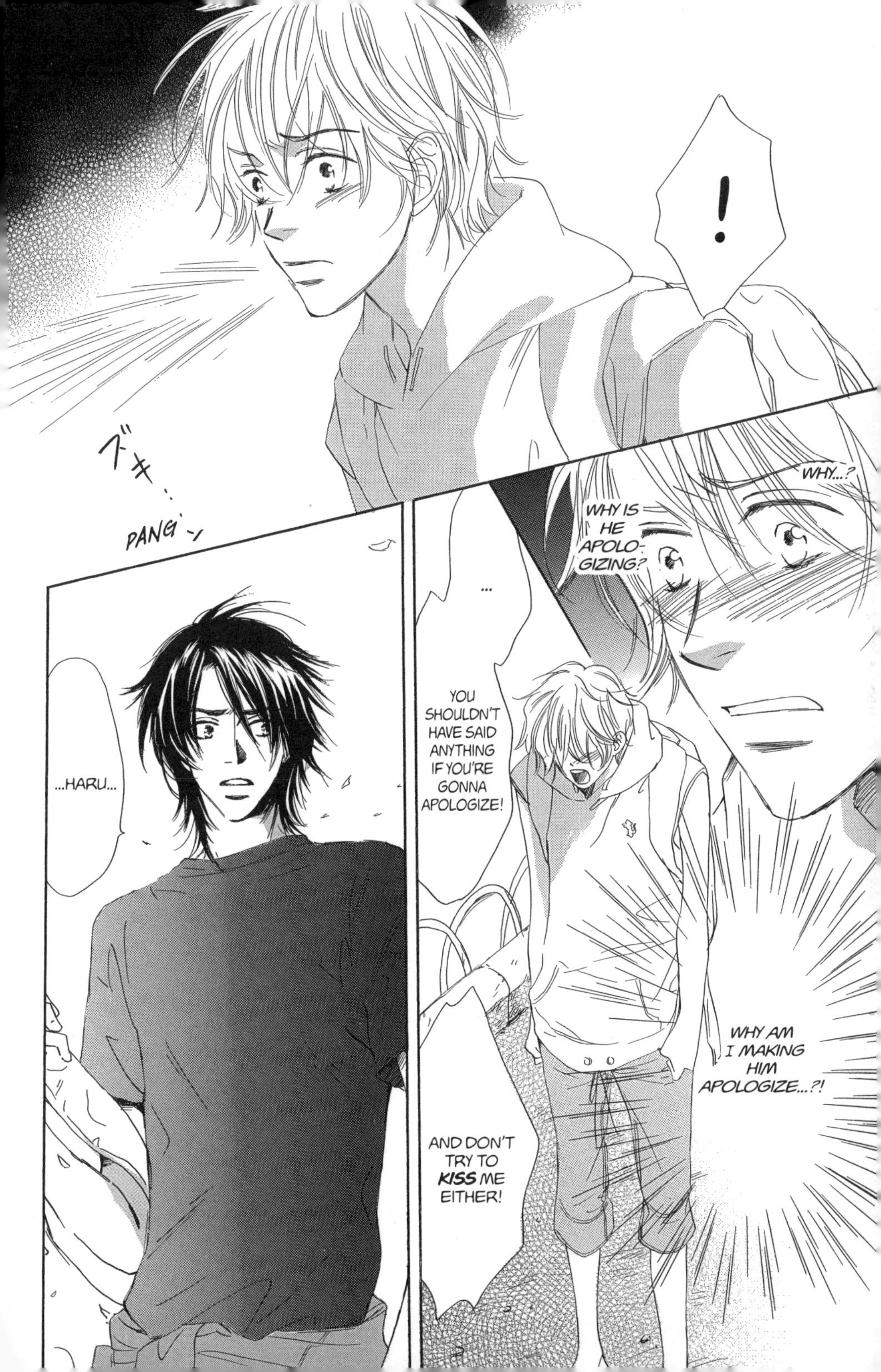
!
ズキ…
PANG
WHY...?
WHY IS HE APOLOGIZING?
...
YOU SHOULDN'T HAVE SAID ANYTHING IF YOU'RE GONNA APOLOGIZE!
WHY AM I MAKING HIM APOLOGIZE...?!
AND DON'T TRY TO **KISS** ME EITHER!
...HARU...

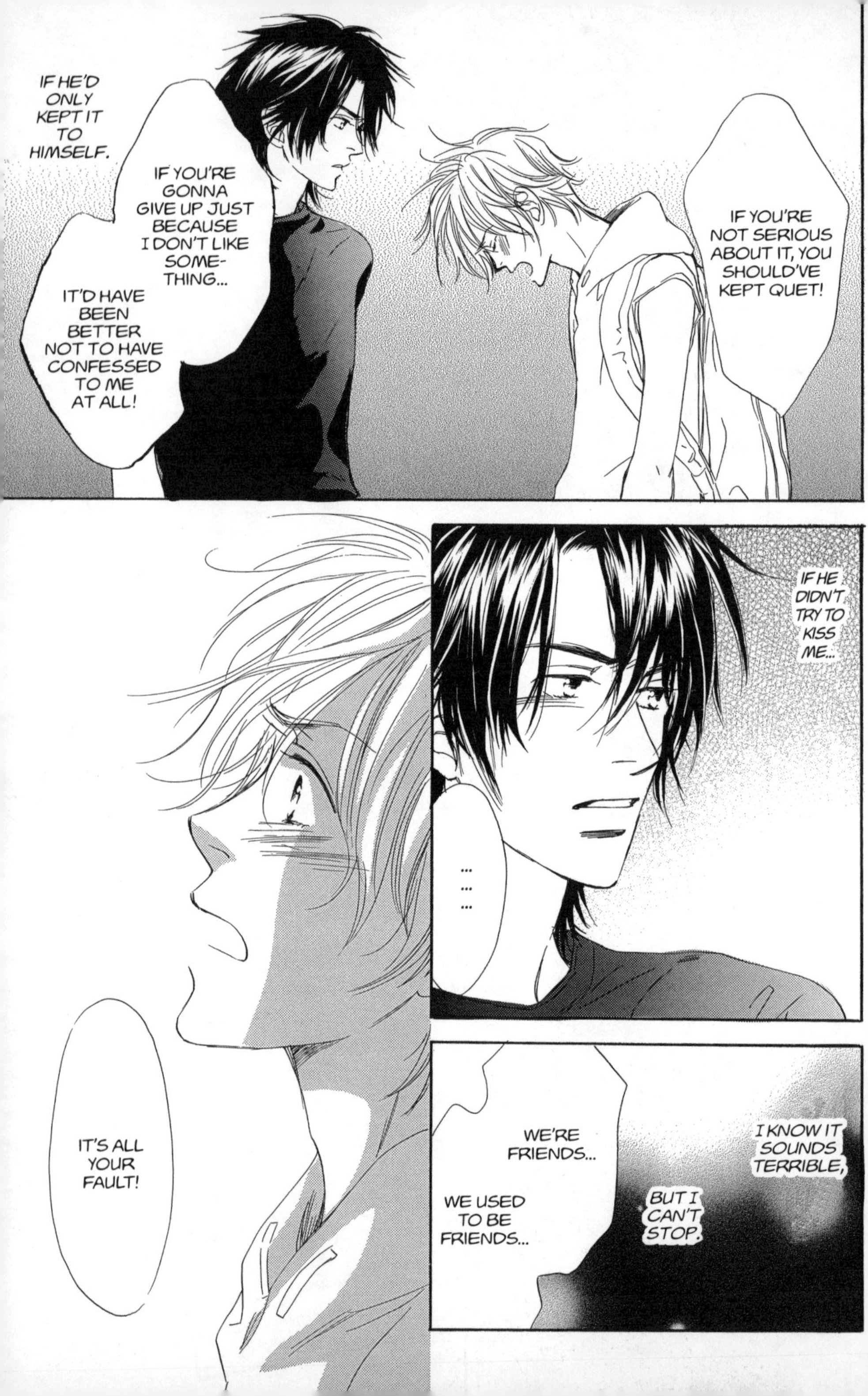
IF YOU'RE NOT SERIOUS ABOUT IT, YOU SHOULD'VE KEPT QUET!
IF YOU'RE GONNA GIVE UP JUST BECAUSE I DON'T LIKE SOME-THING...
IT'D HAVE BEEN BETTER NOT TO HAVE CONFESSED TO ME AT ALL!
IF HE'D ONLY KEPT IT TO HIMSELF.
IF HE DIDN'T TRY TO KISS ME...
... ...
I KNOW IT SOUNDS TERRIBLE,
BUT I CAN'T STOP.
WE'RE FRIENDS...
WE USED TO BE FRIENDS...
IT'S ALL YOUR FAULT!

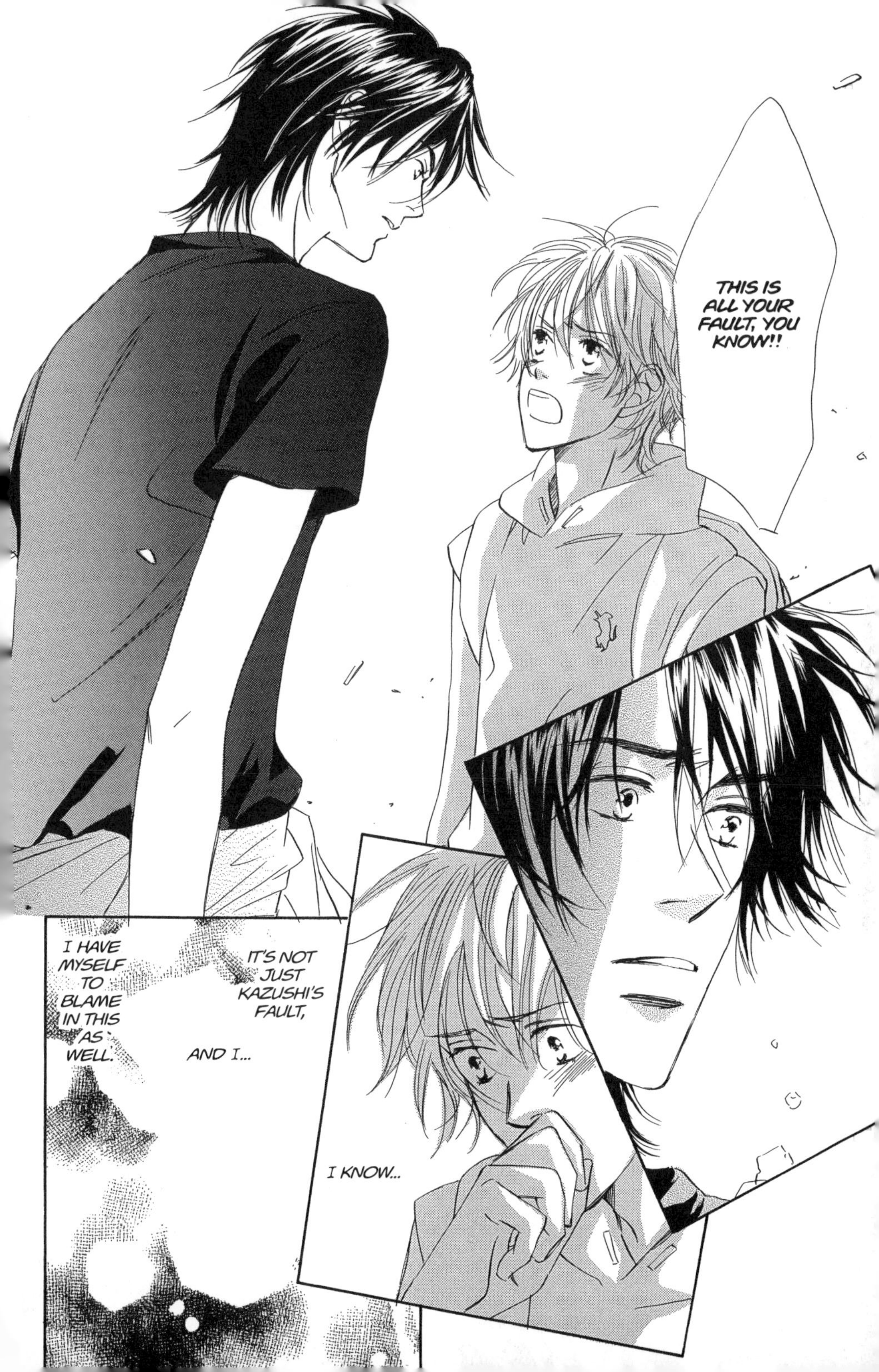
THIS IS ALL YOUR FAULT, YOU KNOW!!
I KNOW...
IT'S NOT JUST KAZUSHI'S FAULT,
AND I...
I HAVE MYSELF TO BLAME IN THIS AS WELL.

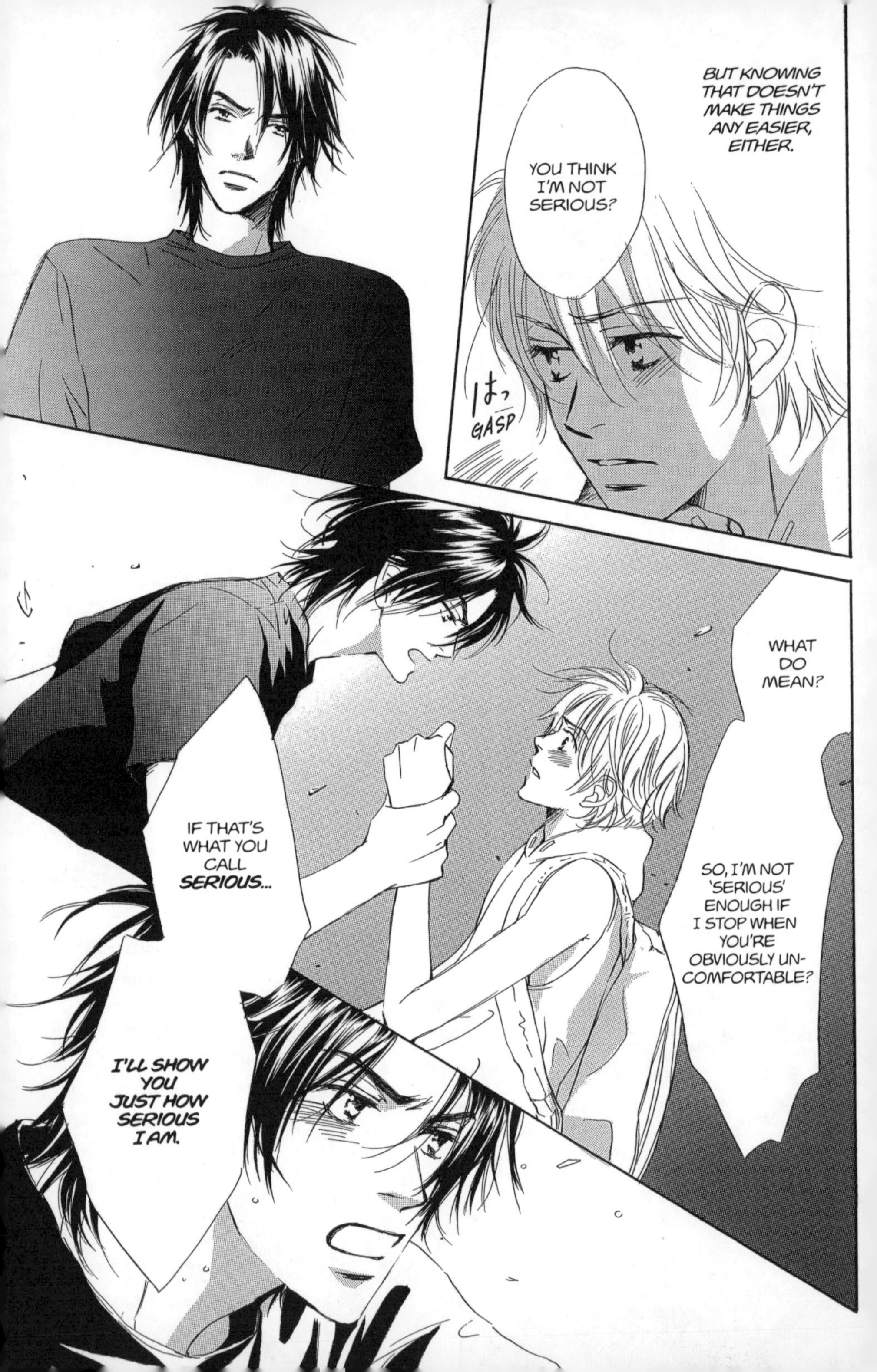
BUT KNOWING THAT DOESN'T MAKE THINGS ANY EASIER, EITHER.
YOU THINK I'M NOT SERIOUS?
はっ
GASP
WHAT DO MEAN?
SO, I'M NOT 'SERIOUS' ENOUGH IF I STOP WHEN YOU'RE OBVIOUSLY UN-COMFORTABLE?
IF THAT'S WHAT YOU CALL SERIOUS...
I'LL SHOW YOU JUST HOW SERIOUS I AM.

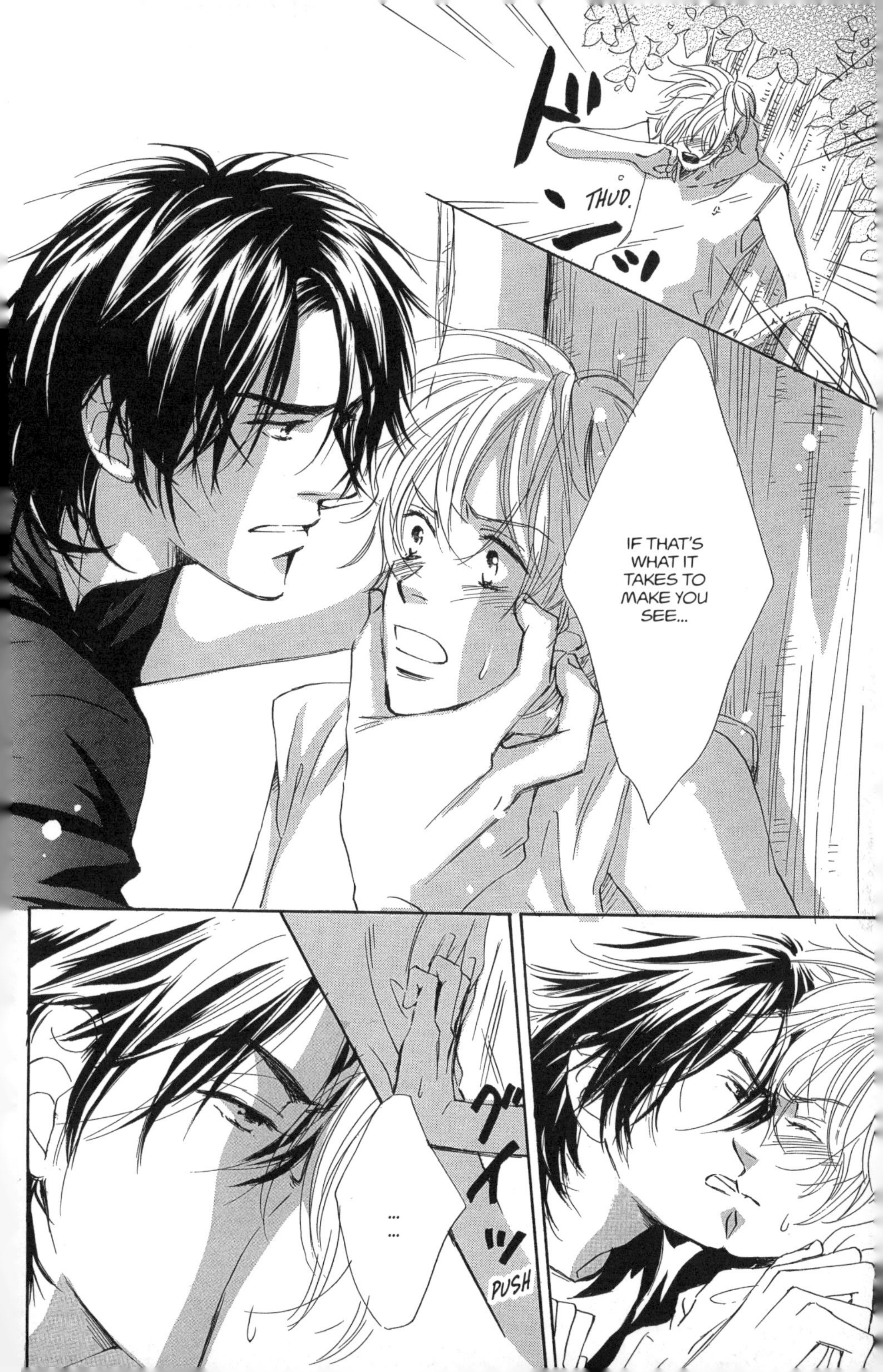
THUD.
IF THAT'S WHAT IT TAKES TO MAKE YOU SEE...
...
...
PUSH

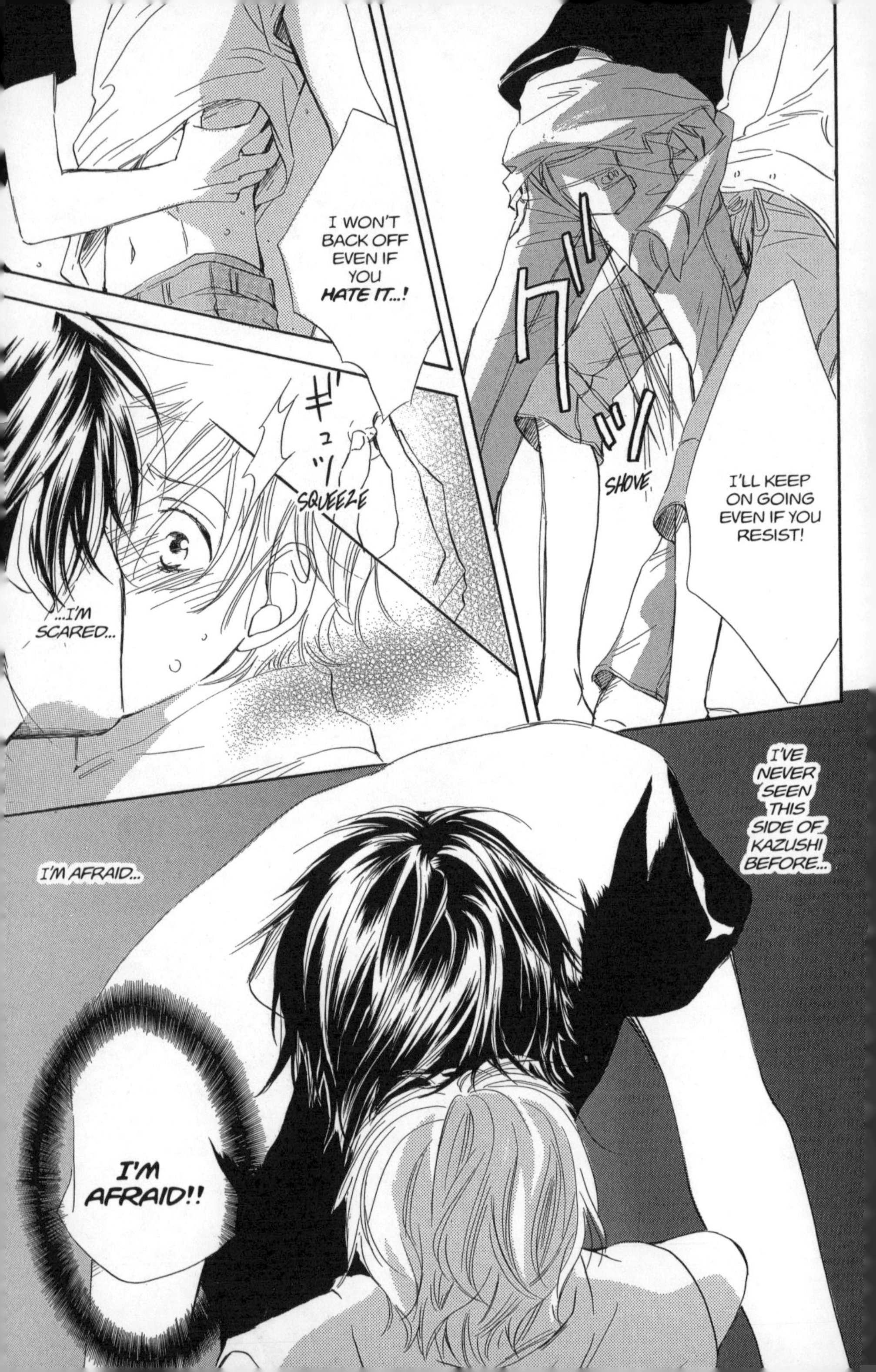
SHOVE
I'LL KEEP ON GOING EVEN IF YOU RESIST!
I WON'T BACK OFF EVEN IF YOU HATE IT...!
ギュッ
SQUEEZE
...I'M SCARED...
I'VE NEVER SEEN THIS SIDE OF KAZUSHI BEFORE...
I'M AFRAID...
I'M AFRAID!!

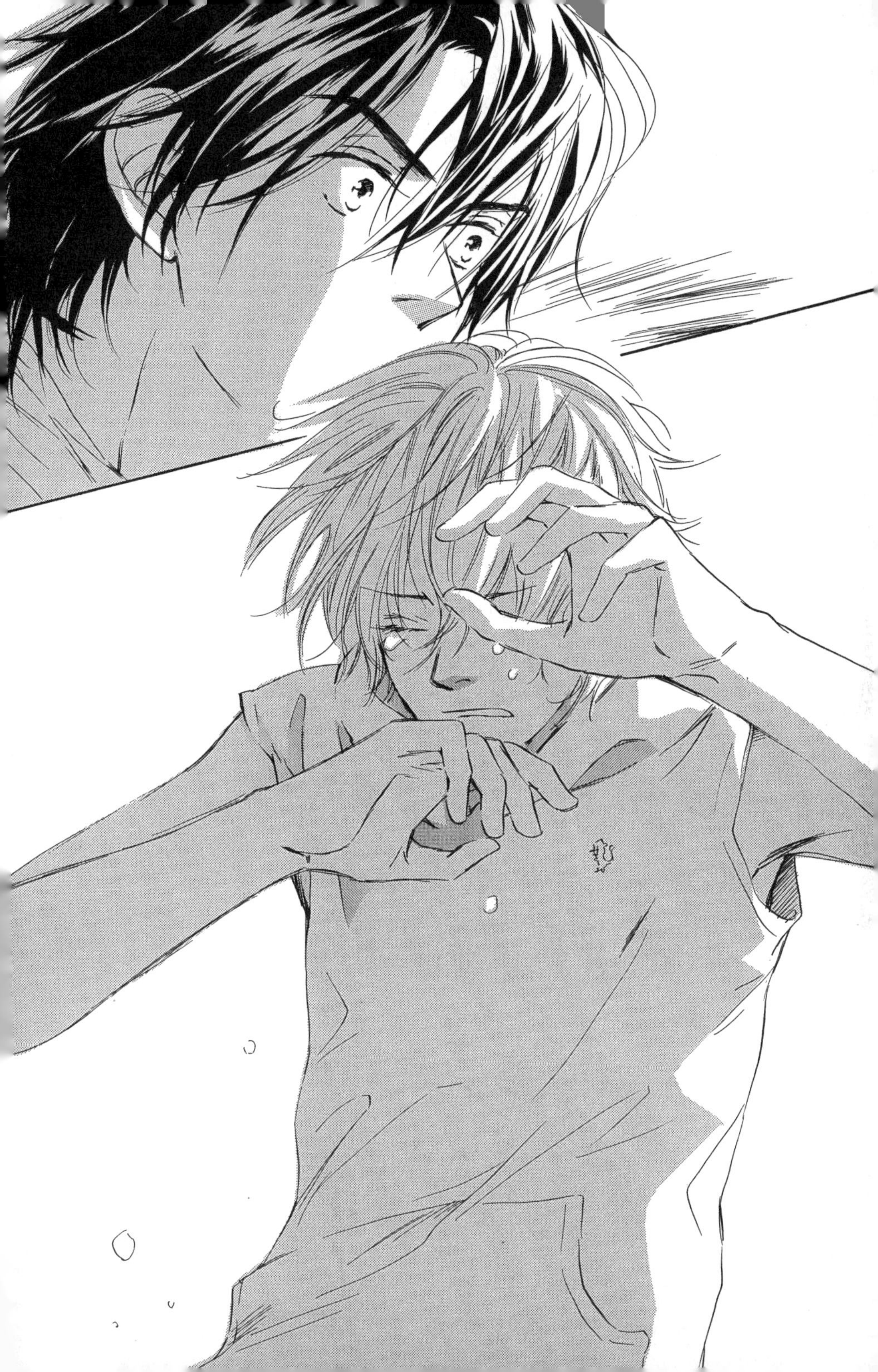

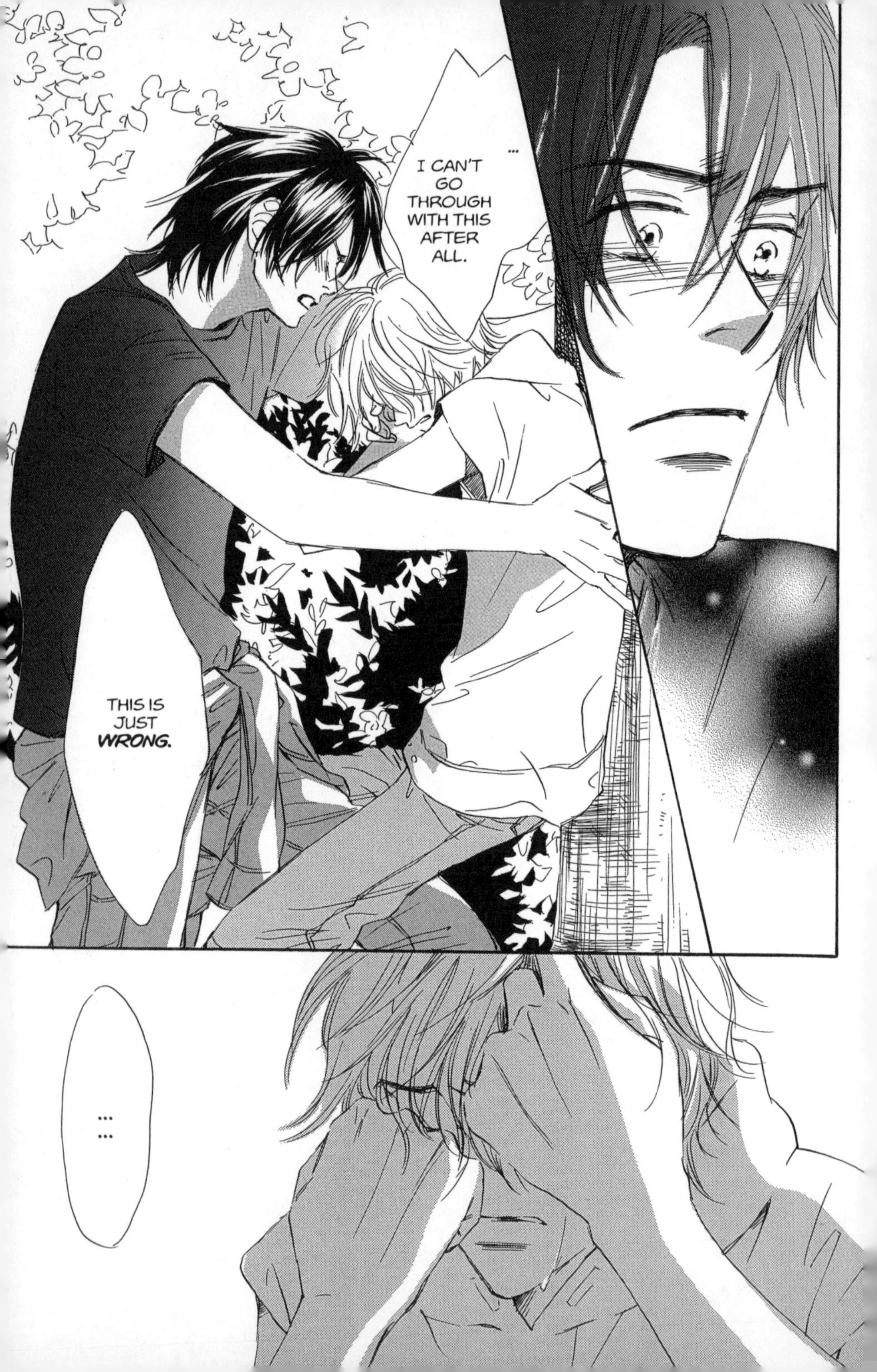
...
I CAN'T GO THROUGH WITH THIS AFTER ALL.
THIS IS JUST **WRONG.**
......

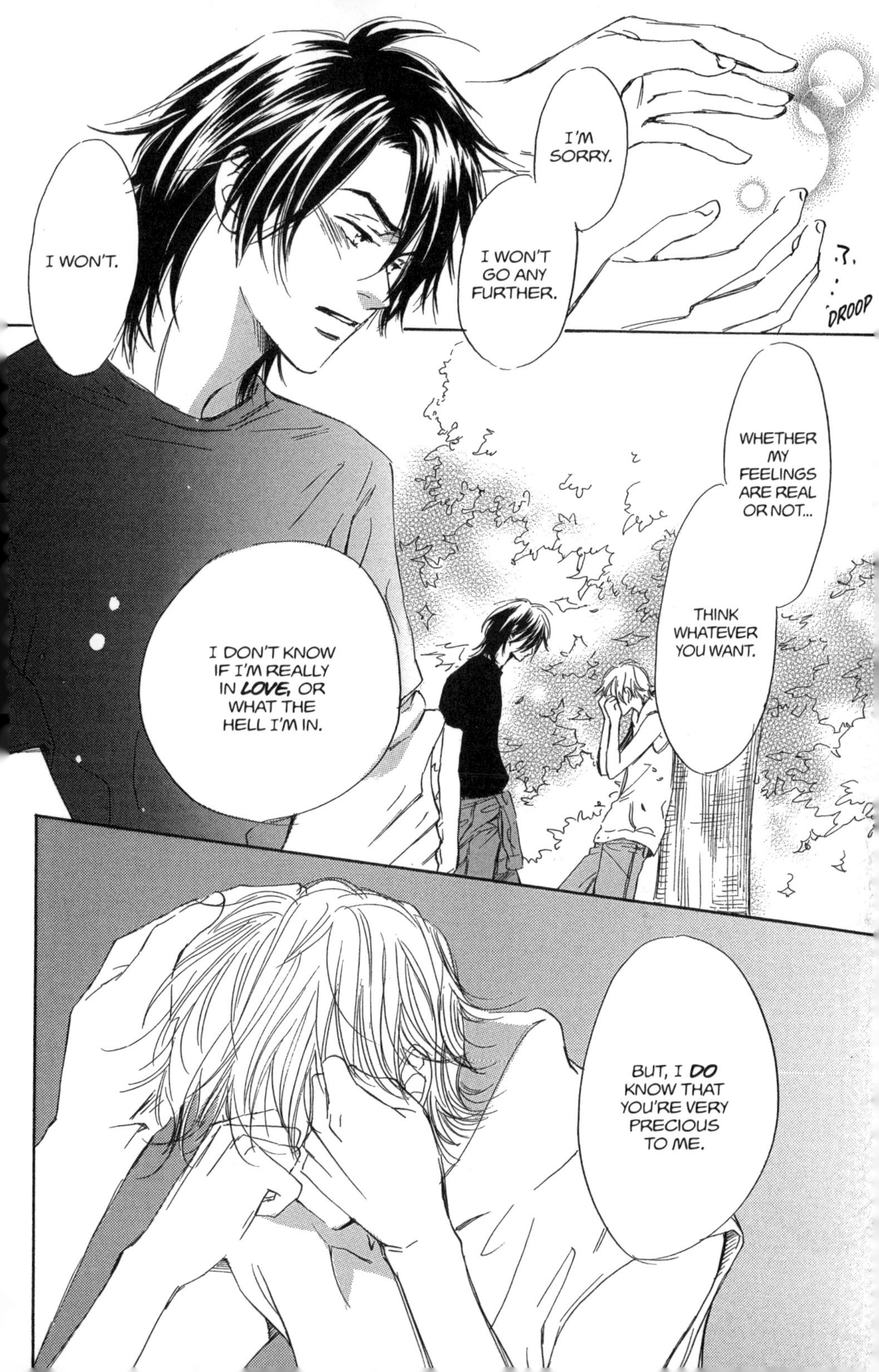

I'M SORRY.
?
DROOP
I WON'T GO ANY FURTHER.
I WON'T.
WHETHER MY FEELINGS ARE REAL OR NOT...
THINK WHATEVER YOU WANT.
I DON'T KNOW IF I'M REALLY IN **LOVE**, OR WHAT THE HELL I'M IN.
BUT, I **DO** KNOW THAT YOU'RE VERY PRECIOUS TO ME.

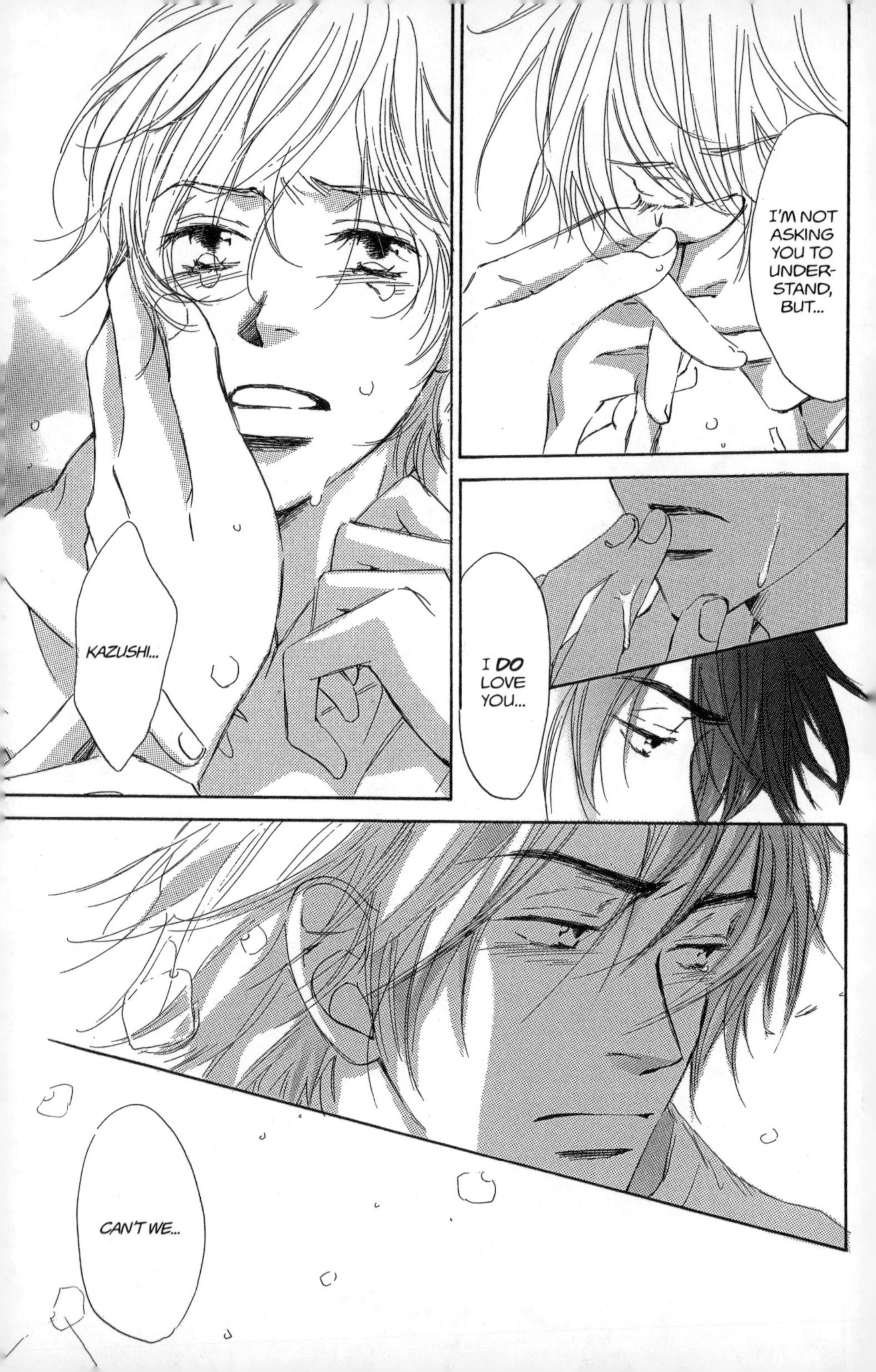
I'M NOT ASKING YOU TO UNDER-STAND, BUT...
I **DO** LOVE YOU...
KAZUSHI...
CAN'T WE...

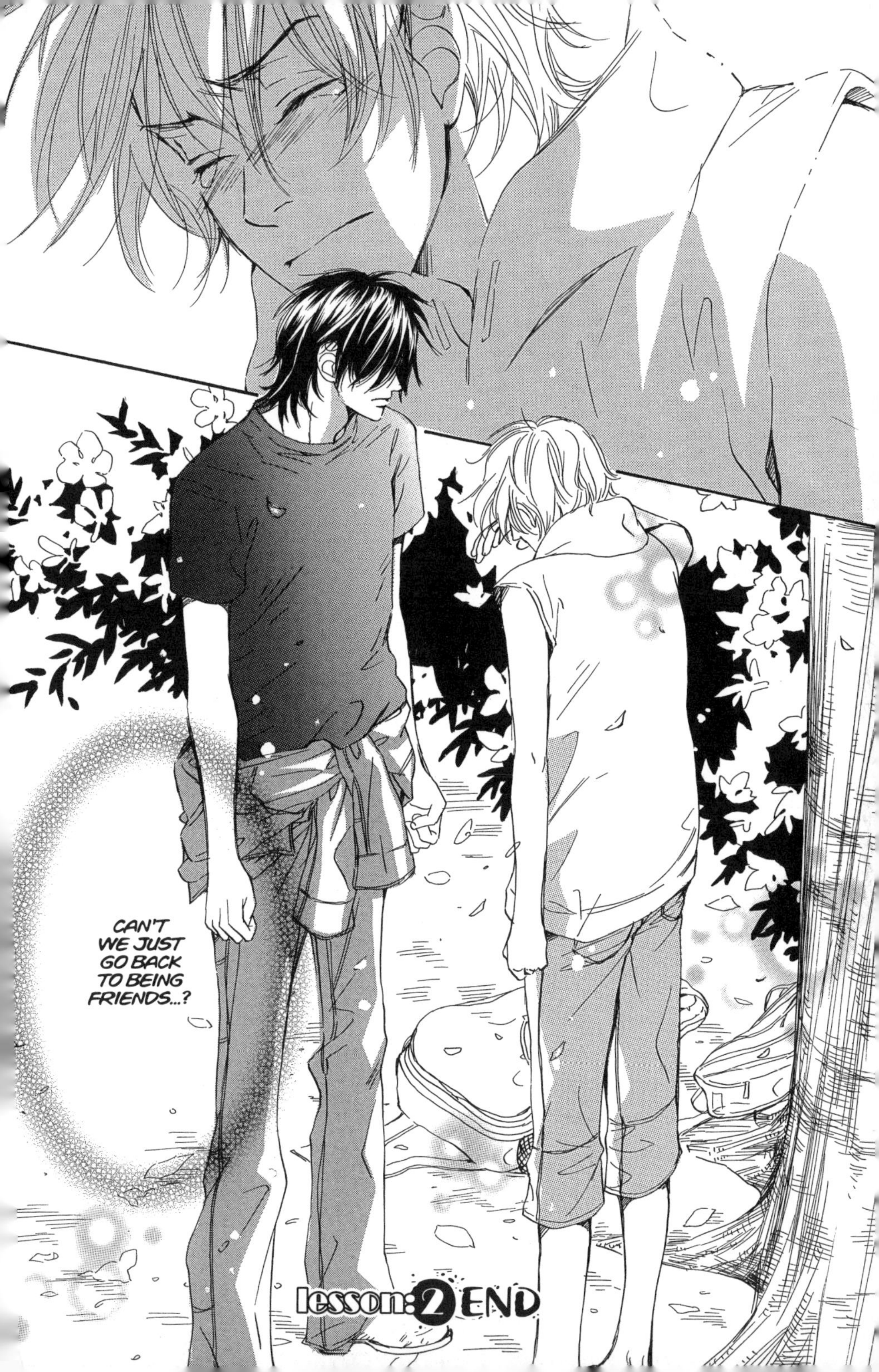
CAN'T WE JUST GO BACK TO BEING FRIENDS...?
lesson:2 END

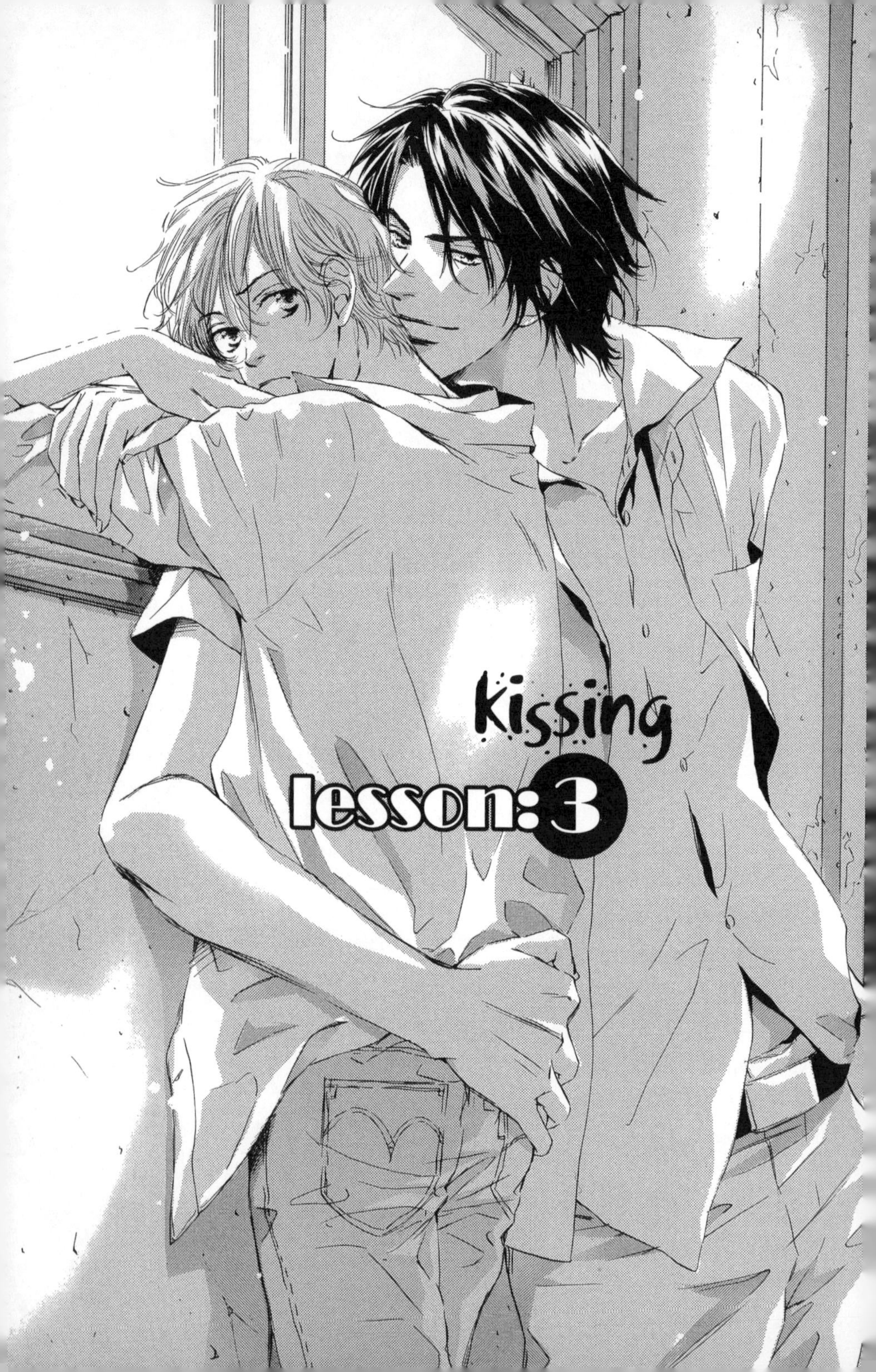
Kissing
lesson: 3

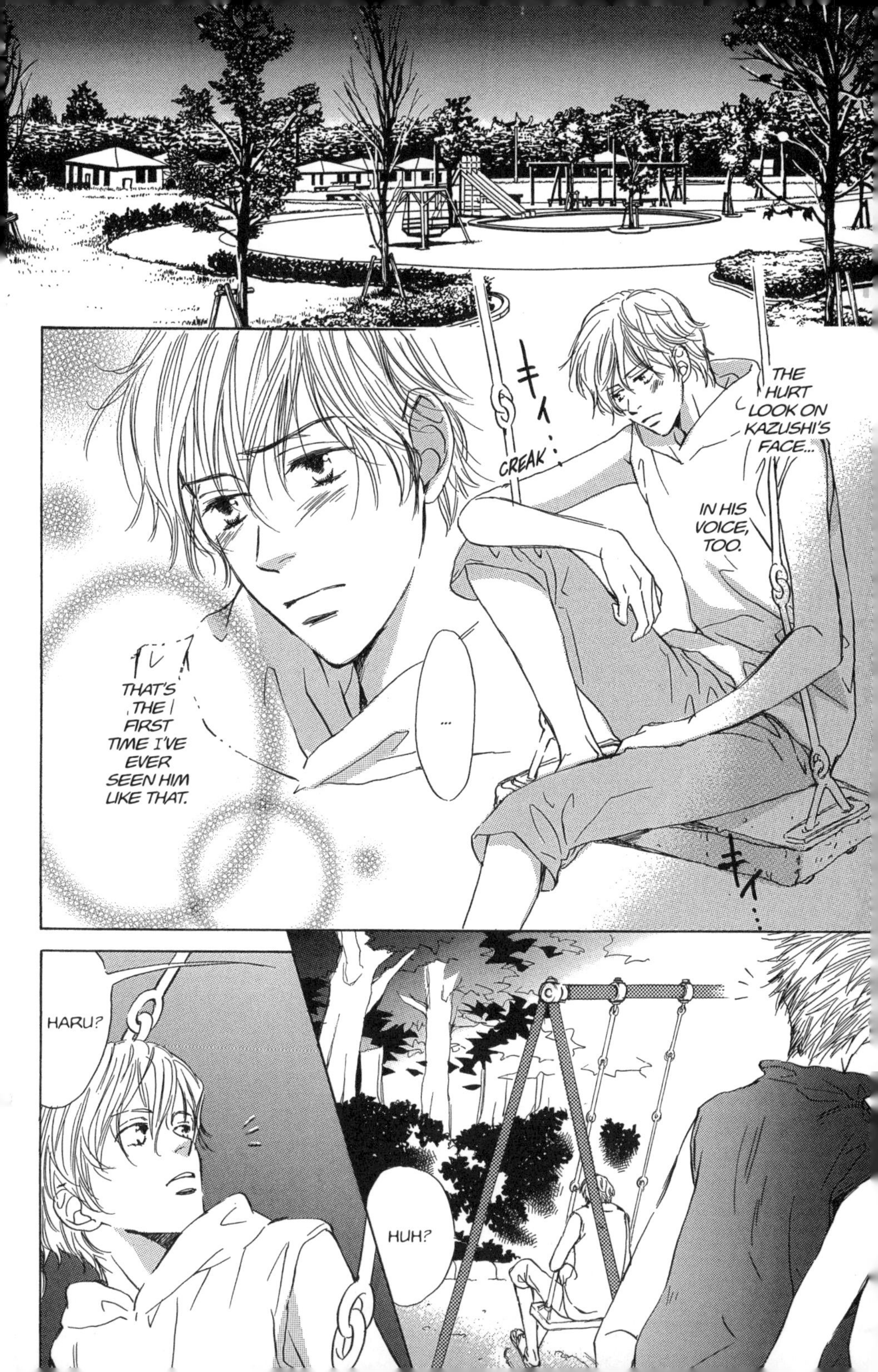

キイ…
CREAK
THE HURT LOOK ON KAZUSHI'S FACE...
IN HIS VOICE, TOO.
...
THAT'S THE FIRST TIME I'VE EVER SEEN HIM LIKE THAT.
キイ…
HARU?
HUH?

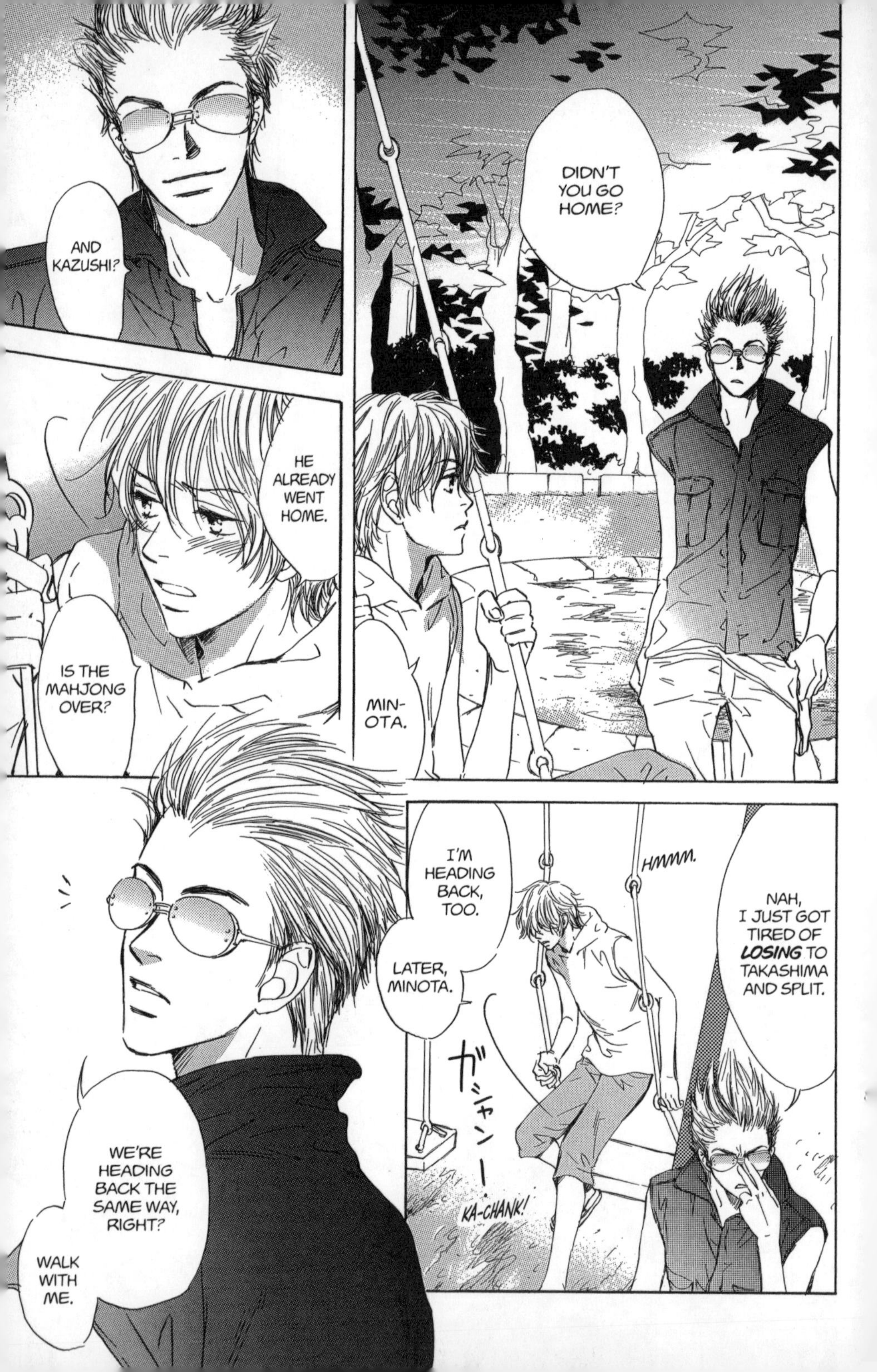
DIDN'T YOU GO HOME?
MIN-OTA.
AND KAZUSHI?
HE ALREADY WENT HOME.
IS THE MAHJONG OVER?
NAH, I JUST GOT TIRED OF ***LOSING*** TO TAKASHIMA AND SPLIT.
HMMM.
I'M HEADING BACK, TOO.
LATER, MINOTA.
ガシャン
KA-CHANK!
WE'RE HEADING BACK THE SAME WAY, RIGHT?
WALK WITH ME.

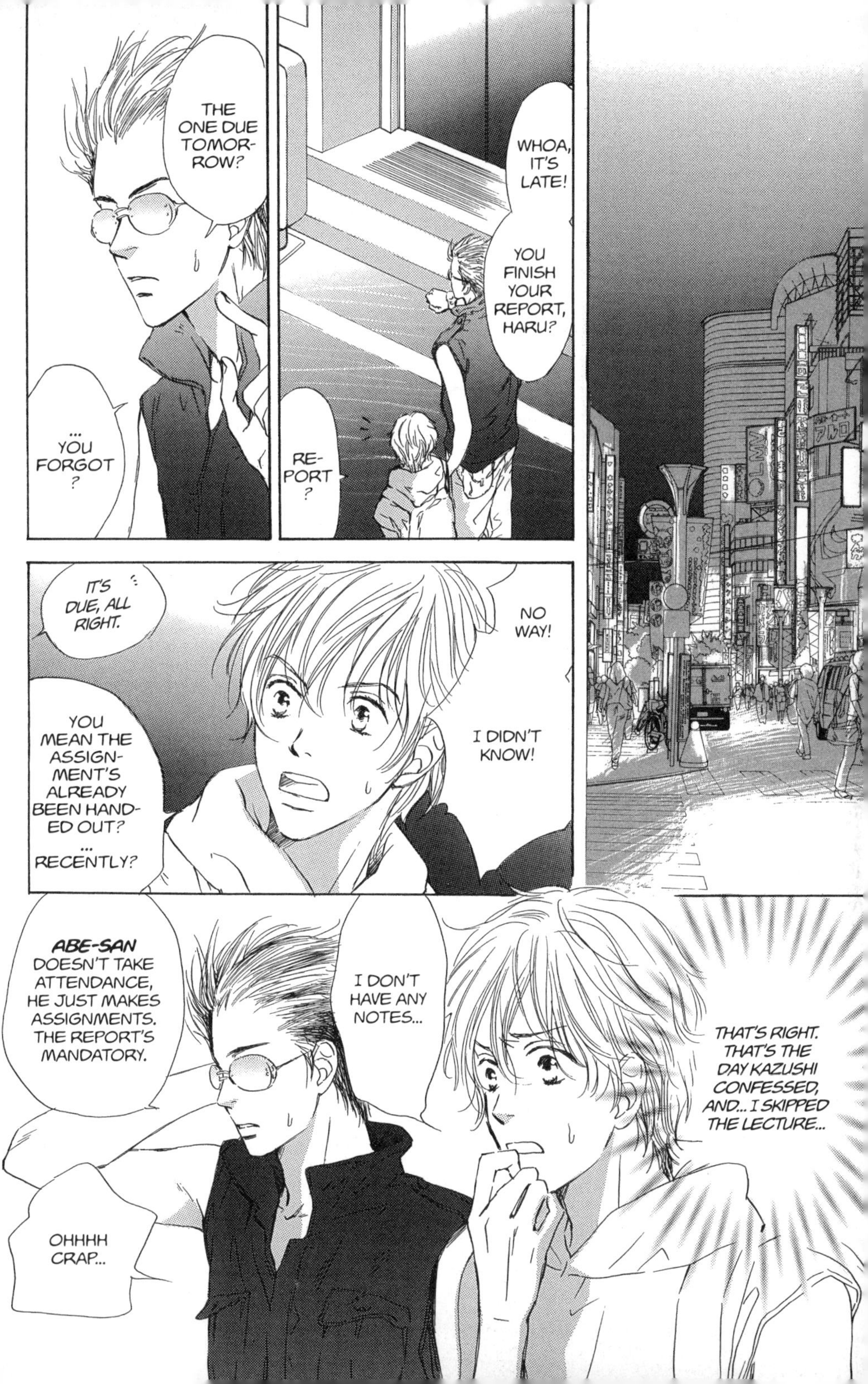
WHOA, IT'S LATE!
YOU FINISH YOUR REPORT, HARU?
REPORT?
THE ONE DUE TOMORROW?
... YOU FORGOT?
NO WAY!
I DIDN'T KNOW!
IT'S DUE, ALL RIGHT.
YOU MEAN THE ASSIGNMENT'S ALREADY BEEN HANDED OUT? ... RECENTLY?
THAT'S RIGHT. THAT'S THE DAY KAZUSHI CONFESSED, AND... I SKIPPED THE LECTURE...
I DON'T HAVE ANY NOTES...
ABE-SAN DOESN'T TAKE ATTENDANCE, HE JUST MAKES ASSIGNMENTS. THE REPORT'S MANDATORY.
OHHHH CRAP...

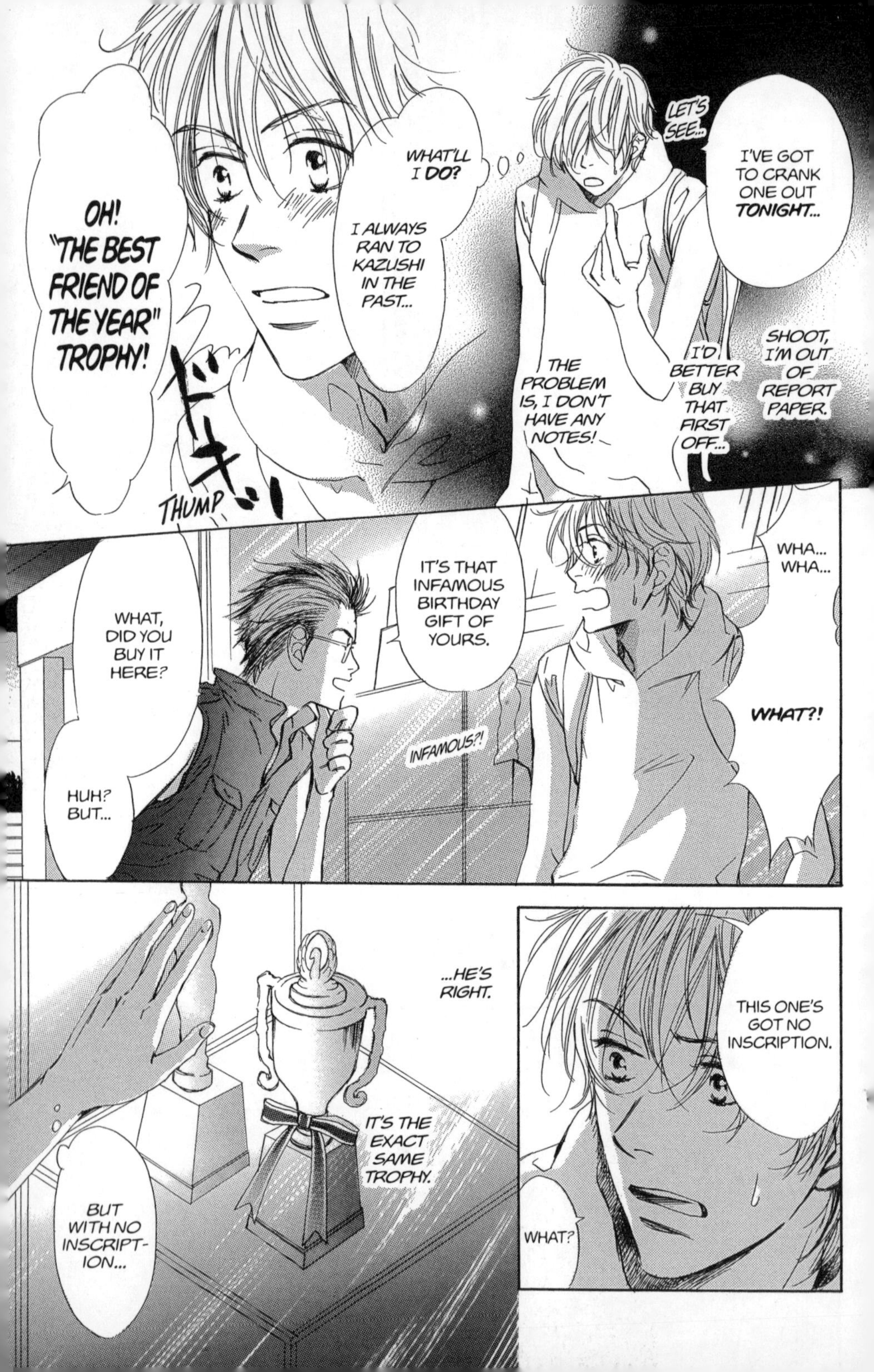
LET'S SEE...
I'VE GOT TO CRANK ONE OUT TONIGHT...
SHOOT, I'M OUT OF REPORT PAPER.
I'D BETTER BUY THAT FIRST OFF...
THE PROBLEM IS, I DON'T HAVE ANY NOTES!
WHAT'LL I DO?
I ALWAYS RAN TO KAZUSHI IN THE PAST...
OH! "THE BEST FRIEND OF THE YEAR" TROPHY!
THUMP
WHA... WHA...
IT'S THAT INFAMOUS BIRTHDAY GIFT OF YOURS.
WHAT?!
INFAMOUS?!
WHAT, DID YOU BUY IT HERE?
HUH? BUT...
THIS ONE'S GOT NO INSCRIPTION.
WHAT?
...HE'S RIGHT.
IT'S THE EXACT SAME TROPHY.
BUT WITH NO INSCRIPTION...

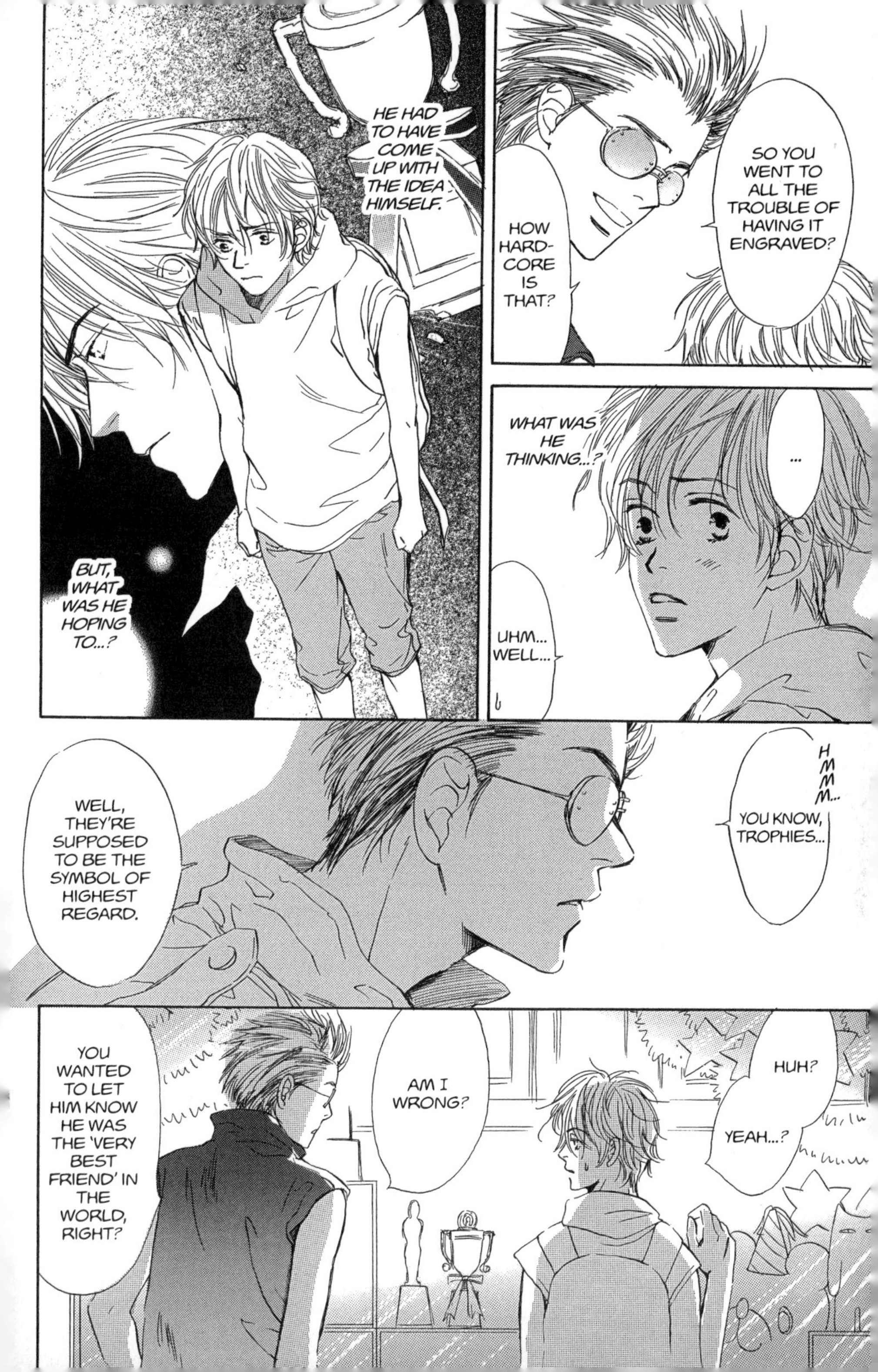
SO YOU WENT TO ALL THE TROUBLE OF HAVING IT ENGRAVED?
HOW HARD-CORE IS THAT?
...
WHAT WAS HE THINKING...?
UHM... WELL...
HE HAD TO HAVE COME UP WITH THE IDEA HIMSELF.
BUT, WHAT WAS HE HOPING TO...?
HMMM...
YOU KNOW, TROPHIES...
WELL, THEY'RE SUPPOSED TO BE THE SYMBOL OF HIGHEST REGARD.
HUH?
YEAH...?
AM I WRONG?
YOU WANTED TO LET HIM KNOW HE WAS THE 'VERY BEST FRIEND' IN THE WORLD, RIGHT?

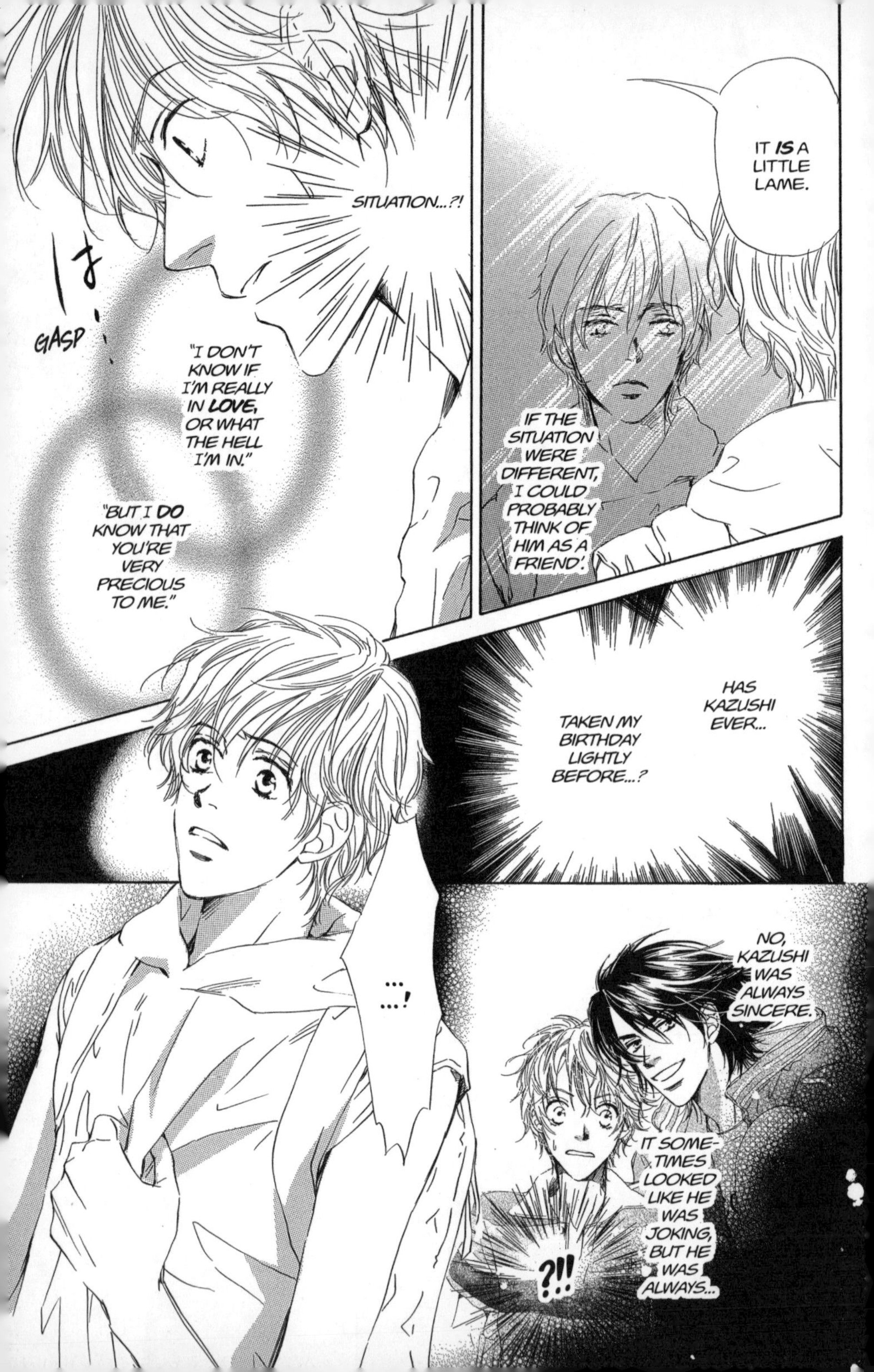
IT **IS** A LITTLE LAME.
IF THE SITUATION WERE DIFFERENT, I COULD PROBABLY THINK OF HIM AS A FRIEND.
SITUATION...?!
は
GASP
"I DON'T KNOW IF I'M REALLY IN **LOVE,** OR WHAT THE HELL I'M IN."
"BUT I **DO** KNOW THAT YOU'RE VERY PRECIOUS TO ME."
HAS KAZUSHI EVER...
TAKEN MY BIRTHDAY LIGHTLY BEFORE...?
...
...!
NO, KAZUSHI WAS ALWAYS SINCERE.
IT SOMETIMES LOOKED LIKE HE WAS JOKING, BUT HE WAS ALWAYS...
?!!

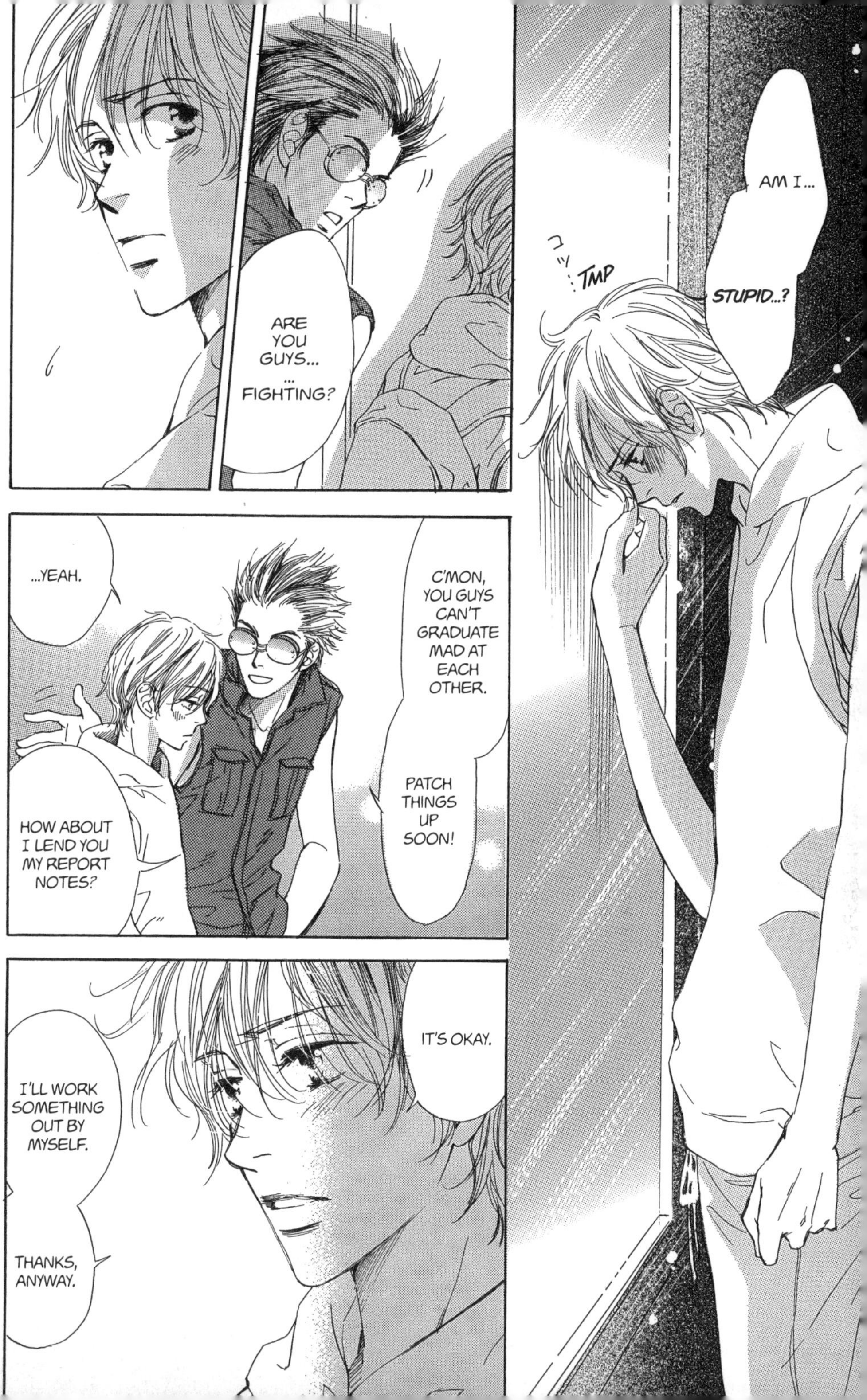
AM I...
STUPID...?
コッ... TMP
ARE YOU GUYS... ...FIGHTING?
C'MON, YOU GUYS CAN'T GRADUATE MAD AT EACH OTHER.
...YEAH.
PATCH THINGS UP SOON!
HOW ABOUT I LEND YOU MY REPORT NOTES?
IT'S OKAY.
I'LL WORK SOMETHING OUT BY MYSELF.
THANKS, ANYWAY.

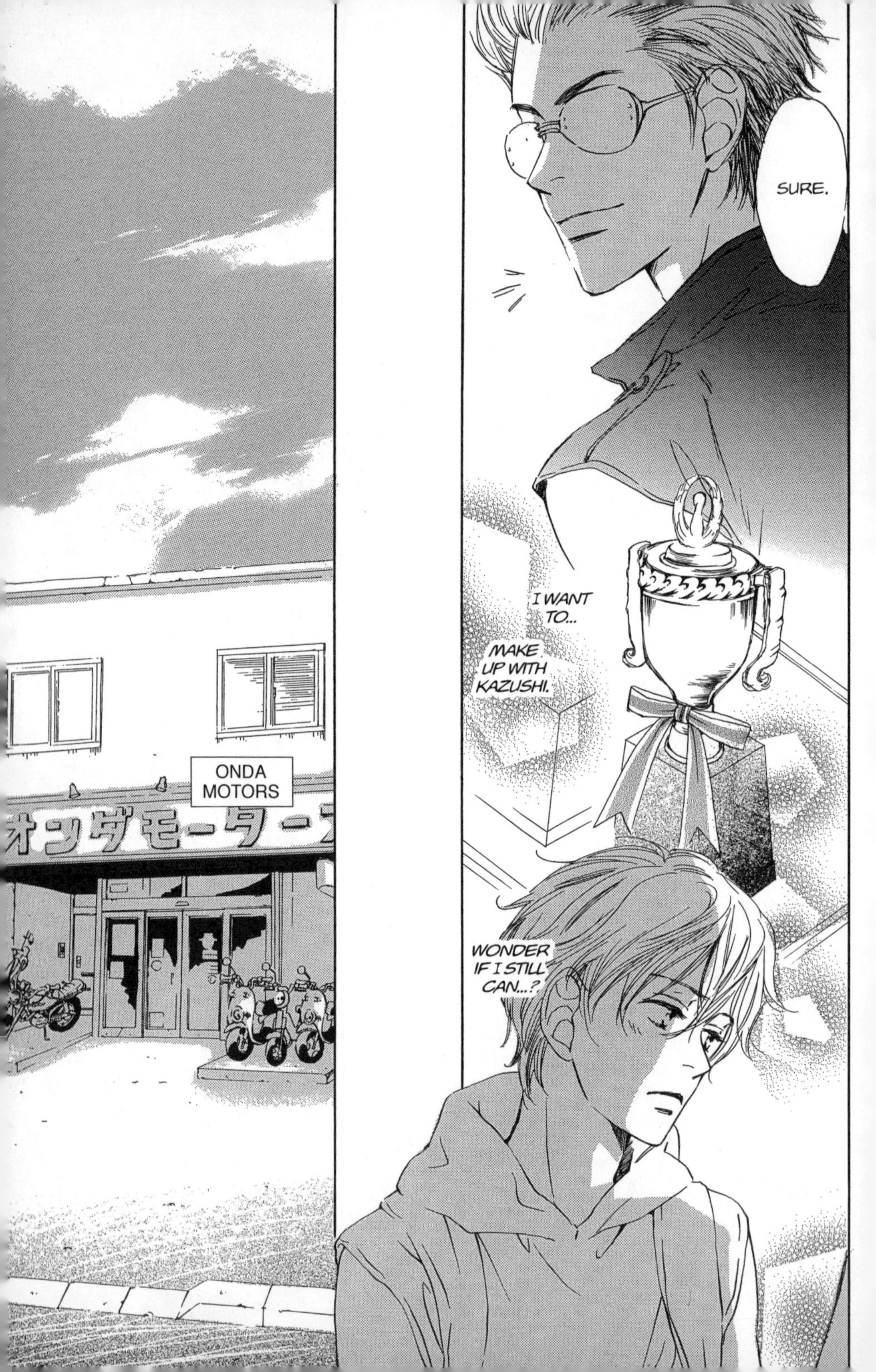
SURE.
I WANT TO...
MAKE UP WITH KAZUSHI.
WONDER IF I STILL CAN...?
ONDA MOTORS
オンダモーター

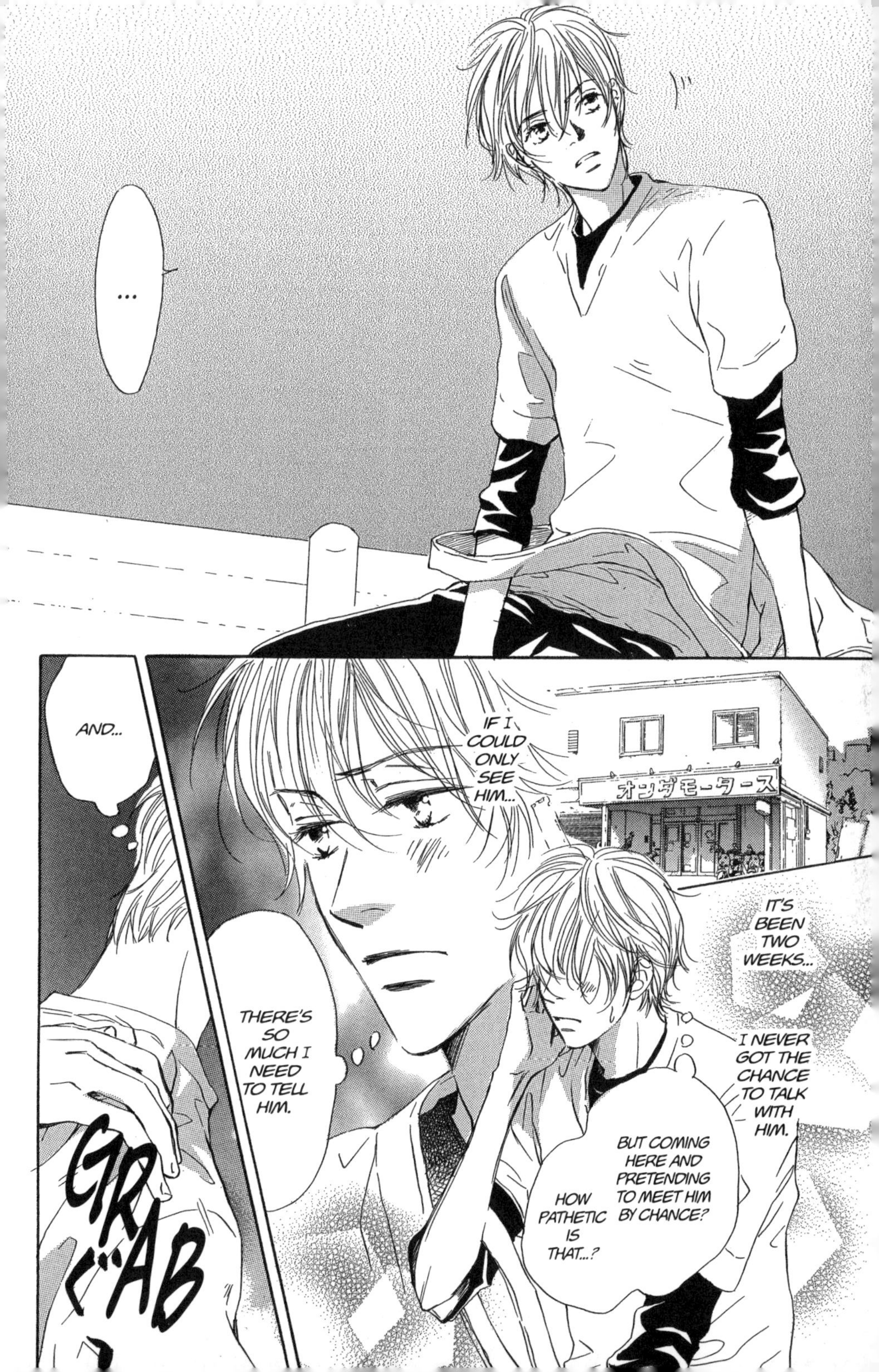
...
オンダモータース
IT'S BEEN TWO WEEKS...
I NEVER GOT THE CHANCE TO TALK WITH HIM.
BUT COMING HERE AND PRETENDING TO MEET HIM BY CHANCE?
HOW PATHETIC IS THAT...?
IF I COULD ONLY SEE HIM...
THERE'S SO MUCH I NEED TO TELL HIM.
AND...
GRAB

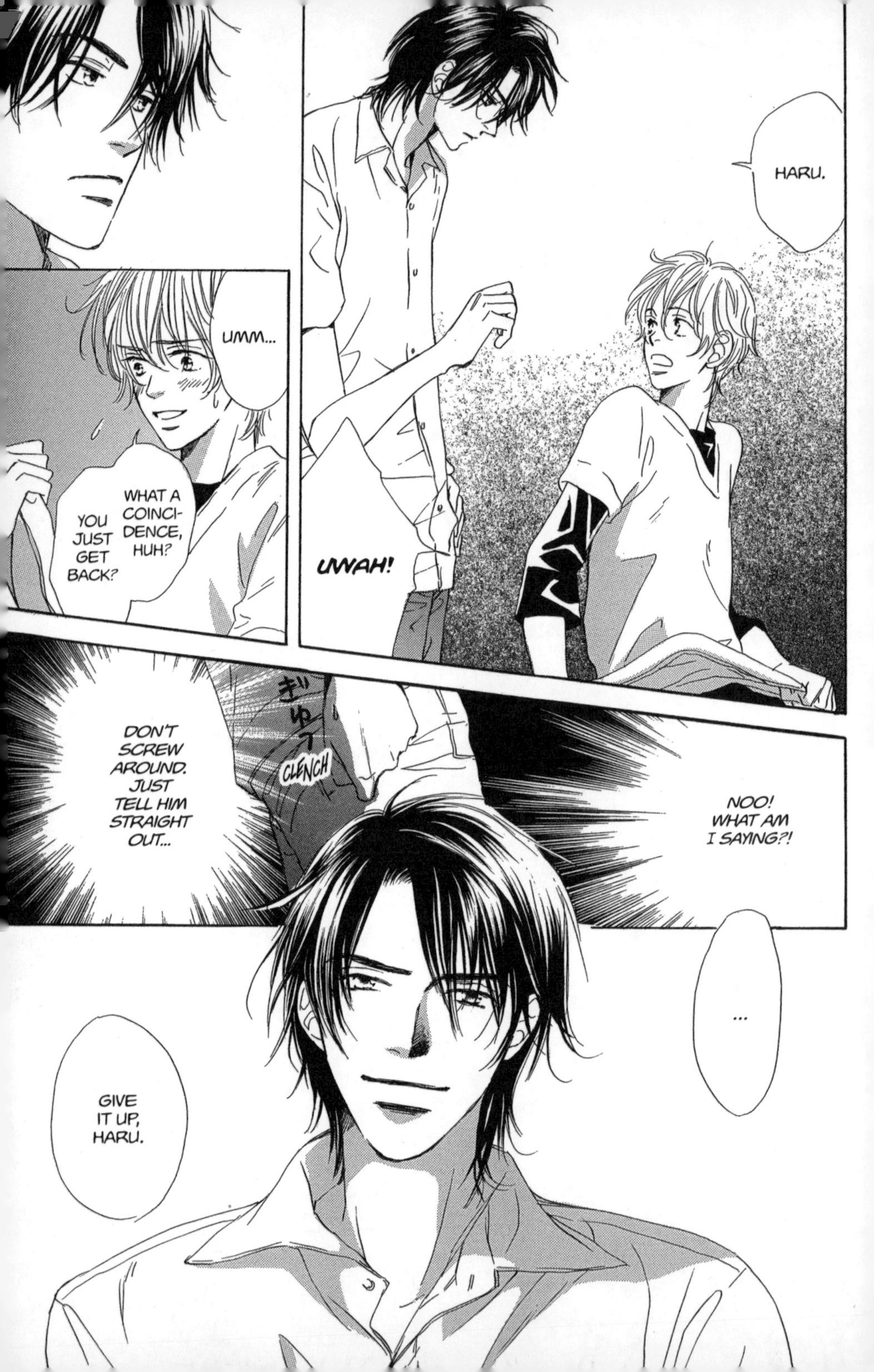
HARU.
UWAH!
UMM...
WHAT A COINCIDENCE, HUH?
YOU JUST GET BACK?
NOO! WHAT AM I SAYING?!
ぎゅっ
CLENCH
DON'T SCREW AROUND. JUST TELL HIM STRAIGHT OUT...
...
GIVE IT UP, HARU.

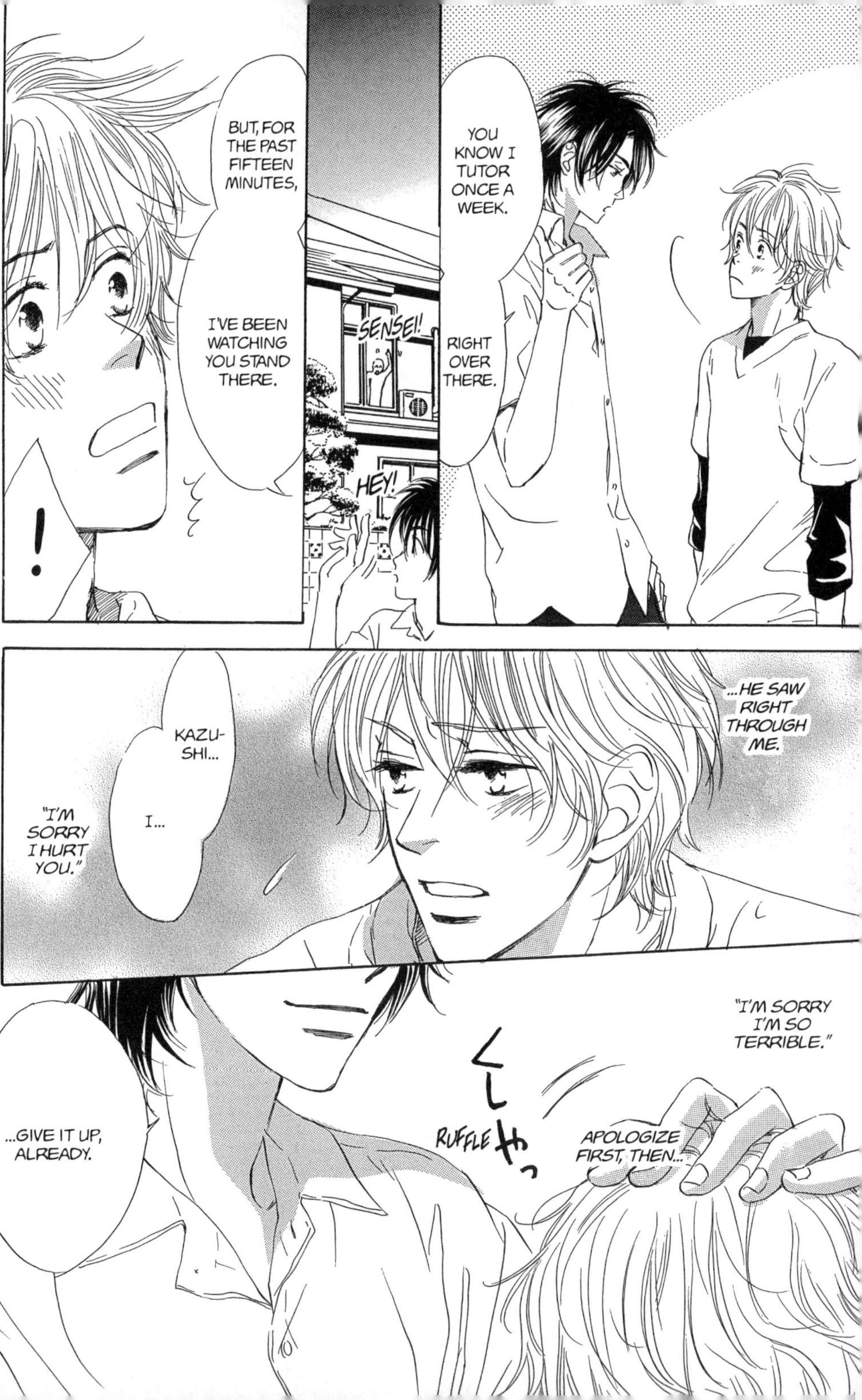
YOU KNOW I TUTOR ONCE A WEEK.
RIGHT OVER THERE.
SENSEI!
HEY!
BUT, FOR THE PAST FIFTEEN MINUTES,
I'VE BEEN WATCHING YOU STAND THERE.
!
...HE SAW RIGHT THROUGH ME.
KAZU-SHI...
I...
"I'M SORRY I HURT YOU."
"I'M SORRY I'M SO TERRIBLE."
APOLOGIZE FIRST, THEN...
RUFFLE
くしやっ
...GIVE IT UP, ALREADY.

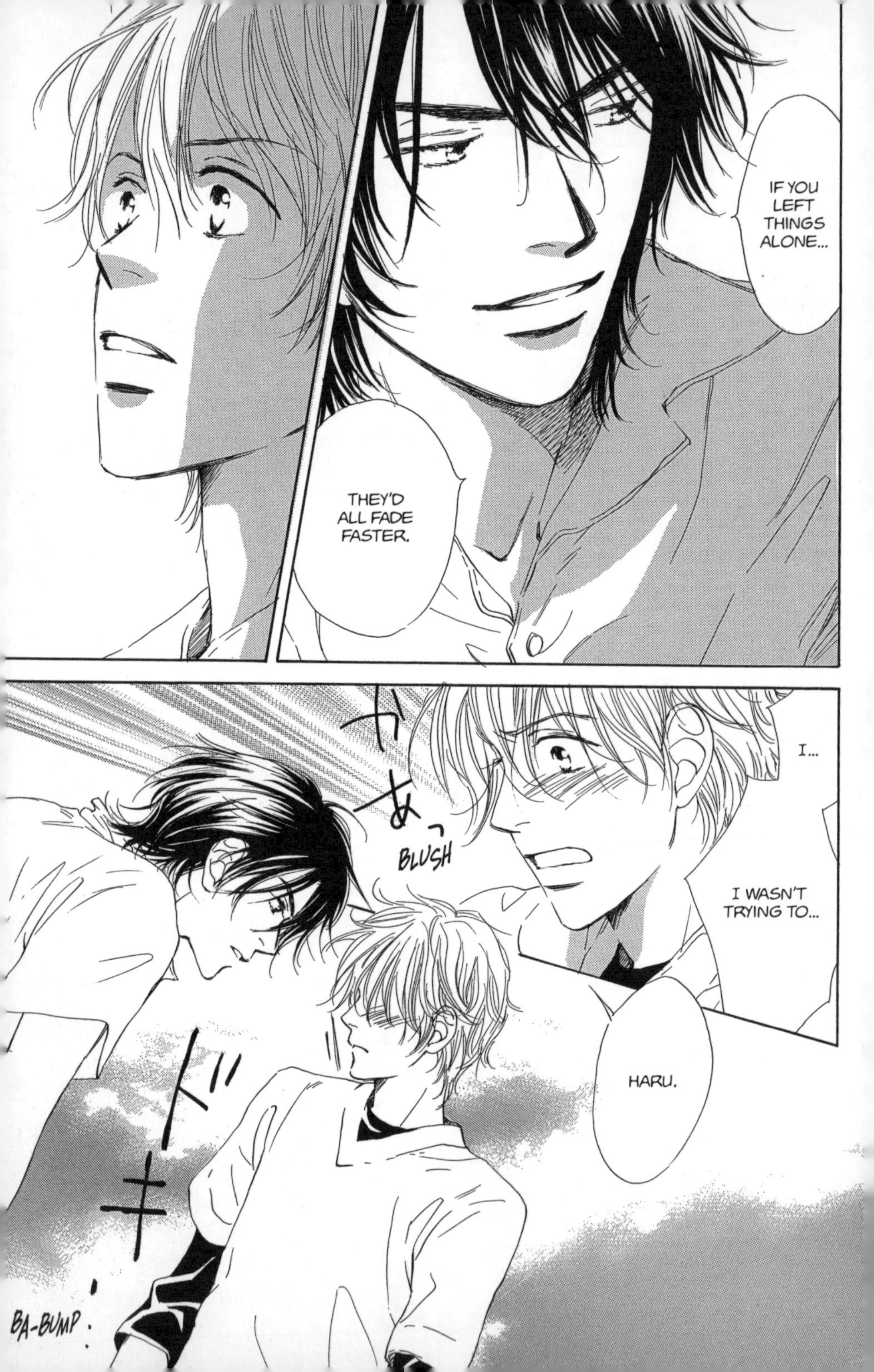
IF YOU LEFT THINGS ALONE...
THEY'D ALL FADE FASTER.
I...
I WASN'T TRYING TO...
BLUSH
HARU.
BA-BUMP

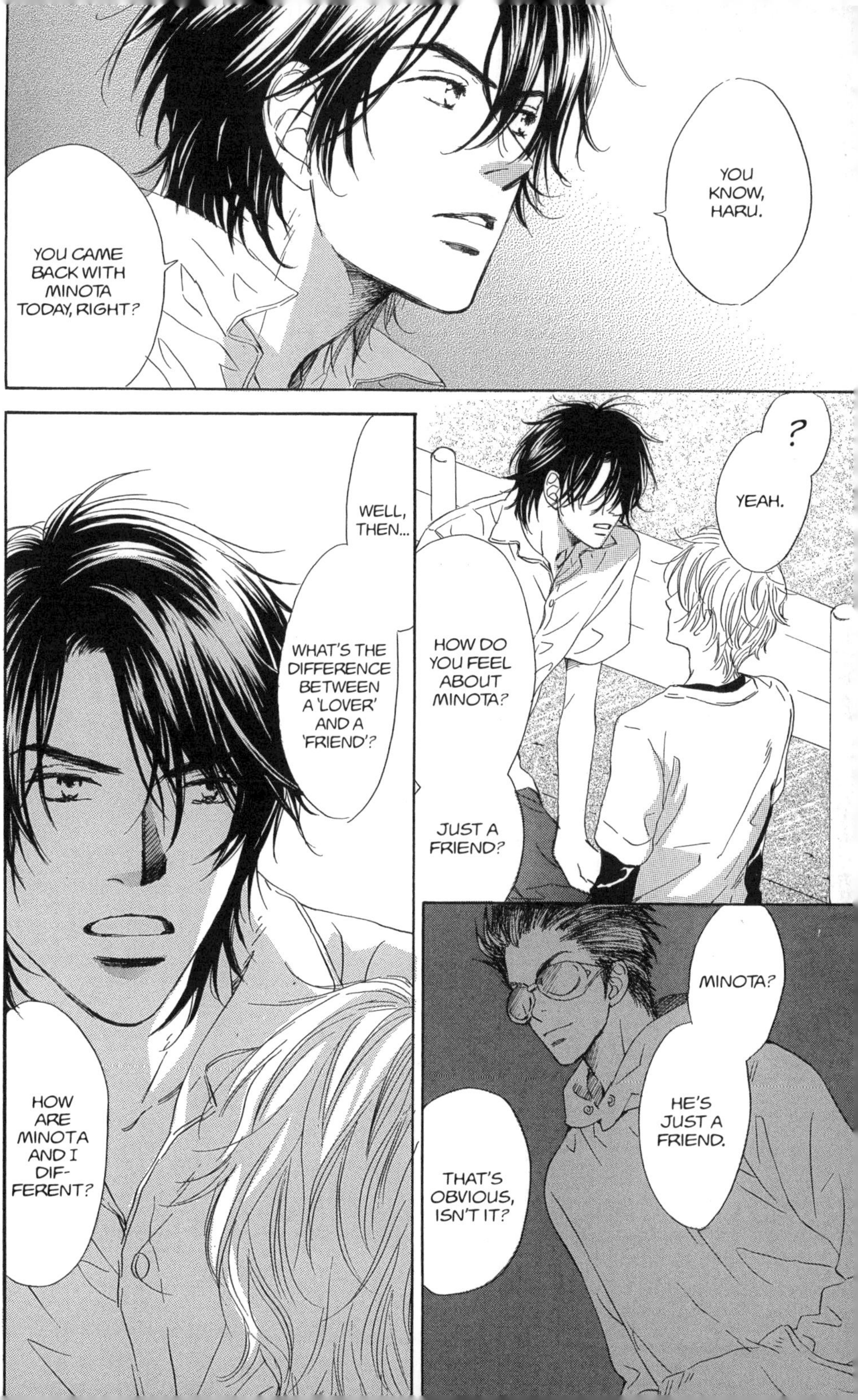
YOU KNOW, HARU.
YOU CAME BACK WITH MINOTA TODAY, RIGHT?
?
YEAH.
HOW DO YOU FEEL ABOUT MINOTA?
JUST A FRIEND?
MINOTA?
HE'S JUST A FRIEND.
THAT'S OBVIOUS, ISN'T IT?
WELL, THEN...
WHAT'S THE DIFFERENCE BETWEEN A 'LOVER' AND A 'FRIEND'?
HOW ARE MINOTA AND I DIF-FERENT?

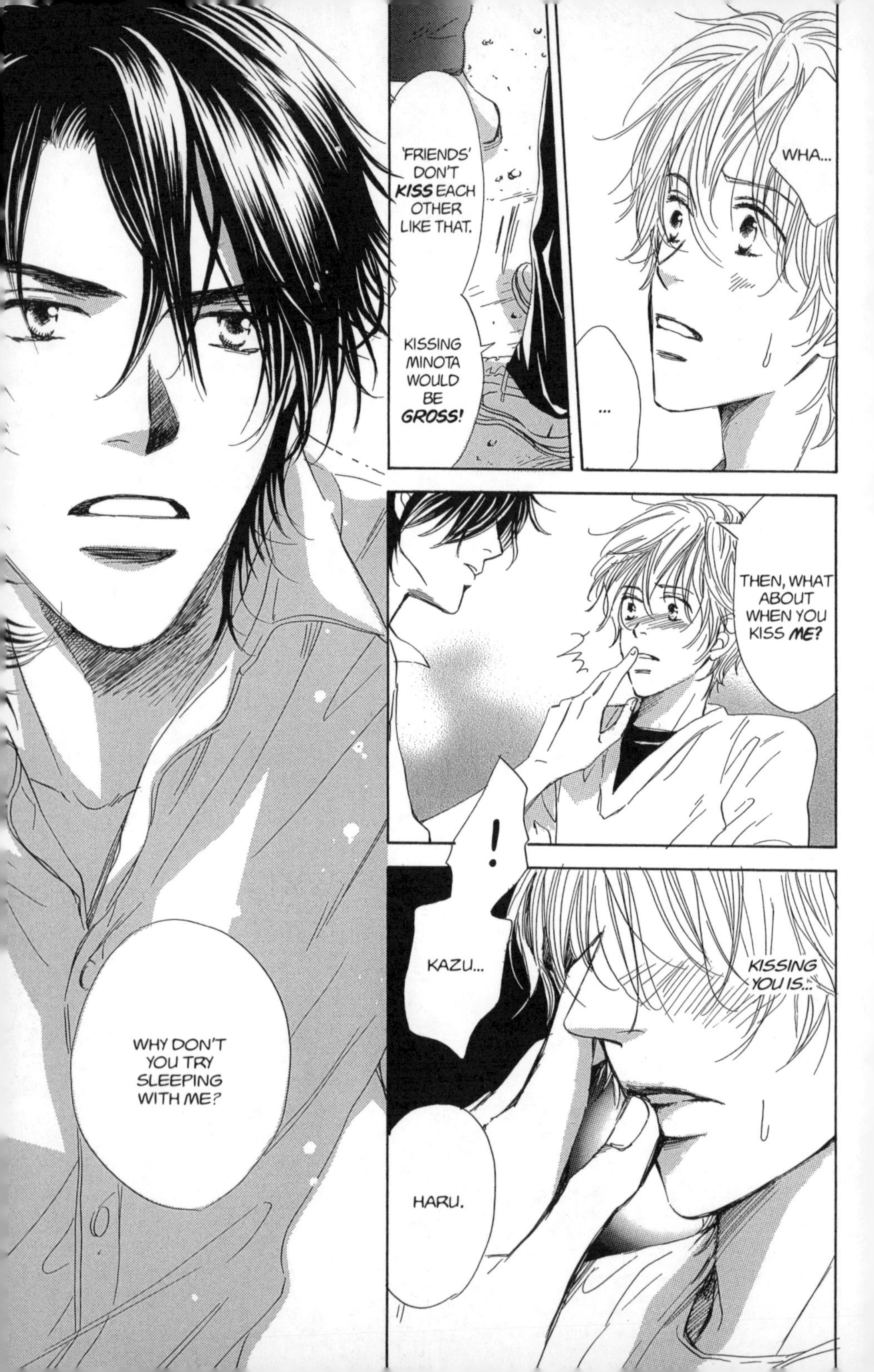
WHA...
...
'FRIENDS' DON'T KISS EACH OTHER LIKE THAT.
KISSING MINOTA WOULD BE GROSS!
THEN, WHAT ABOUT WHEN YOU KISS ME?
!
KISSING YOU IS...
KAZU...
HARU.
WHY DON'T YOU TRY SLEEPING WITH ME?

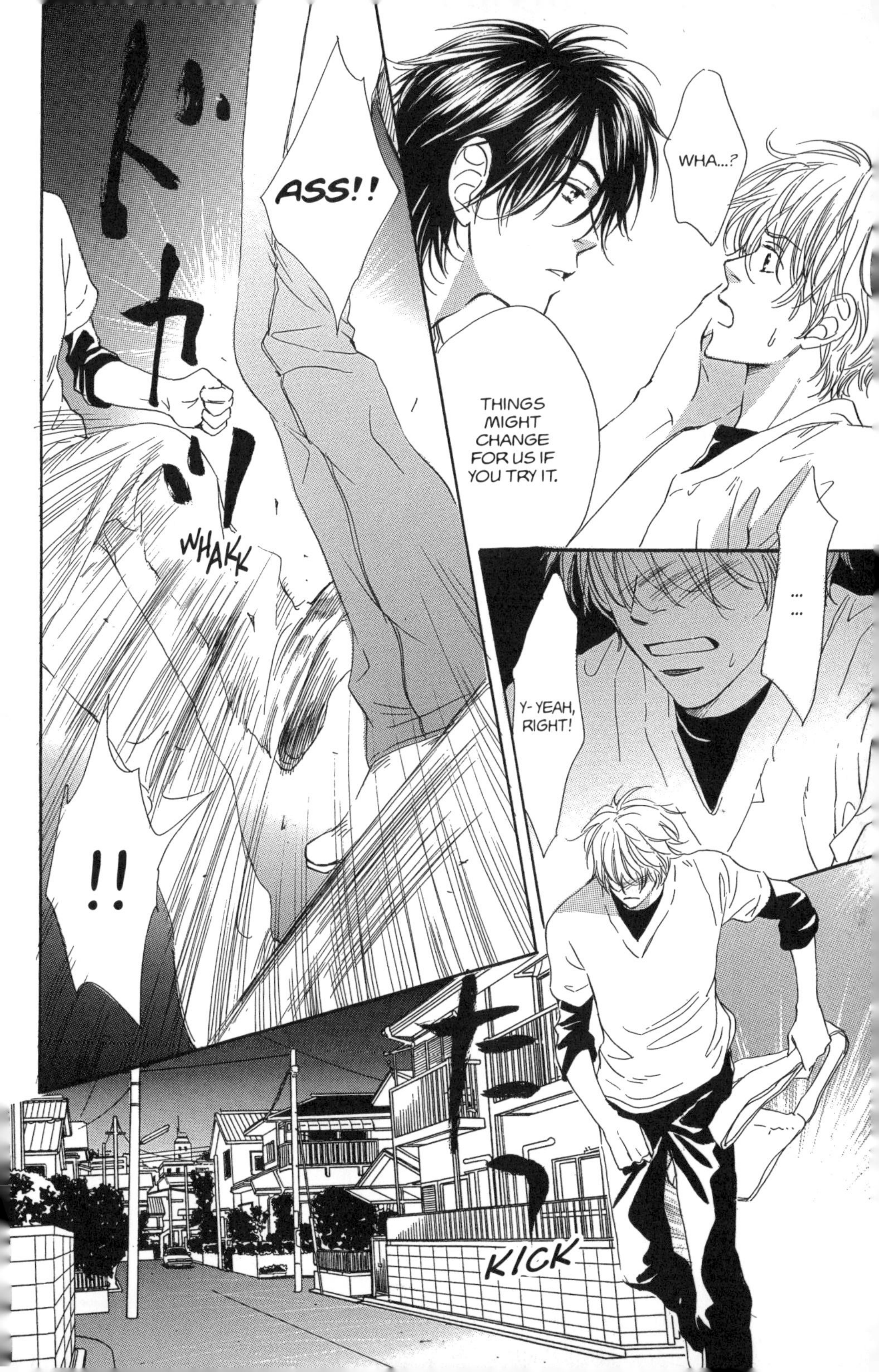
WHA...?
THINGS MIGHT CHANGE FOR US IF YOU TRY IT.
...
...
Y- YEAH, RIGHT!
ASS!!
ドカッ!
WHAKK
!!
KICK

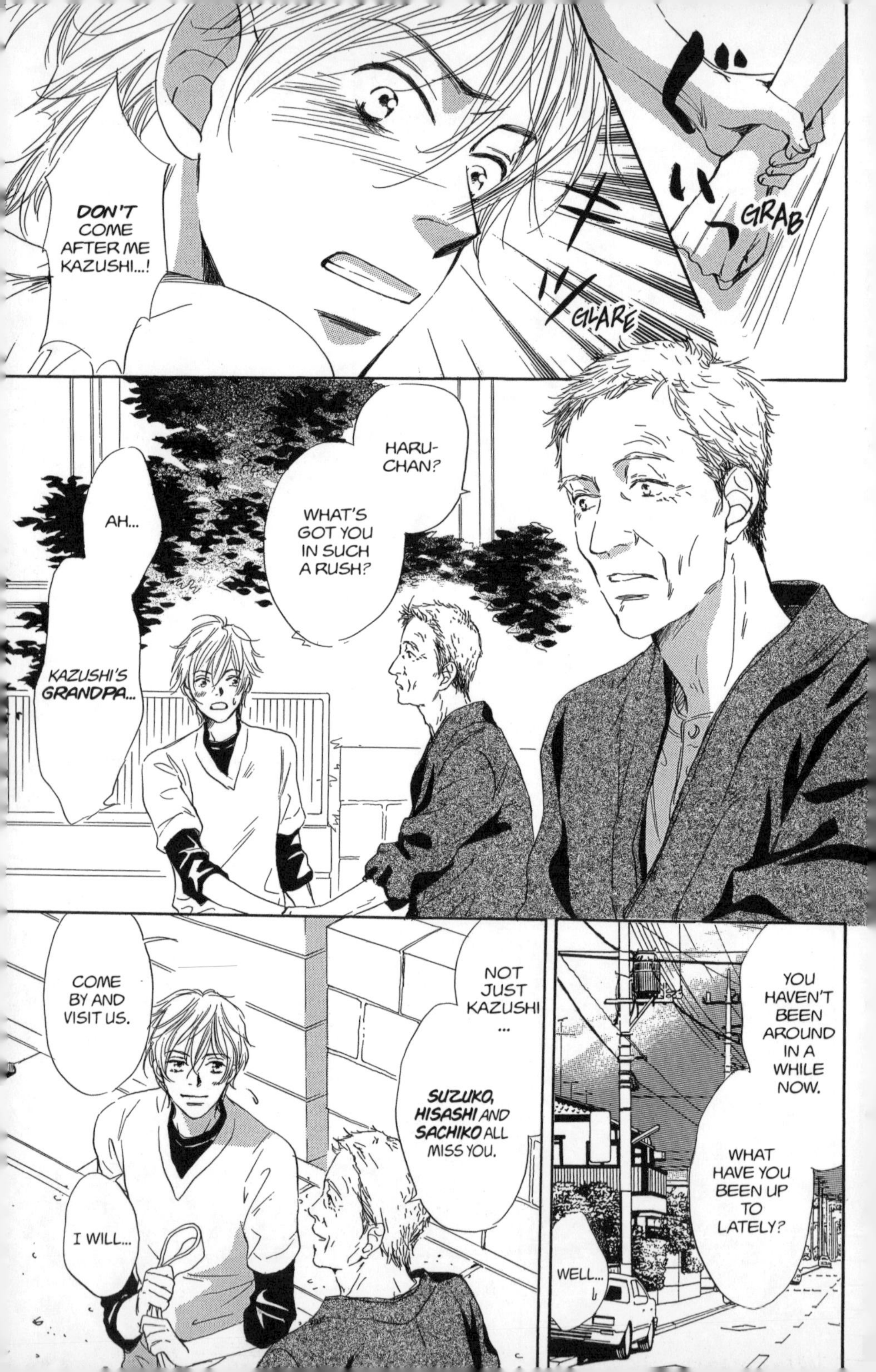
GRAB
GLARE
DON'T COME AFTER ME KAZUSHI...!
HARU-CHAN?
WHAT'S GOT YOU IN SUCH A RUSH?
AH...
KAZUSHI'S GRANDPA...
YOU HAVEN'T BEEN AROUND IN A WHILE NOW.
WHAT HAVE YOU BEEN UP TO LATELY?
WELL...
NOT JUST KAZUSHI...
SUZUKO, HISASHI AND SACHIKO ALL MISS YOU.
COME BY AND VISIT US.
I WILL...

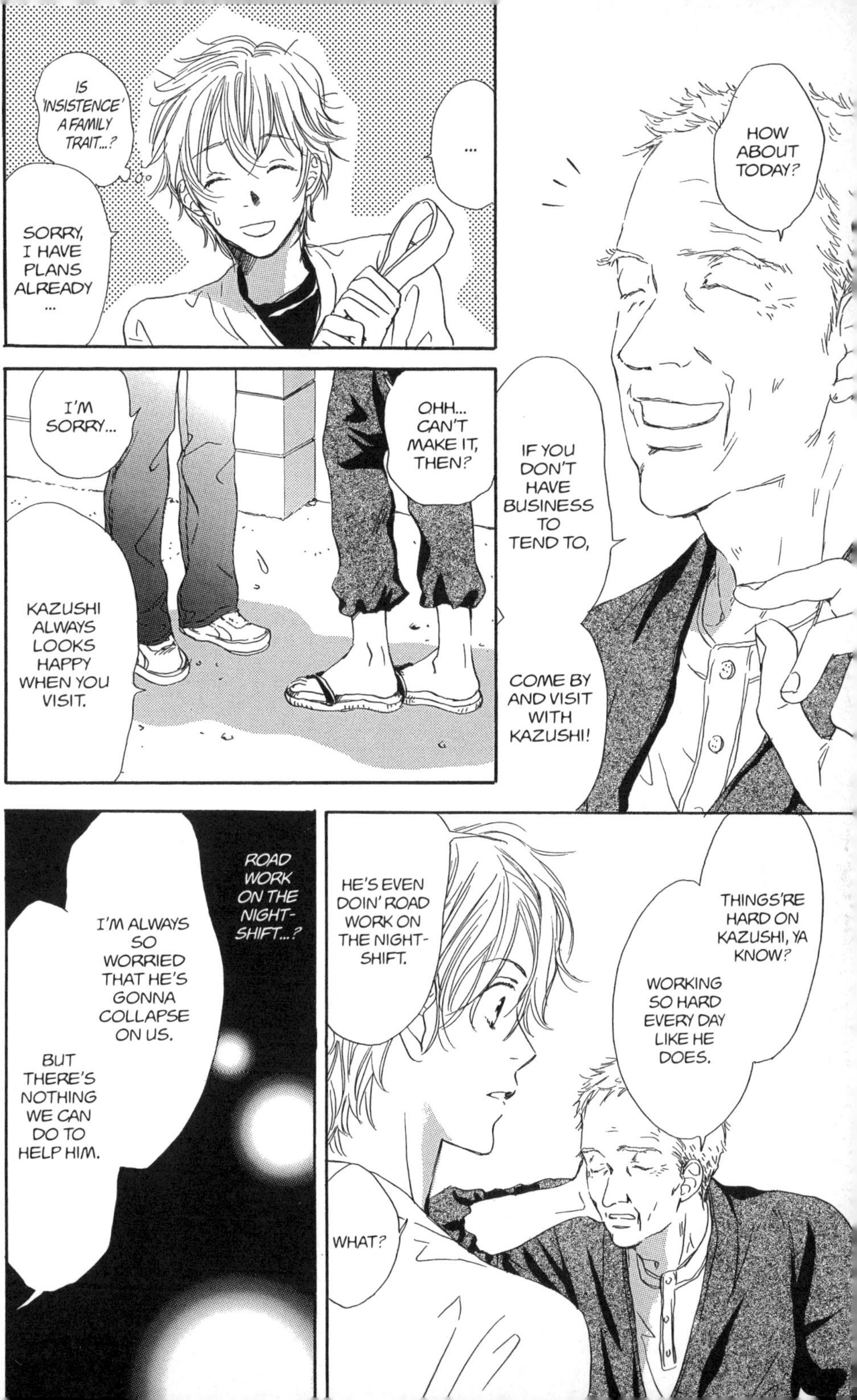
HOW ABOUT TODAY?
IF YOU DON'T HAVE BUSINESS TO TEND TO,
COME BY AND VISIT WITH KAZUSHI!
...
IS 'INSISTENCE' A FAMILY TRAIT...?
SORRY, I HAVE PLANS ALREADY ...
OHH... CAN'T MAKE IT, THEN?
I'M SORRY...
KAZUSHI ALWAYS LOOKS HAPPY WHEN YOU VISIT.
THINGS'RE HARD ON KAZUSHI, YA KNOW?
WORKING SO HARD EVERY DAY LIKE HE DOES.
HE'S EVEN DOIN' ROAD WORK ON THE NIGHT-SHIFT.
WHAT?
ROAD WORK ON THE NIGHT-SHIFT...?
I'M ALWAYS SO WORRIED THAT HE'S GONNA COLLAPSE ON US.
BUT THERE'S NOTHING WE CAN DO TO HELP HIM.

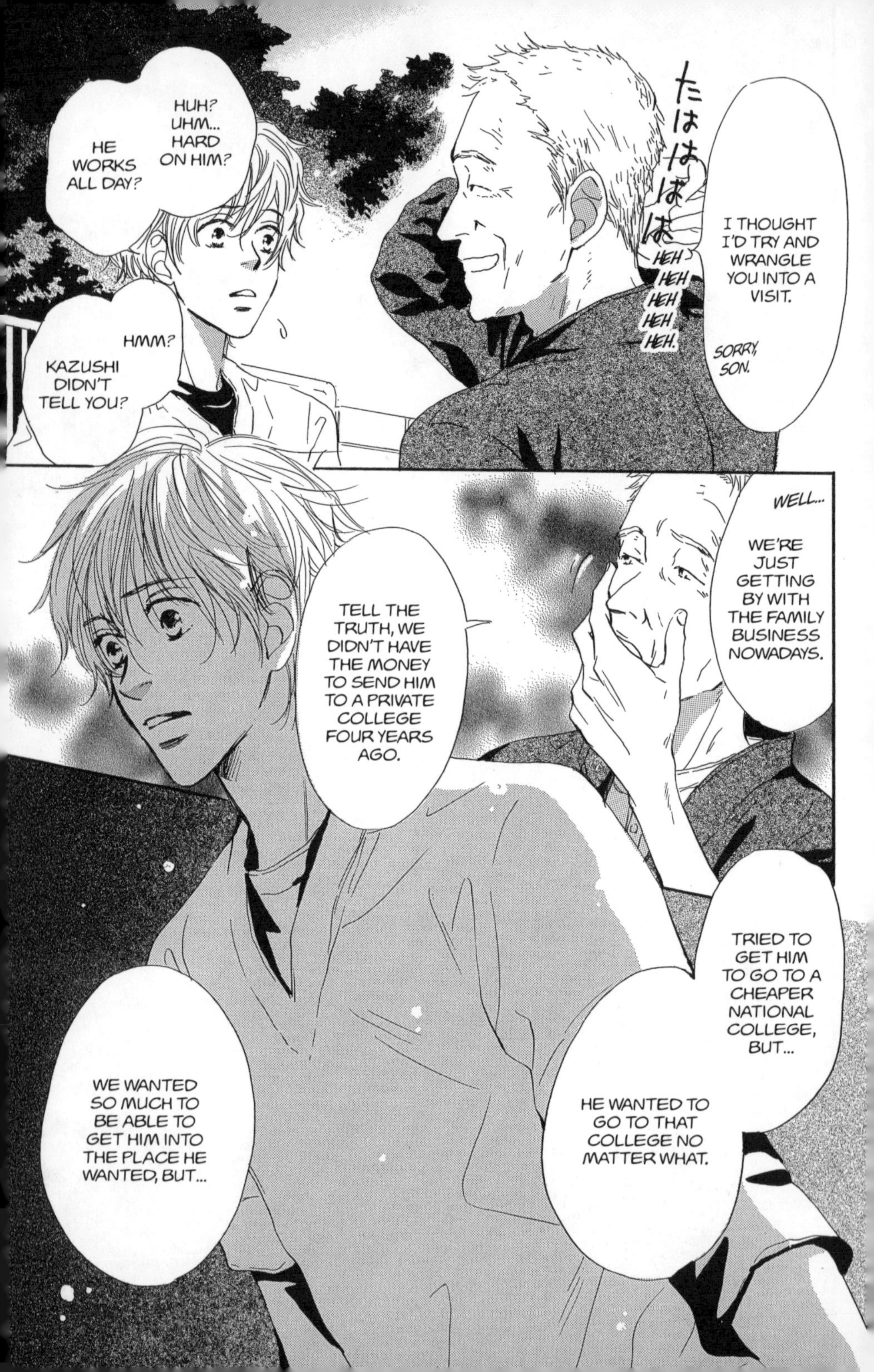

たはははは
HEH HEH HEH HEH HEH.
I THOUGHT I'D TRY AND WRANGLE YOU INTO A VISIT.
SORRY, SON.
HUH? UHM... HARD ON HIM?
HE WORKS ALL DAY?
HMM? KAZUSHI DIDN'T TELL YOU?
WELL...
WE'RE JUST GETTING BY WITH THE FAMILY BUSINESS NOWADAYS.
TELL THE TRUTH, WE DIDN'T HAVE THE MONEY TO SEND HIM TO A PRIVATE COLLEGE FOUR YEARS AGO.
TRIED TO GET HIM TO GO TO A CHEAPER NATIONAL COLLEGE, BUT...
HE WANTED TO GO TO THAT COLLEGE NO MATTER WHAT.
WE WANTED SO MUCH TO BE ABLE TO GET HIM INTO THE PLACE HE WANTED, BUT...

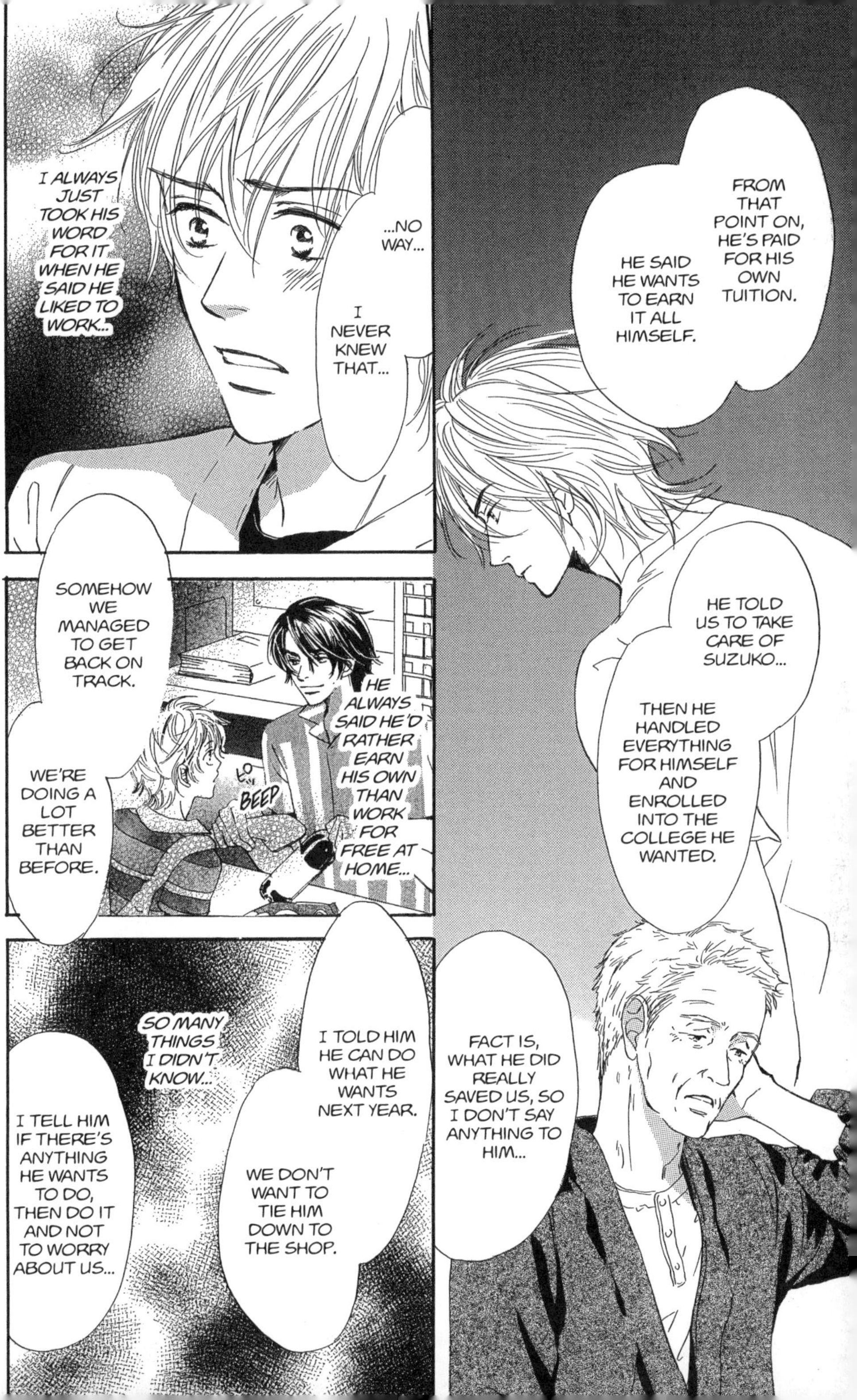
FROM THAT POINT ON, HE'S PAID FOR HIS OWN TUITION.
HE SAID HE WANTS TO EARN IT ALL HIMSELF.
HE TOLD US TO TAKE CARE OF SUZUKO...
THEN HE HANDLED EVERYTHING FOR HIMSELF AND ENROLLED INTO THE COLLEGE HE WANTED.
FACT IS, WHAT HE DID REALLY SAVED US, SO I DON'T SAY ANYTHING TO HIM...
...NO WAY...
I NEVER KNEW THAT...
I ALWAYS JUST TOOK HIS WORD FOR IT WHEN HE SAID HE LIKED TO WORK...
HE ALWAYS SAID HE'D RATHER EARN HIS OWN THAN WORK FOR FREE AT HOME...
BEEP
SOMEHOW WE MANAGED TO GET BACK ON TRACK.
WE'RE DOING A LOT BETTER THAN BEFORE.
I TOLD HIM HE CAN DO WHAT HE WANTS NEXT YEAR.
WE DON'T WANT TO TIE HIM DOWN TO THE SHOP.
SO MANY THINGS I DIDN'T KNOW...
I TELL HIM IF THERE'S ANYTHING HE WANTS TO DO, THEN DO IT AND NOT TO WORRY ABOUT US...

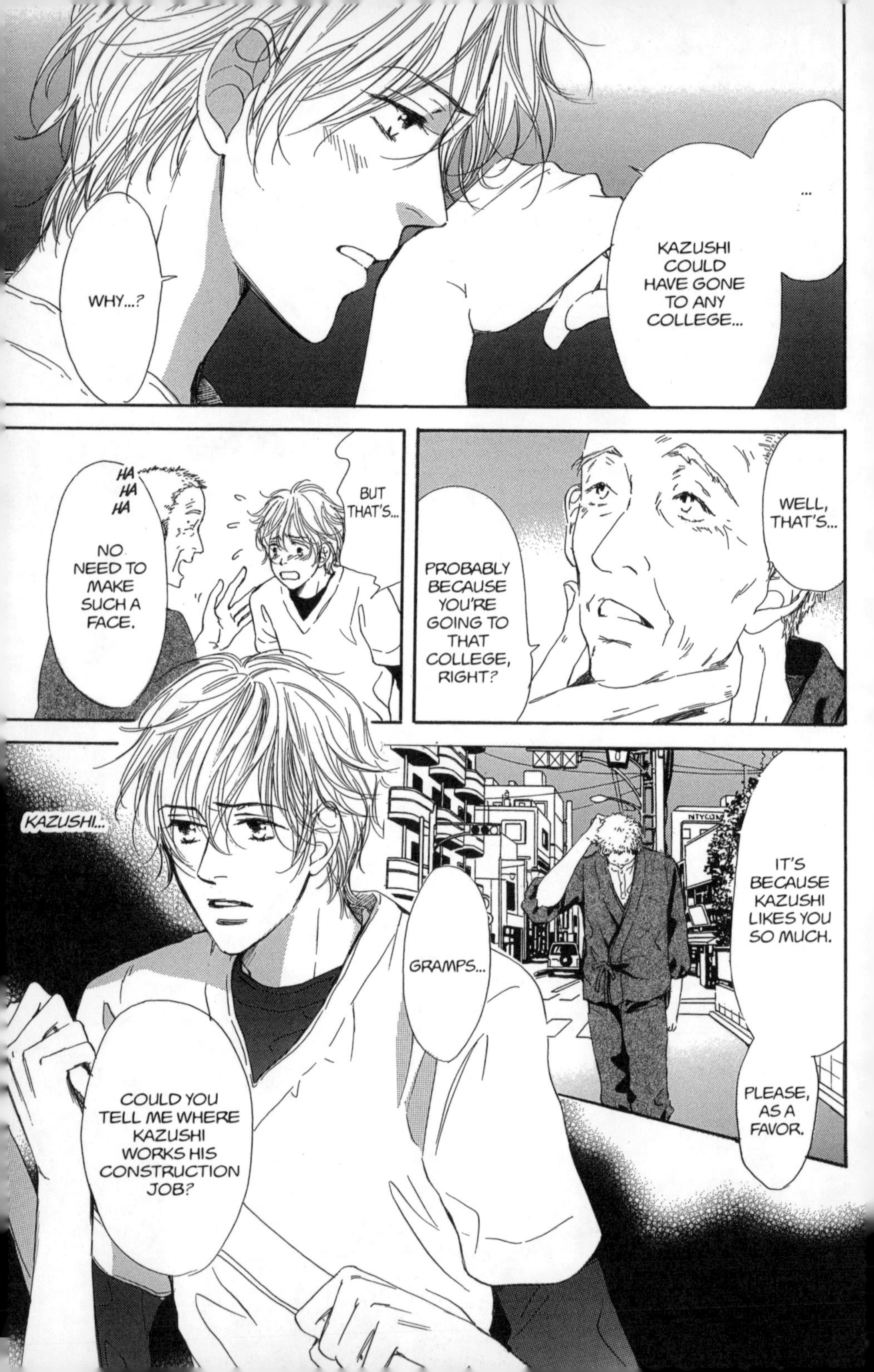
...
KAZUSHI COULD HAVE GONE TO ANY COLLEGE...
WHY...?
WELL, THAT'S...
PROBABLY BECAUSE YOU'RE GOING TO THAT COLLEGE, RIGHT?
BUT THAT'S...
HA HA HA
NO NEED TO MAKE SUCH A FACE.
IT'S BECAUSE KAZUSHI LIKES YOU SO MUCH.
PLEASE, AS A FAVOR.
GRAMPS...
KAZUSHI...
COULD YOU TELL ME WHERE KAZUSHI WORKS HIS CONSTRUCTION JOB?

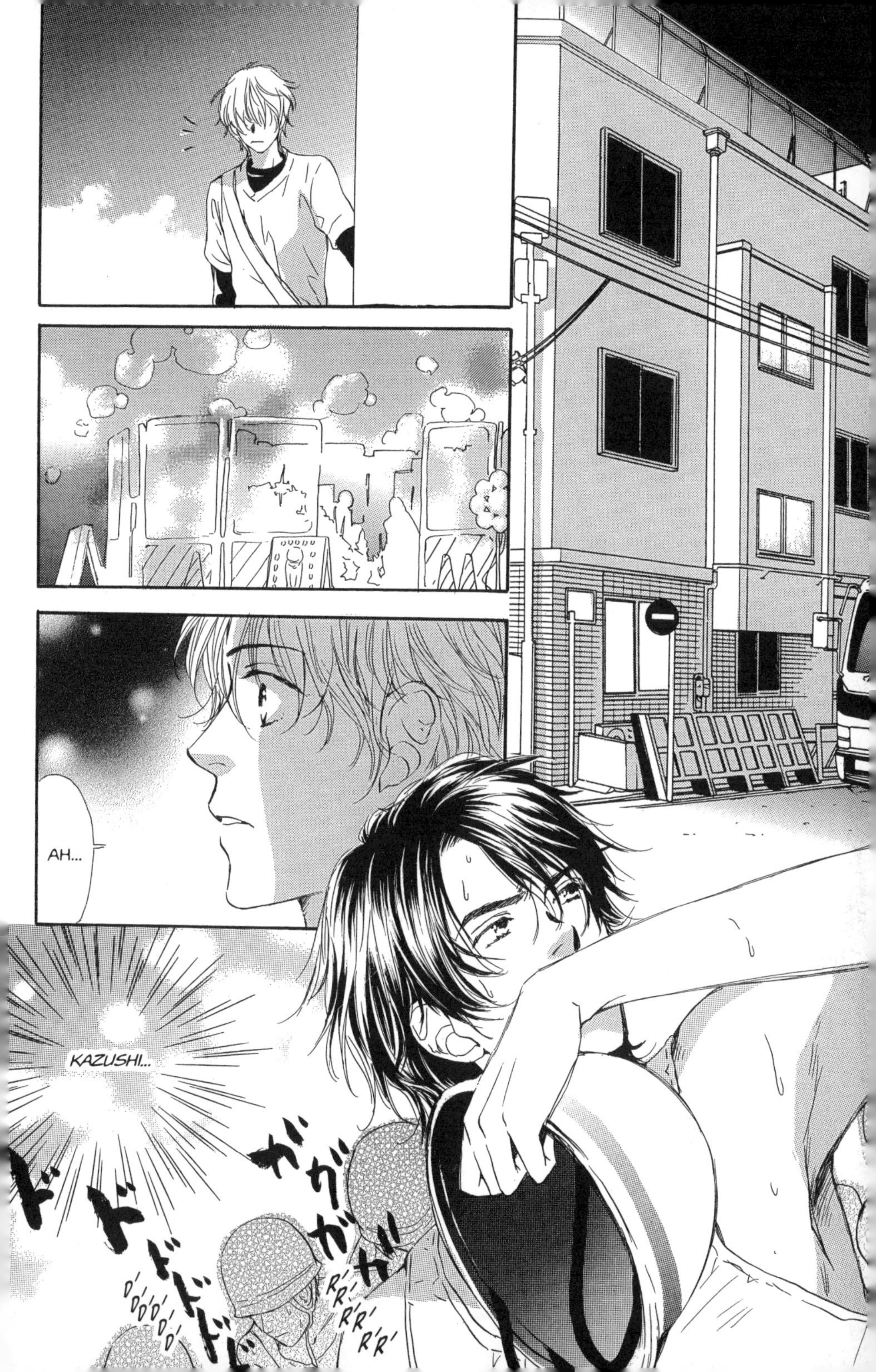
AH...
KAZUSHI...

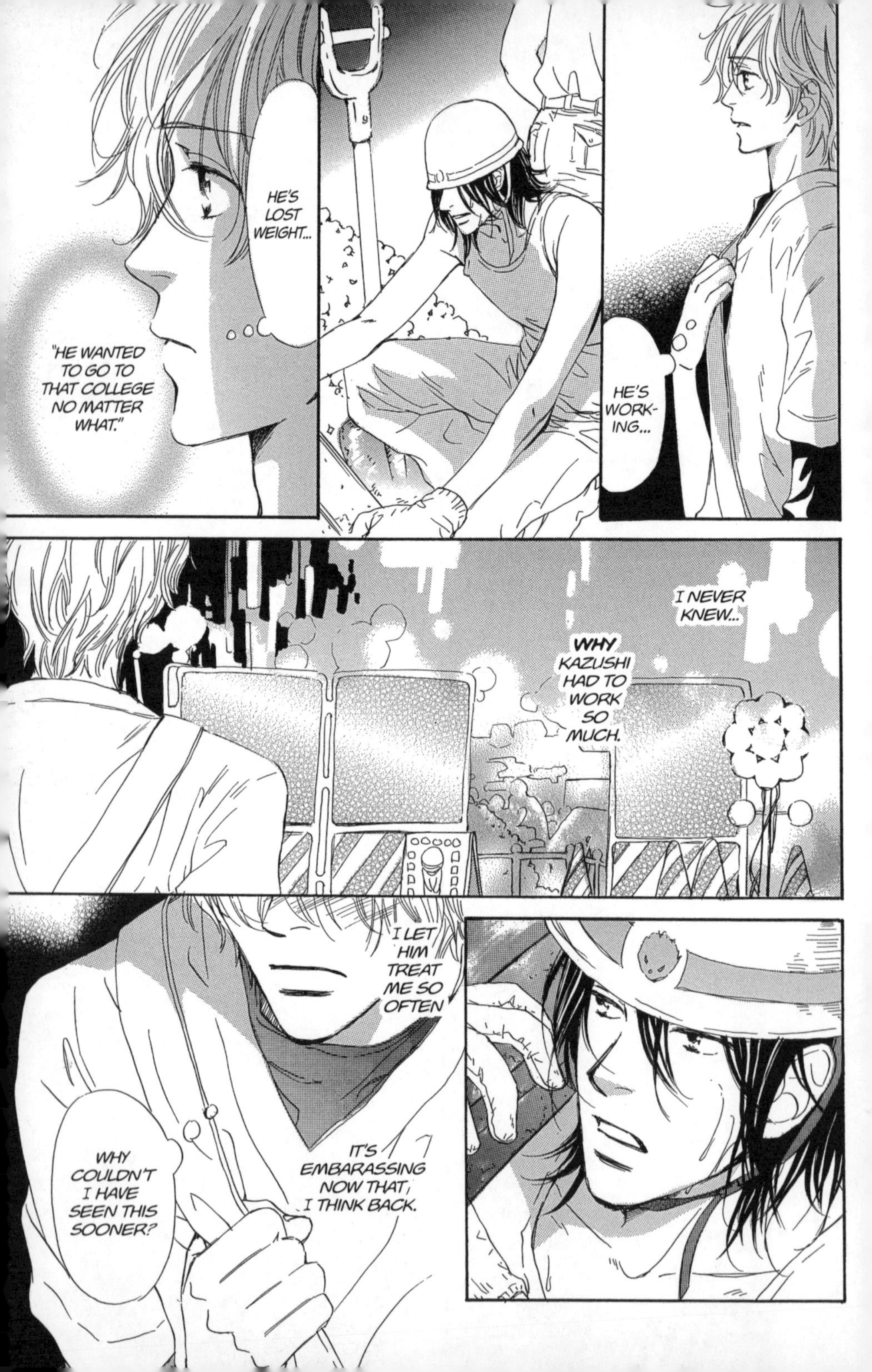
HE'S WORKING...
HE'S LOST WEIGHT...
"HE WANTED TO GO TO THAT COLLEGE NO MATTER WHAT."
I NEVER KNEW...
WHY KAZUSHI HAD TO WORK SO MUCH.
I LET HIM TREAT ME SO OFTEN
IT'S EMBARASSING NOW THAT I THINK BACK.
WHY COULDN'T I HAVE SEEN THIS SOONER?

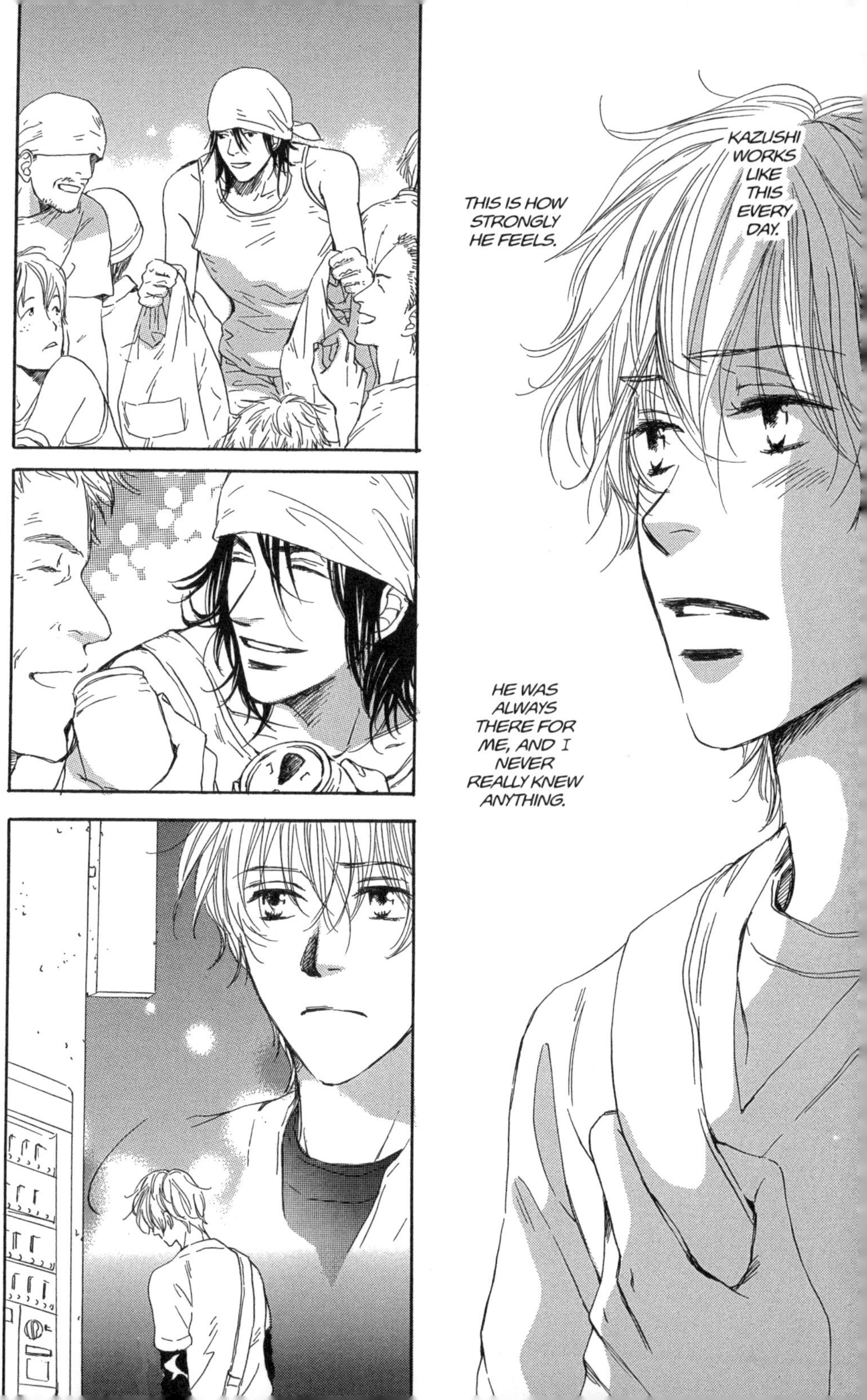
KAZUSHI WORKS LIKE THIS EVERY DAY.
THIS IS HOW STRONGLY HE FEELS.
HE WAS ALWAYS THERE FOR ME, AND I NEVER REALLY KNEW ANYTHING.

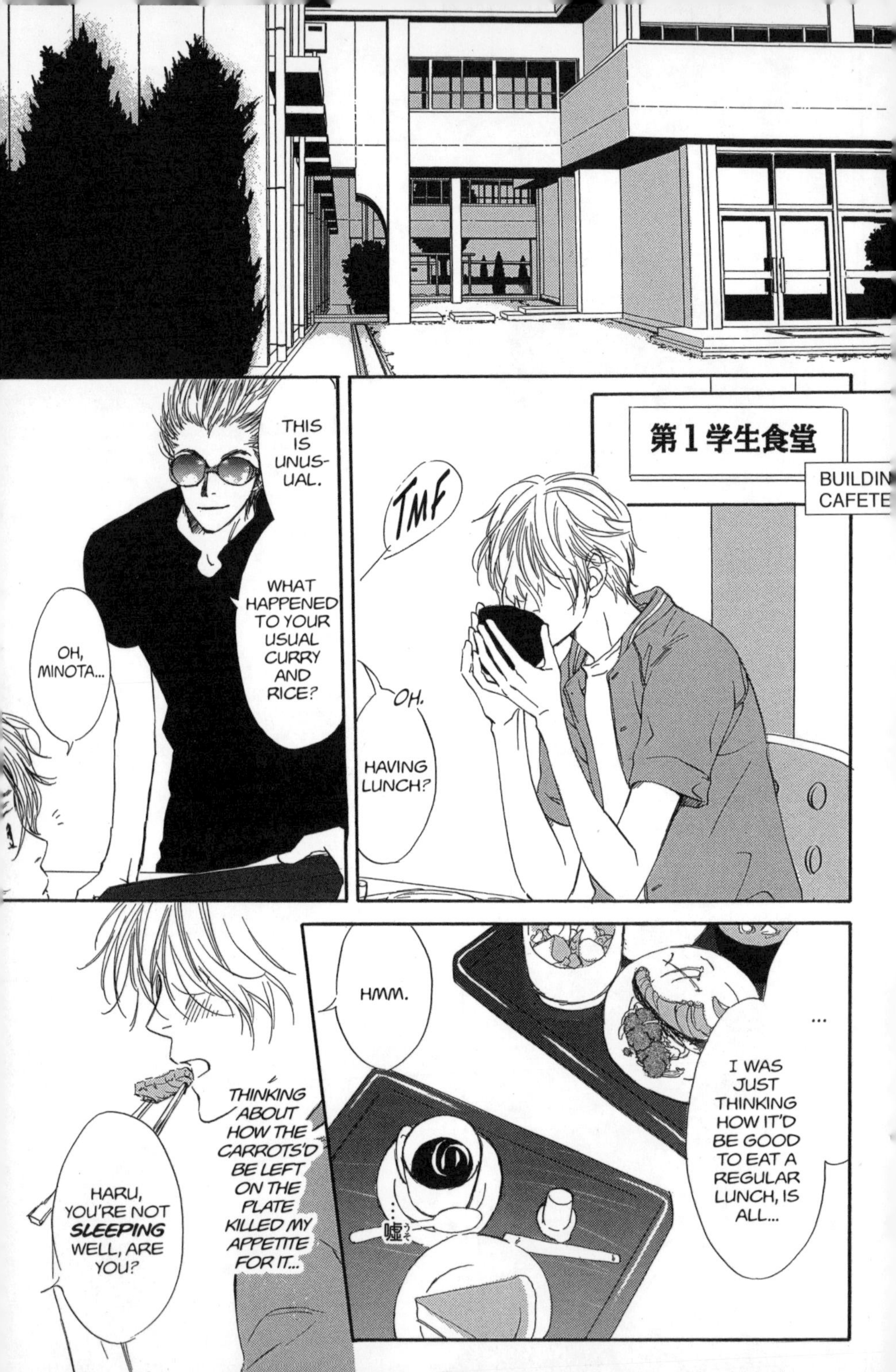
第1学生食堂
BUILDIN
CAFETE
TMF
OH.
HAVING LUNCH?
THIS IS UNUSUAL.
WHAT HAPPENED TO YOUR USUAL CURRY AND RICE?
OH, MINOTA...
HMM.
...
I WAS JUST THINKING HOW IT'D BE GOOD TO EAT A REGULAR LUNCH, IS ALL...
...嘘
THINKING ABOUT HOW THE CARROTS'D BE LEFT ON THE PLATE KILLED MY APPETITE FOR IT...
HARU, YOU'RE NOT **SLEEPING** WELL, ARE YOU?

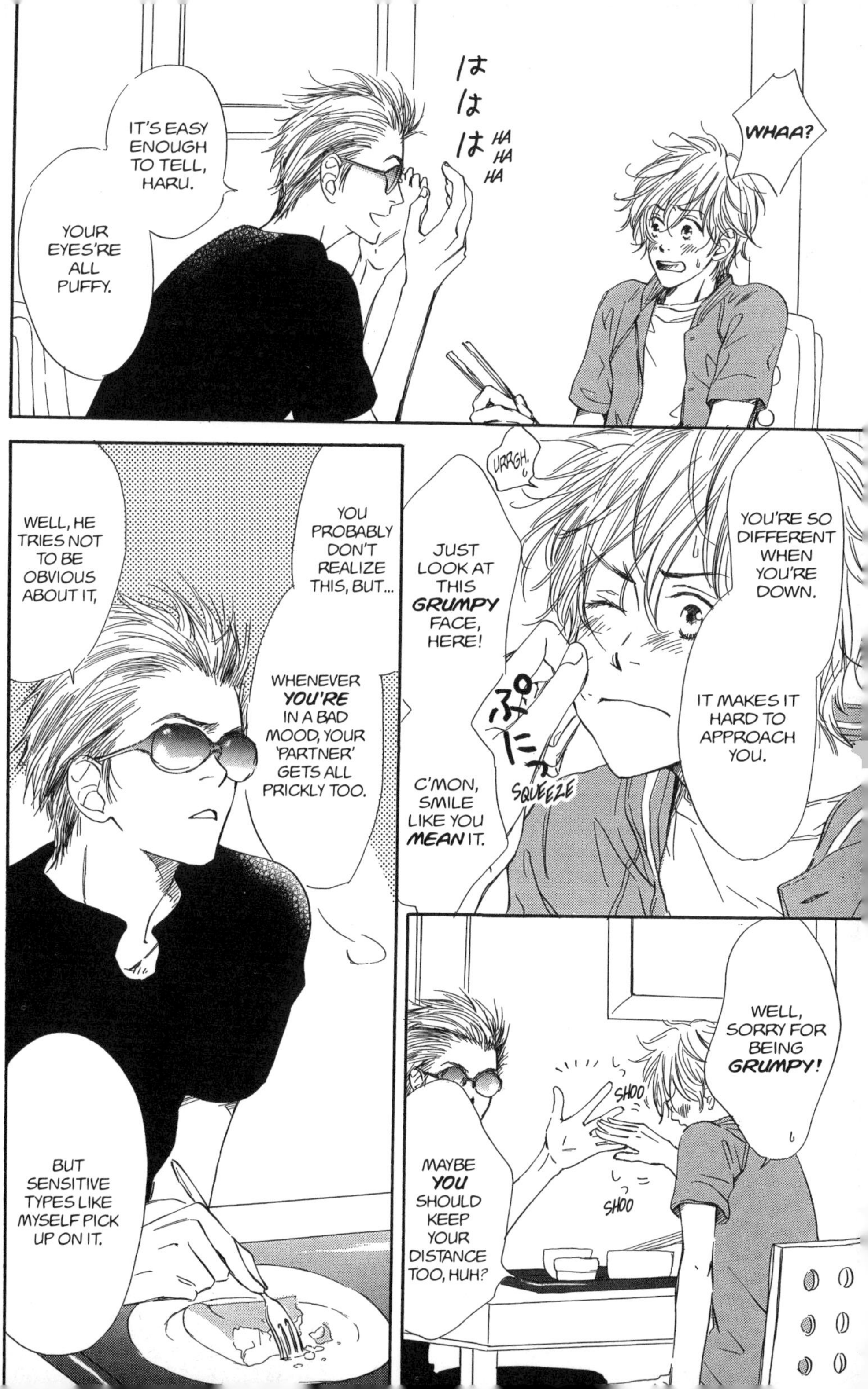

ははは
HA HA HA
IT'S EASY ENOUGH TO TELL, HARU.
YOUR EYES'RE ALL PUFFY.
WHAA?
YOU'RE SO DIFFERENT WHEN YOU'RE DOWN.
URRGH.
JUST LOOK AT THIS GRUMPY FACE, HERE!
IT MAKES IT HARD TO APPROACH YOU.
ぷにっ
SQUEEZE
C'MON, SMILE LIKE YOU MEAN IT.
WELL, SORRY FOR BEING GRUMPY!
SHOO
SHOO
MAYBE YOU SHOULD KEEP YOUR DISTANCE TOO, HUH?
YOU PROBABLY DON'T REALIZE THIS, BUT...
WHENEVER YOU'RE IN A BAD MOOD, YOUR 'PARTNER' GETS ALL PRICKLY TOO.
WELL, HE TRIES NOT TO BE OBVIOUS ABOUT IT,
BUT SENSITIVE TYPES LIKE MYSELF PICK UP ON IT.

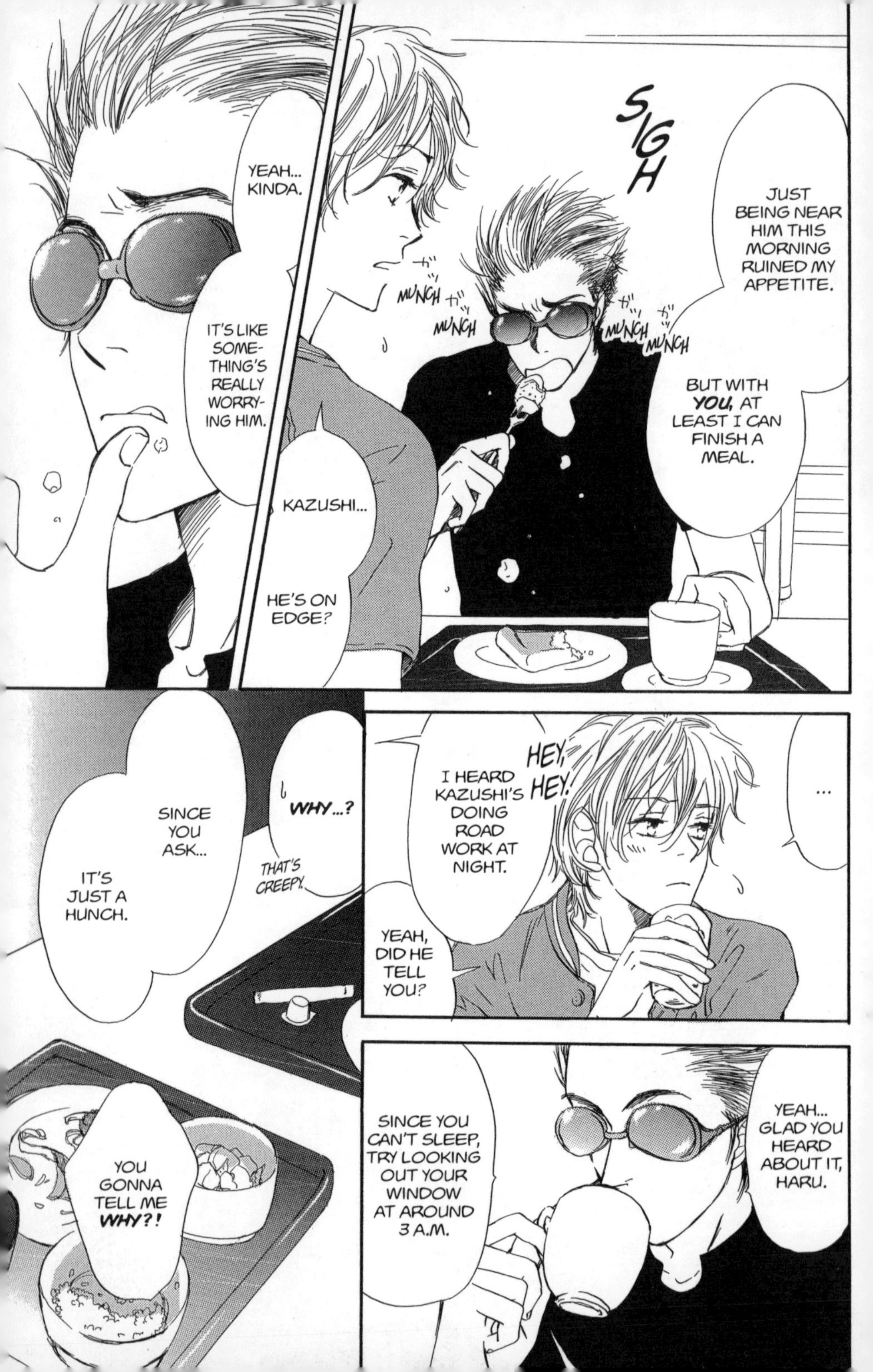
SIGH
JUST BEING NEAR HIM THIS MORNING RUINED MY APPETITE.
MUNCH MUNCH MUNCH MUNCH
BUT WITH **YOU,** AT LEAST I CAN FINISH A MEAL.
KAZUSHI...
HE'S ON EDGE?
YEAH... KINDA.
IT'S LIKE SOMETHING'S REALLY WORRYING HIM.
...
I HEARD KAZUSHI'S DOING ROAD WORK AT NIGHT.
HEY, HEY.
YEAH, DID HE TELL YOU?
YEAH... GLAD YOU HEARD ABOUT IT, HARU.
SINCE YOU CAN'T SLEEP, TRY LOOKING OUT YOUR WINDOW AT AROUND 3 A.M.
WHY...?
THAT'S CREEPY.
YOU GONNA TELL ME **WHY?!**
SINCE YOU ASK...
IT'S JUST A HUNCH.

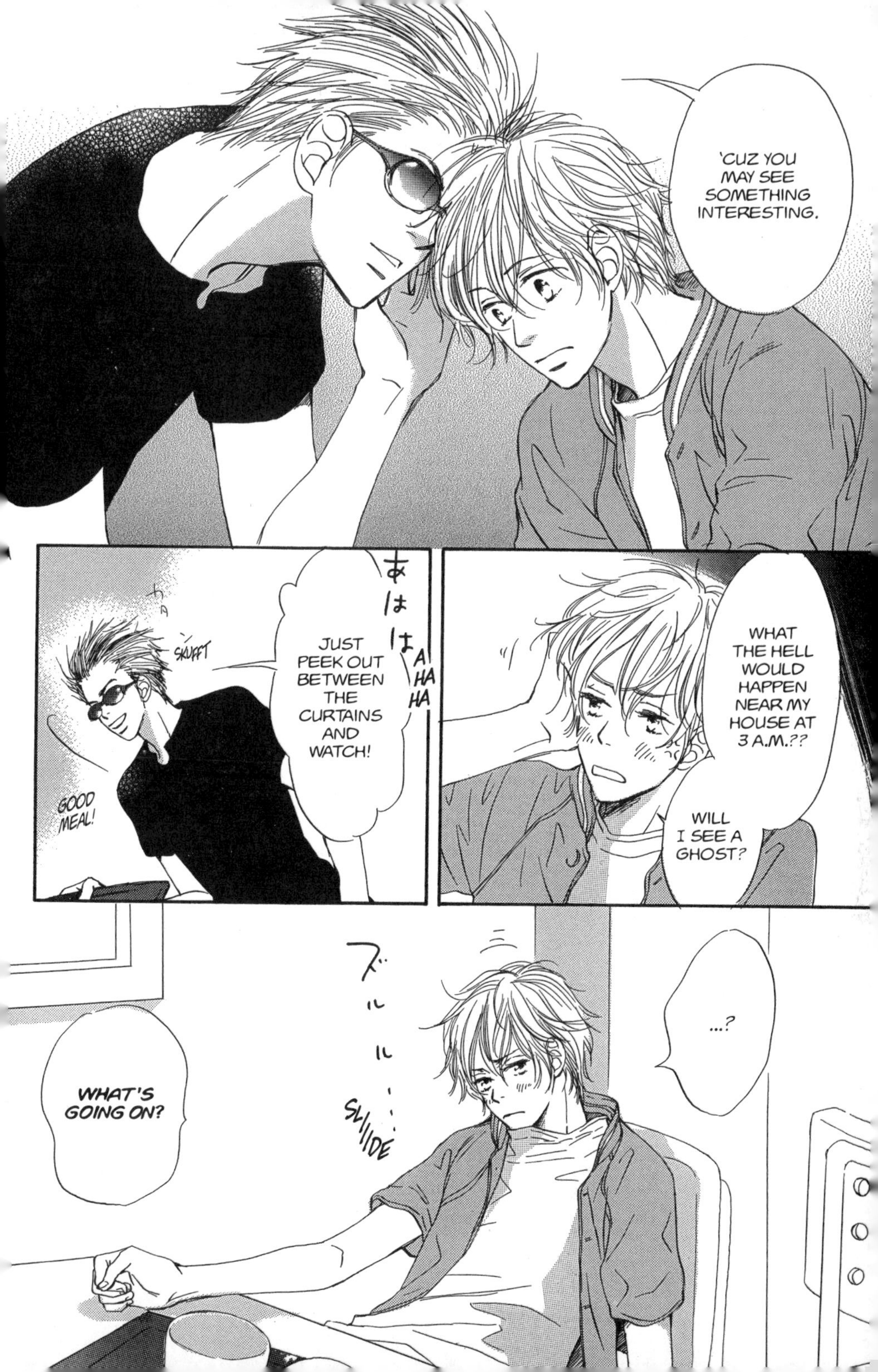
'CUZ YOU MAY SEE SOMETHING INTERESTING.
WHAT THE HELL WOULD HAPPEN NEAR MY HOUSE AT 3 A.M.??
WILL I SEE A GHOST?
あはは
AHAHA
JUST PEEK OUT BETWEEN THE CURTAINS AND WATCH!
SKUFFT
GOOD MEAL!
...?
ズルル・・・
SLIIIDE
WHAT'S GOING ON?

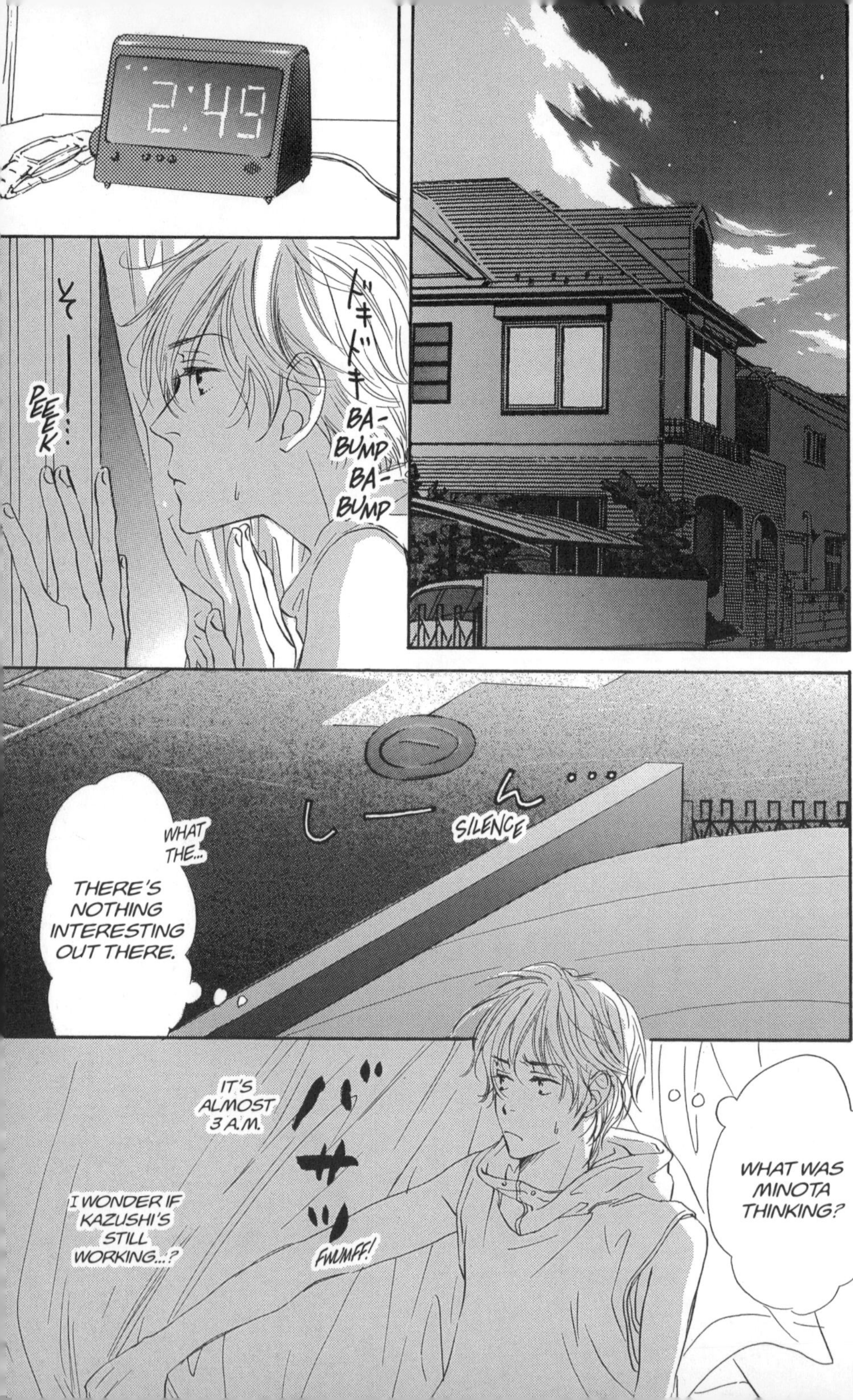
2:49
ドキドキ
BA-BUMP BA-BUMP
そーー…
PEEEK
しーん…
SILENCE
WHAT THE...
THERE'S NOTHING INTERESTING OUT THERE.
WHAT WAS MINOTA THINKING?
バサッ
FWUMFF!
IT'S ALMOST 3 A.M.
I WONDER IF KAZUSHI'S STILL WORKING...?

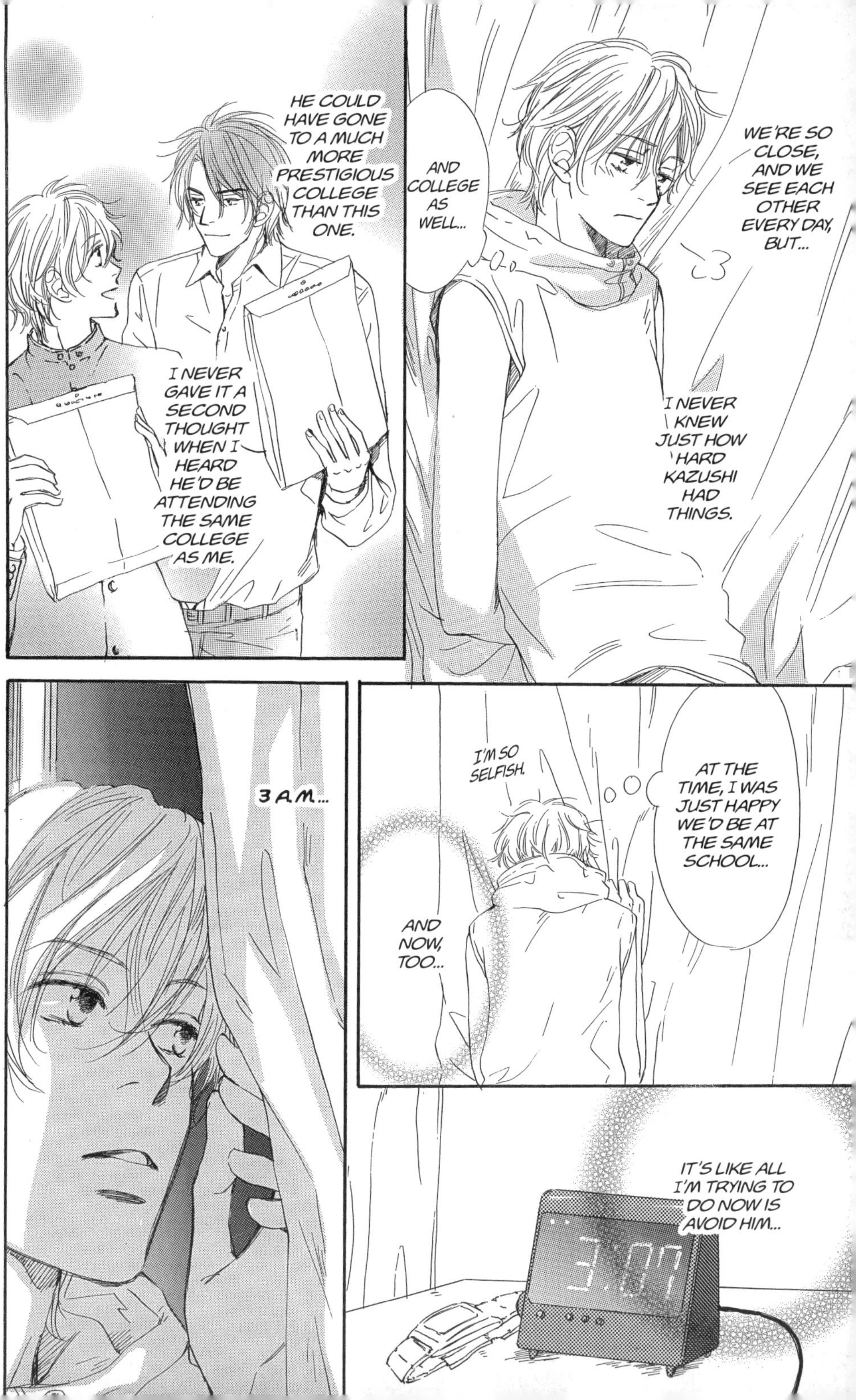
WE'RE SO CLOSE, AND WE SEE EACH OTHER EVERY DAY, BUT...
AND COLLEGE AS WELL...
I NEVER KNEW JUST HOW HARD KAZUSHI HAD THINGS.
HE COULD HAVE GONE TO A MUCH MORE PRESTIGIOUS COLLEGE THAN THIS ONE.
I NEVER GAVE IT A SECOND THOUGHT WHEN I HEARD HE'D BE ATTENDING THE SAME COLLEGE AS ME.
AT THE TIME, I WAS JUST HAPPY WE'D BE AT THE SAME SCHOOL...
I'M SO SELFISH.
AND NOW, TOO...
IT'S LIKE ALL I'M TRYING TO DO NOW IS AVOID HIM...
3 A.M...

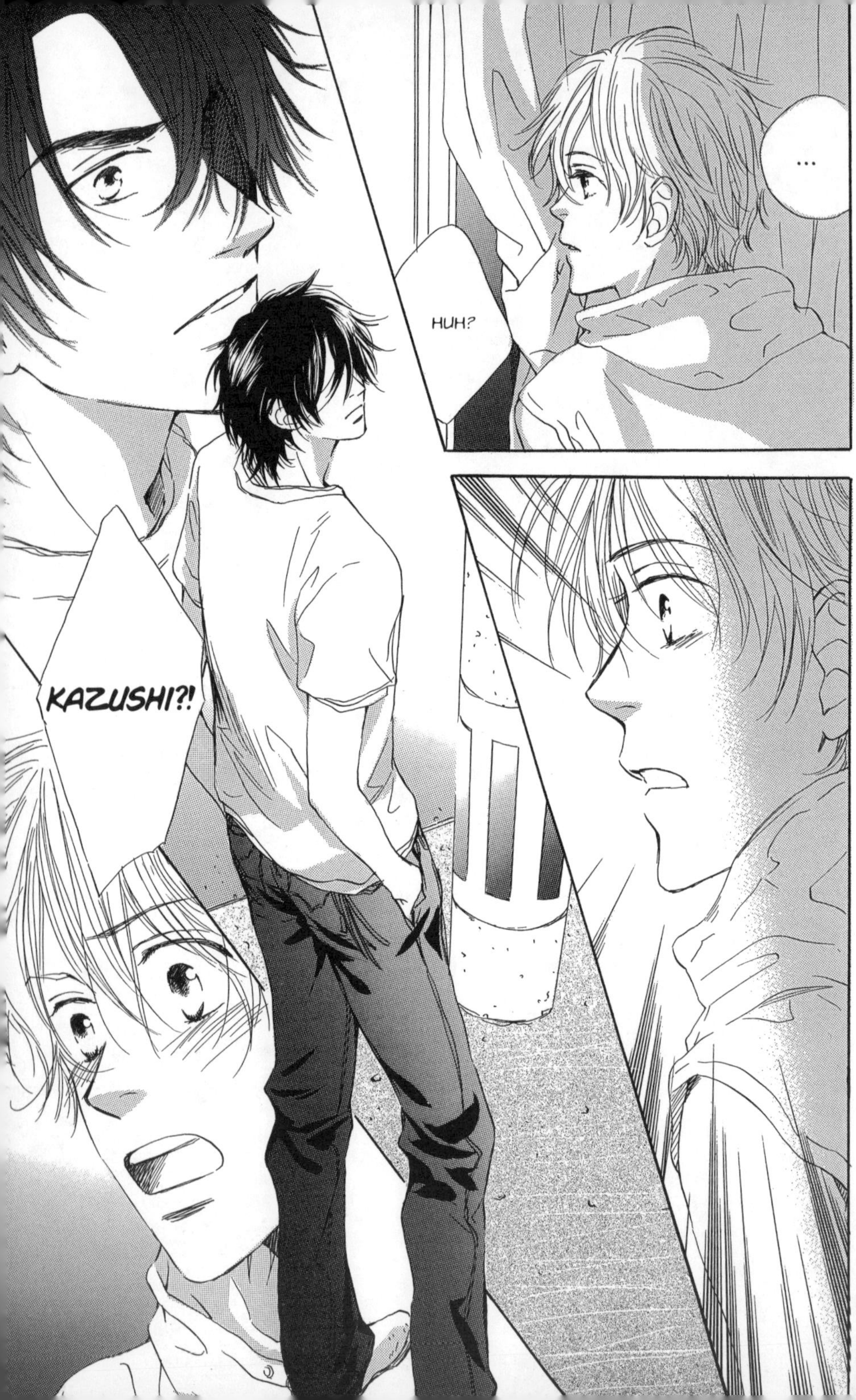
...
HUH?
KAZUSHI?!

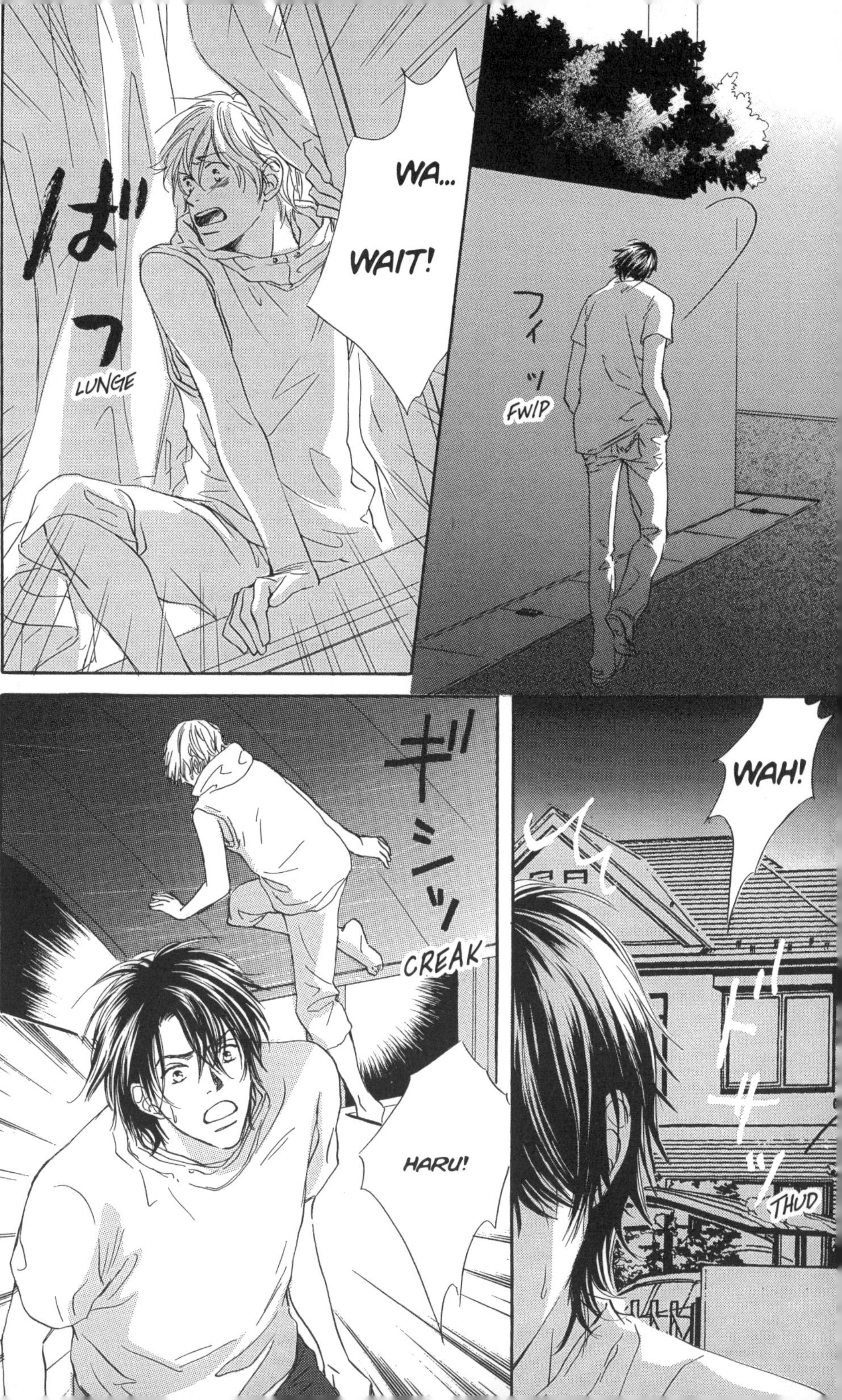
フィッ
FWIP
WA...
WAIT!
ぱっ
LUNGE
WAH!
ドサッ
THUD
ギシッ
CREAK
HARU!

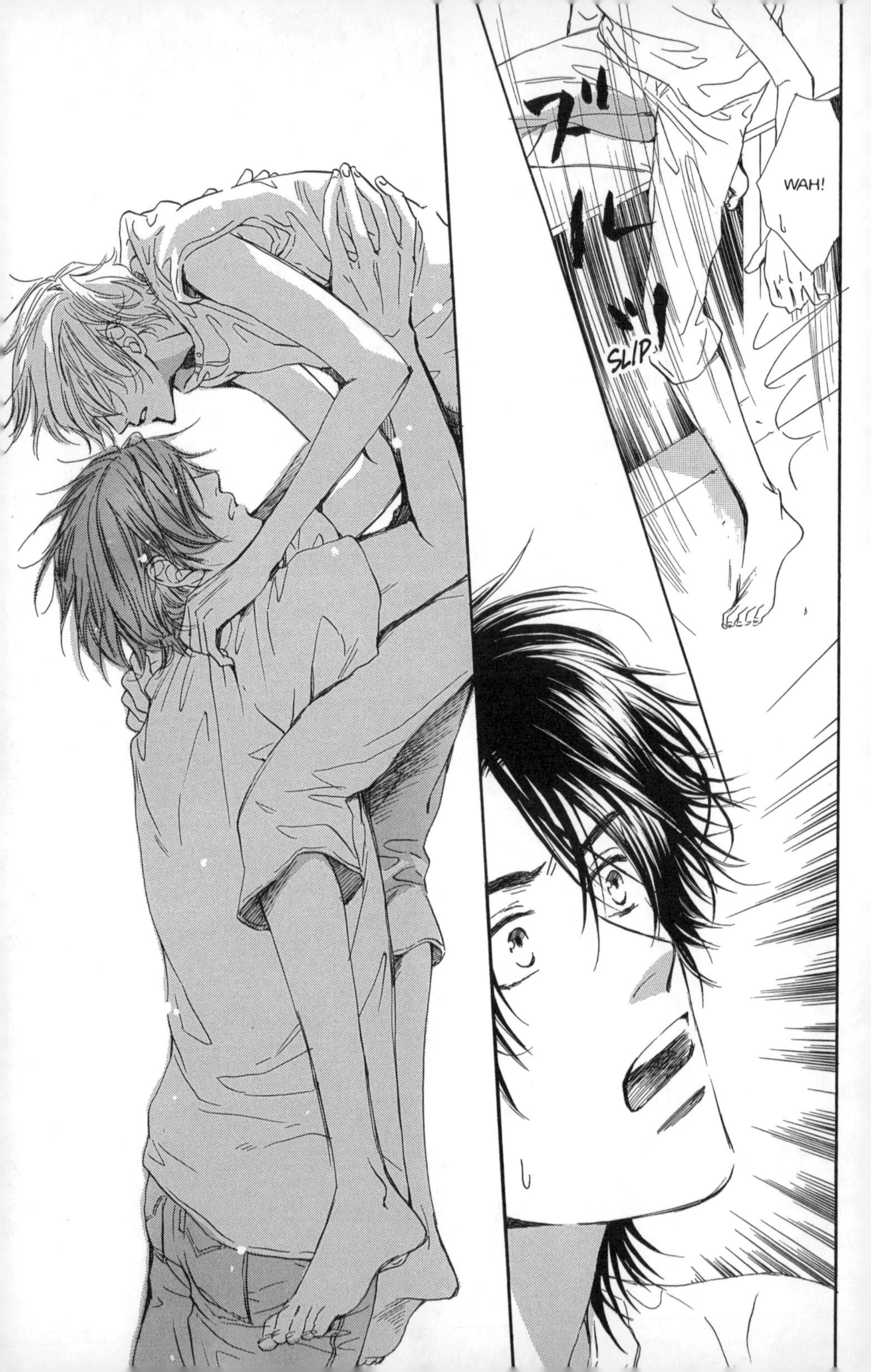
WAH!
ズルッ
SLIP

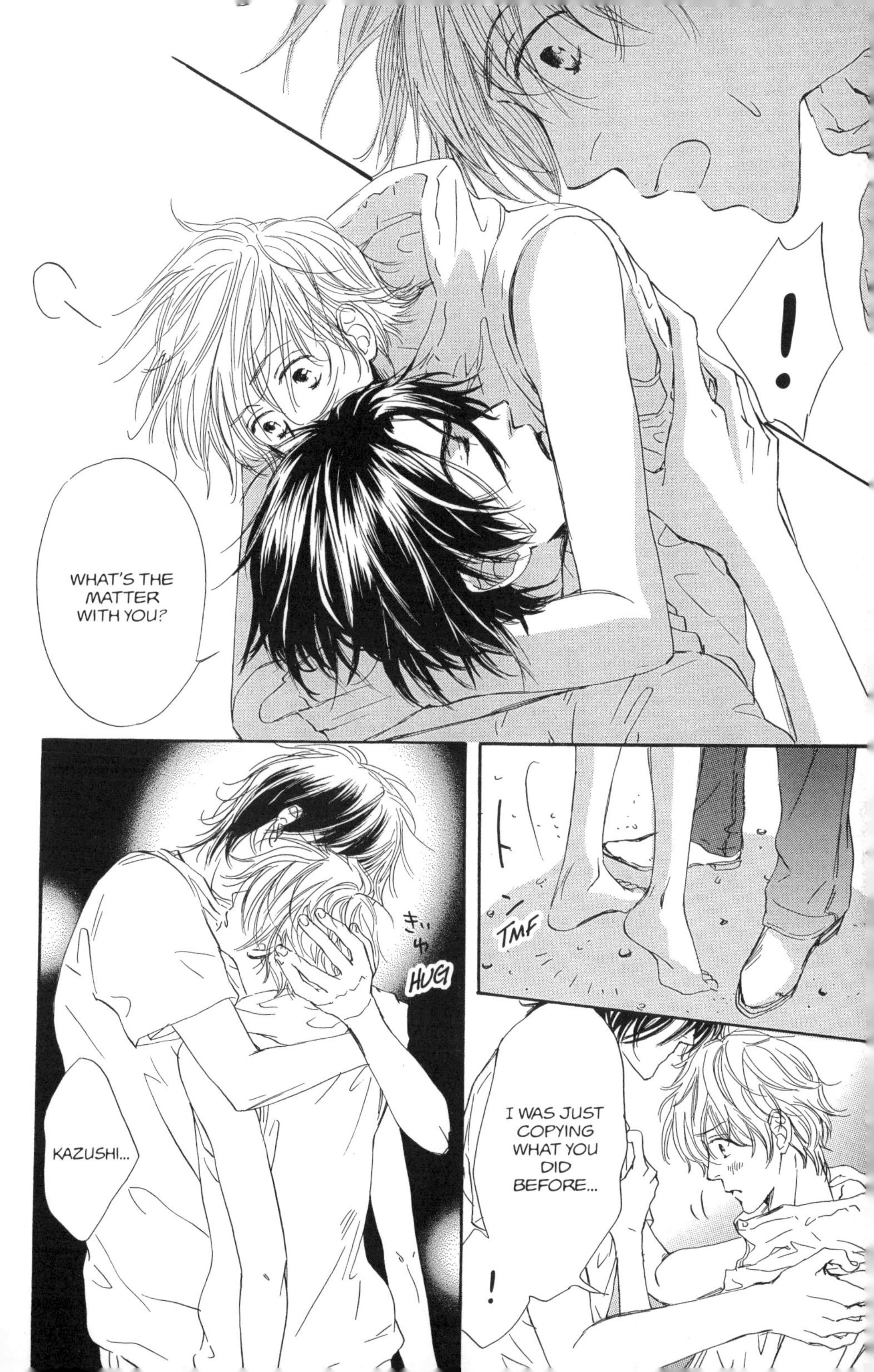
!
WHAT'S THE MATTER WITH YOU?
TMF
I WAS JUST COPYING WHAT YOU DID BEFORE...
!
HUG
KAZUSHI...

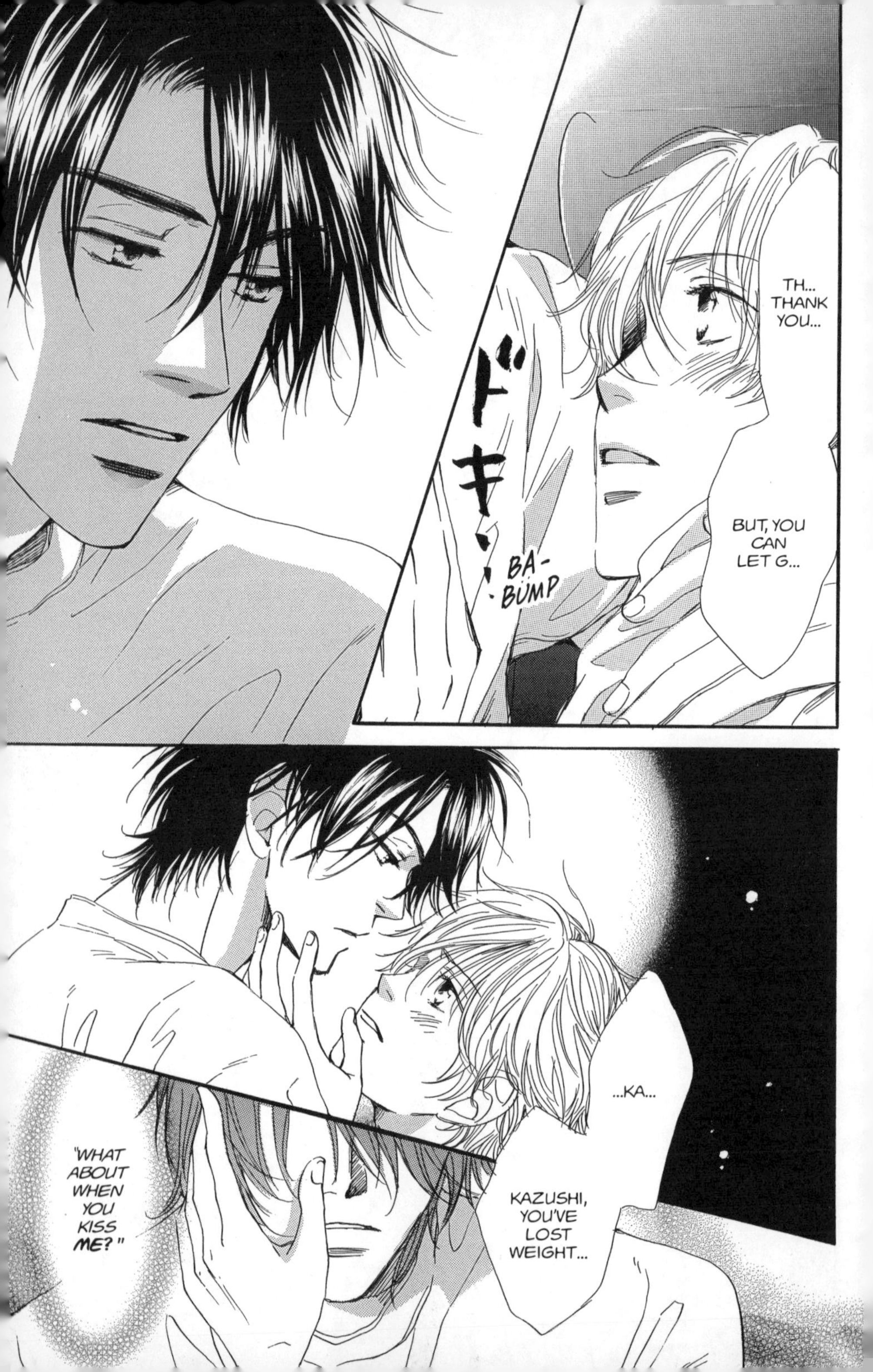
TH... THANK YOU...
ドキ
BA-BUMP
BUT, YOU CAN LET G...
...KA...
KAZUSHI, YOU'VE LOST WEIGHT...
"WHAT ABOUT WHEN YOU KISS ME?"

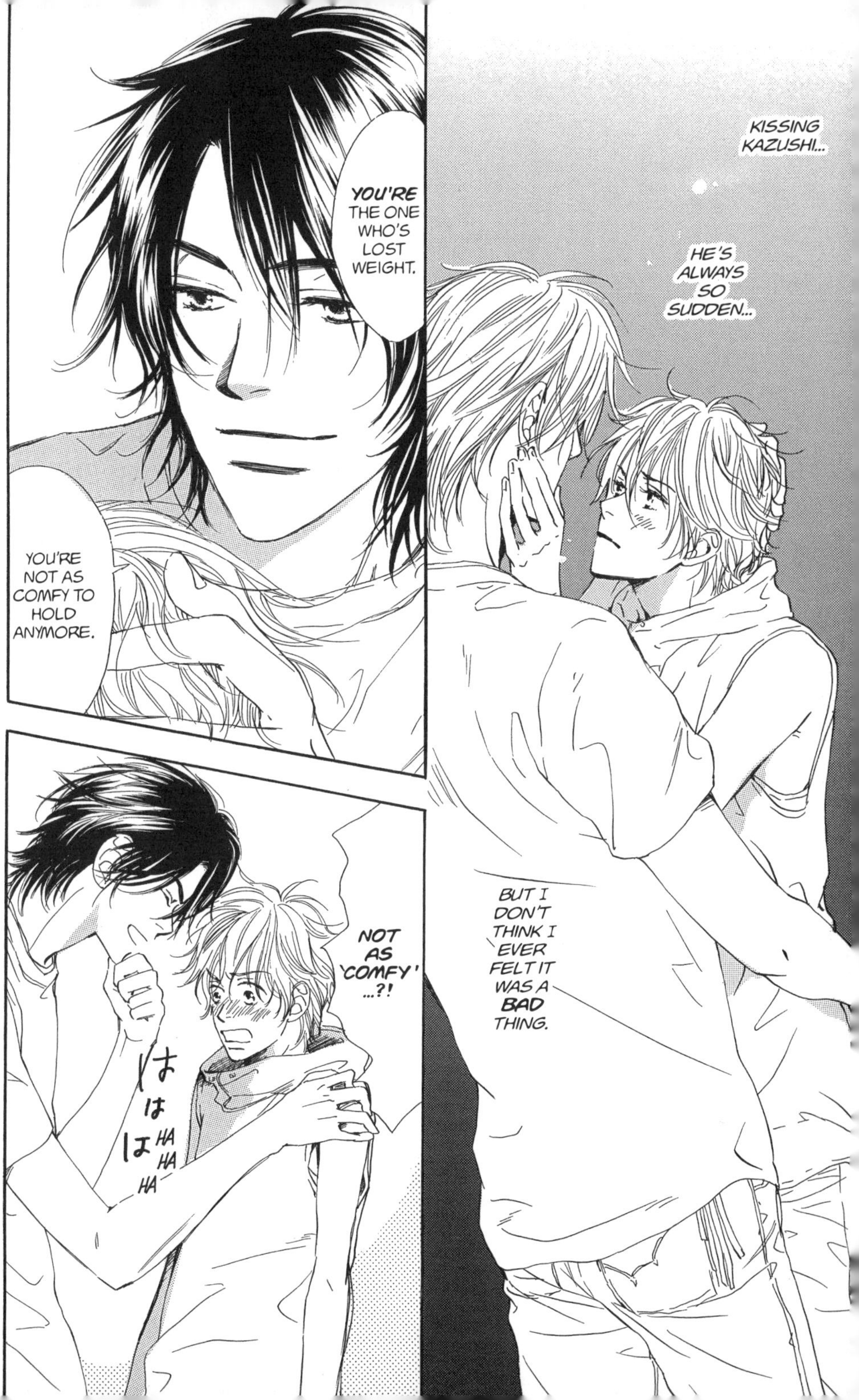

KISSING KAZUSHI...
HE'S ALWAYS SO SUDDEN...
BUT I DON'T THINK I EVER FELT IT WAS A BAD THING.
YOU'RE THE ONE WHO'S LOST WEIGHT.
YOU'RE NOT AS COMFY TO HOLD ANYMORE.
NOT AS 'COMFY' ...?!
ははは HA HA HA

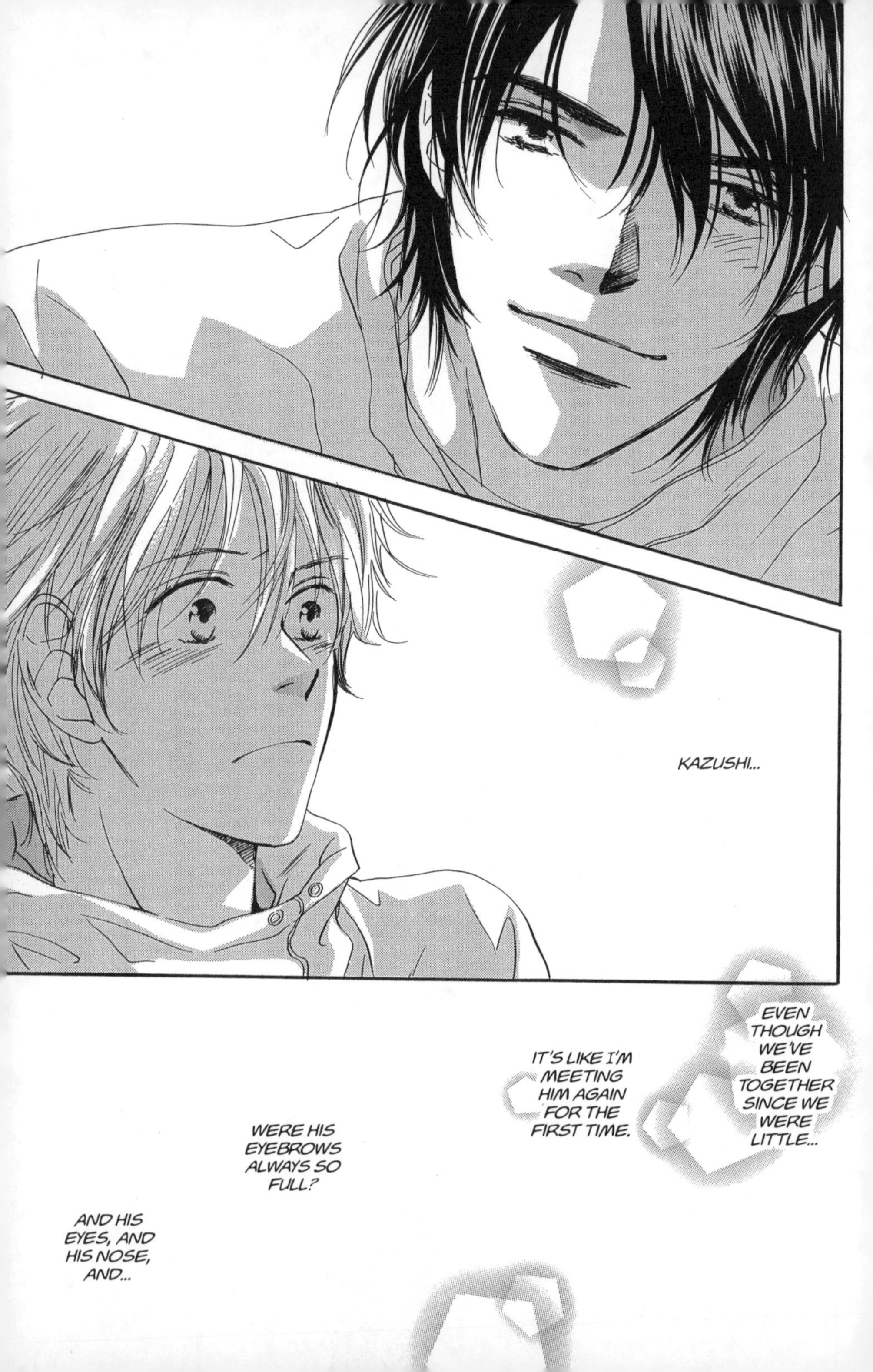
KAZUSHI...
EVEN THOUGH WE'VE BEEN TOGETHER SINCE WE WERE LITTLE...
IT'S LIKE I'M MEETING HIM AGAIN FOR THE FIRST TIME.
WERE HIS EYEBROWS ALWAYS SO FULL?
AND HIS EYES, AND HIS NOSE, AND...

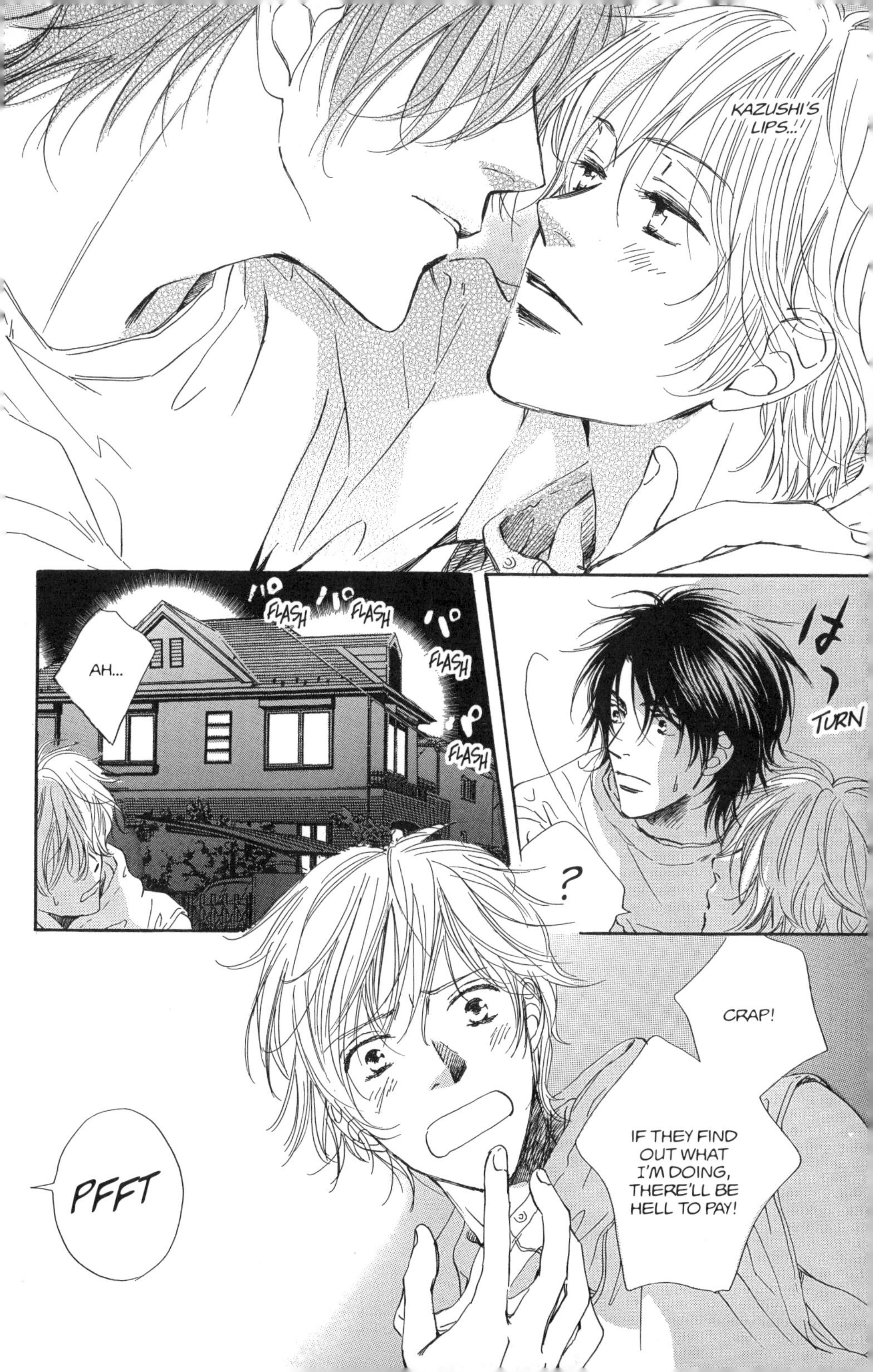
KAZUSHI'S LIPS...
はっ
TURN
?
パ
FLASH
パ
FLASH
パ
FLASH
パ
FLASH
AH...
CRAP!
IF THEY FIND OUT WHAT I'M DOING, THERE'LL BE HELL TO PAY!
PFFT

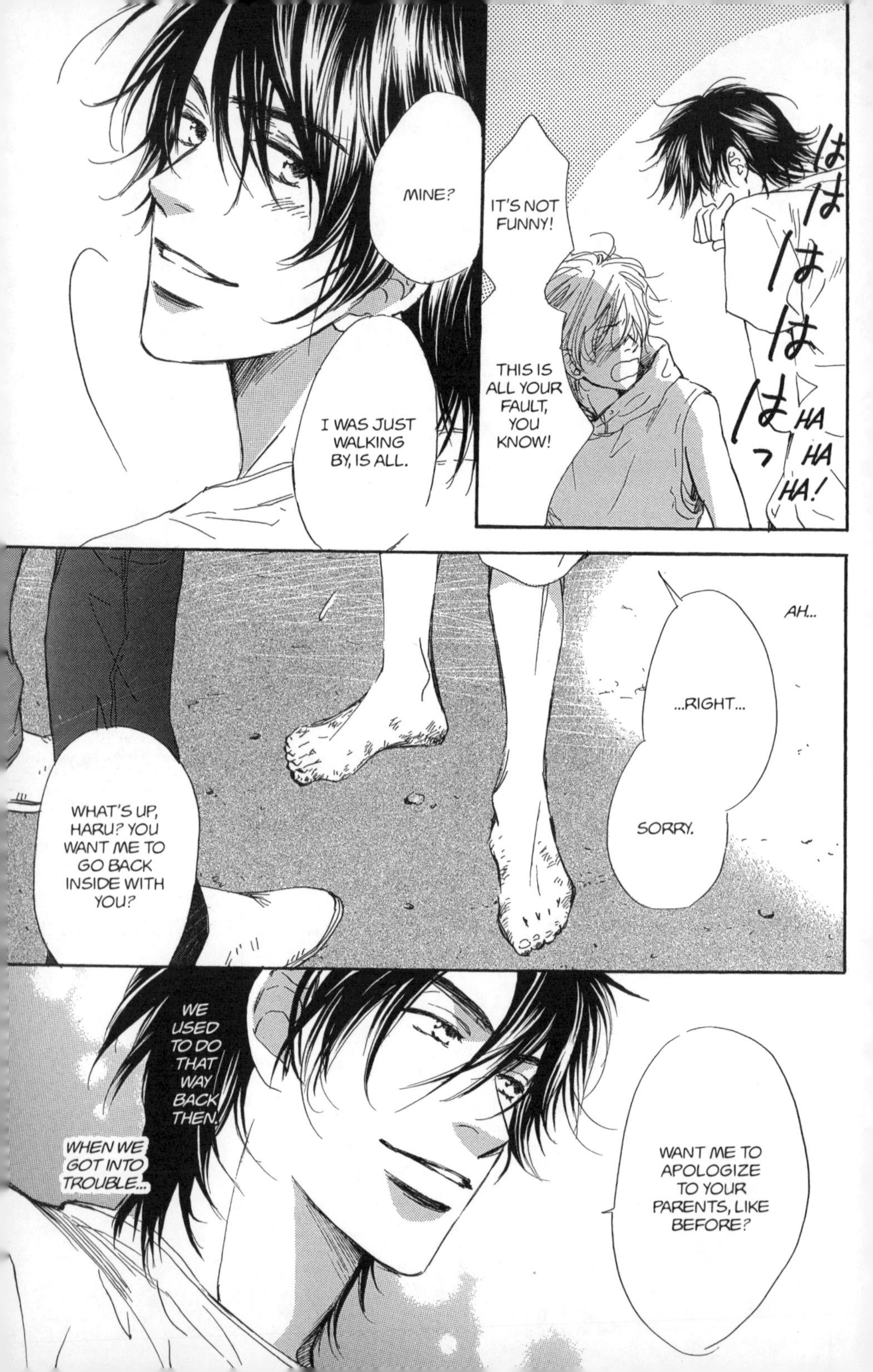
ははははっ
HA HA HA!
IT'S NOT FUNNY!
THIS IS ALL YOUR FAULT, YOU KNOW!
MINE?
I WAS JUST WALKING BY, IS ALL.
AH...
...RIGHT...
SORRY.
WHAT'S UP, HARU? YOU WANT ME TO GO BACK INSIDE WITH YOU?
WANT ME TO APOLOGIZE TO YOUR PARENTS, LIKE BEFORE?
WE USED TO DO THAT WAY BACK THEN.
WHEN WE GOT INTO TROUBLE...

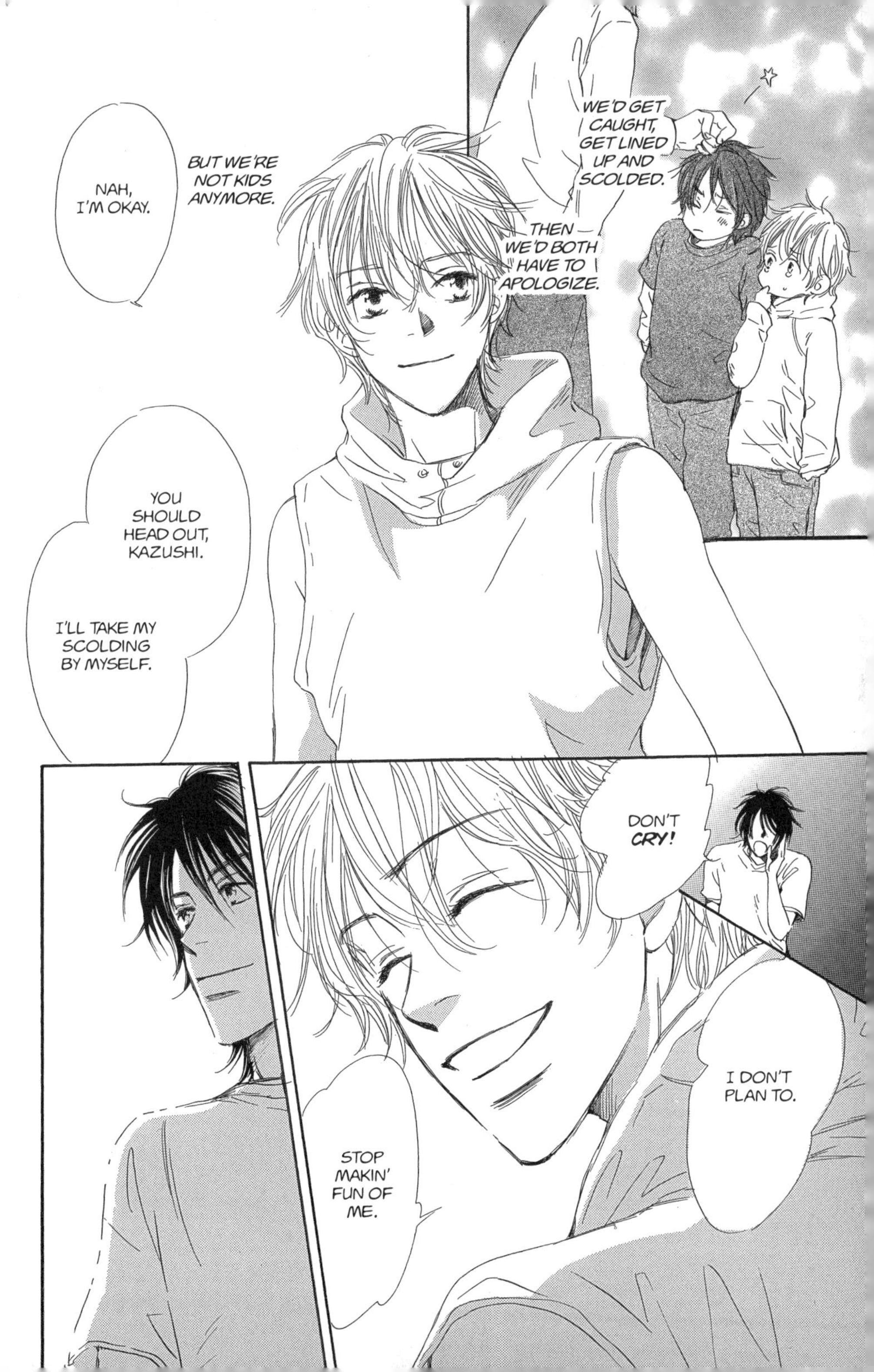
WE'D GET CAUGHT, GET LINED UP AND SCOLDED.
THEN WE'D BOTH HAVE TO APOLOGIZE.
BUT WE'RE NOT KIDS ANYMORE.
NAH, I'M OKAY.
YOU SHOULD HEAD OUT, KAZUSHI.
I'LL TAKE MY SCOLDING BY MYSELF.
DON'T **CRY**!
I DON'T PLAN TO.
STOP MAKIN' FUN OF ME.

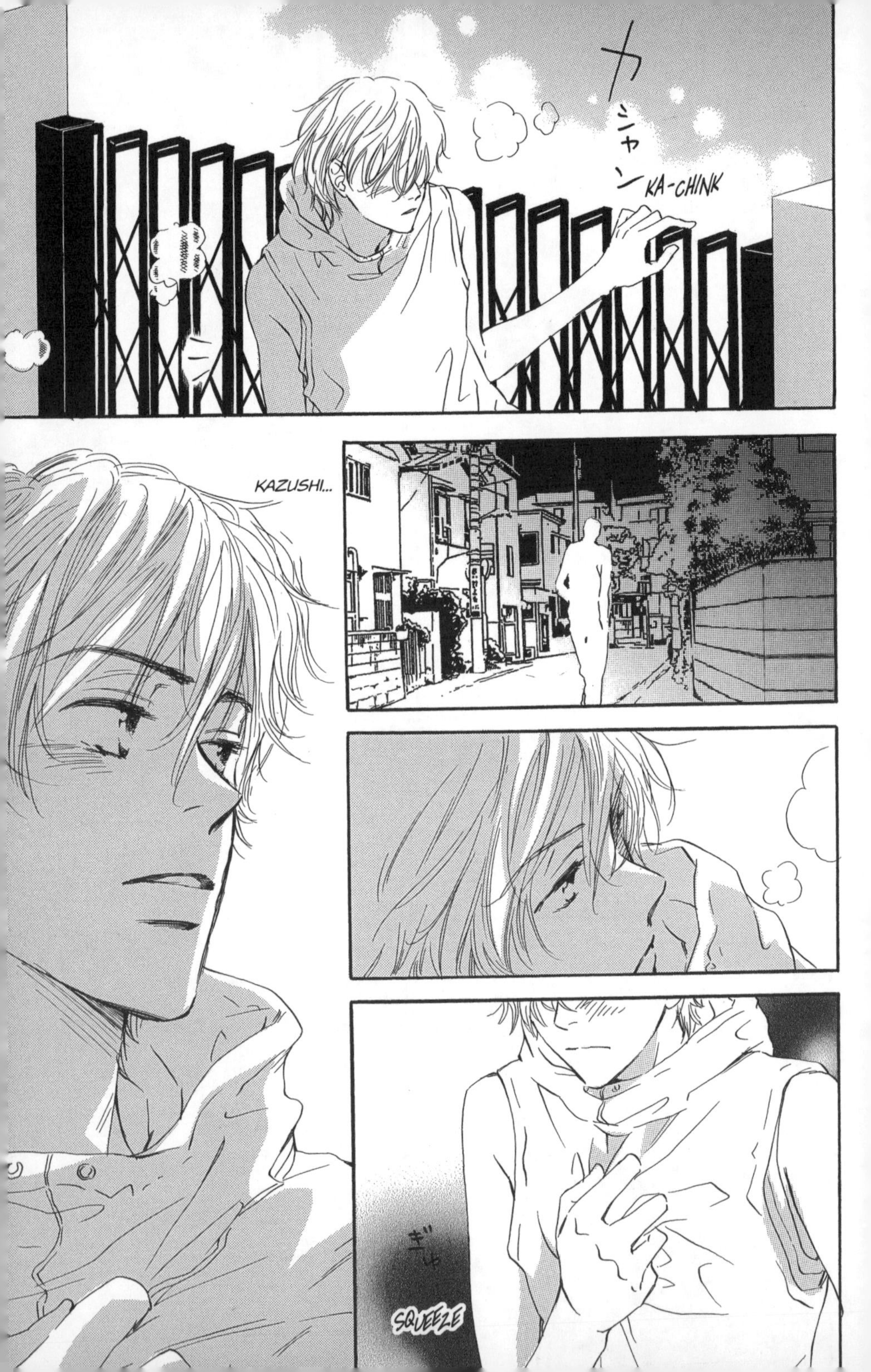
カシャン
KA-CHINK
ぎゅ
SQUEEZE
KAZUSHI...

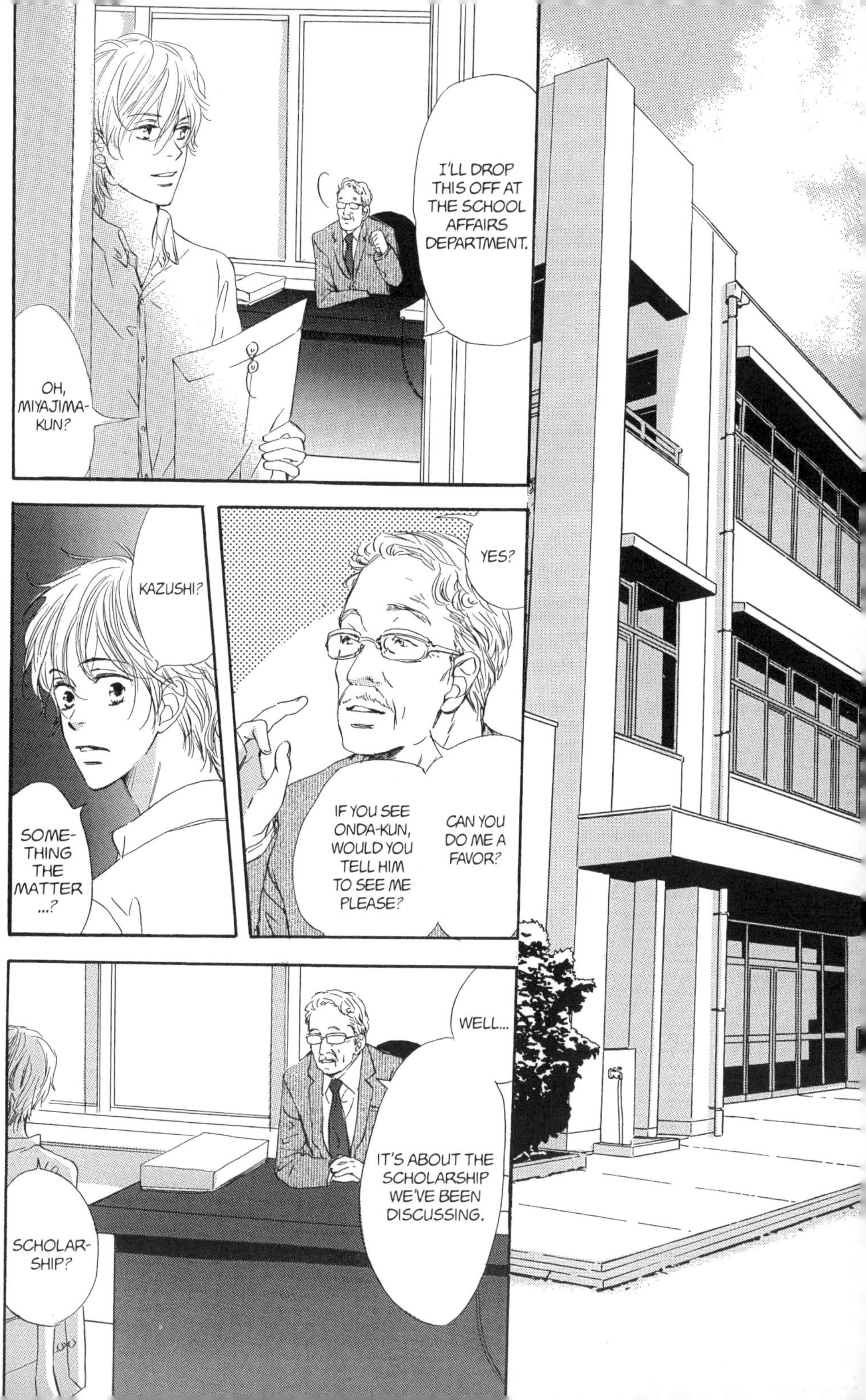
I'LL DROP THIS OFF AT THE SCHOOL AFFAIRS DEPARTMENT.
OH, MIYAJIMA-KUN?
YES?
CAN YOU DO ME A FAVOR?
IF YOU SEE ONDA-KUN, WOULD YOU TELL HIM TO SEE ME PLEASE?
KAZUSHI?
SOME-THING THE MATTER ...?
WELL...
IT'S ABOUT THE SCHOLARSHIP WE'VE BEEN DISCUSSING.
SCHOLAR-SHIP?

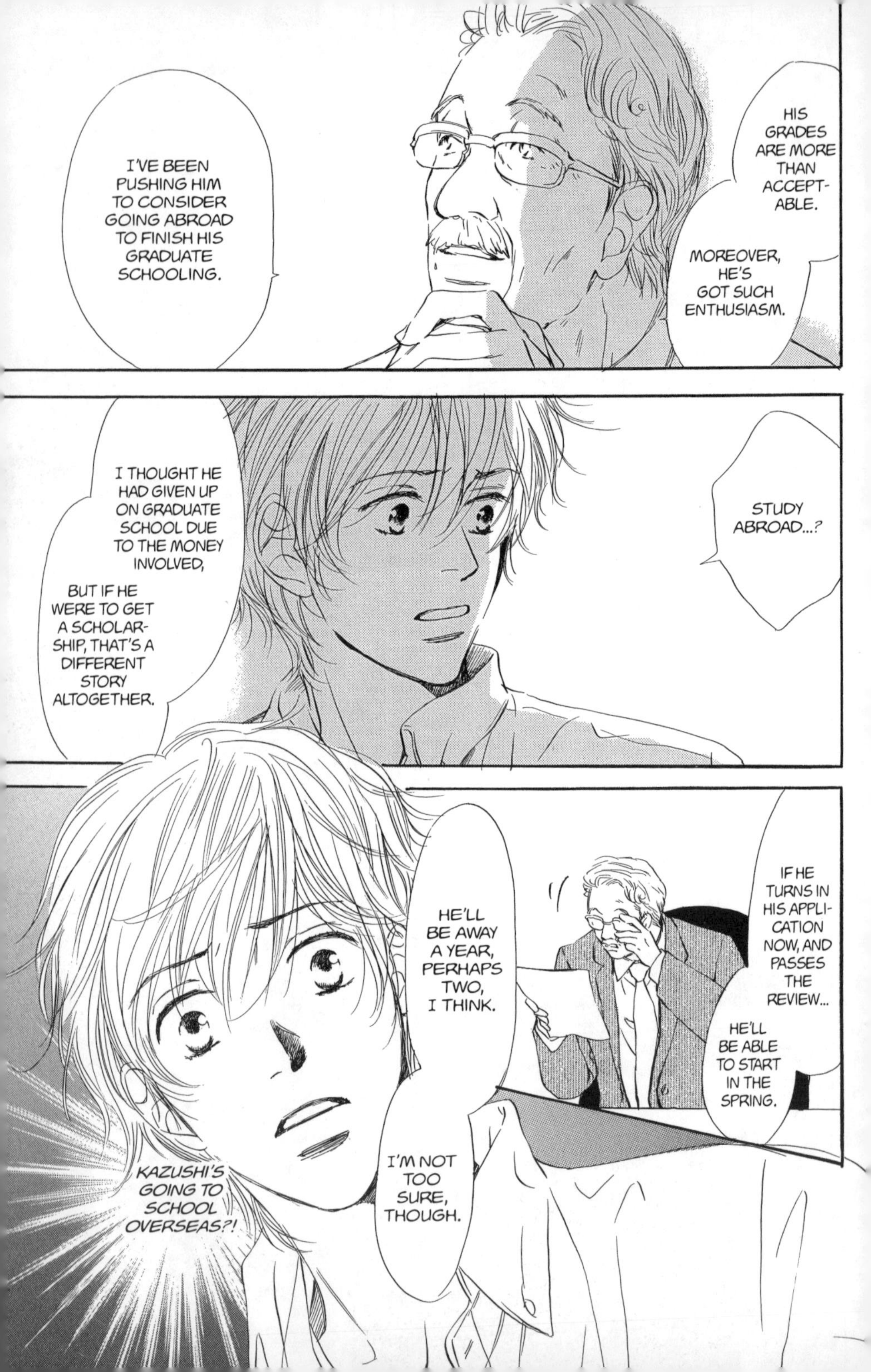
HIS GRADES ARE MORE THAN ACCEPT-ABLE.
MOREOVER, HE'S GOT SUCH ENTHUSIASM.
I'VE BEEN PUSHING HIM TO CONSIDER GOING ABROAD TO FINISH HIS GRADUATE SCHOOLING.
STUDY ABROAD...?
I THOUGHT HE HAD GIVEN UP ON GRADUATE SCHOOL DUE TO THE MONEY INVOLVED,
BUT IF HE WERE TO GET A SCHOLAR-SHIP, THAT'S A DIFFERENT STORY ALTOGETHER.
IF HE TURNS IN HIS APPLI-CATION NOW, AND PASSES THE REVIEW...
HE'LL BE ABLE TO START IN THE SPRING.
HE'LL BE AWAY A YEAR, PERHAPS TWO, I THINK.
I'M NOT TOO SURE, THOUGH.
KAZUSHI'S GOING TO SCHOOL OVERSEAS?!

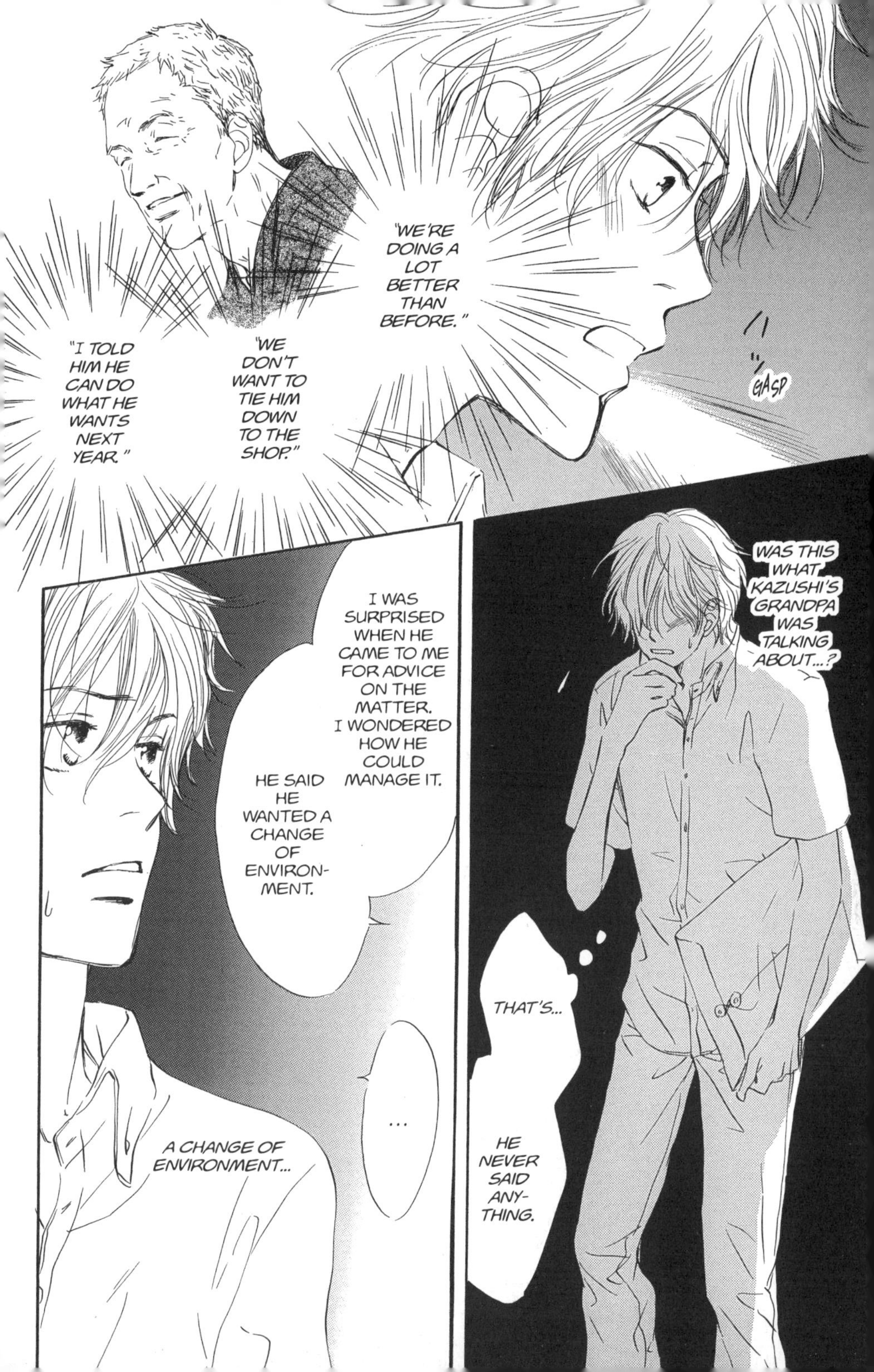
"WE'RE DOING A LOT BETTER THAN BEFORE."
GASP
"WE DON'T WANT TO TIE HIM DOWN TO THE SHOP."
"I TOLD HIM HE CAN DO WHAT HE WANTS NEXT YEAR."
WAS THIS WHAT KAZUSHI'S GRANDPA WAS TALKING ABOUT...?
THAT'S...
HE NEVER SAID ANY-THING.
I WAS SURPRISED WHEN HE CAME TO ME FOR ADVICE ON THE MATTER. I WONDERED HOW HE COULD MANAGE IT.
HE SAID HE WANTED A CHANGE OF ENVIRON-MENT.
...
A CHANGE OF ENVIRONMENT...

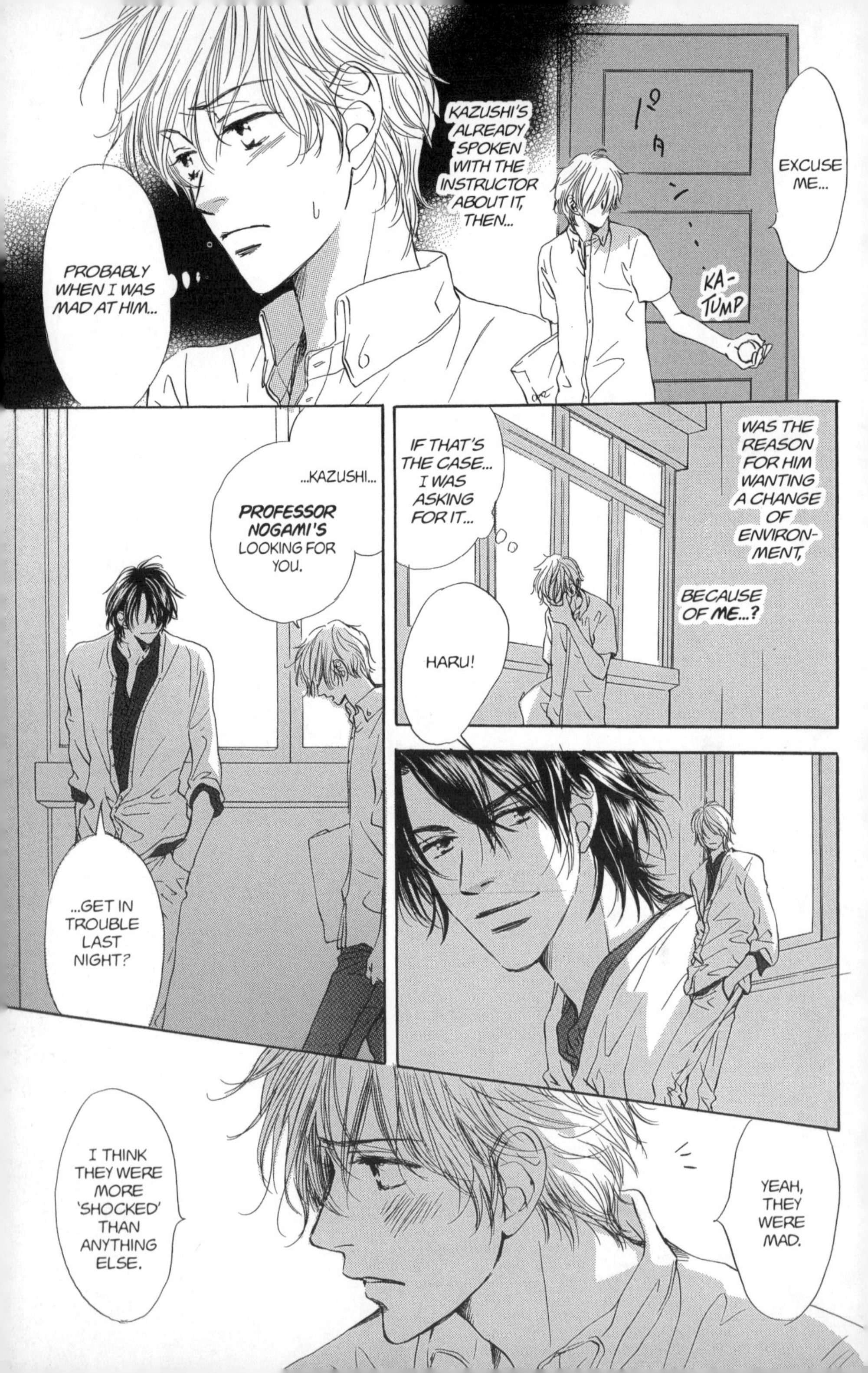
EXCUSE ME...
KA-TUMP
KAZUSHI'S ALREADY SPOKEN WITH THE INSTRUCTOR ABOUT IT, THEN...
PROBABLY WHEN I WAS MAD AT HIM...
WAS THE REASON FOR HIM WANTING A CHANGE OF ENVIRON-MENT,
BECAUSE OF ME...?
IF THAT'S THE CASE... I WAS ASKING FOR IT...
HARU!
...KAZUSHI...
PROFESSOR NOGAMI'S LOOKING FOR YOU.
...GET IN TROUBLE LAST NIGHT?
YEAH, THEY WERE MAD.
I THINK THEY WERE MORE 'SHOCKED' THAN ANYTHING ELSE.

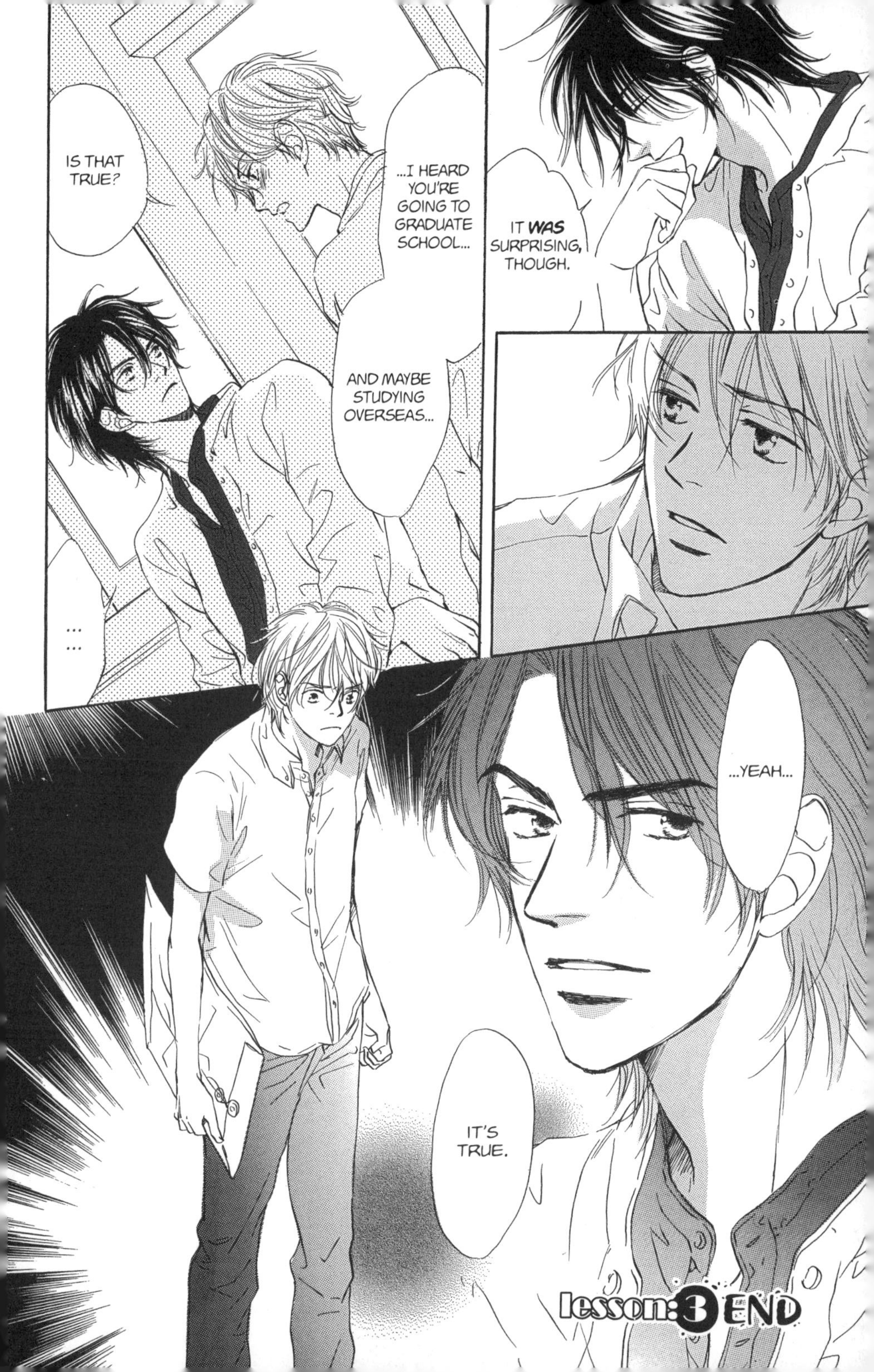
IT WAS SURPRISING, THOUGH.
...I HEARD YOU'RE GOING TO GRADUATE SCHOOL...
IS THAT TRUE?
AND MAYBE STUDYING OVERSEAS...
... ...
...YEAH...
IT'S TRUE.
lesson:3 END

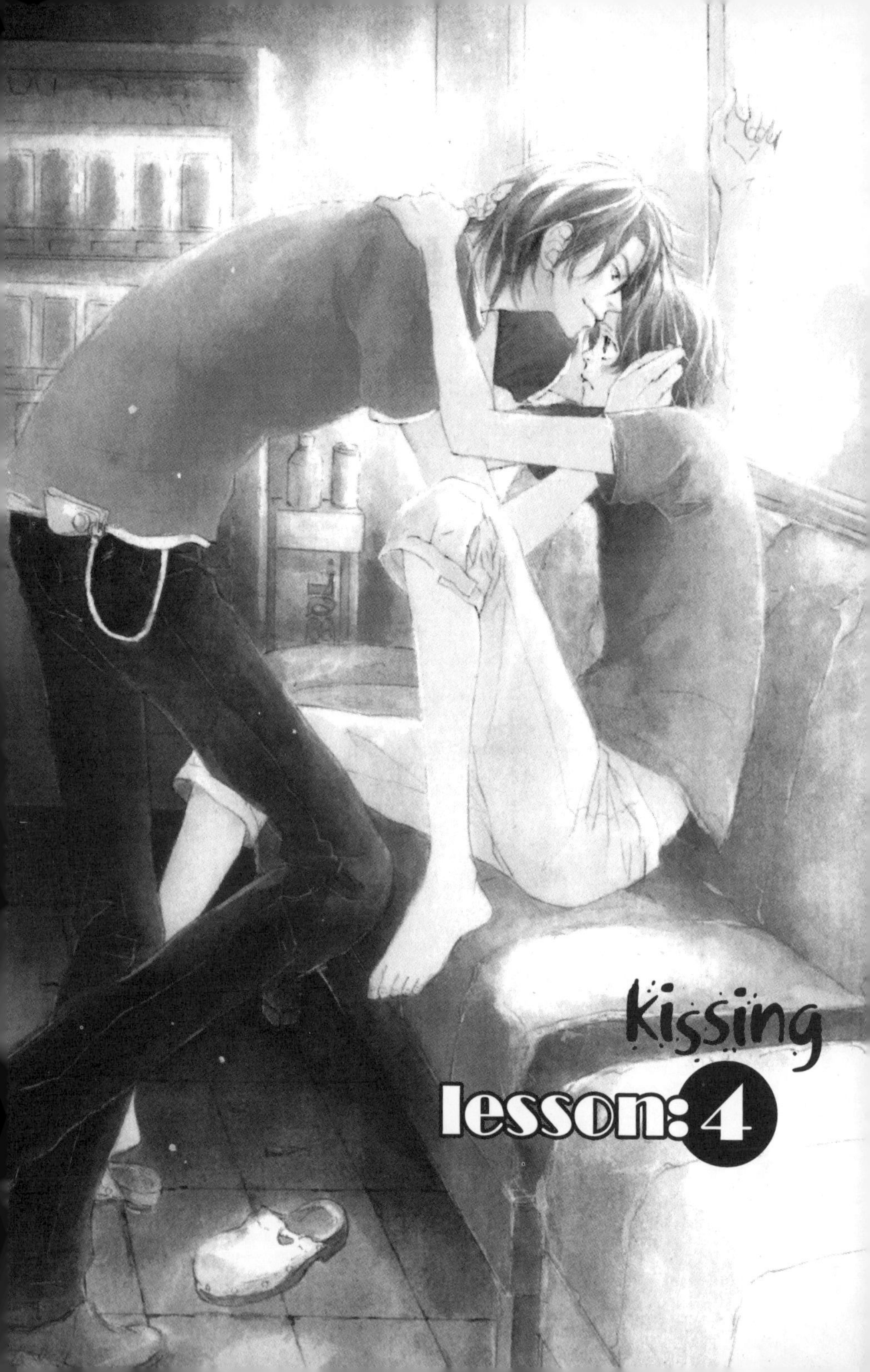
Kissing
lesson: 4

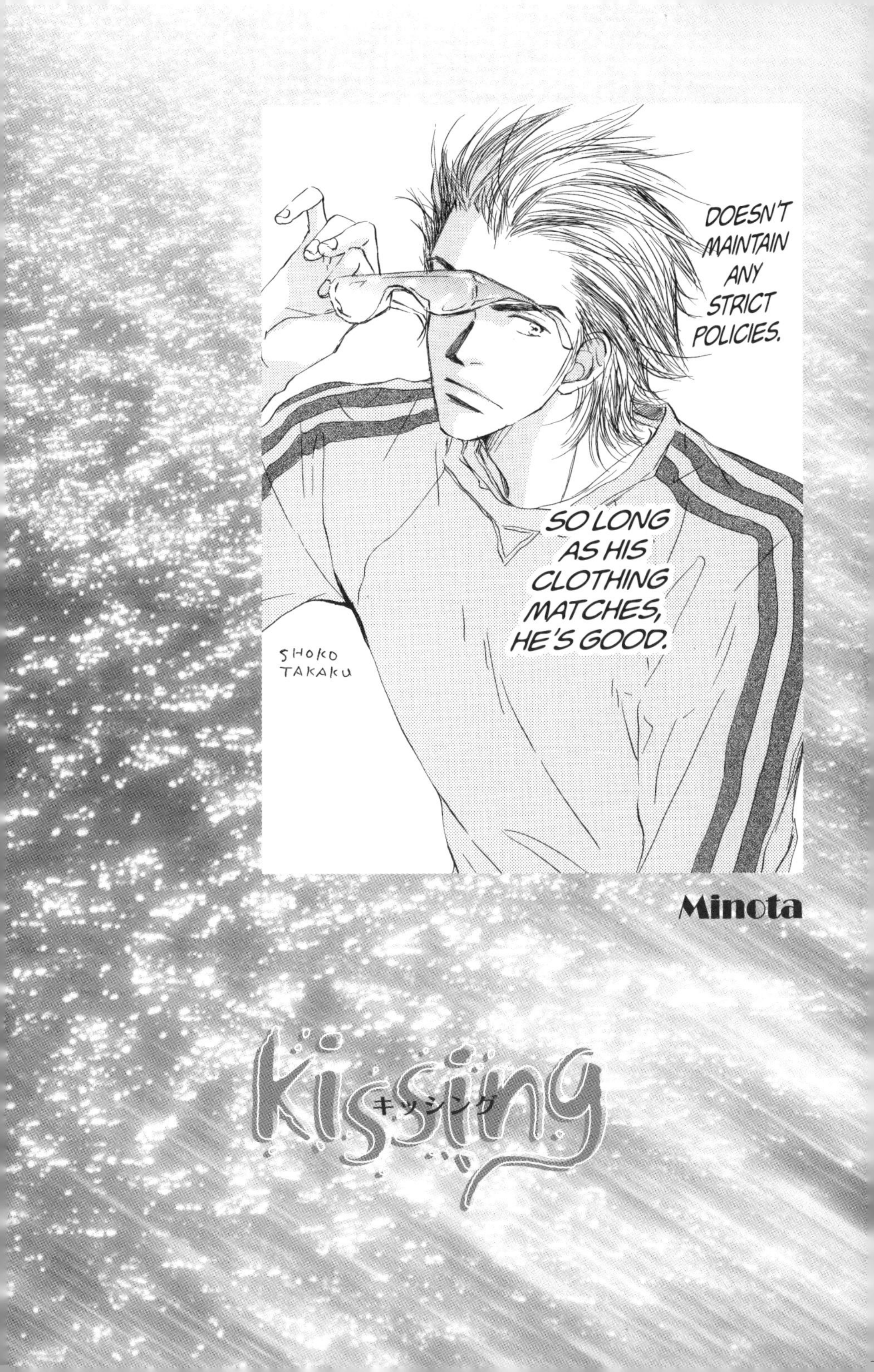
DOESN'T MAINTAIN ANY STRICT POLICIES.
SO LONG AS HIS CLOTHING MATCHES, HE'S GOOD.
SHOKO TAKAKU
Minota
kissing
キッシング

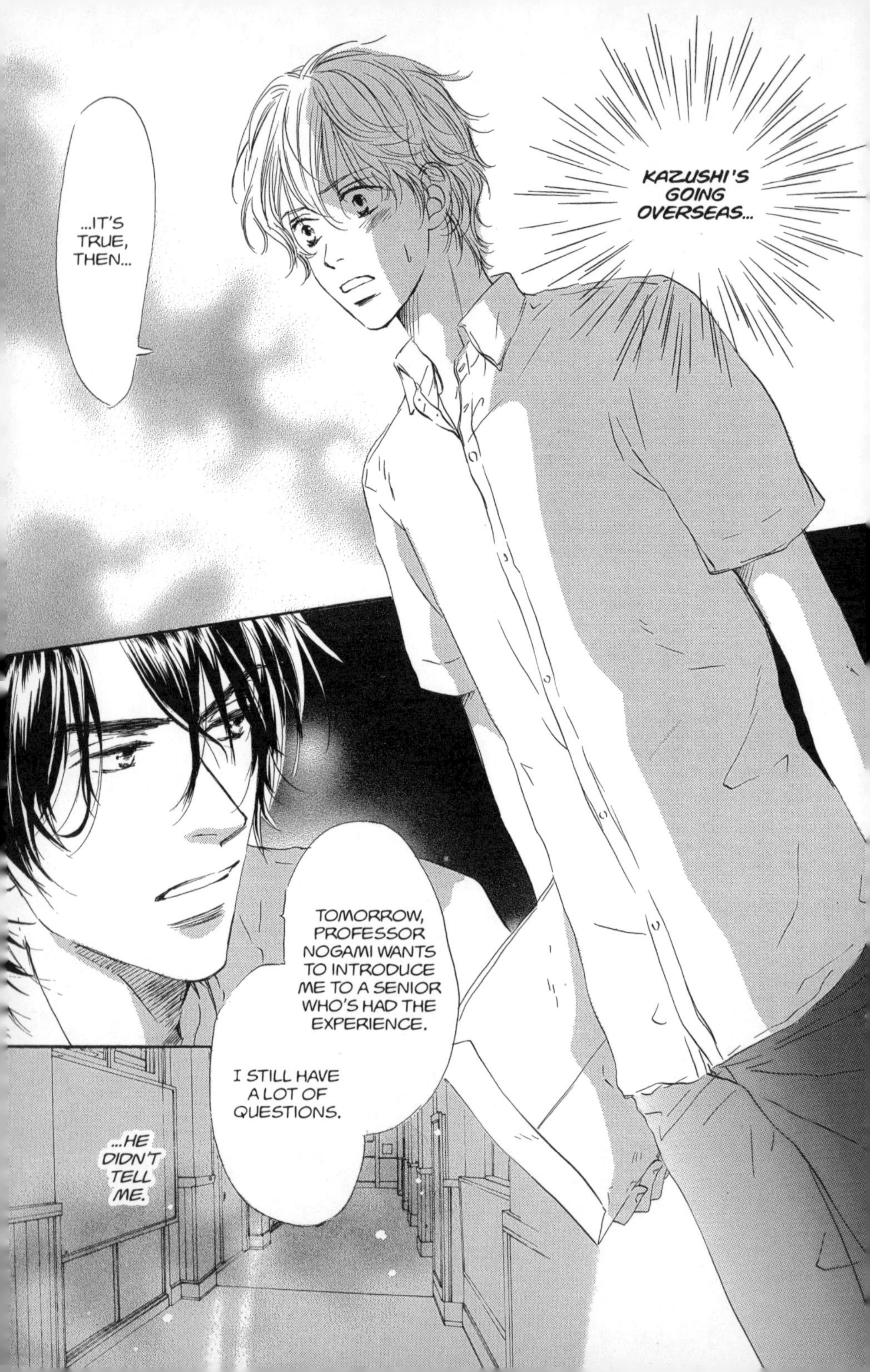
KAZUSHI'S GOING OVERSEAS...
...IT'S TRUE, THEN...
TOMORROW, PROFESSOR NOGAMI WANTS TO INTRODUCE ME TO A SENIOR WHO'S HAD THE EXPERIENCE.
I STILL HAVE A LOT OF QUESTIONS.
...HE DIDN'T TELL ME.

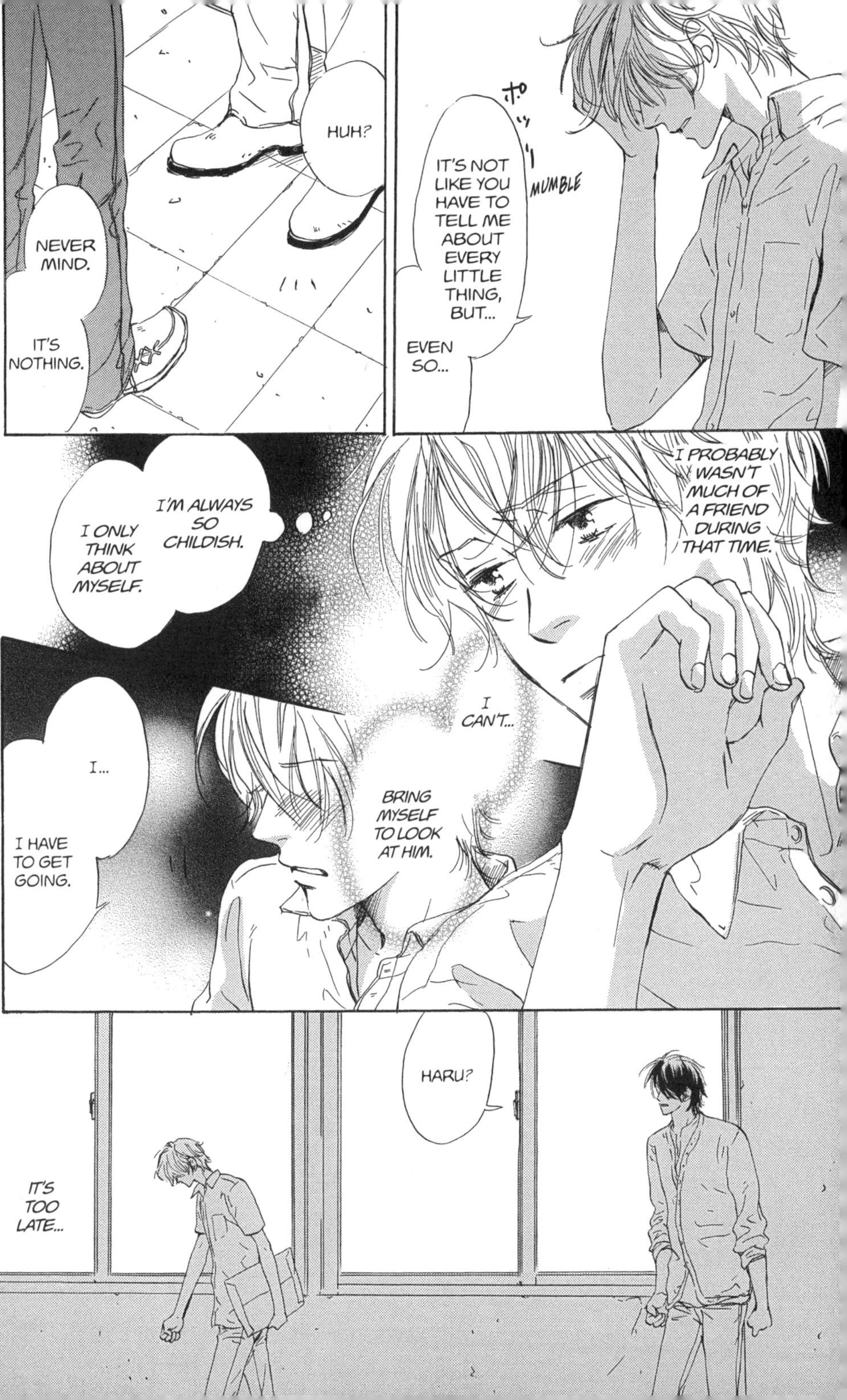
IT'S NOT LIKE YOU HAVE TO TELL ME ABOUT EVERY LITTLE THING, BUT...
MUMBLE
EVEN SO...
HUH?
NEVER MIND.
IT'S NOTHING.
I PROBABLY WASN'T MUCH OF A FRIEND DURING THAT TIME.
I'M ALWAYS SO CHILDISH.
I ONLY THINK ABOUT MYSELF.
I CAN'T...
BRING MYSELF TO LOOK AT HIM.
I...
I HAVE TO GET GOING.
HARU?
IT'S TOO LATE...

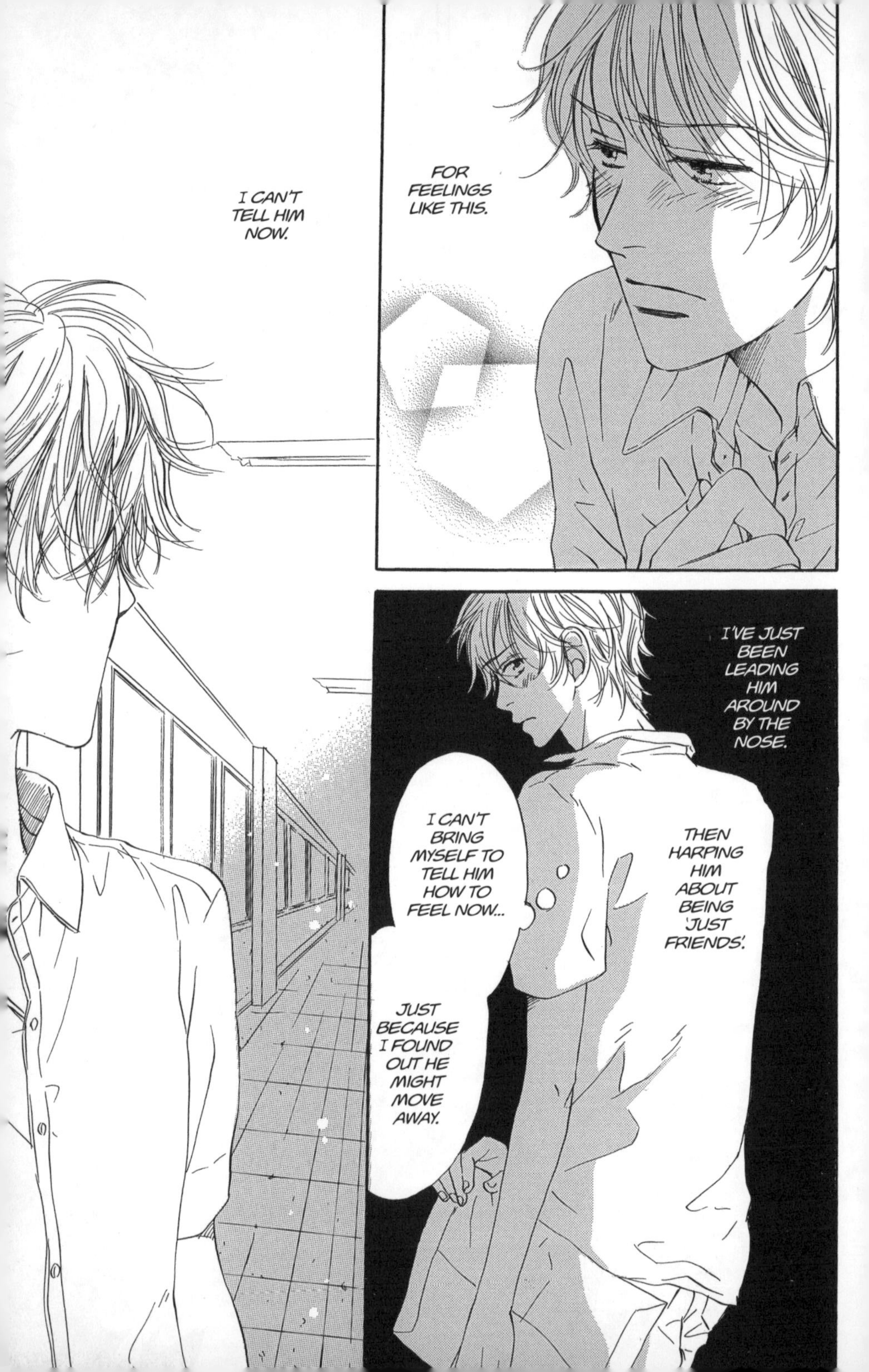
FOR FEELINGS LIKE THIS.
I'VE JUST BEEN LEADING HIM AROUND BY THE NOSE.
THEN HARPING HIM ABOUT BEING 'JUST FRIENDS'.
I CAN'T BRING MYSELF TO TELL HIM HOW TO FEEL NOW...
JUST BECAUSE I FOUND OUT HE MIGHT MOVE AWAY.
I CAN'T TELL HIM NOW.

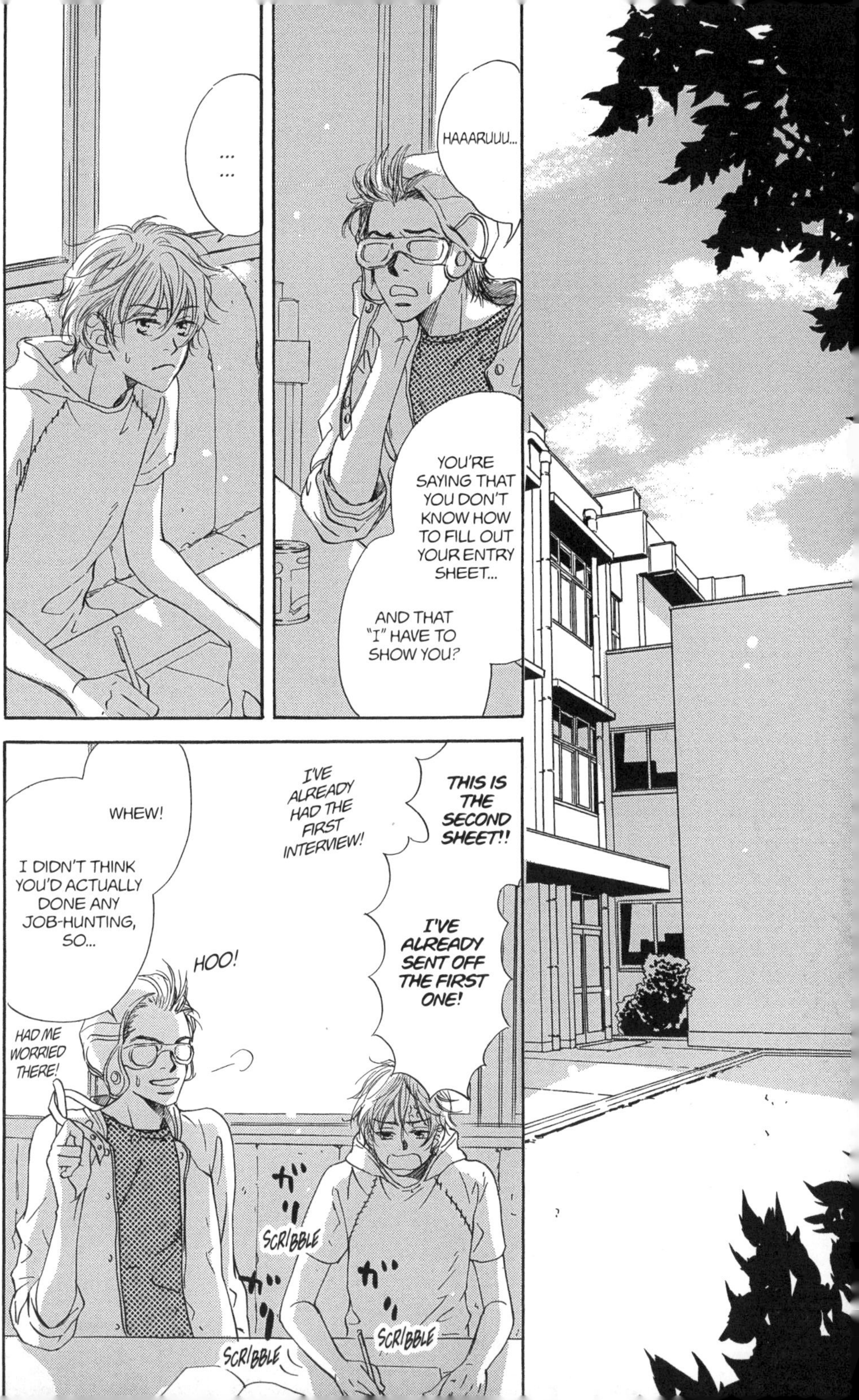
HAAARUUU...
YOU'RE SAYING THAT YOU DON'T KNOW HOW TO FILL OUT YOUR ENTRY SHEET...
AND THAT "I" HAVE TO SHOW YOU?
...
...
THIS IS THE SECOND SHEET!!
I'VE ALREADY HAD THE FIRST INTERVIEW!
I'VE ALREADY SENT OFF THE FIRST ONE!
WHEW!
I DIDN'T THINK YOU'D ACTUALLY DONE ANY JOB-HUNTING, SO...
HOO!
HAD ME WORRIED THERE!
ガリ
SCRIBBLE
ガリ
SCRIBBLE
ガリ
SCRIBBLE

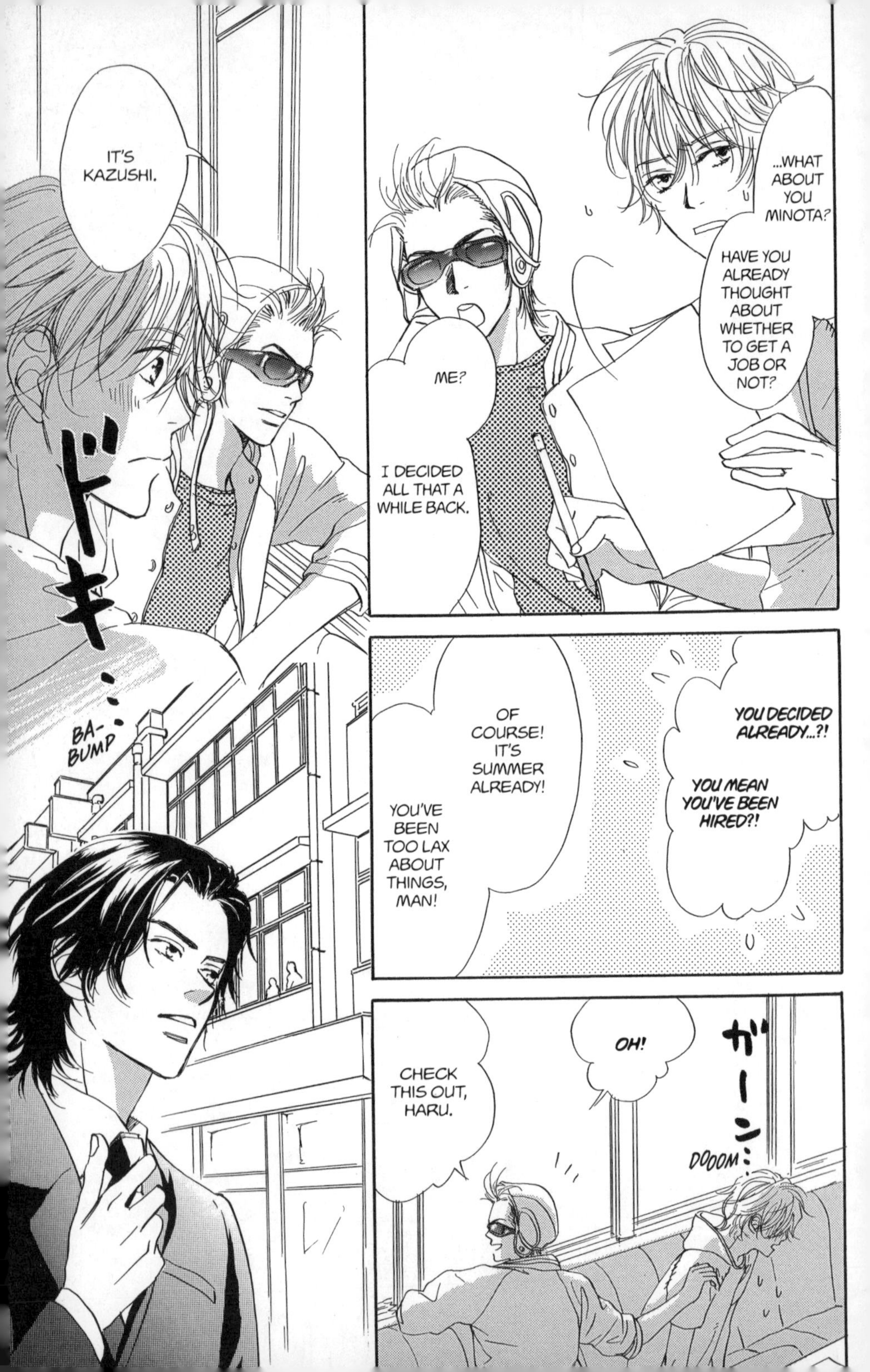

...WHAT ABOUT YOU MINOTA?
HAVE YOU ALREADY THOUGHT ABOUT WHETHER TO GET A JOB OR NOT?
ME?
I DECIDED ALL THAT A WHILE BACK.
YOU DECIDED ALREADY...?!
YOU MEAN YOU'VE BEEN HIRED?!
OF COURSE! IT'S SUMMER ALREADY!
YOU'VE BEEN TOO LAX ABOUT THINGS, MAN!
ガーン…
DOOOM...
OH!
CHECK THIS OUT, HARU.
IT'S KAZUSHI.
ドキ…
BA-BUMP

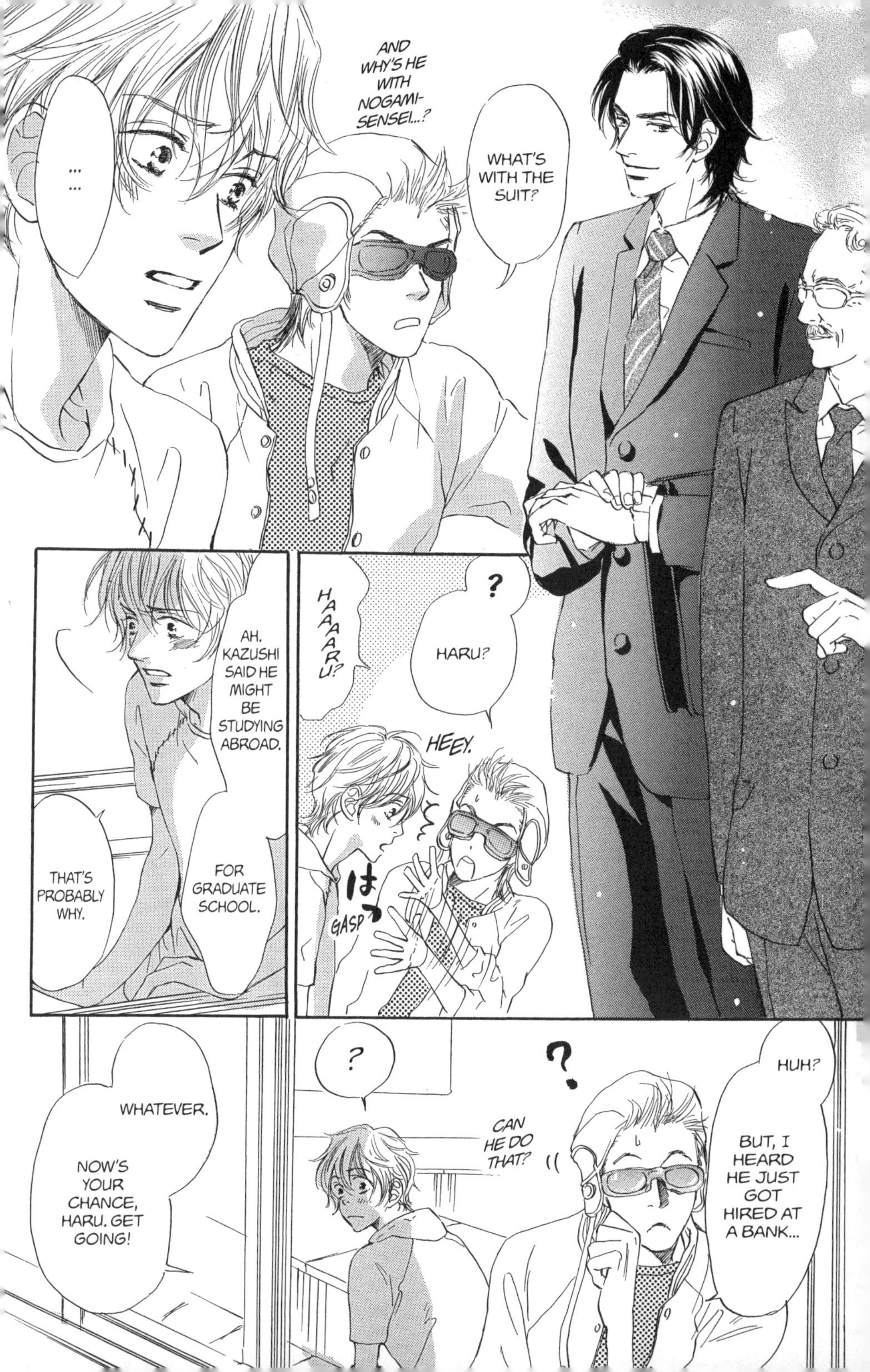
WHAT'S WITH THE SUIT?
AND WHY'S HE WITH NOGAMI-SENSEI...?
... ...
?
HARU?
HAAAARU?
HEEY.
は GASP
AH. KAZUSHI SAID HE MIGHT BE STUDYING ABROAD.
FOR GRADUATE SCHOOL.
THAT'S PROBABLY WHY.
HUH?
BUT, I HEARD HE JUST GOT HIRED AT A BANK...
?
CAN HE DO THAT?
?
WHATEVER.
NOW'S YOUR CHANCE, HARU. GET GOING!

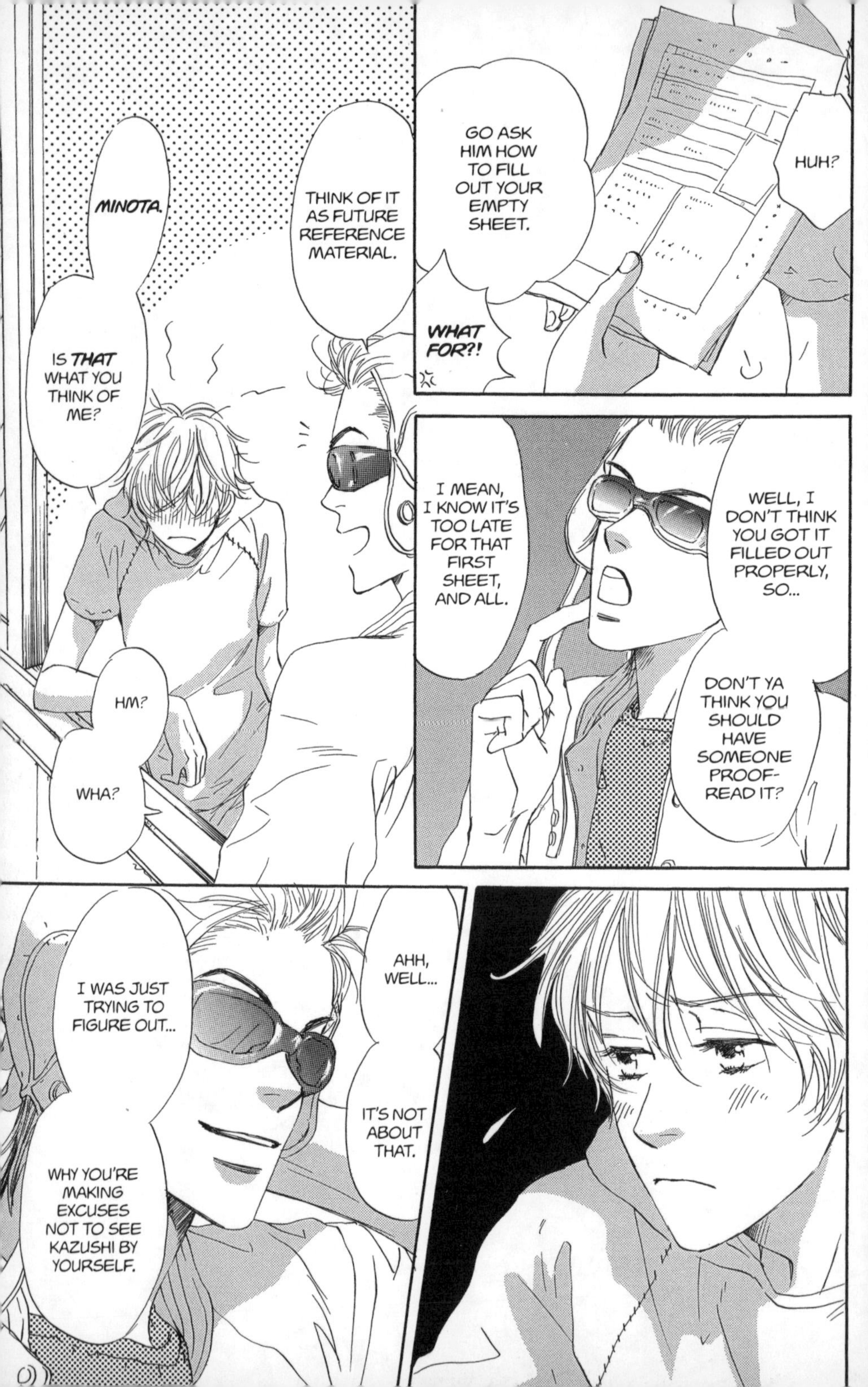
HUH?
GO ASK HIM HOW TO FILL OUT YOUR EMPTY SHEET.
WHAT FOR?!
WELL, I DON'T THINK YOU GOT IT FILLED OUT PROPERLY, SO...
I MEAN, I KNOW IT'S TOO LATE FOR THAT FIRST SHEET, AND ALL.
DON'T YA THINK YOU SHOULD HAVE SOMEONE PROOF-READ IT?
THINK OF IT AS FUTURE REFERENCE MATERIAL.
MINOTA.
IS THAT WHAT YOU THINK OF ME?
HM?
WHA?
AHH, WELL...
IT'S NOT ABOUT THAT.
I WAS JUST TRYING TO FIGURE OUT...
WHY YOU'RE MAKING EXCUSES NOT TO SEE KAZUSHI BY YOURSELF.

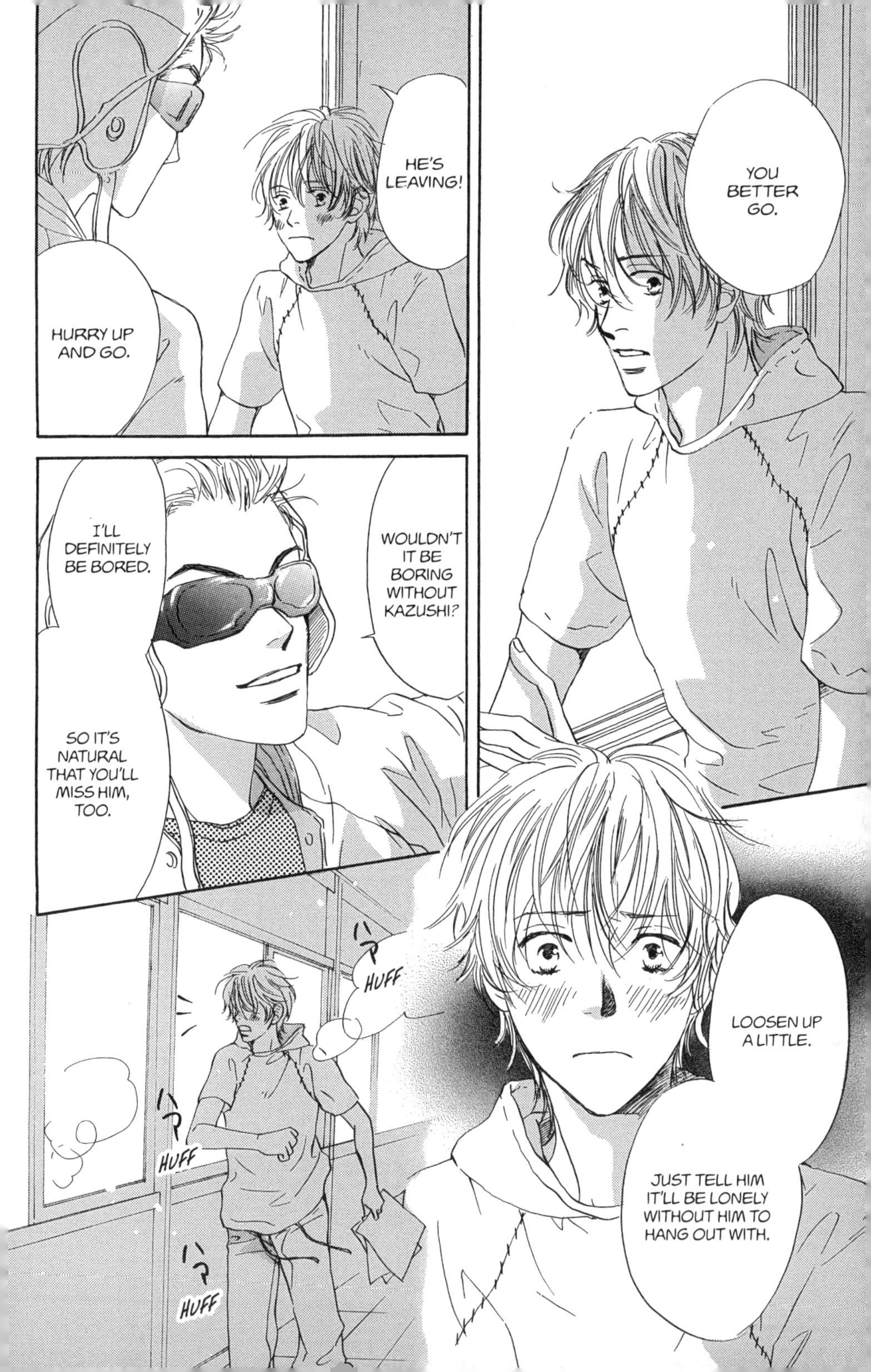
YOU BETTER GO.
HE'S LEAVING!
HURRY UP AND GO.
WOULDN'T IT BE BORING WITHOUT KAZUSHI?
I'LL DEFINITELY BE BORED.
SO IT'S NATURAL THAT YOU'LL MISS HIM, TOO.
LOOSEN UP A LITTLE.
ハア HUFF
JUST TELL HIM IT'LL BE LONELY WITHOUT HIM TO HANG OUT WITH.
ハア HUFF
ハア HUFF

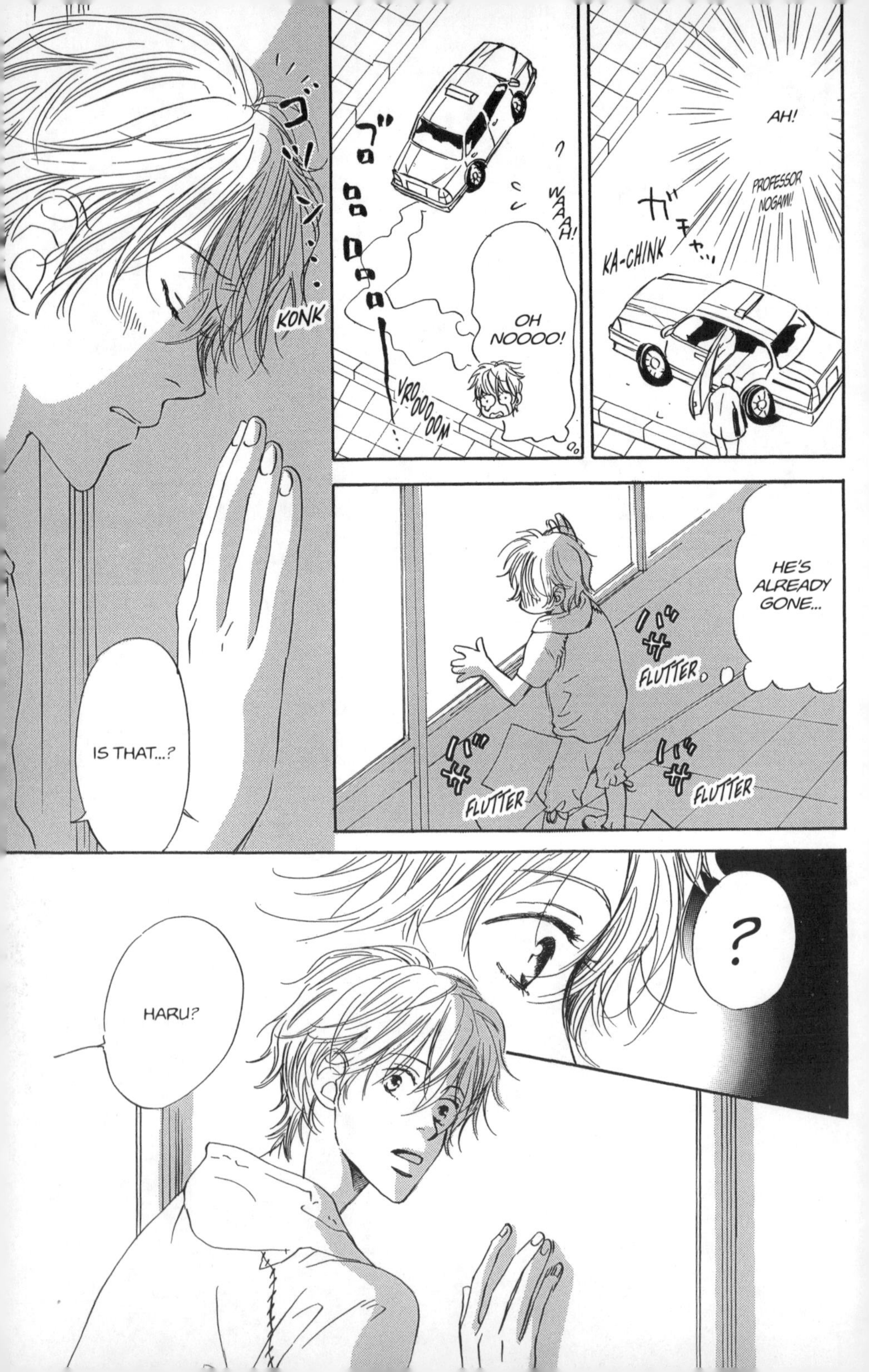
AH!
PROFESSOR NOGAMI!
KA-CHINK
WAAAH!
OH NOOOO!
VROOOOOOM
HE'S ALREADY GONE...
FLUTTER
FLUTTER
FLUTTER
KONK
IS THAT...?
?
HARU?

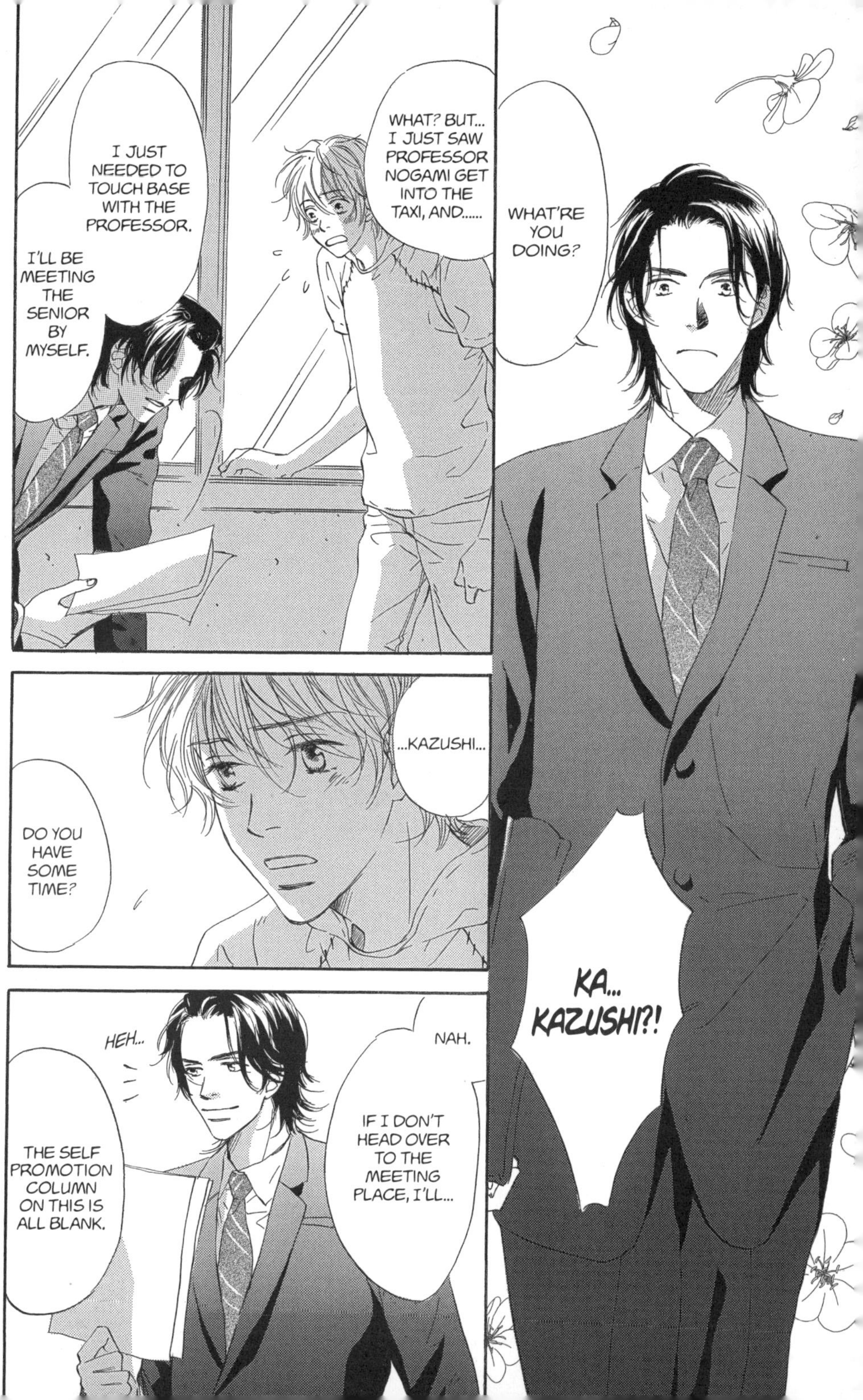
WHAT'RE YOU DOING?
KA... KAZUSHI?!
WHAT? BUT... I JUST SAW PROFESSOR NOGAMI GET INTO THE TAXI, AND......
I JUST NEEDED TO TOUCH BASE WITH THE PROFESSOR.
I'LL BE MEETING THE SENIOR BY MYSELF.
...KAZUSHI...
DO YOU HAVE SOME TIME?
NAH.
IF I DON'T HEAD OVER TO THE MEETING PLACE, I'LL...
HEH...
THE SELF PROMOTION COLUMN ON THIS IS ALL BLANK.

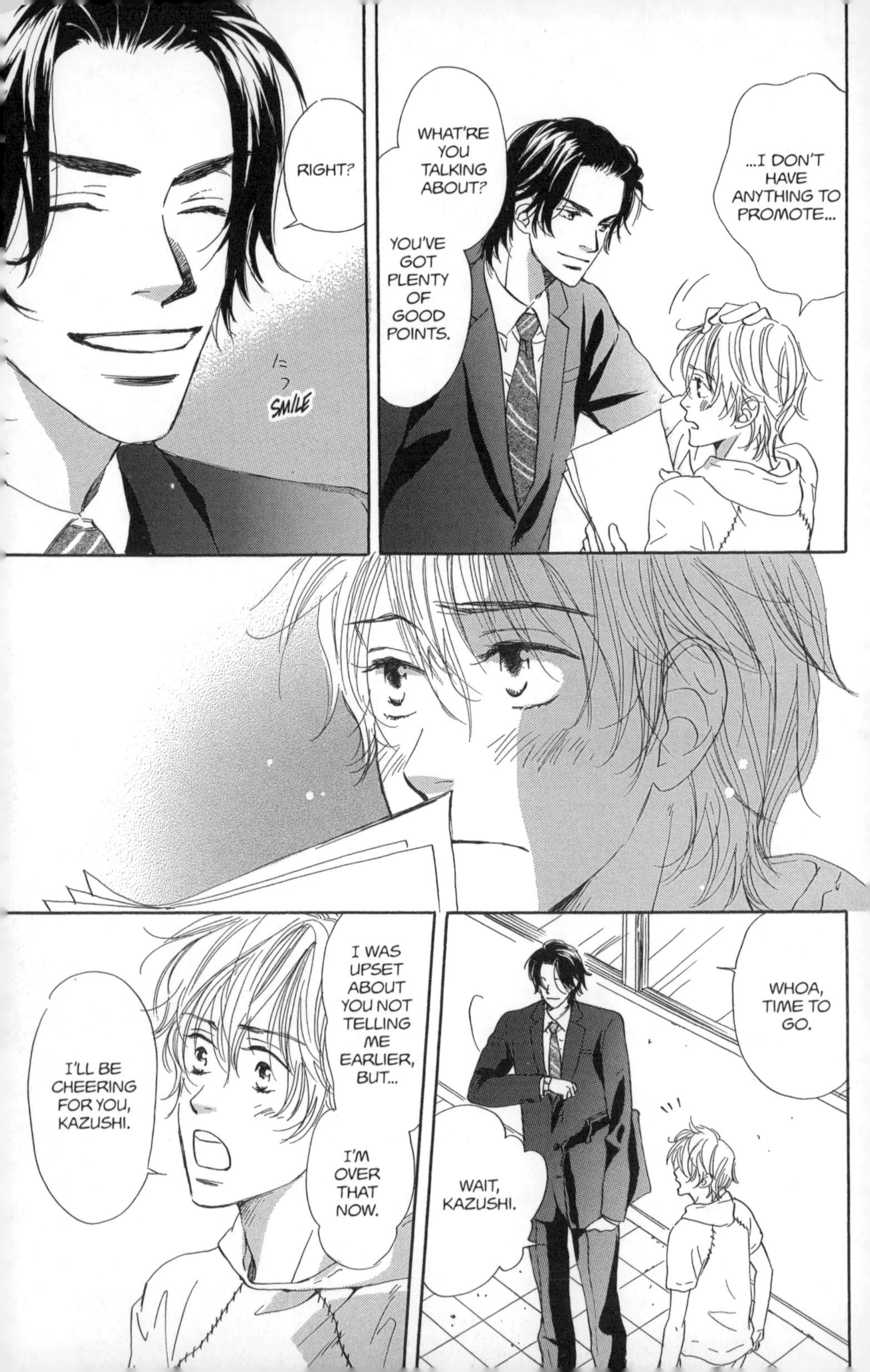
...I DON'T HAVE ANYTHING TO PROMOTE...
WHAT'RE YOU TALKING ABOUT?
YOU'VE GOT PLENTY OF GOOD POINTS.
RIGHT?
にっ
SMILE
WHOA, TIME TO GO.
WAIT, KAZUSHI.
I WAS UPSET ABOUT YOU NOT TELLING ME EARLIER, BUT...
I'M OVER THAT NOW.
I'LL BE CHEERING FOR YOU, KAZUSHI.

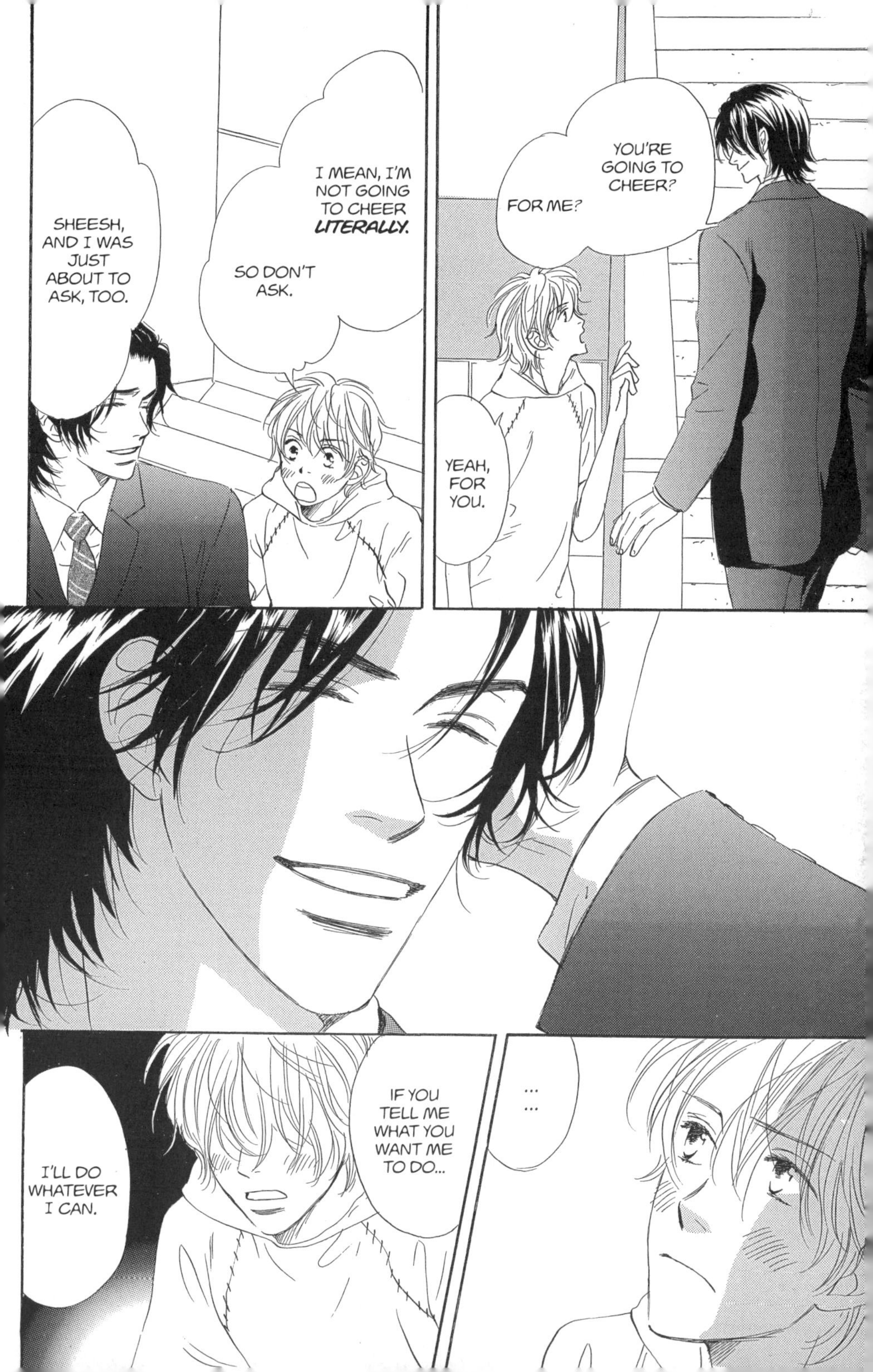
YOU'RE GOING TO CHEER?
FOR ME?
YEAH, FOR YOU.
I MEAN, I'M NOT GOING TO CHEER **LITERALLY.**
SO DON'T ASK.
SHEESH, AND I WAS JUST ABOUT TO ASK, TOO.
......
IF YOU TELL ME WHAT YOU WANT ME TO DO...
I'LL DO WHATEVER I CAN.

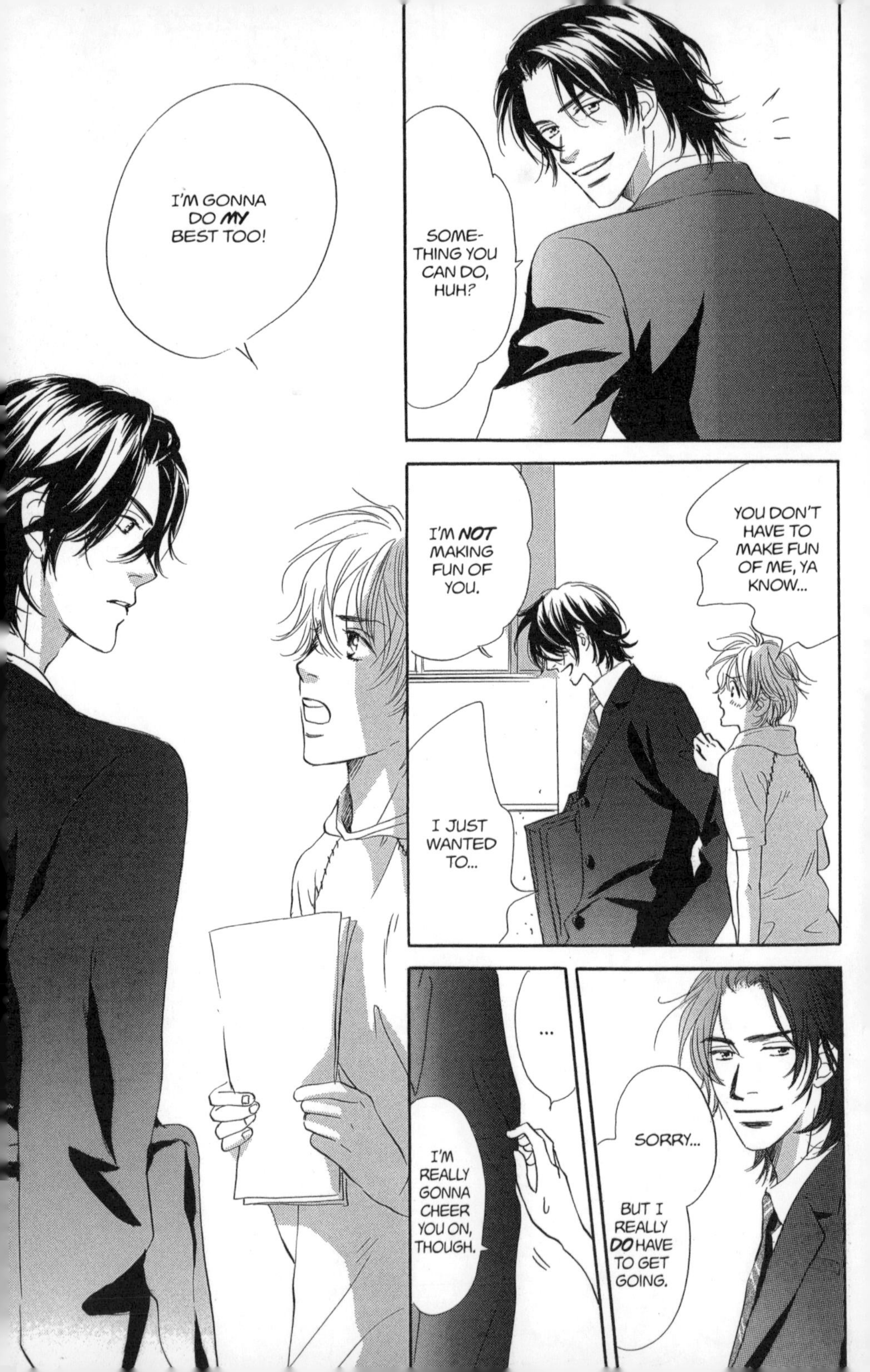
I'M GONNA DO **MY** BEST TOO!
SOME-THING YOU CAN DO, HUH?
YOU DON'T HAVE TO MAKE FUN OF ME, YA KNOW...
I'M **NOT** MAKING FUN OF YOU.
I JUST WANTED TO...
SORRY...
BUT I REALLY **DO** HAVE TO GET GOING.
...
I'M REALLY GONNA CHEER YOU ON, THOUGH.

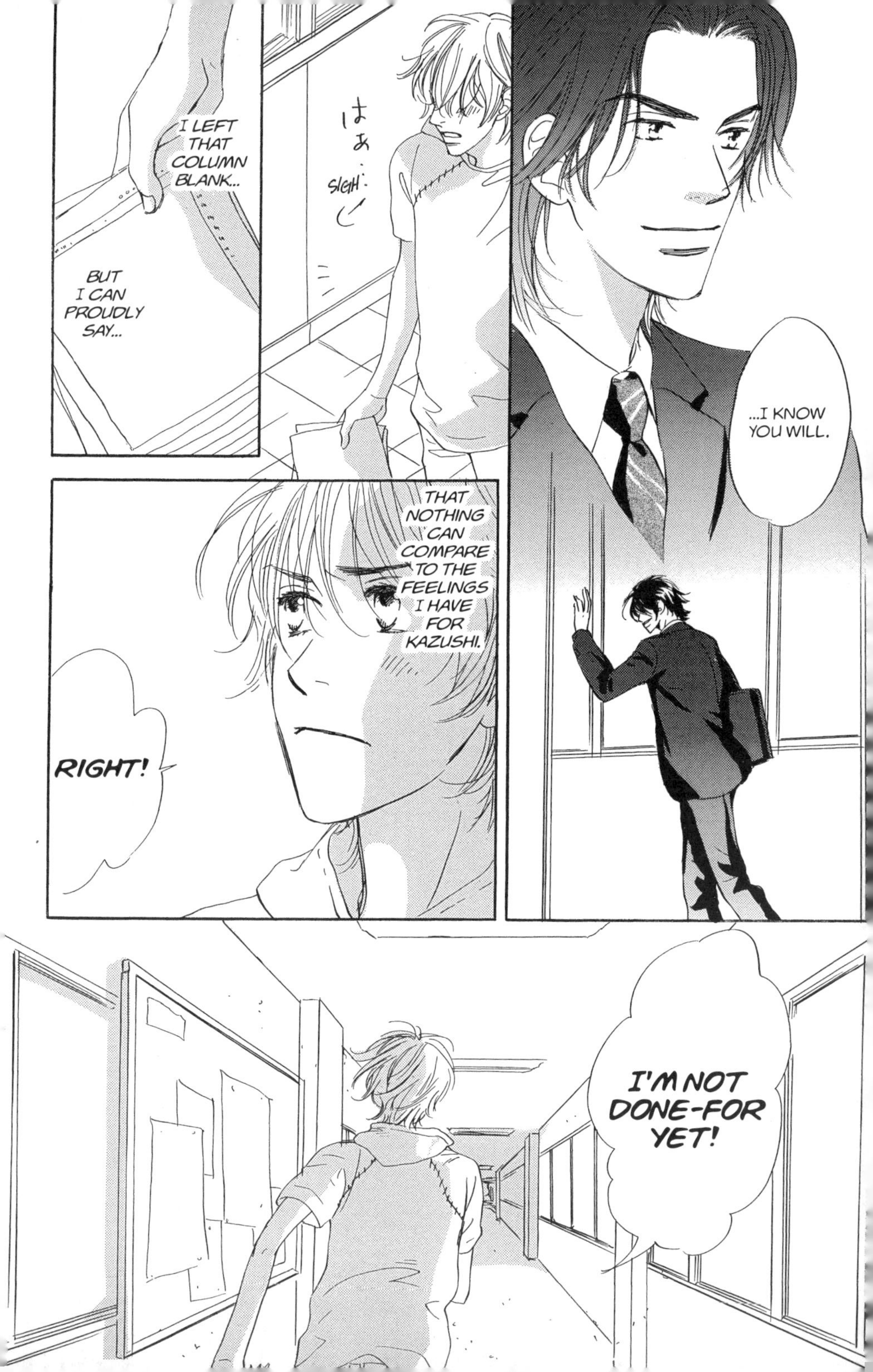
...I KNOW YOU WILL.
はあ
SIGH
I LEFT THAT COLUMN BLANK...
BUT I CAN PROUDLY SAY...
THAT NOTHING CAN COMPARE TO THE FEELINGS I HAVE FOR KAZUSHI.
RIGHT!
I'M NOT DONE-FOR YET!

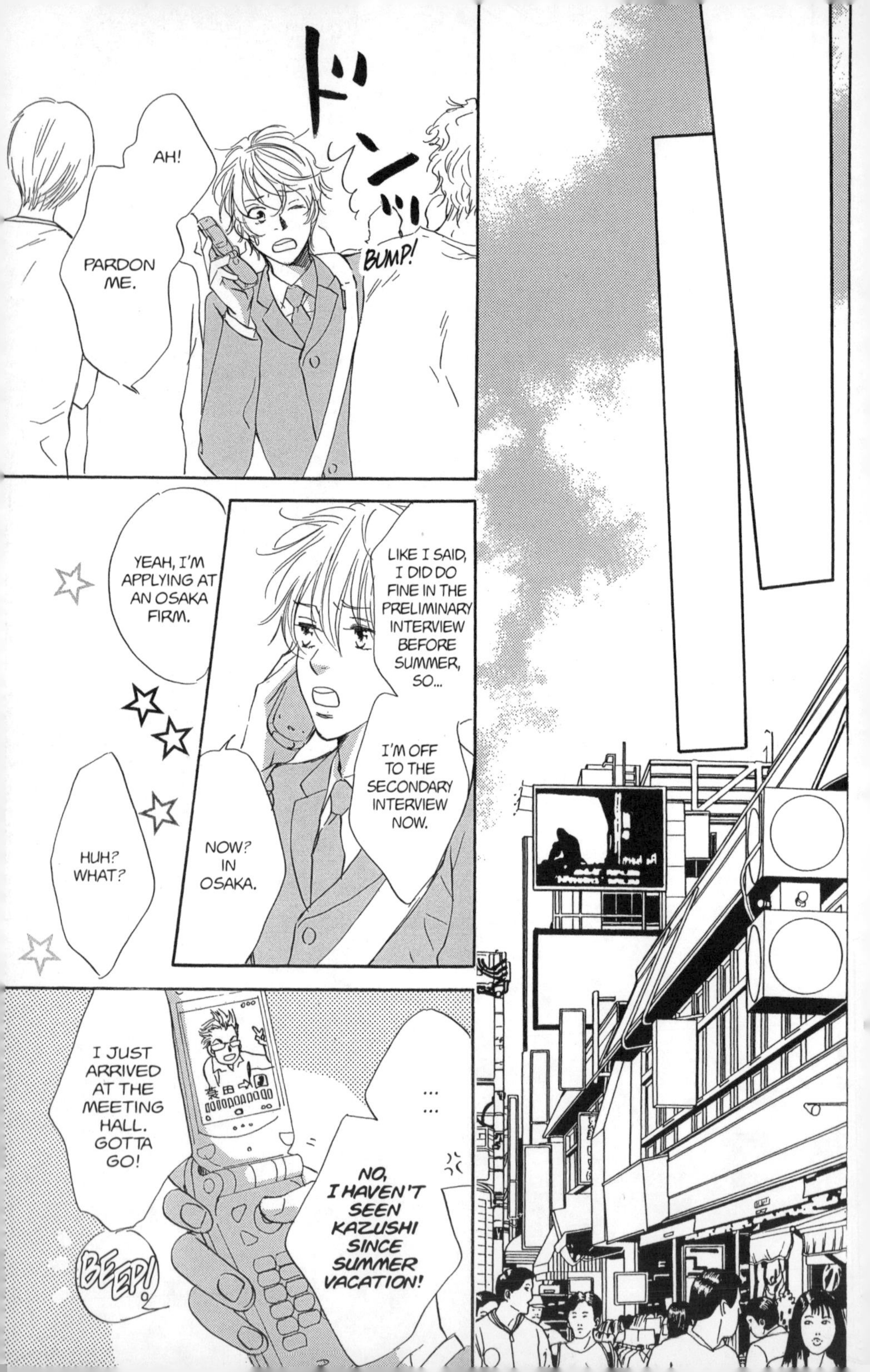
BUMP!
AH!
PARDON ME.
LIKE I SAID, I DID DO FINE IN THE PRELIMINARY INTERVIEW BEFORE SUMMER, SO...
YEAH, I'M APPLYING AT AN OSAKA FIRM.
I'M OFF TO THE SECONDARY INTERVIEW NOW.
NOW? IN OSAKA.
HUH? WHAT?
... ...
NO, I HAVEN'T SEEN KAZUSHI SINCE SUMMER VACATION!
I JUST ARRIVED AT THE MEETING HALL. GOTTA GO!
BEEP!

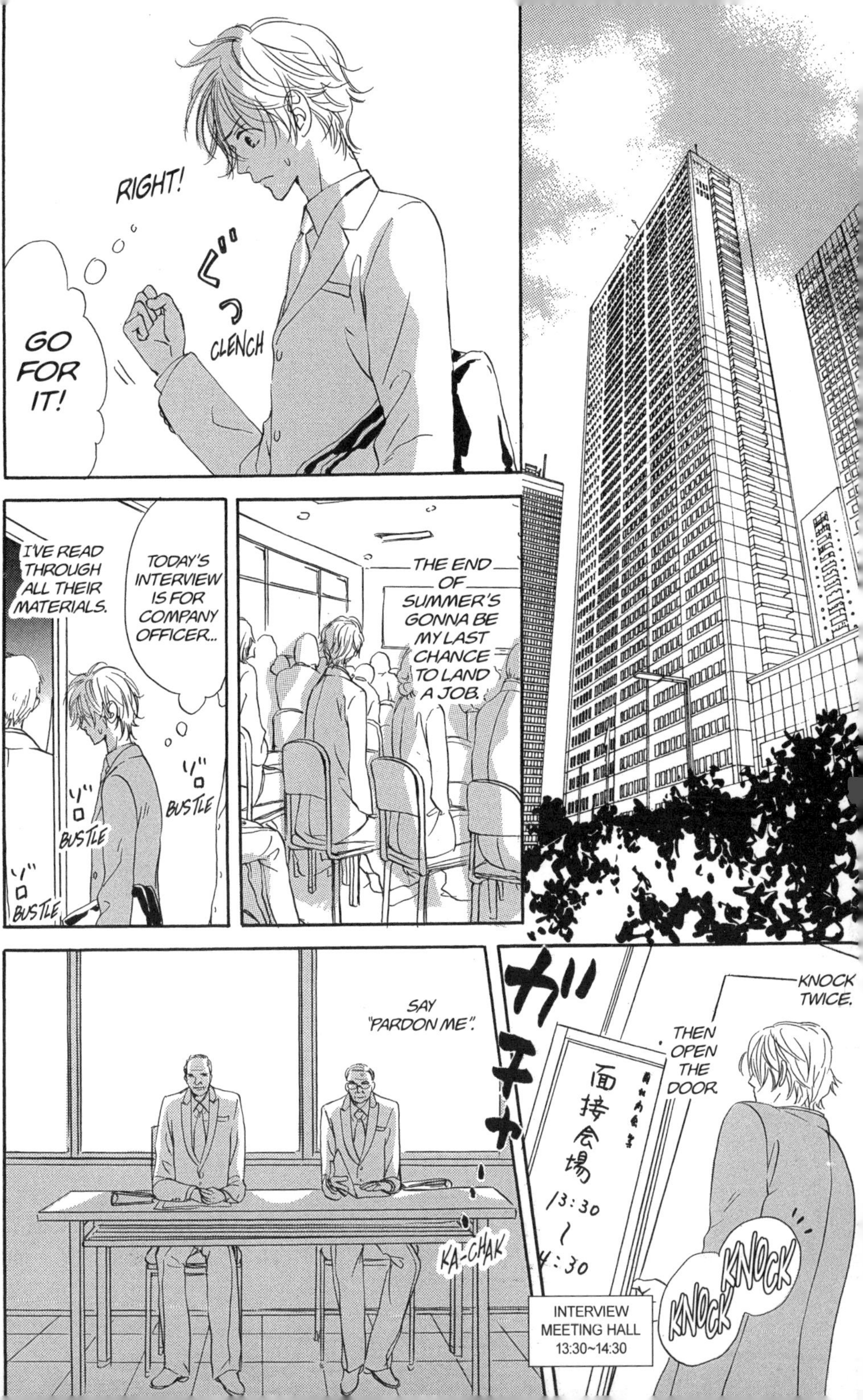
RIGHT!
GO FOR IT!
ぐっ
CLENCH
THE END OF SUMMER'S GONNA BE MY LAST CHANCE TO LAND A JOB.
I'VE READ THROUGH ALL THEIR MATERIALS.
TODAY'S INTERVIEW IS FOR COMPANY OFFICER...
ゾロ
BUSTLE
ゾロ
BUSTLE
ゾロ
BUSTLE
KNOCK TWICE.
THEN OPEN THE DOOR.
KNOCK KNOCK
面接会場
13:30 ~ 14:30
INTERVIEW MEETING HALL 13:30~14:30
ガチャ
SAY "PARDON ME".
KA-CHAK

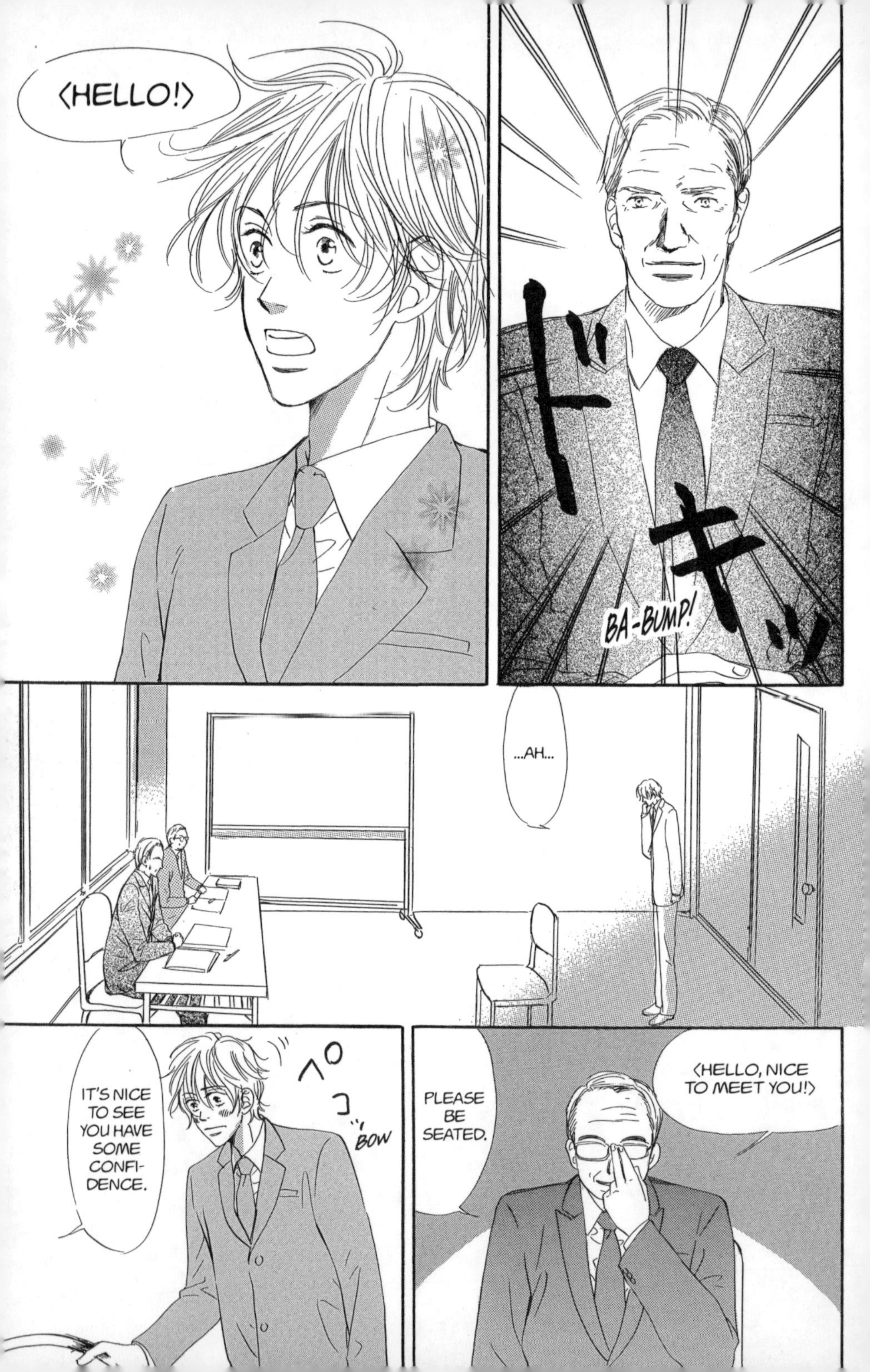
ドキッ
BA-BUMP!
⟨HELLO!⟩
...AH...
⟨HELLO, NICE TO MEET YOU!⟩
PLEASE BE SEATED.
IT'S NICE TO SEE YOU HAVE SOME CONFIDENCE.
ペコ
BOW

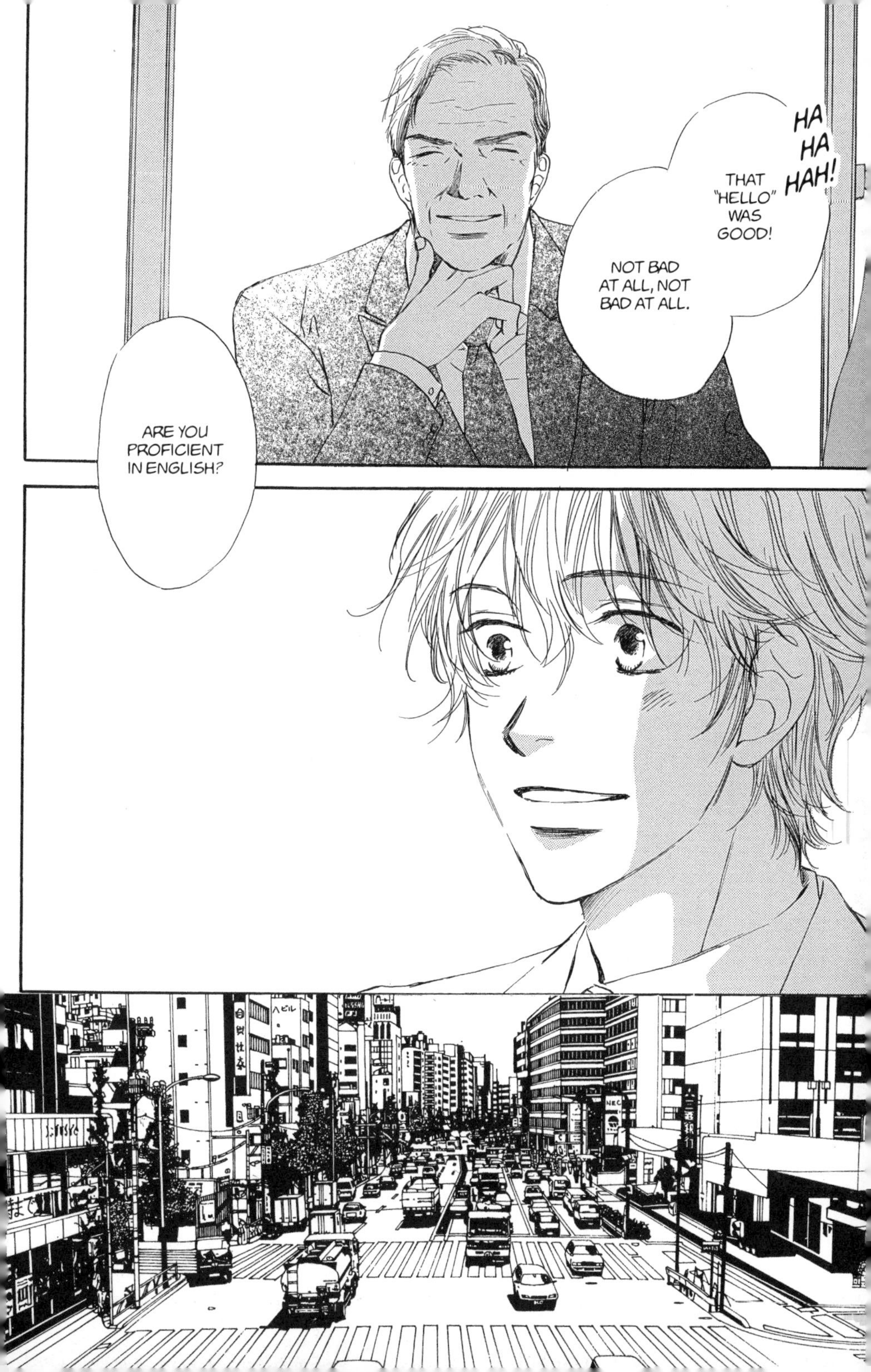
HA HA HAH!
THAT "HELLO" WAS GOOD!
NOT BAD AT ALL, NOT BAD AT ALL.
ARE YOU PROFICIENT IN ENGLISH?

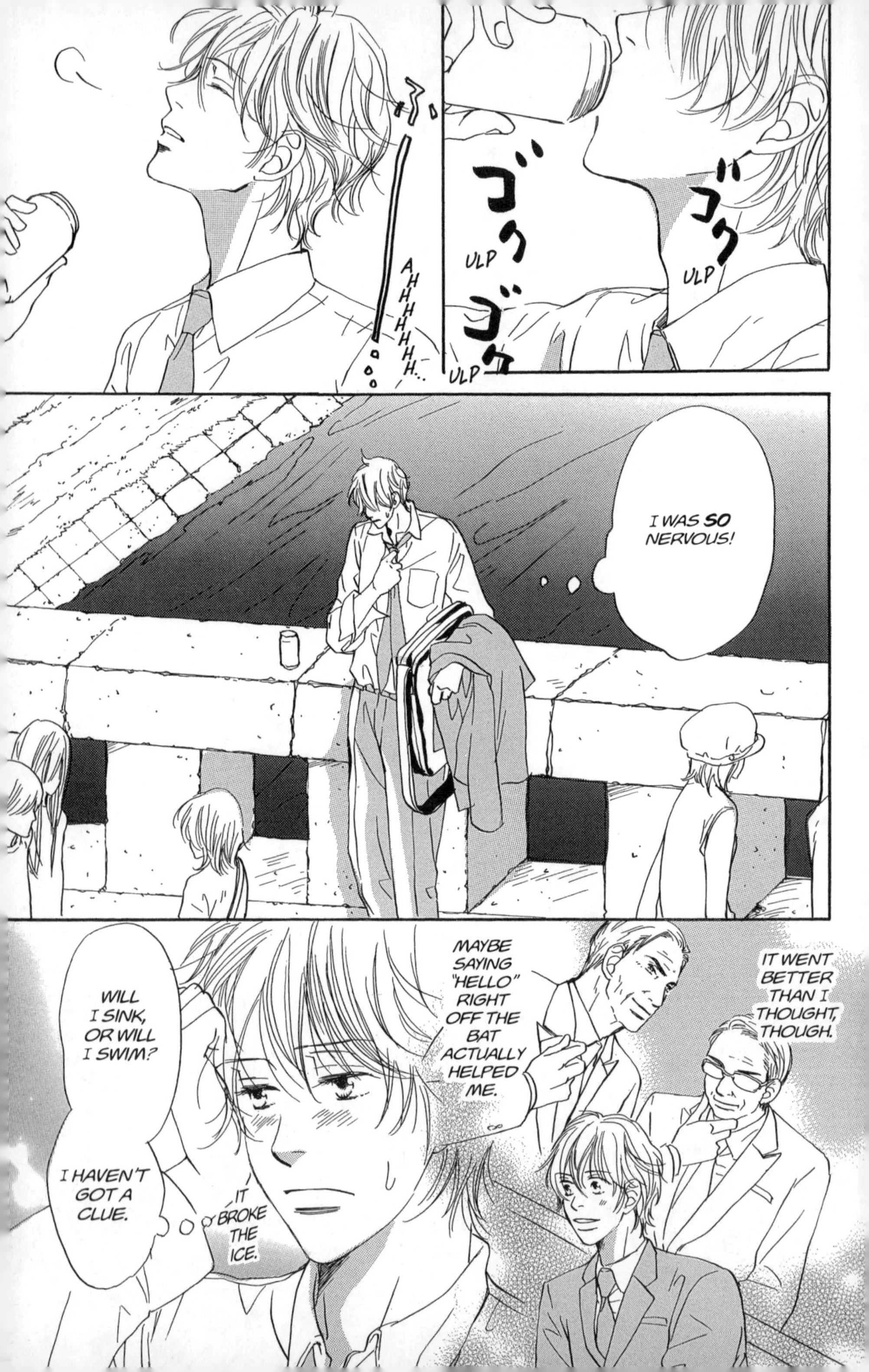
ゴク
ULP
ゴクゴク
ULP
ULP
AHHHHHHH...
I WAS **SO** NERVOUS!
IT WENT BETTER THAN I THOUGHT, THOUGH.
MAYBE SAYING "HELLO" RIGHT OFF THE BAT ACTUALLY HELPED ME.
IT BROKE THE ICE.
WILL I SINK, OR WILL I SWIM?
I HAVEN'T GOT A CLUE.

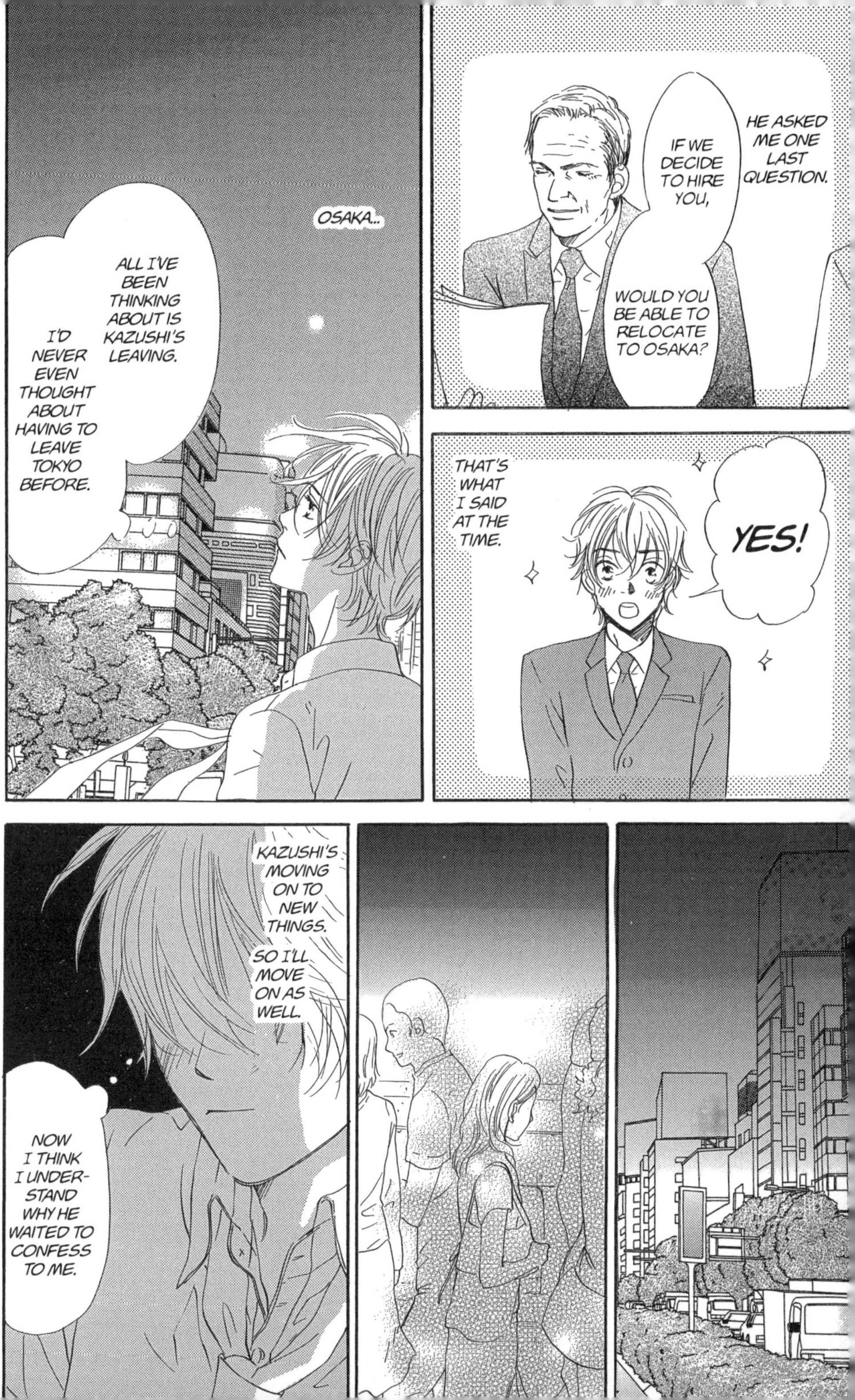
HE ASKED ME ONE LAST QUESTION.
IF WE DECIDE TO HIRE YOU,
WOULD YOU BE ABLE TO RELOCATE TO OSAKA?
YES!
THAT'S WHAT I SAID AT THE TIME.
OSAKA...
ALL I'VE BEEN THINKING ABOUT IS KAZUSHI'S LEAVING.
I'D NEVER EVEN THOUGHT ABOUT HAVING TO LEAVE TOKYO BEFORE.
KAZUSHI'S MOVING ON TO NEW THINGS.
SO I'LL MOVE ON AS WELL.
NOW I THINK I UNDER-STAND WHY HE WAITED TO CONFESS TO ME.

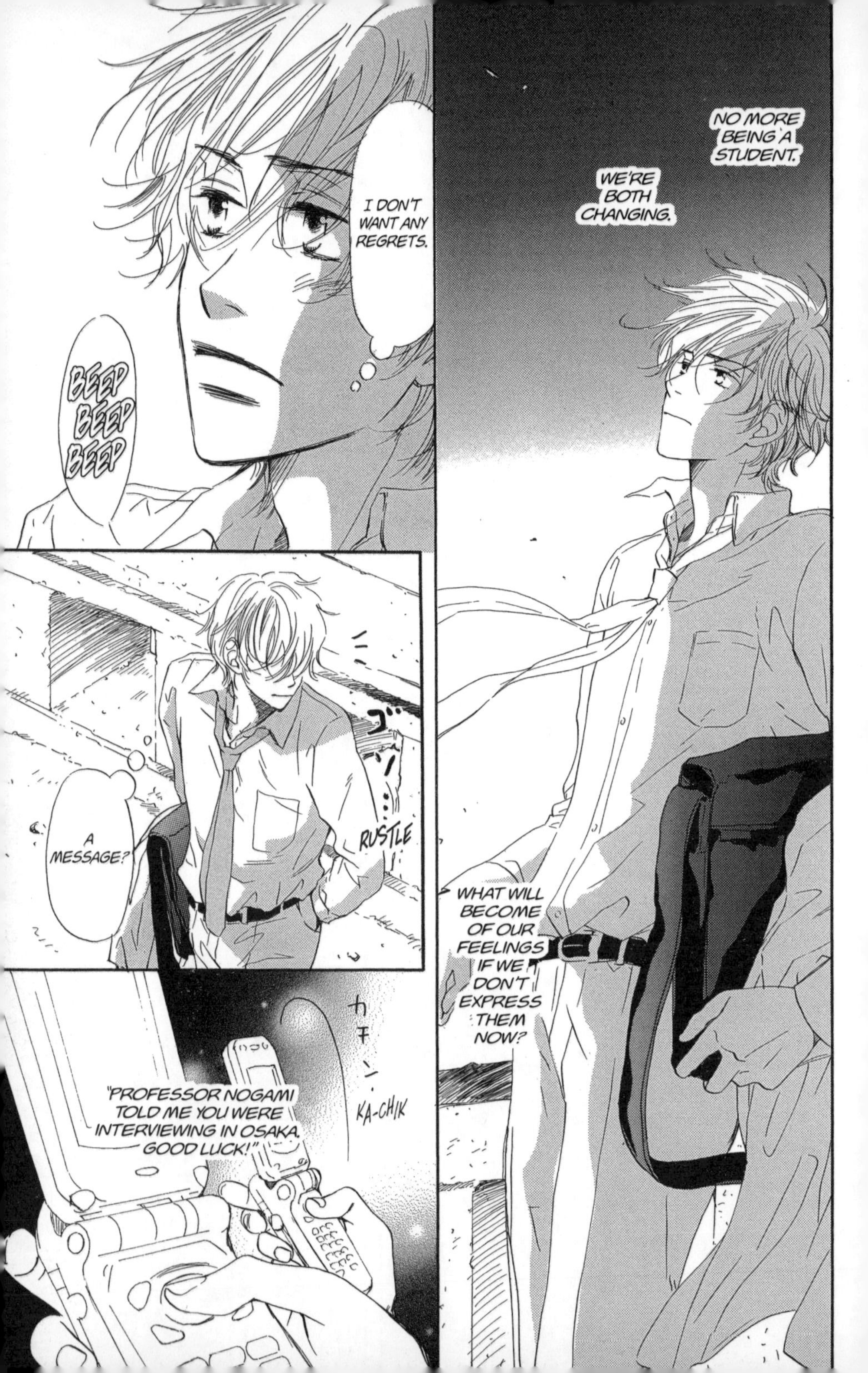
NO MORE BEING A STUDENT.
WE'RE BOTH CHANGING.
WHAT WILL BECOME OF OUR FEELINGS IF WE DON'T EXPRESS THEM NOW?
I DON'T WANT ANY REGRETS.
BEEP BEEP BEEP
RUSTLE
A MESSAGE?
KA-CHIK
"PROFESSOR NOGAMI TOLD ME YOU WERE INTERVIEWING IN OSAKA. GOOD LUCK!"

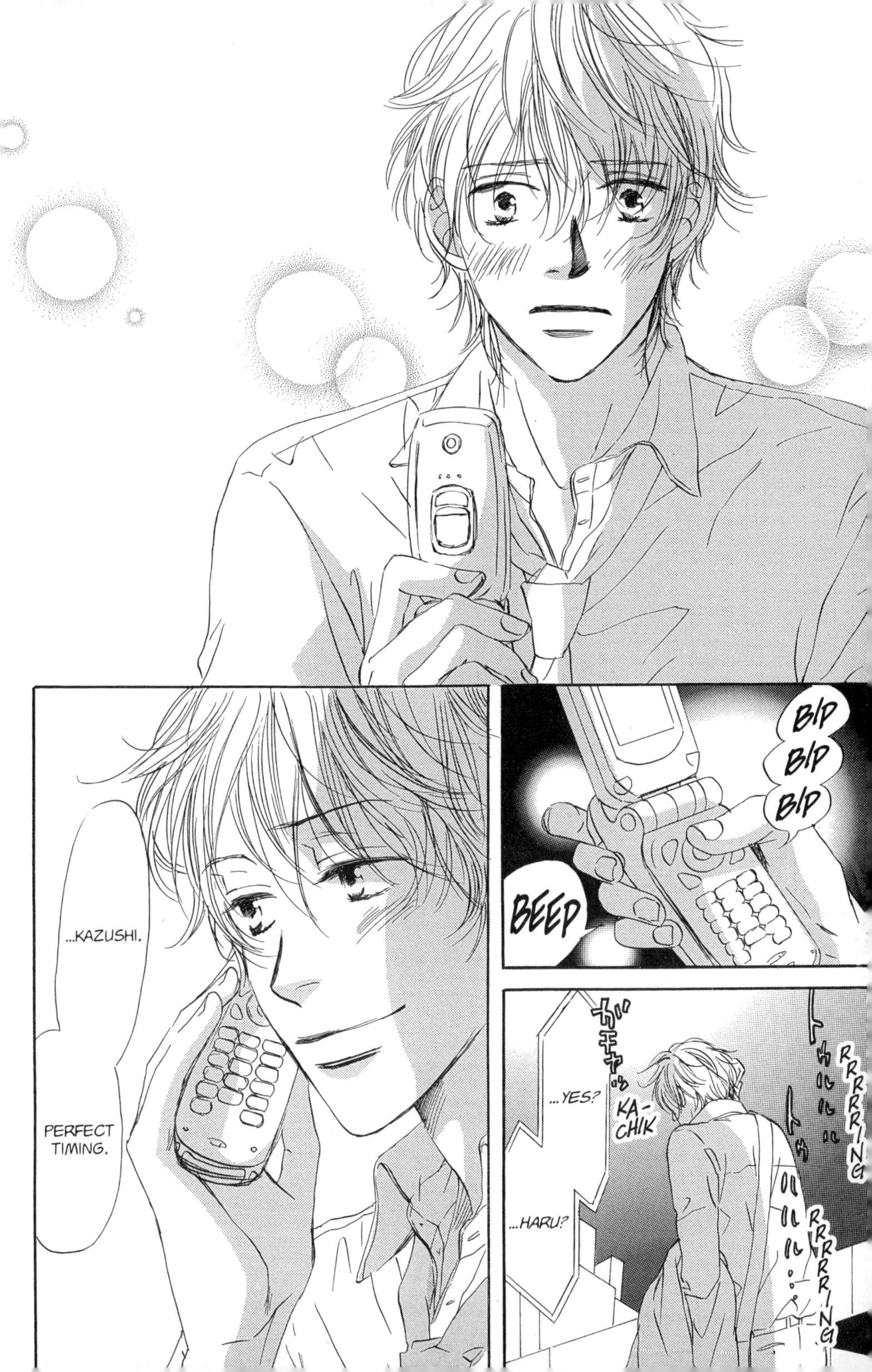
BIP
BIP
BIP
BEEP
RRRRING
RRRRING
KA-CHIK
...YES?
...HARU?
...KAZUSHI.
PERFECT TIMING.

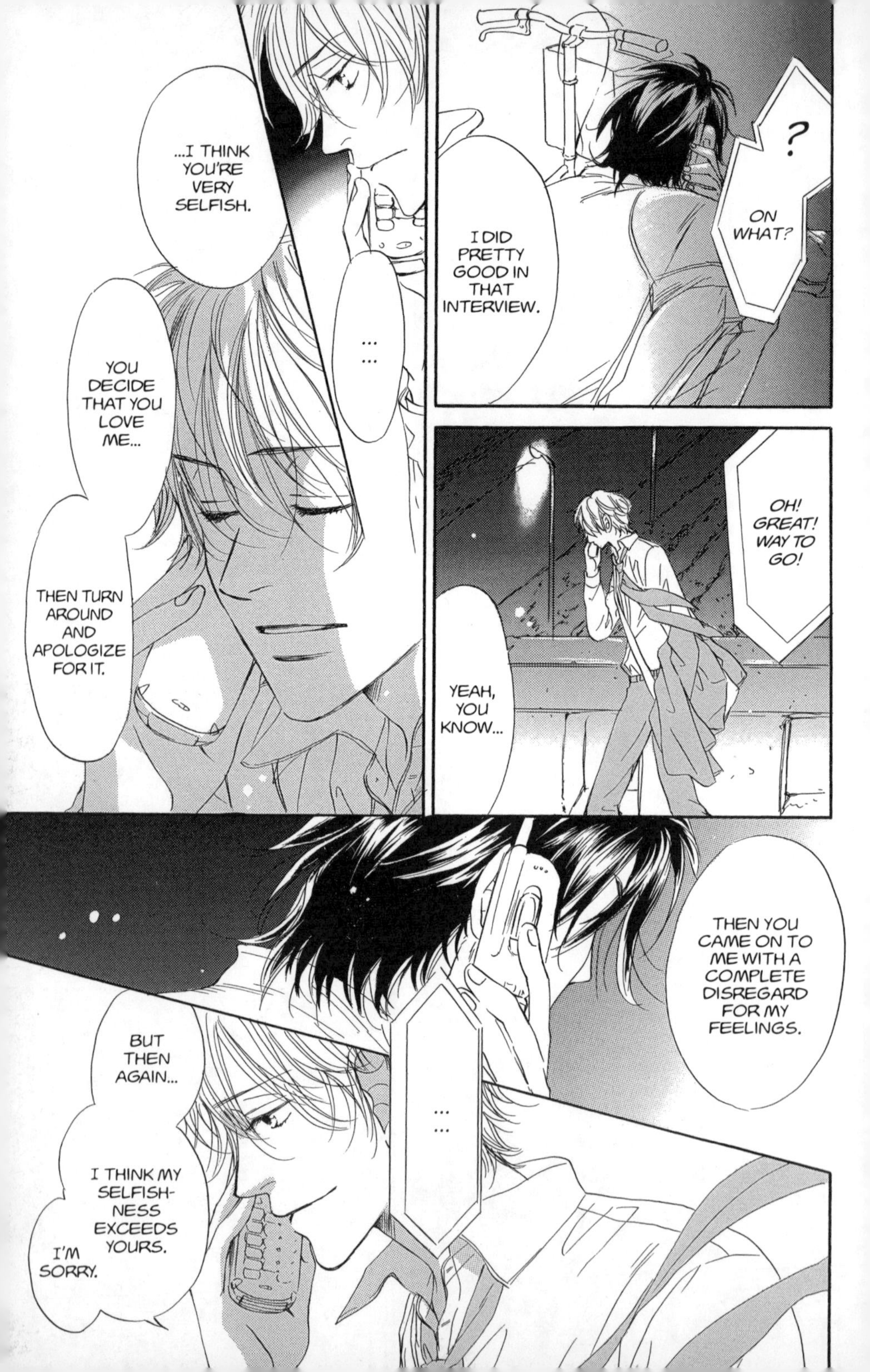
?
ON WHAT?
I DID PRETTY GOOD IN THAT INTERVIEW.
OH! GREAT! WAY TO GO!
YEAH, YOU KNOW...
...I THINK YOU'RE VERY SELFISH.
......
YOU DECIDE THAT YOU LOVE ME...
THEN TURN AROUND AND APOLOGIZE FOR IT.
THEN YOU CAME ON TO ME WITH A COMPLETE DISREGARD FOR MY FEELINGS.
......
BUT THEN AGAIN...
I THINK MY SELFISH-NESS EXCEEDS YOURS.
I'M SORRY.

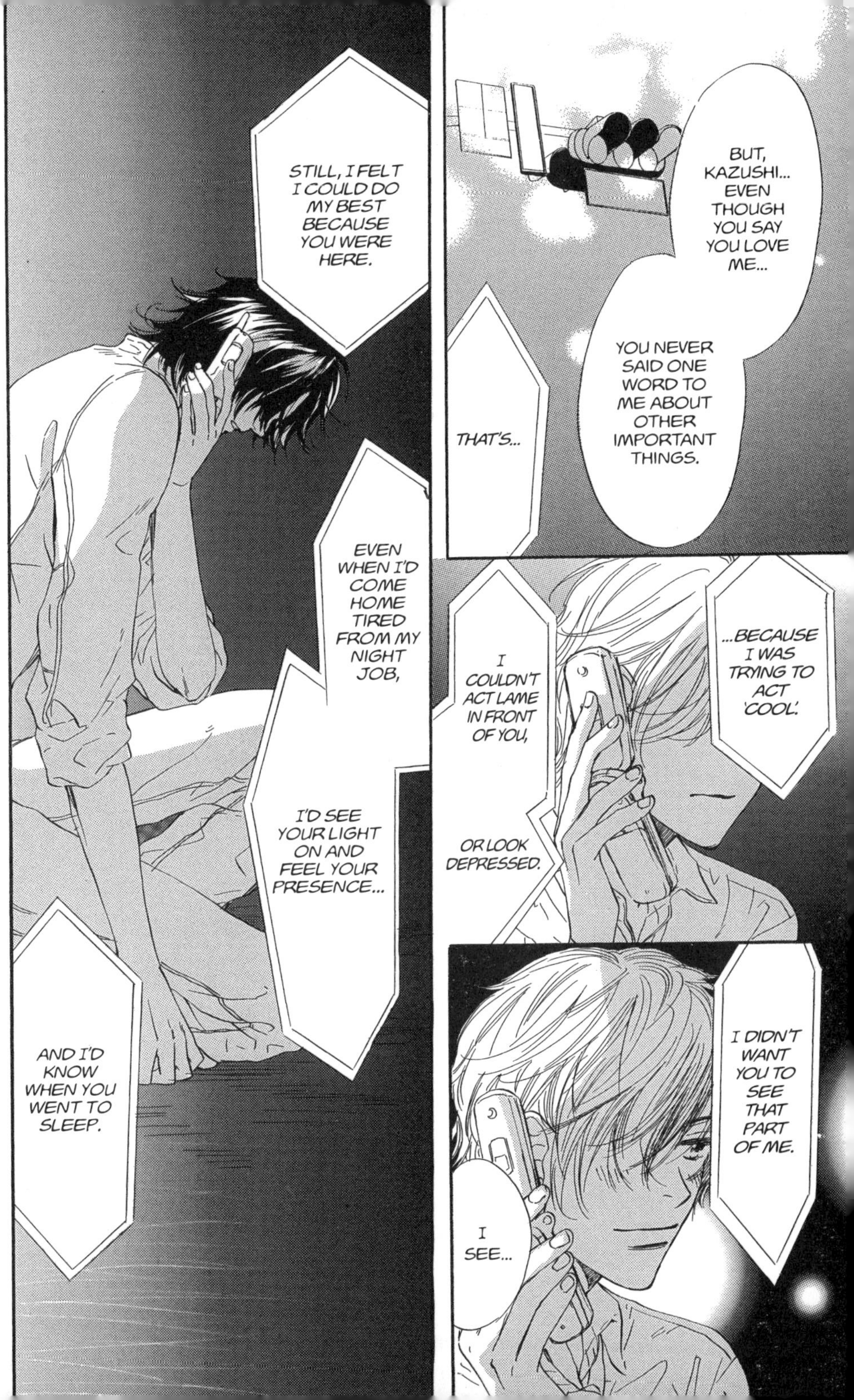
BUT, KAZUSHI... EVEN THOUGH YOU SAY YOU LOVE ME...
YOU NEVER SAID ONE WORD TO ME ABOUT OTHER IMPORTANT THINGS.
THAT'S...
...BECAUSE I WAS TRYING TO ACT 'COOL.'
I COULDN'T ACT LAME IN FRONT OF YOU,
OR LOOK DEPRESSED.
I DIDN'T WANT YOU TO SEE THAT PART OF ME.
I SEE...
STILL, I FELT I COULD DO MY BEST BECAUSE YOU WERE HERE.
EVEN WHEN I'D COME HOME TIRED FROM MY NIGHT JOB,
I'D SEE YOUR LIGHT ON AND FEEL YOUR PRESENCE...
AND I'D KNOW WHEN YOU WENT TO SLEEP.

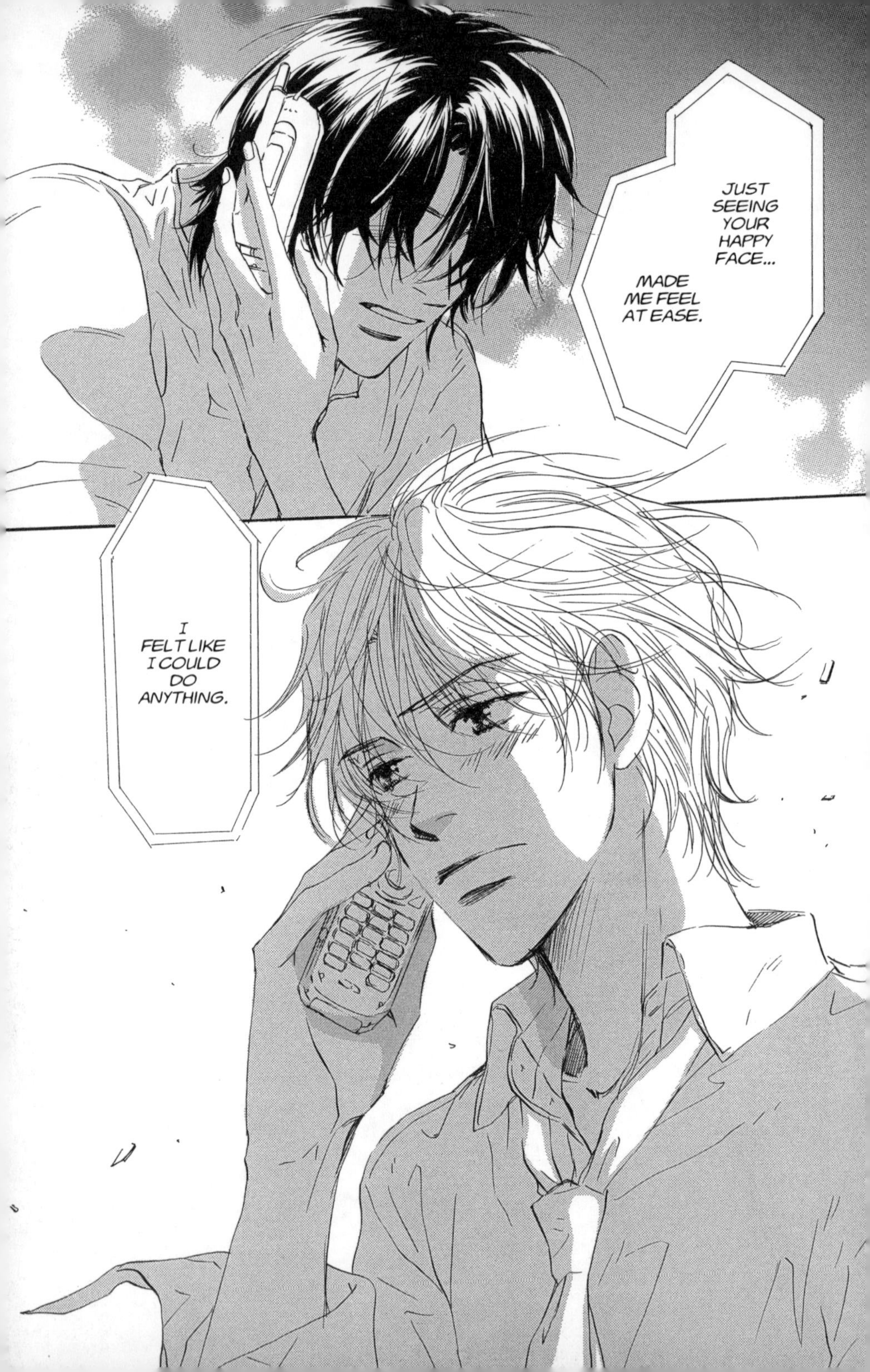
JUST SEEING YOUR HAPPY FACE...
MADE ME FEEL AT EASE.
I FELT LIKE I COULD DO ANYTHING.

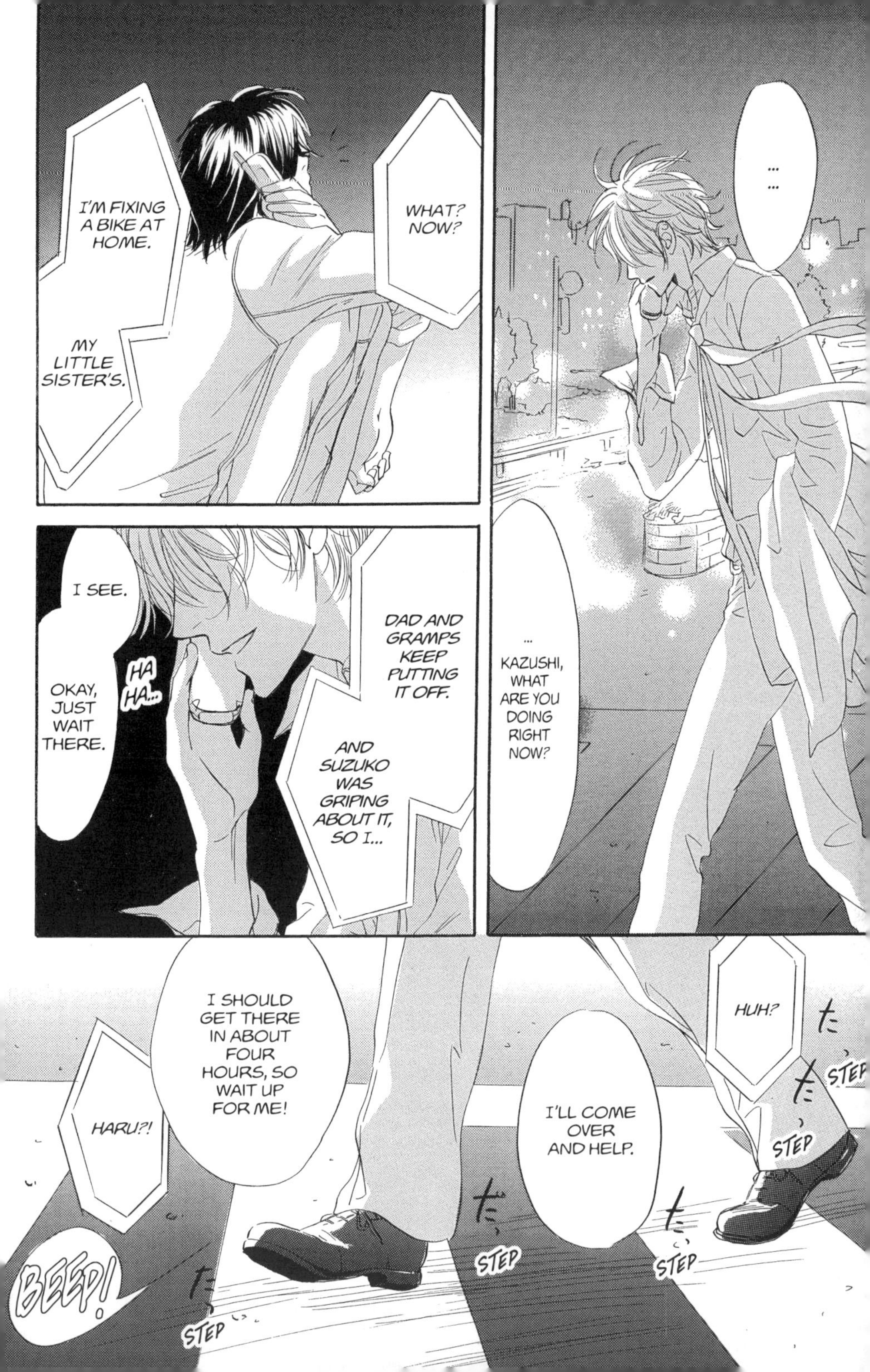
……
… KAZUSHI, WHAT ARE YOU DOING RIGHT NOW?
WHAT? NOW?
I'M FIXING A BIKE AT HOME.
MY LITTLE SISTER'S.
DAD AND GRAMPS KEEP PUTTING IT OFF.
AND SUZUKO WAS GRIPING ABOUT IT, SO I...
I SEE.
HA HA...
OKAY, JUST WAIT THERE.
HUH?
STEP
STEP
I'LL COME OVER AND HELP.
STEP
STEP
I SHOULD GET THERE IN ABOUT FOUR HOURS, SO WAIT UP FOR ME!
HARU?!
BEEP!
STEP

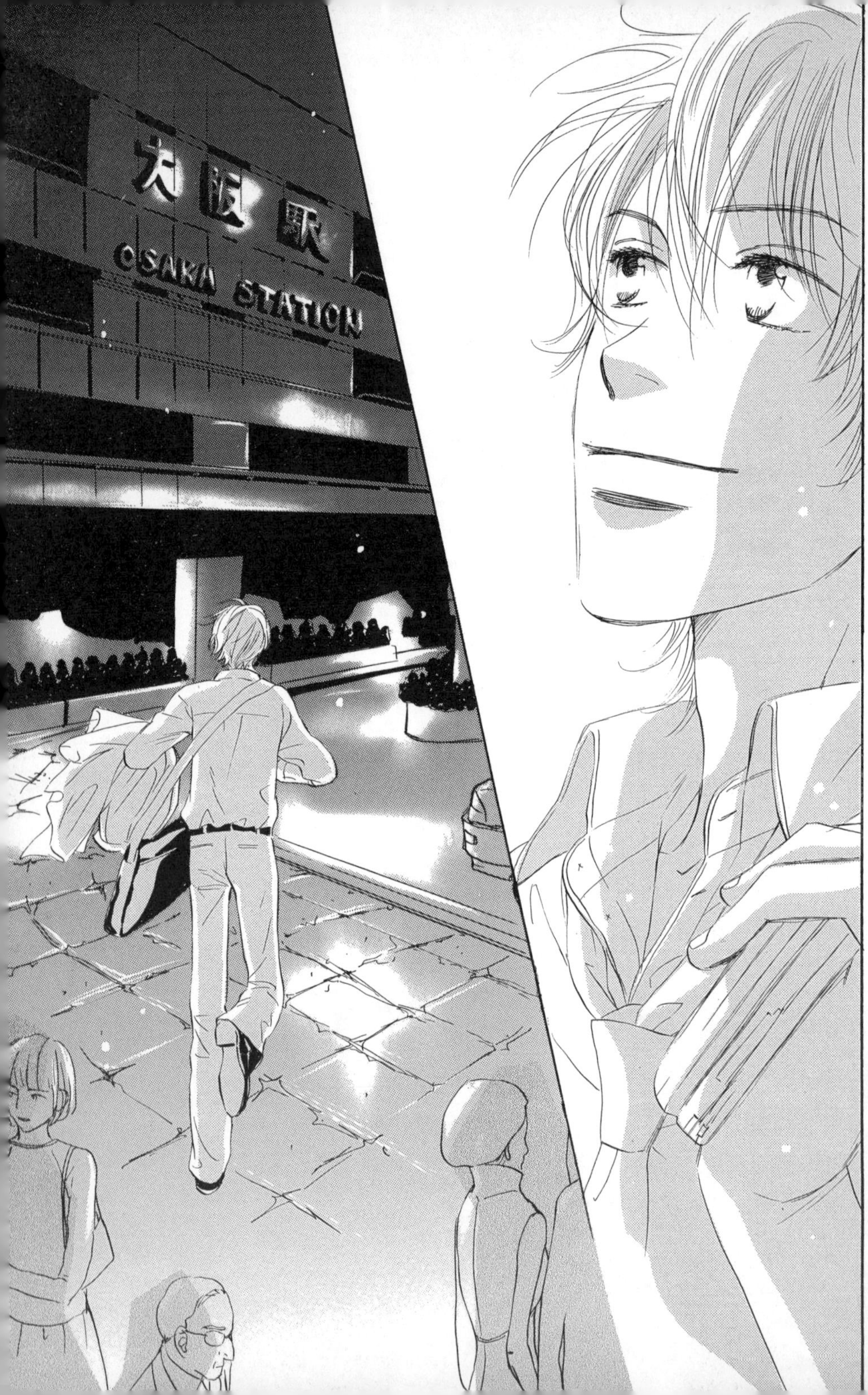
大阪駅
OSAKA STATION

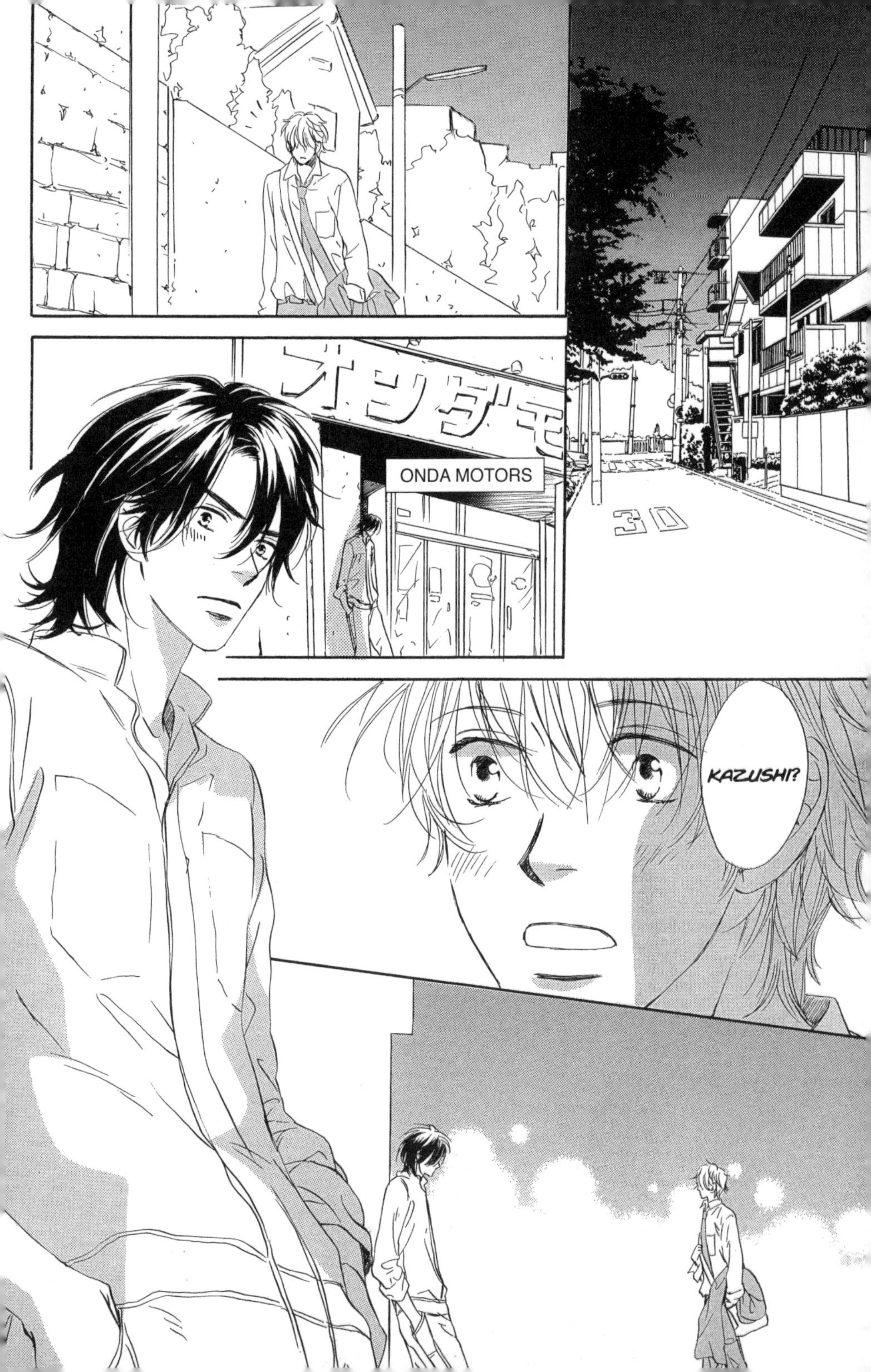
オンダモ
ONDA MOTORS
30
KAZUSHI?

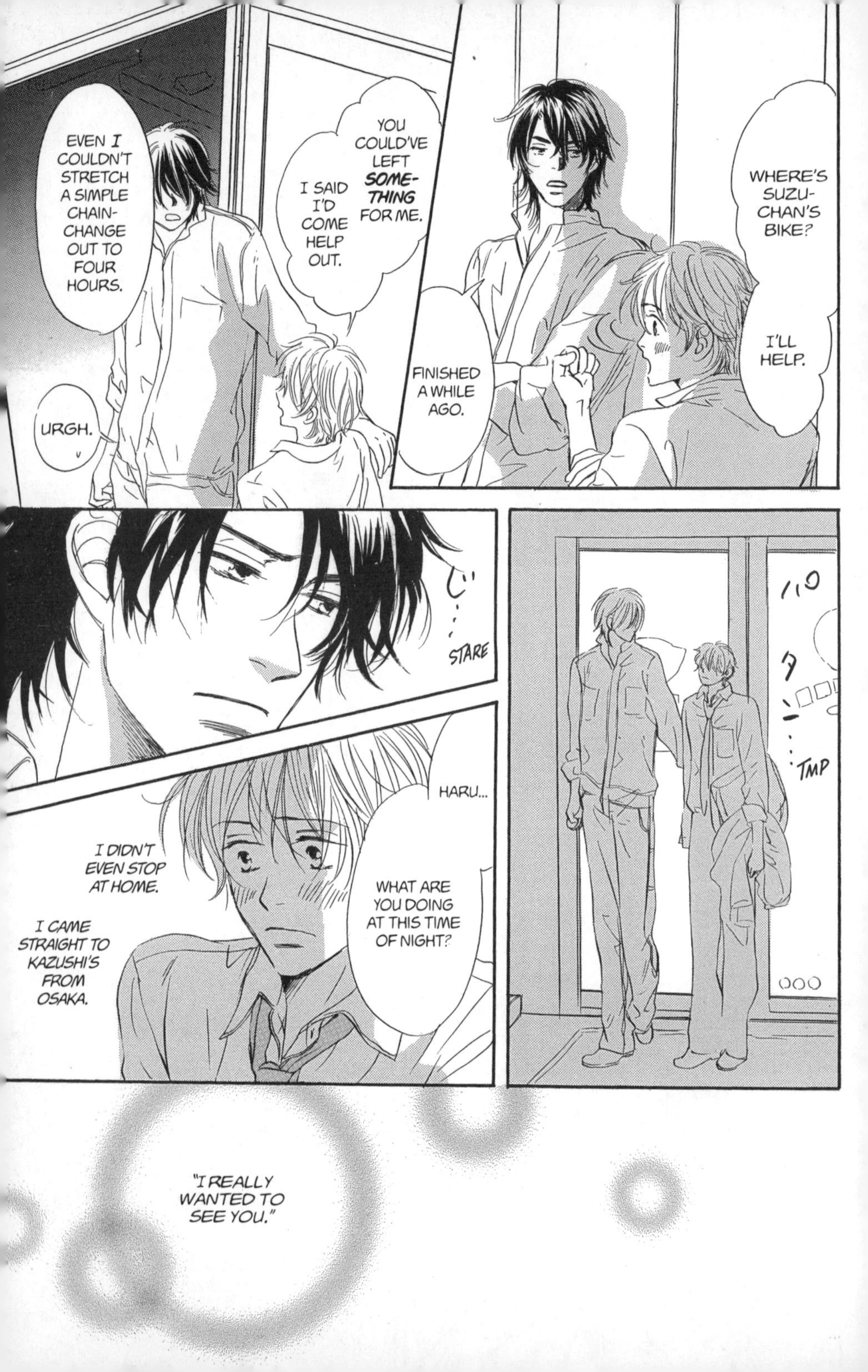
WHERE'S SUZU-CHAN'S BIKE?
I'LL HELP.
FINISHED A WHILE AGO.
YOU COULD'VE LEFT SOMETHING FOR ME.
I SAID I'D COME HELP OUT.
EVEN I COULDN'T STRETCH A SIMPLE CHAIN-CHANGE OUT TO FOUR HOURS.
URGH.
パタン…
TMP
じ…
STARE
HARU...
WHAT ARE YOU DOING AT THIS TIME OF NIGHT?
I DIDN'T EVEN STOP AT HOME.
I CAME STRAIGHT TO KAZUSHI'S FROM OSAKA.
"I REALLY WANTED TO SEE YOU."

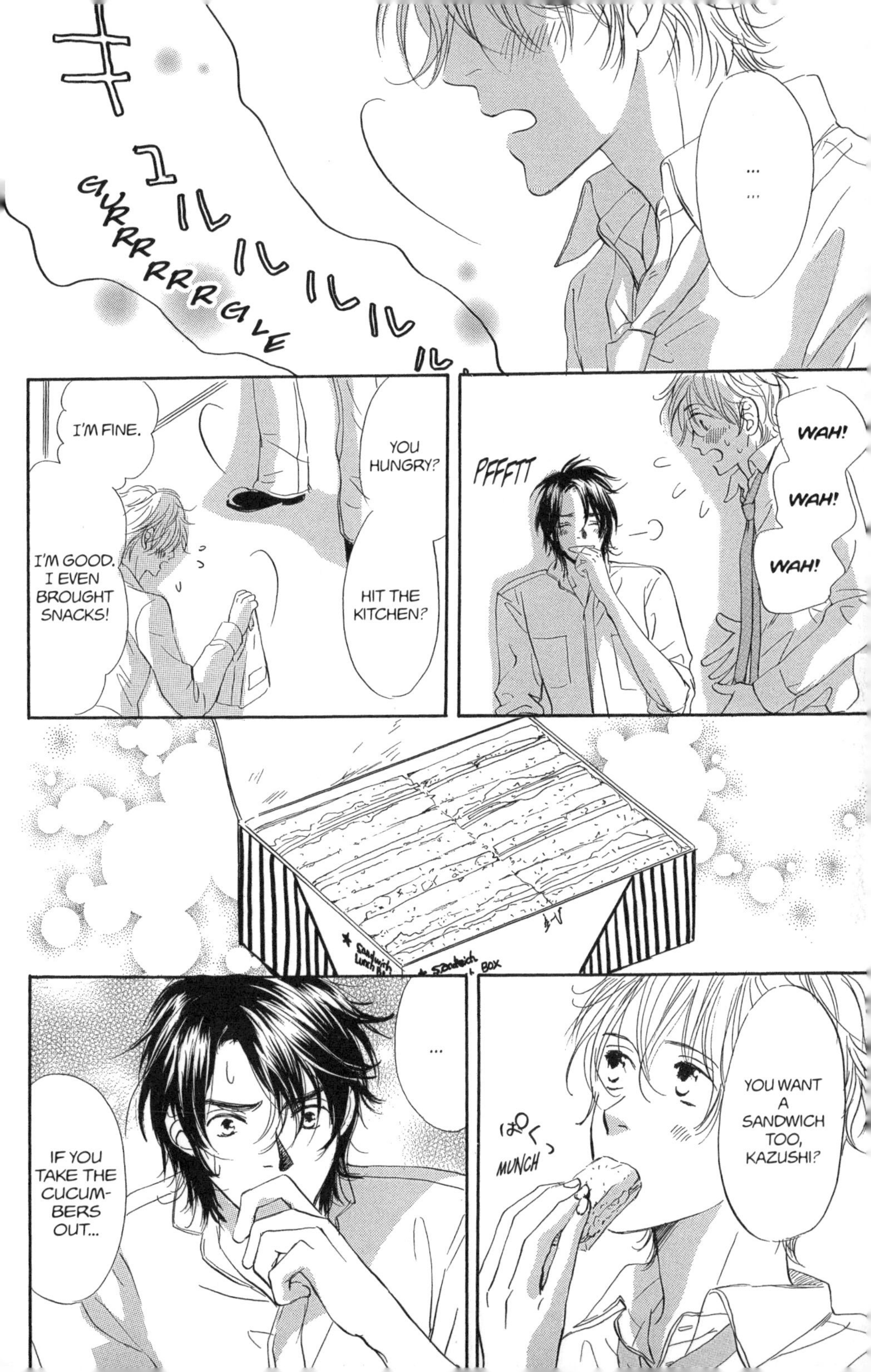
キュルルルルル
GURRRRRRRGLE
... ...
WAH!
WAH!
WAH!
PFFFTT
YOU HUNGRY?
HIT THE KITCHEN?
I'M FINE.
I'M GOOD. I EVEN BROUGHT SNACKS!
YOU WANT A SANDWICH TOO, KAZUSHI?
ぱくっ
MUNCH
...
IF YOU TAKE THE CUCUMBERS OUT...

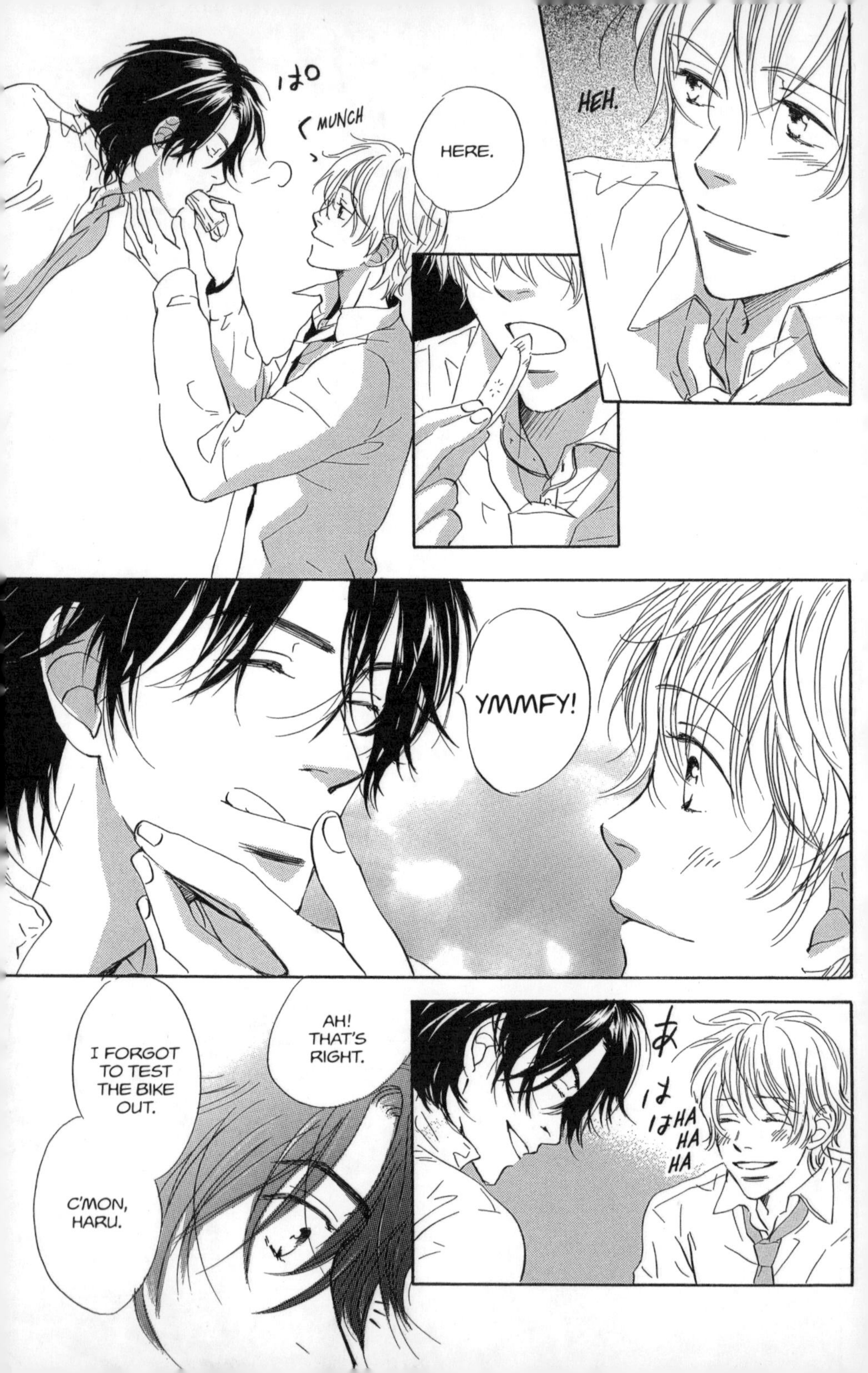
HEH.
ぱ
MUNCH
HERE.
YMMFY!
あはは
HA HA HA
AH! THAT'S RIGHT.
I FORGOT TO TEST THE BIKE OUT.
C'MON, HARU.

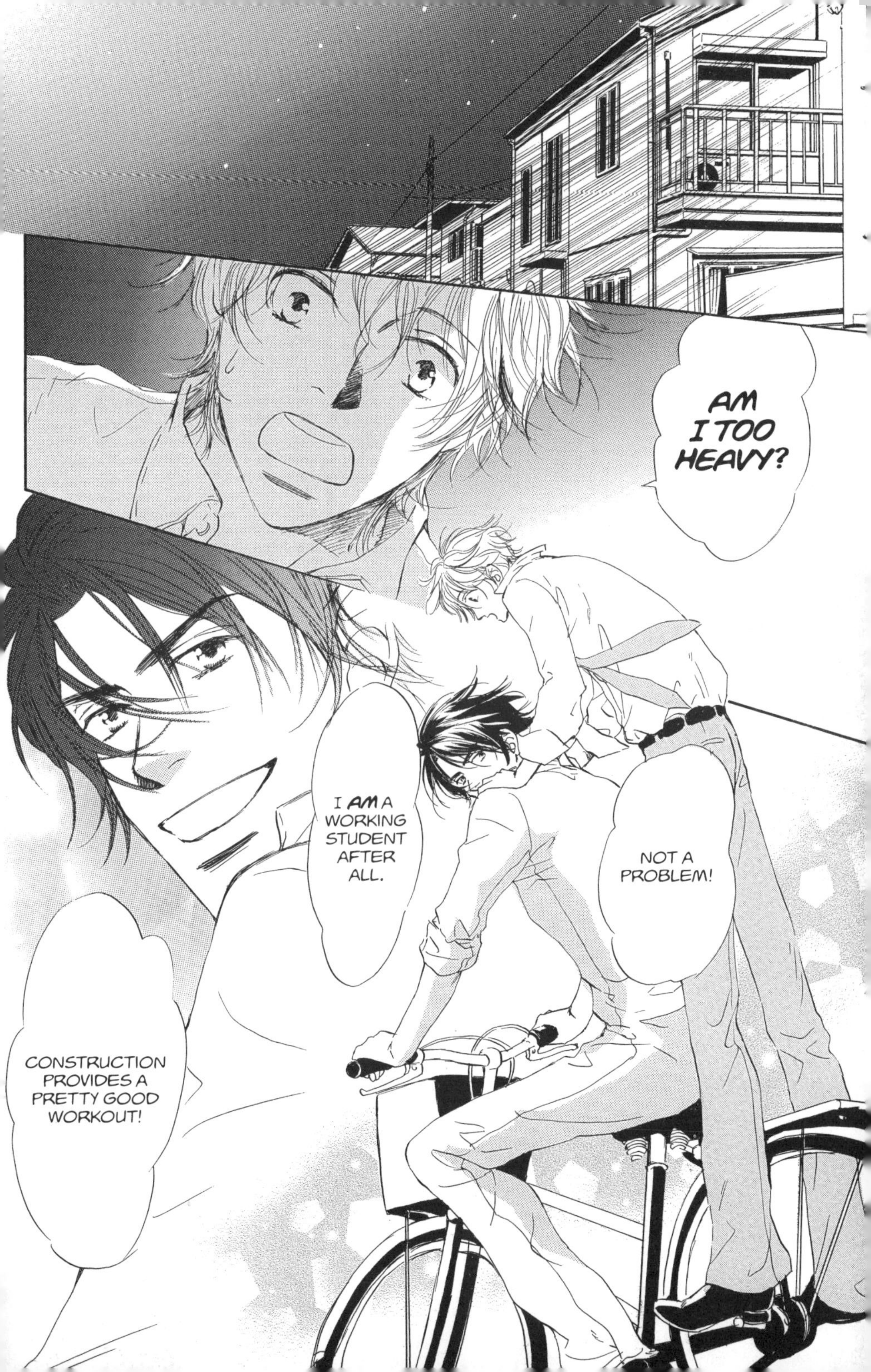
AM I TOO HEAVY?
NOT A PROBLEM!
I **AM** A WORKING STUDENT AFTER ALL.
CONSTRUCTION PROVIDES A PRETTY GOOD WORKOUT!

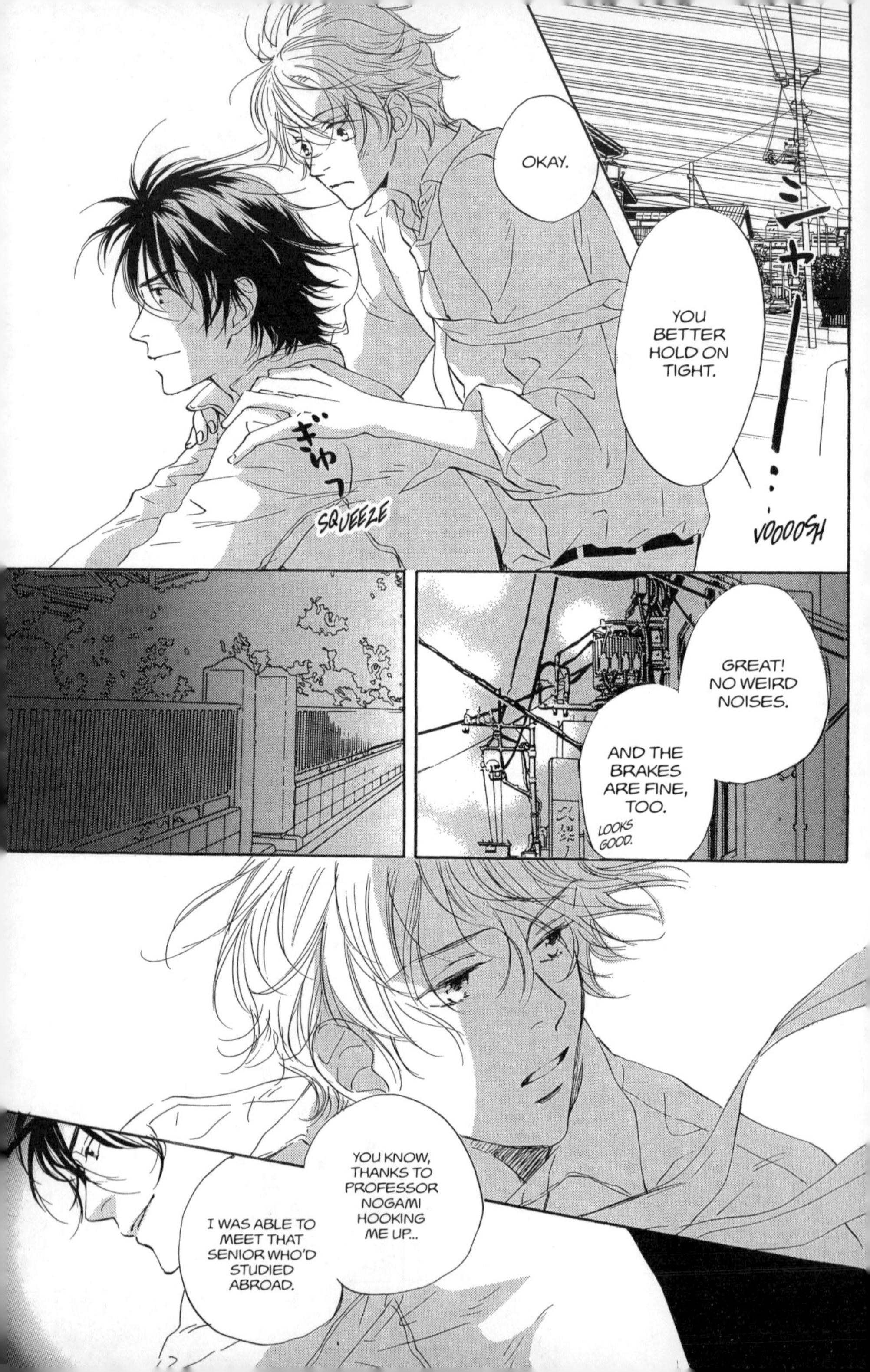
YOU BETTER HOLD ON TIGHT.
OKAY.
VOOOOSH
ぎゅっ
SQUEEZE
GREAT! NO WEIRD NOISES.
AND THE BRAKES ARE FINE, TOO.
LOOKS GOOD.
YOU KNOW, THANKS TO PROFESSOR NOGAMI HOOKING ME UP...
I WAS ABLE TO MEET THAT SENIOR WHO'D STUDIED ABROAD.

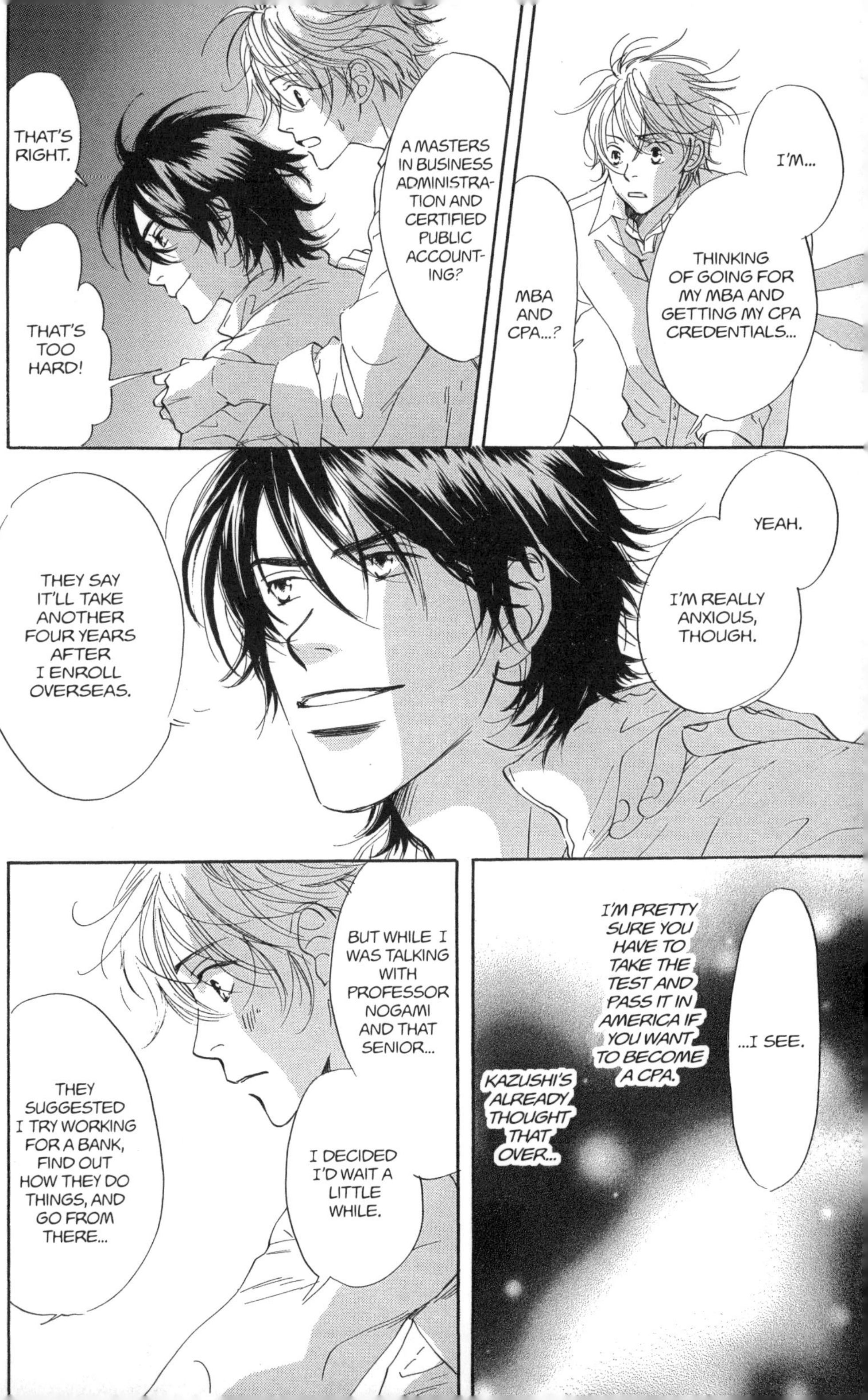
I'M...
THINKING OF GOING FOR MY MBA AND GETTING MY CPA CREDENTIALS...
MBA AND CPA...?
A MASTERS IN BUSINESS ADMINISTRATION AND CERTIFIED PUBLIC ACCOUNTING?
THAT'S RIGHT.
THAT'S TOO HARD!
YEAH.
I'M REALLY ANXIOUS, THOUGH.
THEY SAY IT'LL TAKE ANOTHER FOUR YEARS AFTER I ENROLL OVERSEAS.
...I SEE.
I'M PRETTY SURE YOU HAVE TO TAKE THE TEST AND PASS IT IN AMERICA IF YOU WANT TO BECOME A CPA.
KAZUSHI'S ALREADY THOUGHT THAT OVER...
BUT WHILE I WAS TALKING WITH PROFESSOR NOGAMI AND THAT SENIOR...
I DECIDED I'D WAIT A LITTLE WHILE.
THEY SUGGESTED I TRY WORKING FOR A BANK, FIND OUT HOW THEY DO THINGS, AND GO FROM THERE...

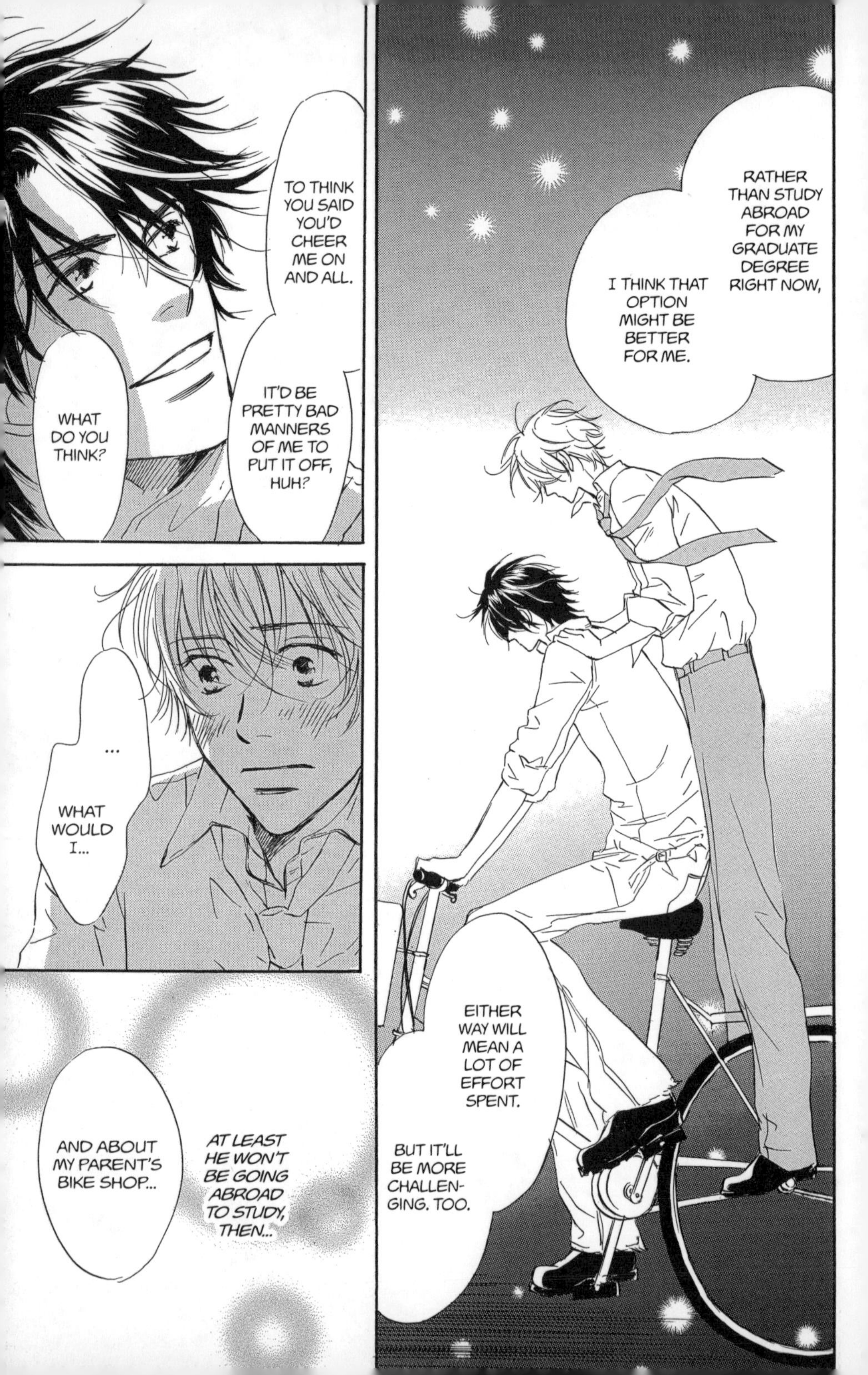
RATHER THAN STUDY ABROAD FOR MY GRADUATE DEGREE RIGHT NOW,
I THINK THAT OPTION MIGHT BE BETTER FOR ME.
EITHER WAY WILL MEAN A LOT OF EFFORT SPENT.
BUT IT'LL BE MORE CHALLENG-ING. TOO.
TO THINK YOU SAID YOU'D CHEER ME ON AND ALL.
IT'D BE PRETTY BAD MANNERS OF ME TO PUT IT OFF, HUH?
WHAT DO YOU THINK?
...
WHAT WOULD I...
AT LEAST HE WON'T BE GOING ABROAD TO STUDY, THEN...
AND ABOUT MY PARENT'S BIKE SHOP...

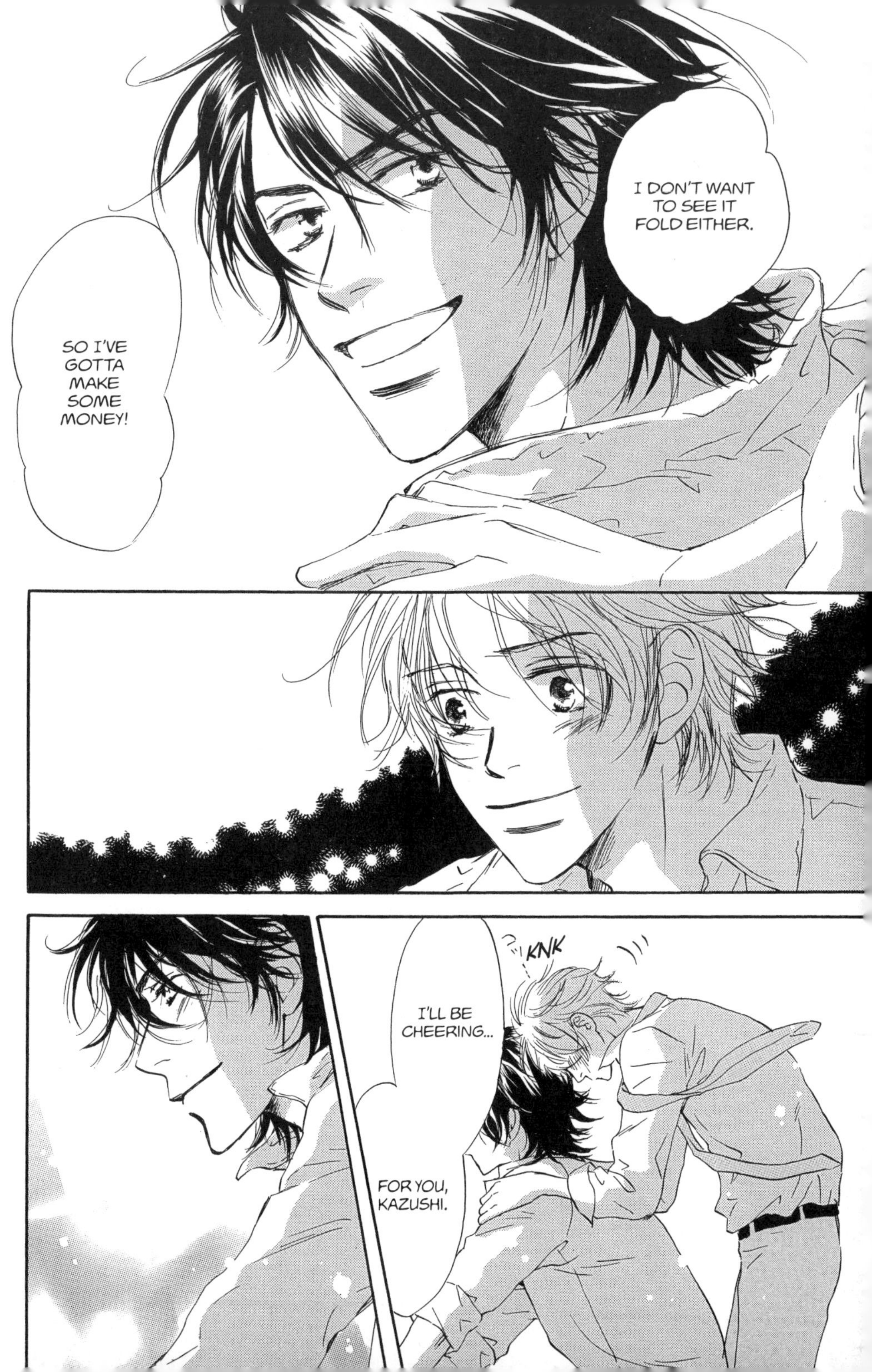
I DON'T WANT TO SEE IT FOLD EITHER.
SO I'VE GOTTA MAKE SOME MONEY!
KNK
I'LL BE CHEERING...
FOR YOU, KAZUSHI.

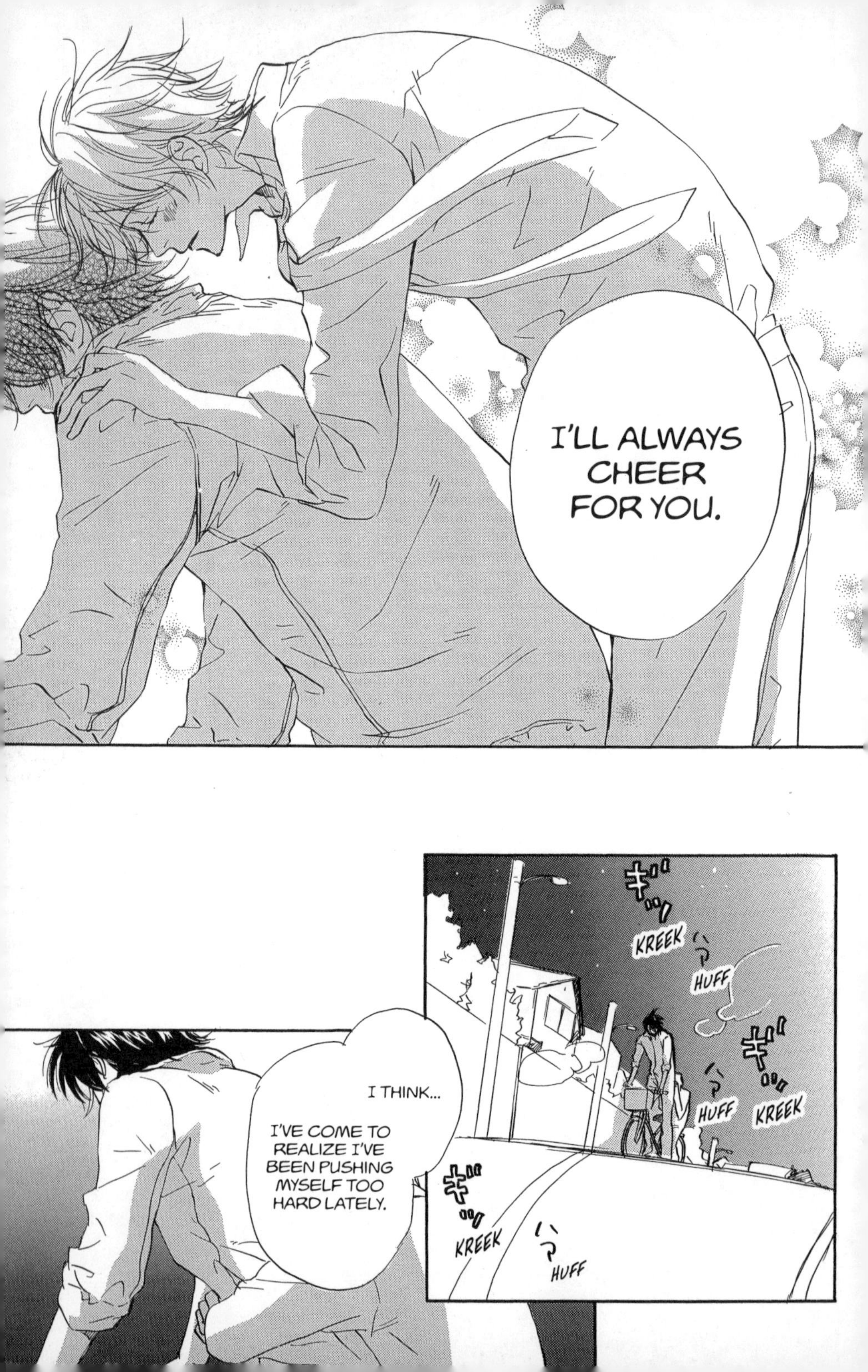
I'LL ALWAYS CHEER FOR YOU.
KREEK
HUFF
KREEK
HUFF
KREEK
HUFF
I THINK...
I'VE COME TO REALIZE I'VE BEEN PUSHING MYSELF TOO HARD LATELY.

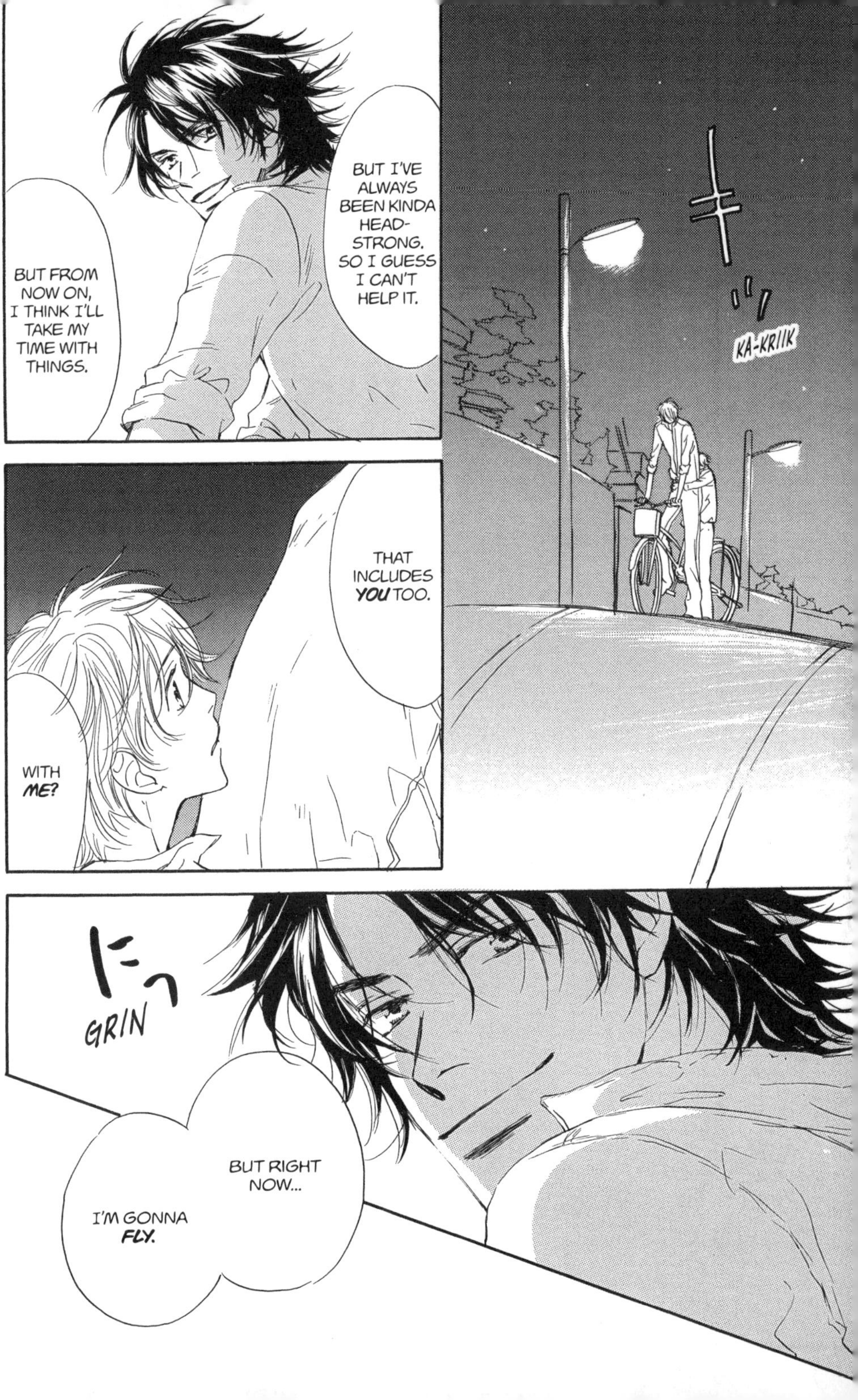
KA-KRIIK
BUT I'VE ALWAYS BEEN KINDA HEAD-STRONG. SO I GUESS I CAN'T HELP IT.
BUT FROM NOW ON, I THINK I'LL TAKE MY TIME WITH THINGS.
THAT INCLUDES YOU TOO.
WITH ME?
GRIN
BUT RIGHT NOW...
I'M GONNA FLY.

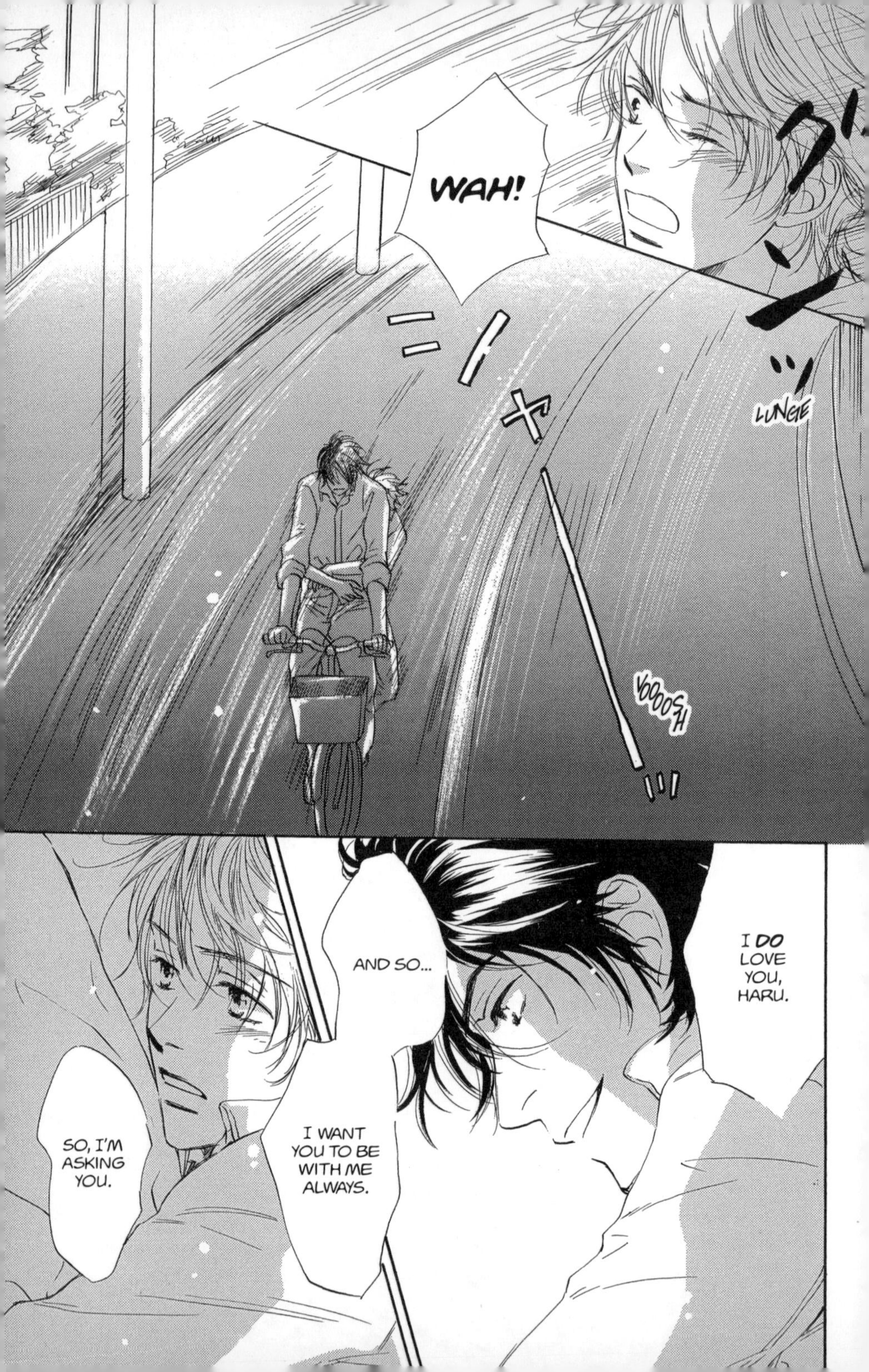
WAH!
LUNGE
VOOOOSH
I DO LOVE YOU, HARU.
AND SO...
I WANT YOU TO BE WITH ME ALWAYS.
SO, I'M ASKING YOU.

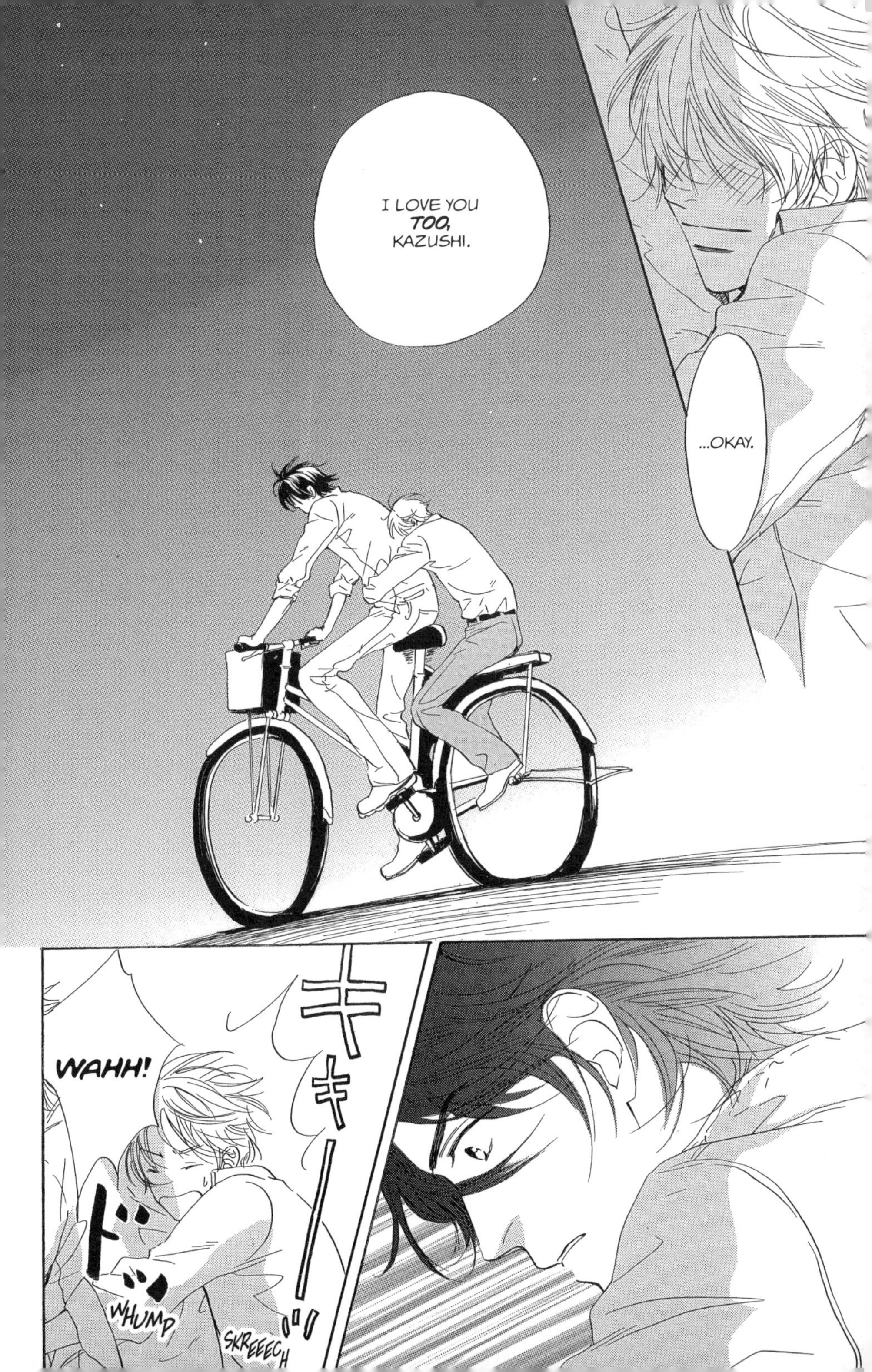
...OKAY.
I LOVE YOU **TOO,** KAZUSHI.
キキー
WAHH!
ドッ
WHUMP
SKREEECH

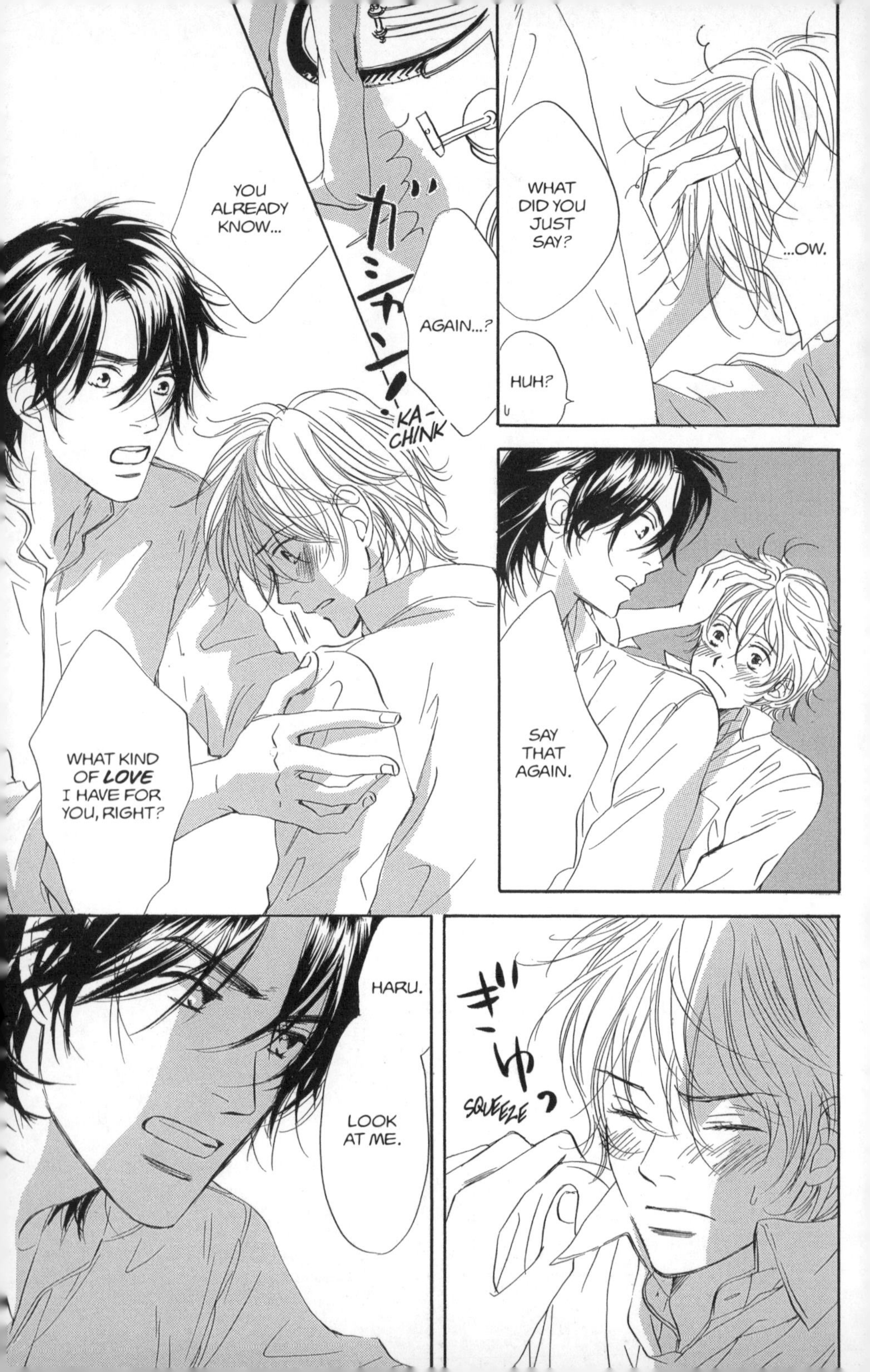

WHAT DID YOU JUST SAY?
...OW.
HUH?
SAY THAT AGAIN.
AGAIN...?
ガシャン
KA-CHINK
YOU ALREADY KNOW...
WHAT KIND OF **LOVE** I HAVE FOR YOU, RIGHT?
ぎゅっ
SQUEEZE
HARU.
LOOK AT ME.

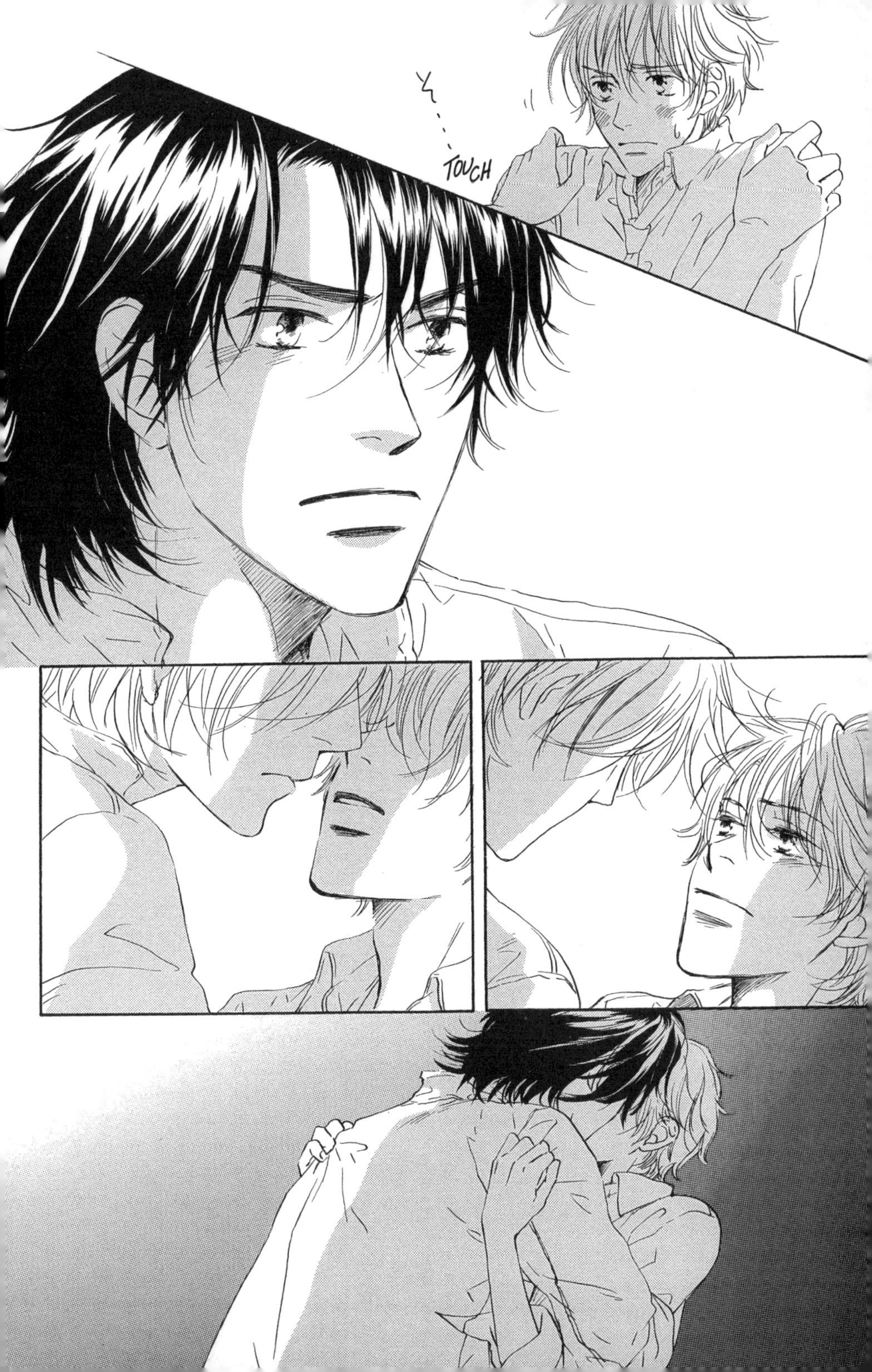
TOUCH

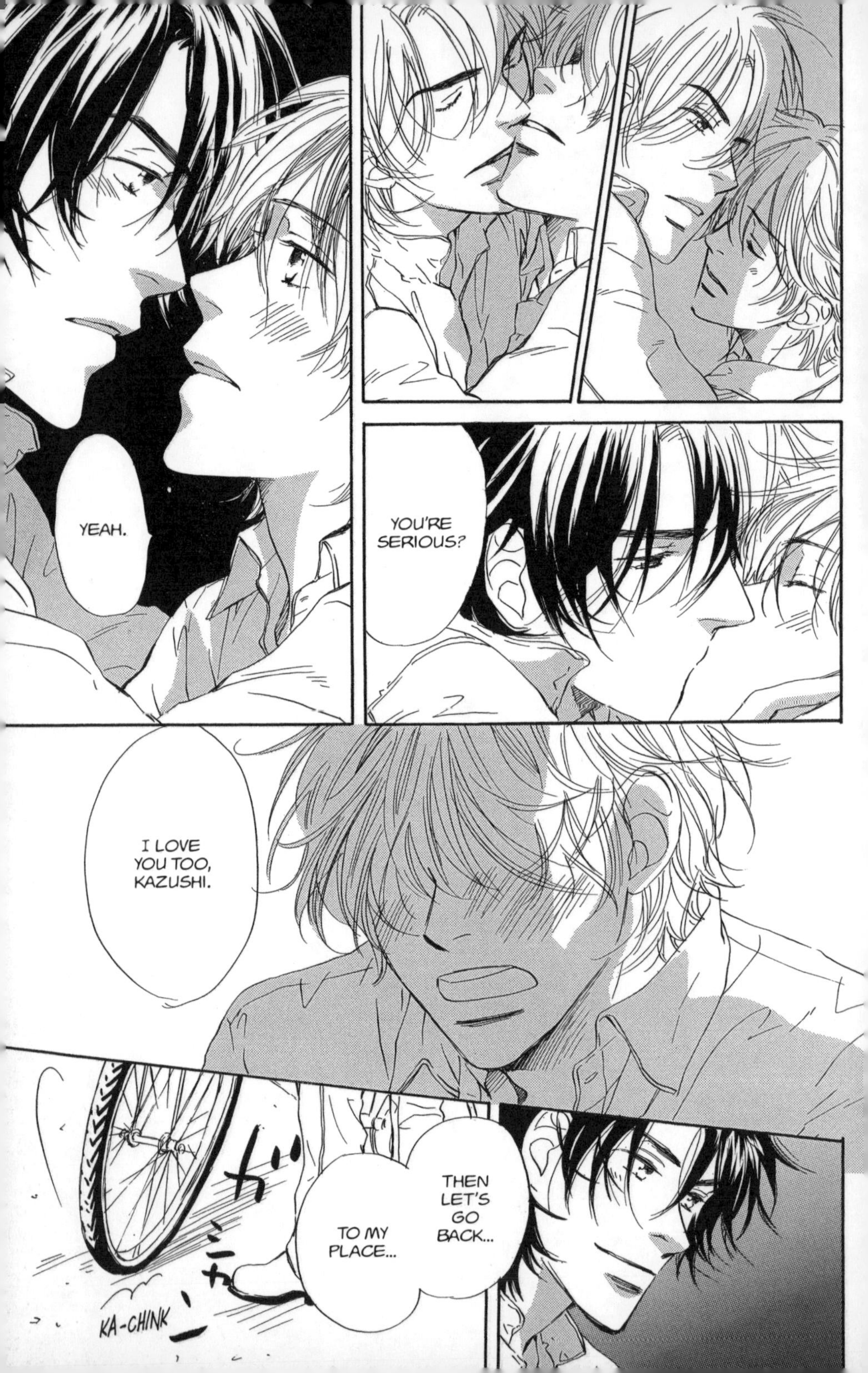
YOU'RE SERIOUS?
YEAH.
I LOVE YOU TOO, KAZUSHI.
THEN LET'S GO BACK...
TO MY PLACE...
KA-CHINK

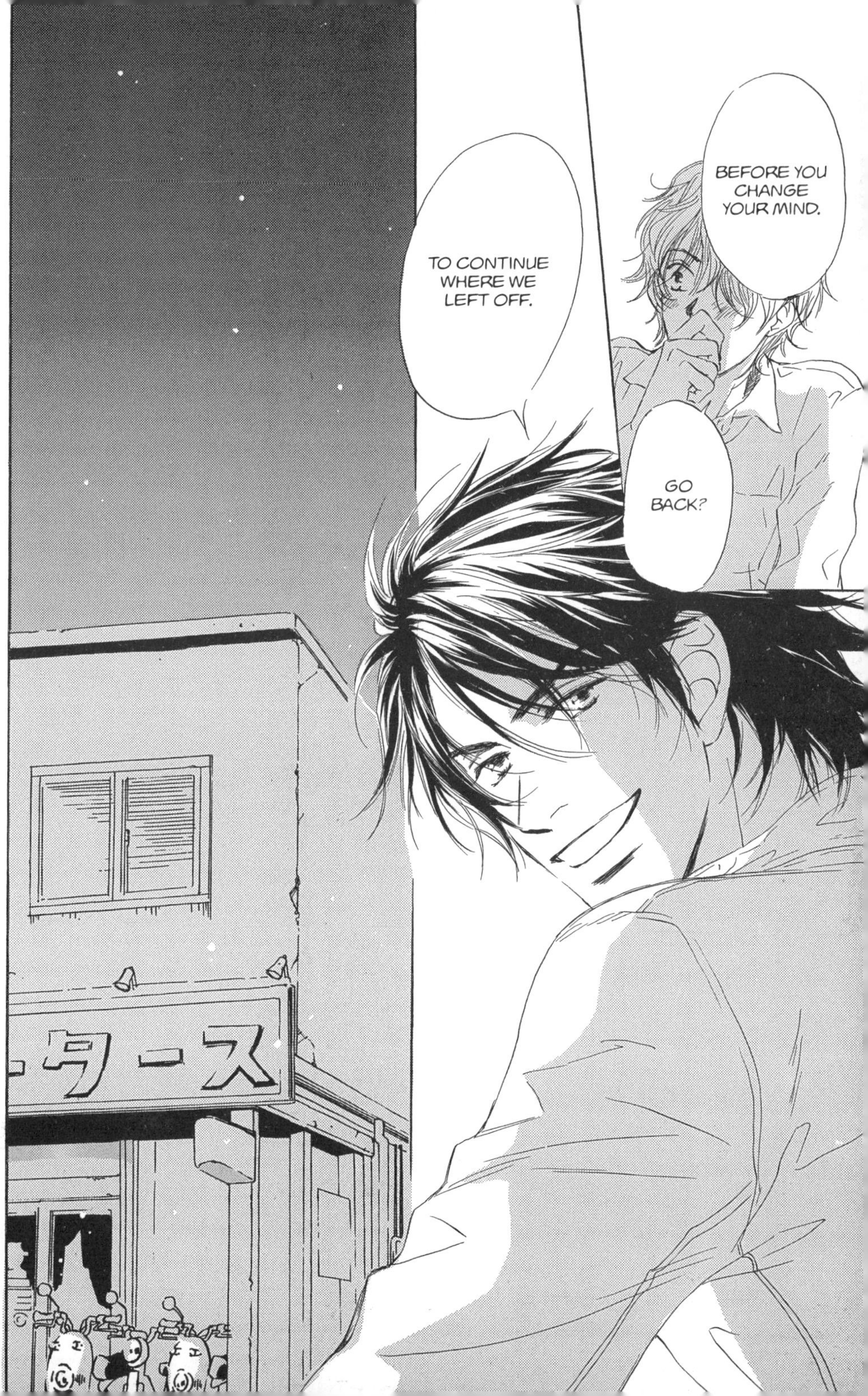
BEFORE YOU CHANGE YOUR MIND.
GO BACK?
TO CONTINUE WHERE WE LEFT OFF.
タース

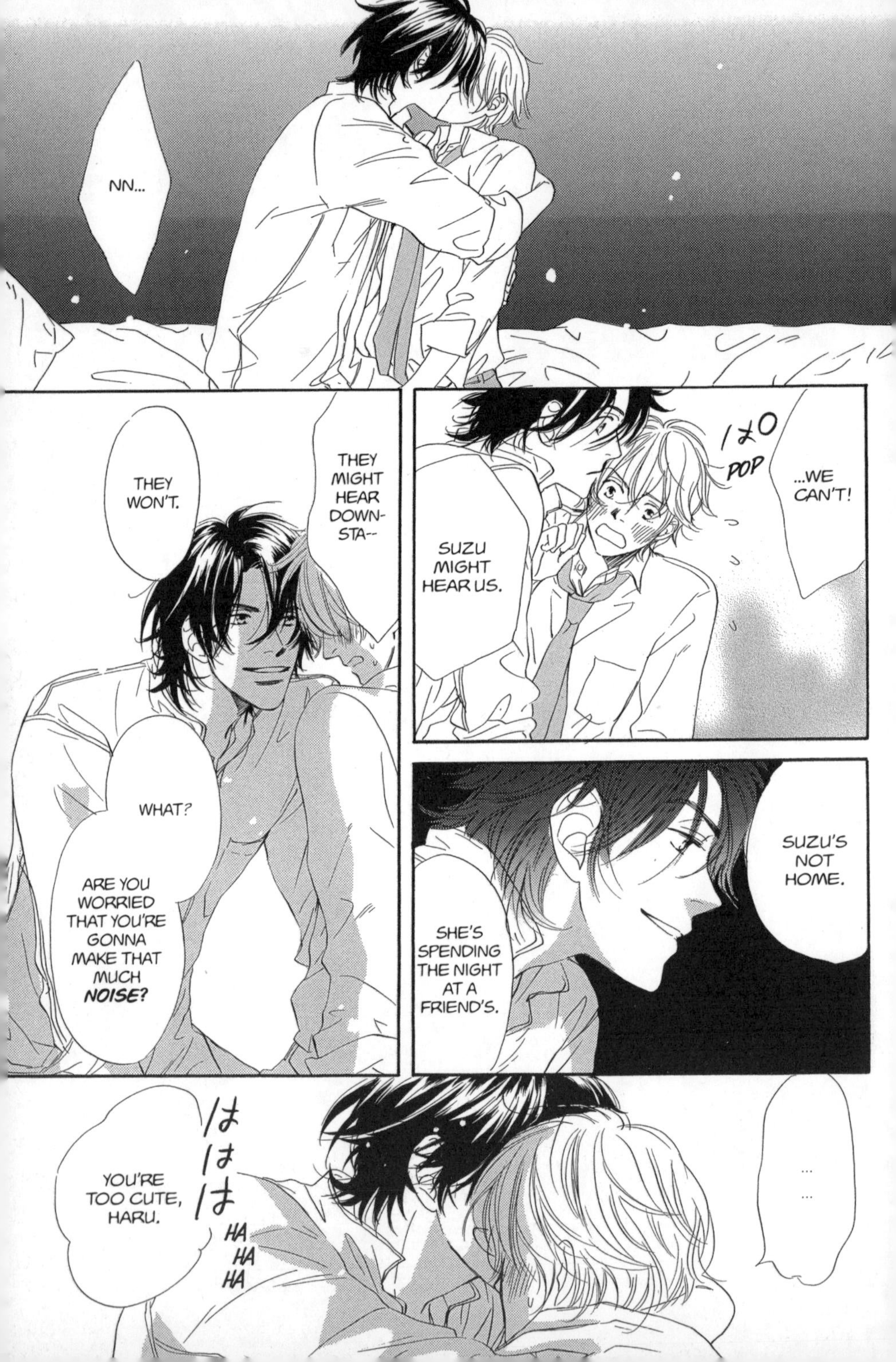
NN...
...WE CAN'T!
POP
SUZU MIGHT HEAR US.
SUZU'S NOT HOME.
SHE'S SPENDING THE NIGHT AT A FRIEND'S.
THEY MIGHT HEAR DOWNSTA--
THEY WON'T.
WHAT?
ARE YOU WORRIED THAT YOU'RE GONNA MAKE THAT MUCH **NOISE?**
... ...
ははは
HA HA HA
YOU'RE TOO CUTE, HARU.

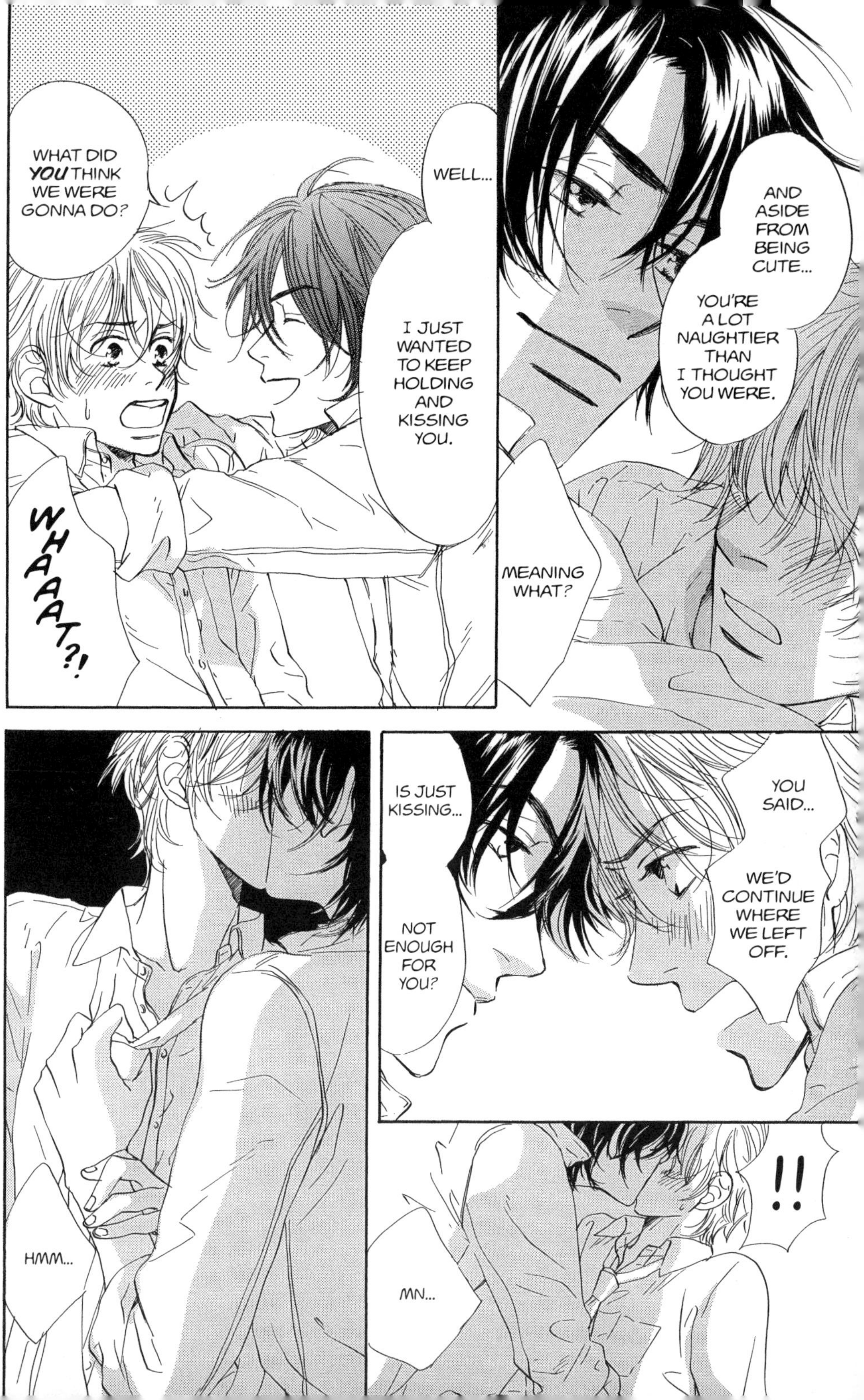
AND ASIDE FROM BEING CUTE...
YOU'RE A LOT NAUGHTIER THAN I THOUGHT YOU WERE.
MEANING WHAT?
WELL...
I JUST WANTED TO KEEP HOLDING AND KISSING YOU.
WHAT DID *YOU* THINK WE WERE GONNA DO?
WHAAAT?!
YOU SAID...
WE'D CONTINUE WHERE WE LEFT OFF.
IS JUST KISSING...
NOT ENOUGH FOR YOU?
!!
MN...
HMM...

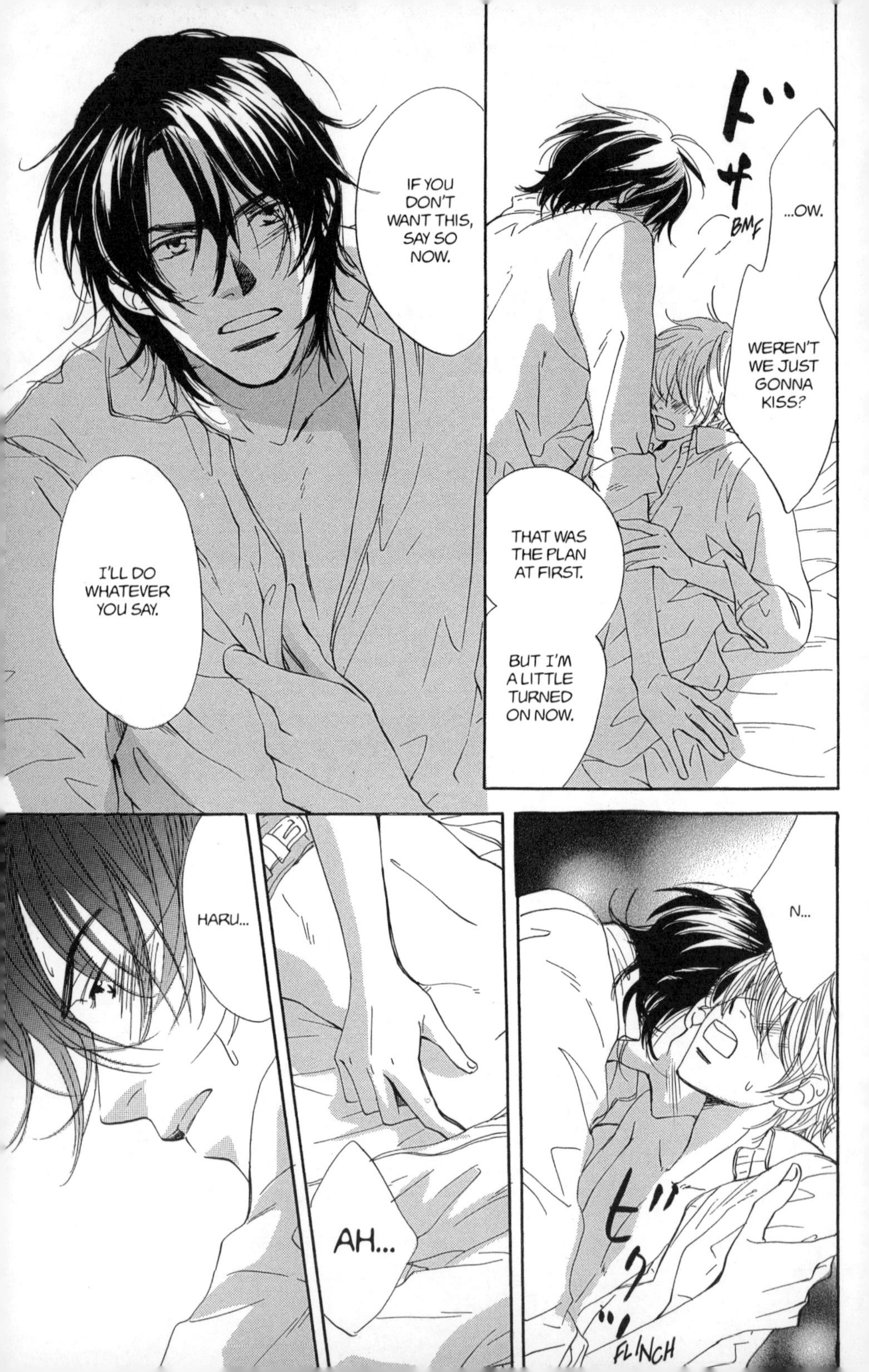
ドサ
BMF
...OW.
WEREN'T WE JUST GONNA KISS?
THAT WAS THE PLAN AT FIRST.
BUT I'M A LITTLE TURNED ON NOW.
IF YOU DON'T WANT THIS, SAY SO NOW.
I'LL DO WHATEVER YOU SAY.
N...
ビクッ
FLINCH
AH...
HARU...

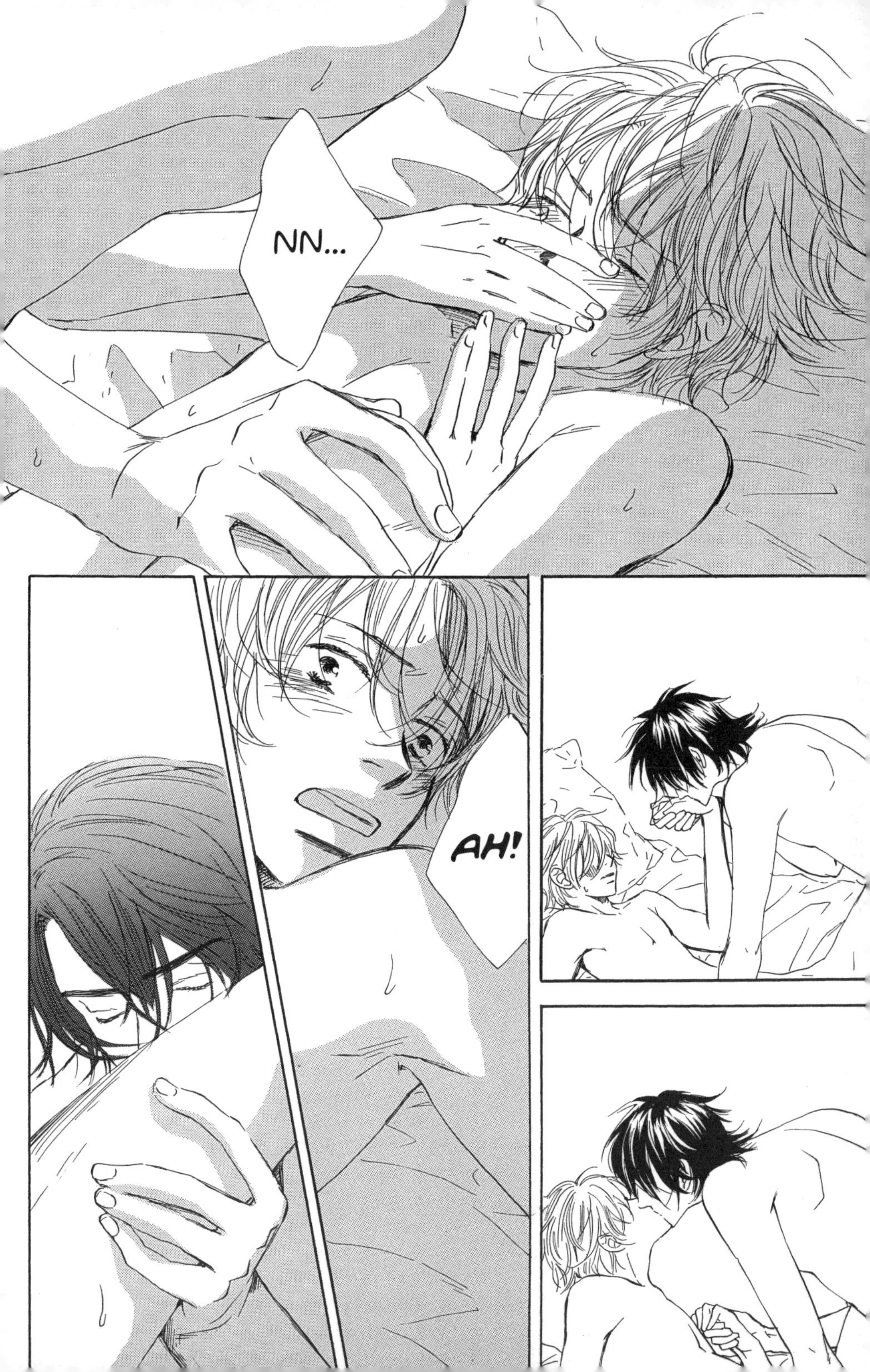
NN...
AH!

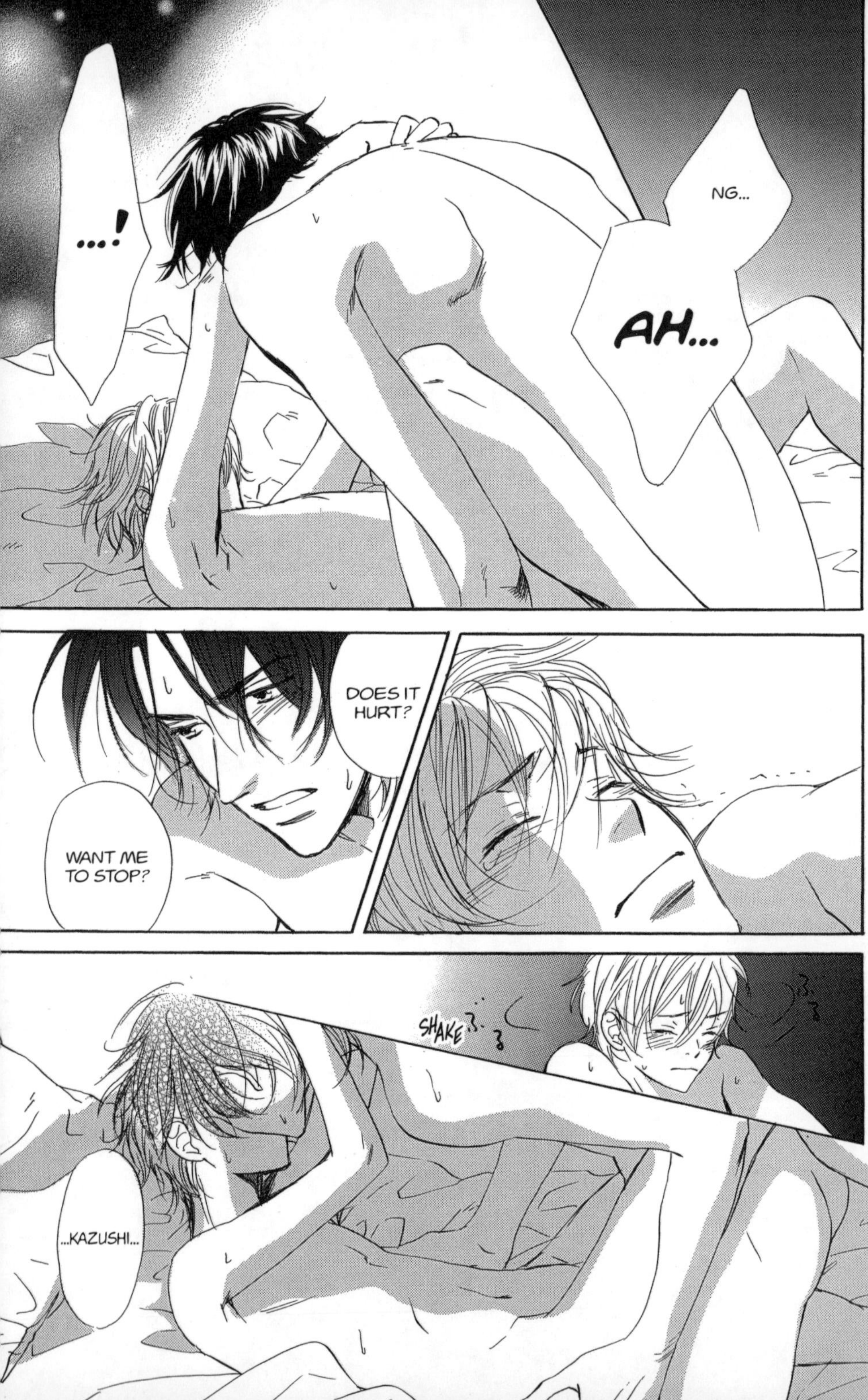
NG...
AH...
...!
DOES IT HURT?
WANT ME TO STOP?
SHAKE
...KAZUSHI...

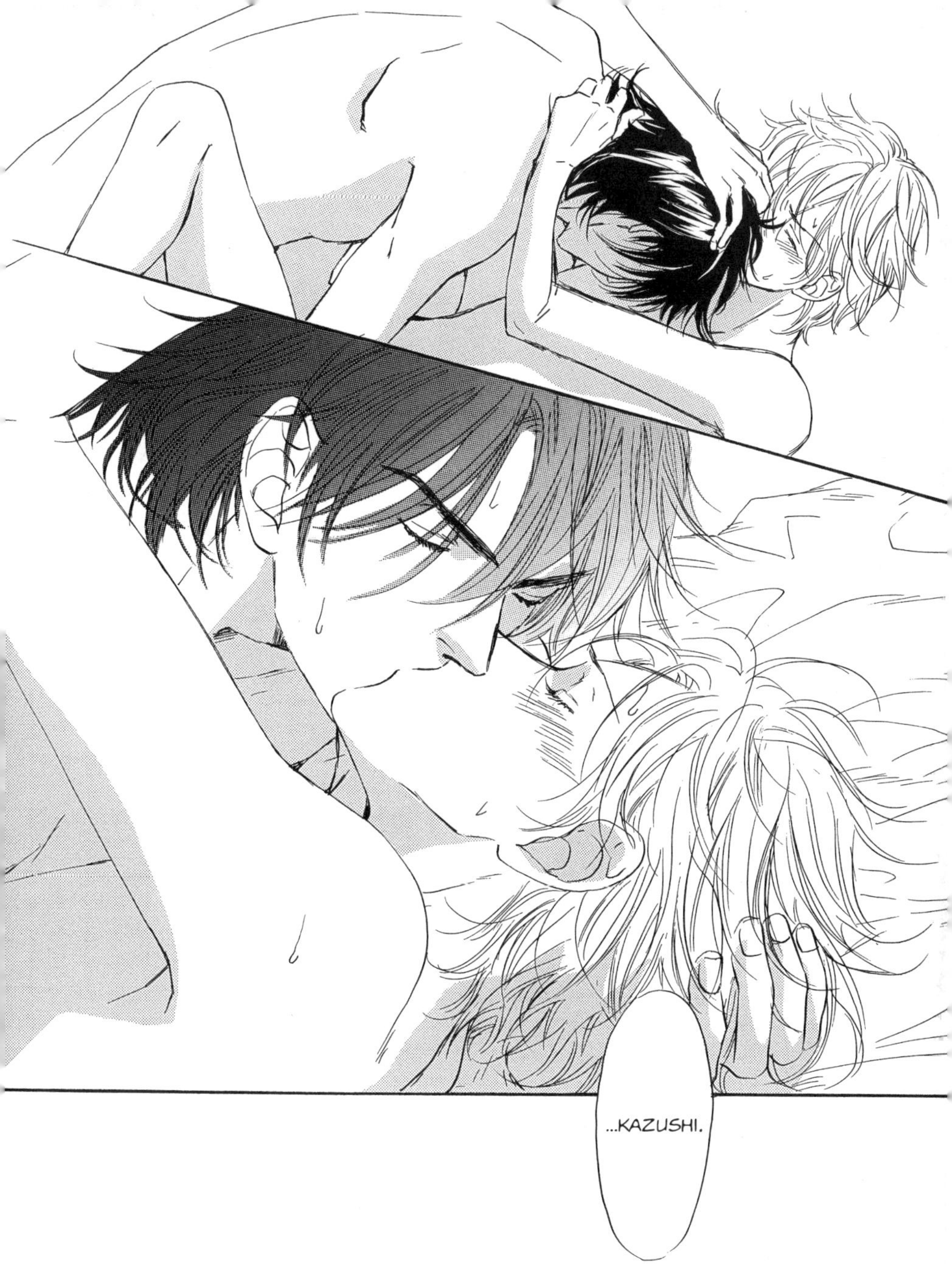
...KAZUSHI.

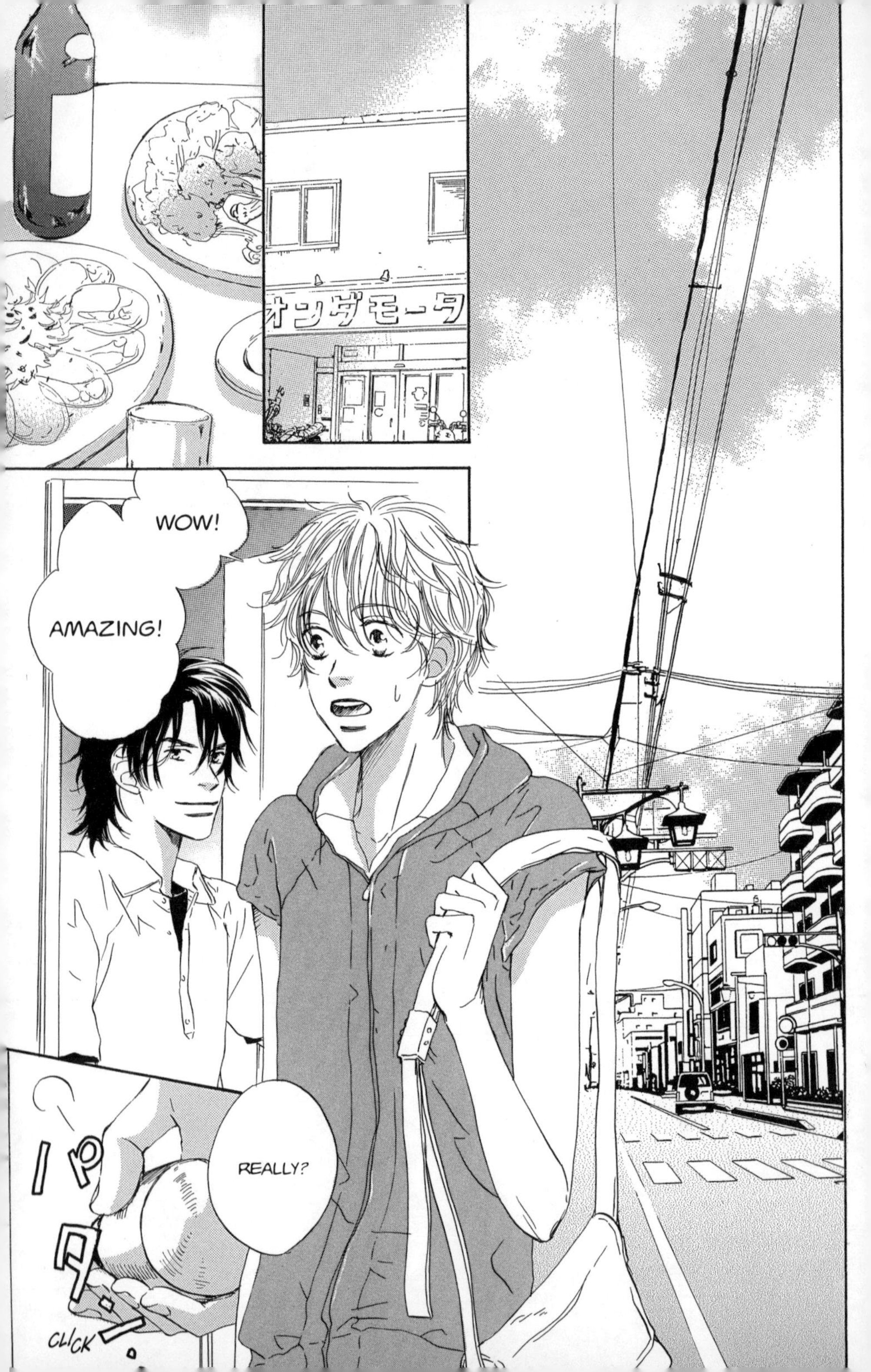
オンダモータ
WOW!
AMAZING!
REALLY?
CLICK

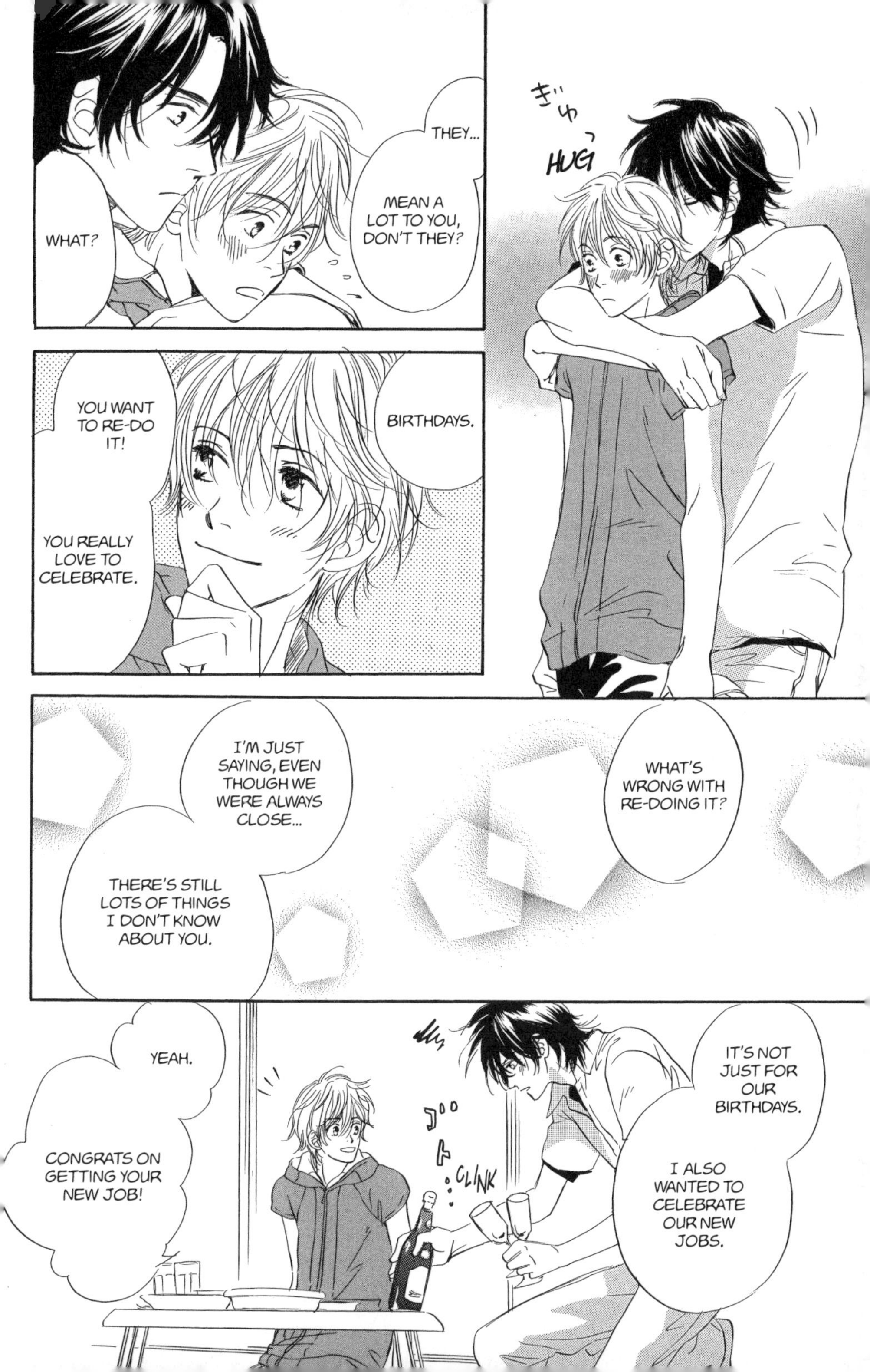
ぎゅっ
HUG
THEY...
MEAN A LOT TO YOU, DON'T THEY?
WHAT?
BIRTHDAYS.
YOU WANT TO RE-DO IT!
YOU REALLY LOVE TO CELEBRATE.
WHAT'S WRONG WITH RE-DOING IT?
I'M JUST SAYING, EVEN THOUGH WE WERE ALWAYS CLOSE...
THERE'S STILL LOTS OF THINGS I DON'T KNOW ABOUT YOU.
IT'S NOT JUST FOR OUR BIRTHDAYS.
I ALSO WANTED TO CELEBRATE OUR NEW JOBS.
CLINK
YEAH.
CONGRATS ON GETTING YOUR NEW JOB!

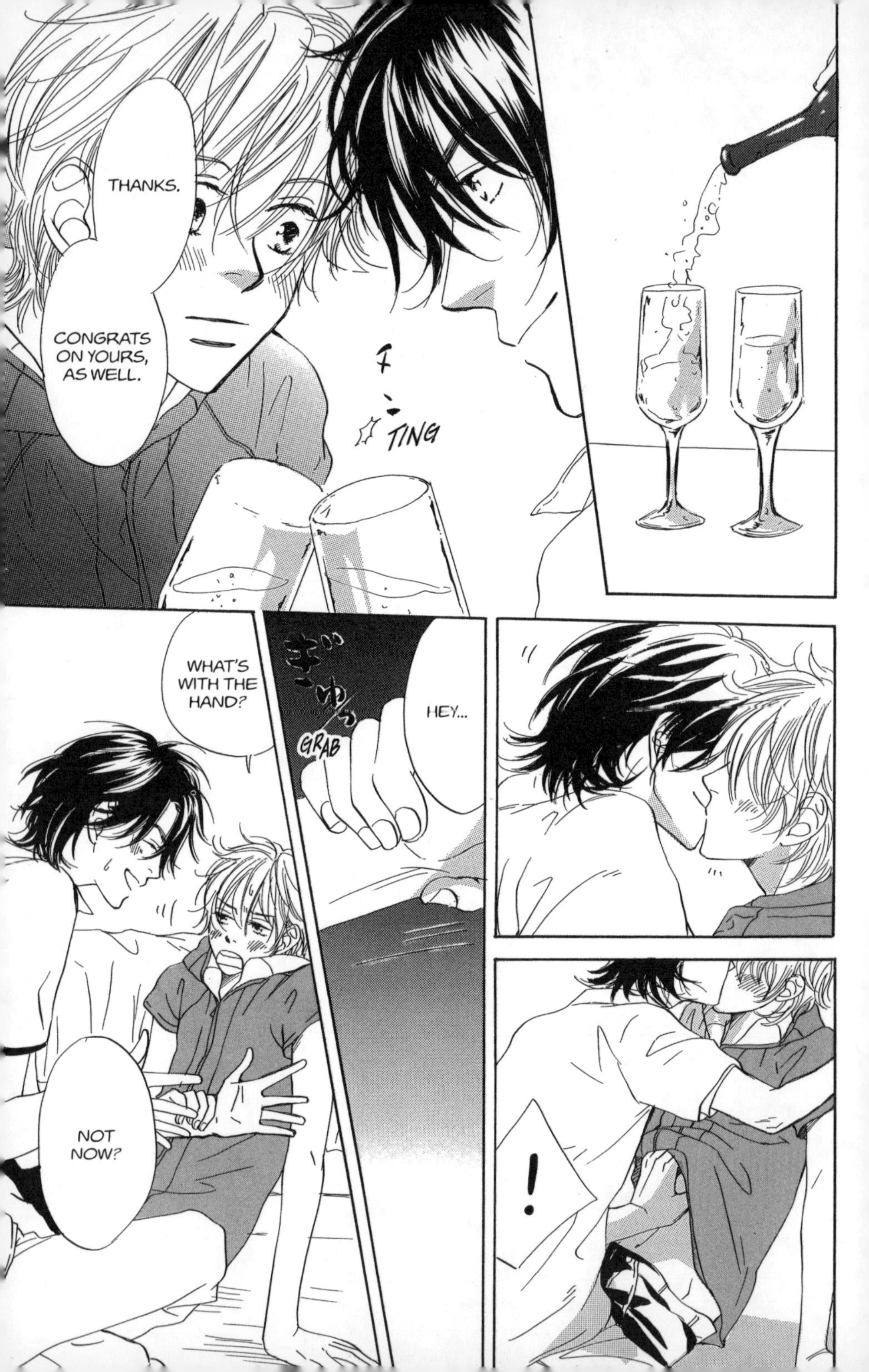
THANKS.
CONGRATS ON YOURS, AS WELL.
TING
!
HEY...
ぎゅっ
GRAB
WHAT'S WITH THE HAND?
NOT NOW?

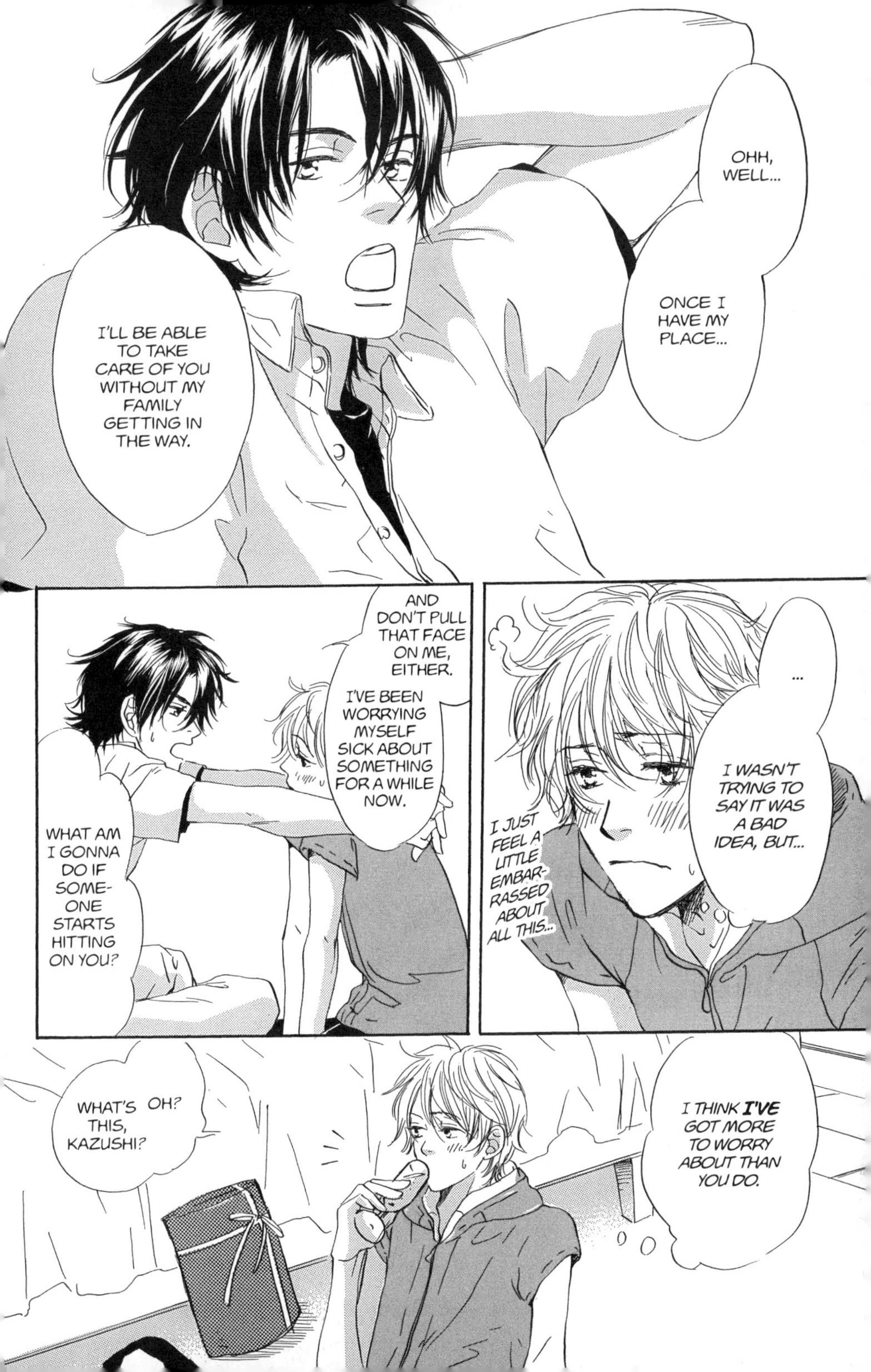
OHH, WELL...
ONCE I HAVE MY PLACE...
I'LL BE ABLE TO TAKE CARE OF YOU WITHOUT MY FAMILY GETTING IN THE WAY.
...
I WASN'T TRYING TO SAY IT WAS A BAD IDEA, BUT...
I JUST FEEL A LITTLE EMBARRASSED ABOUT ALL THIS...
AND DON'T PULL THAT FACE ON ME, EITHER.
I'VE BEEN WORRYING MYSELF SICK ABOUT SOMETHING FOR A WHILE NOW.
WHAT AM I GONNA DO IF SOMEONE STARTS HITTING ON YOU?
I THINK **I'VE** GOT MORE TO WORRY ABOUT THAN YOU DO.
OH?
WHAT'S THIS, KAZUSHI?

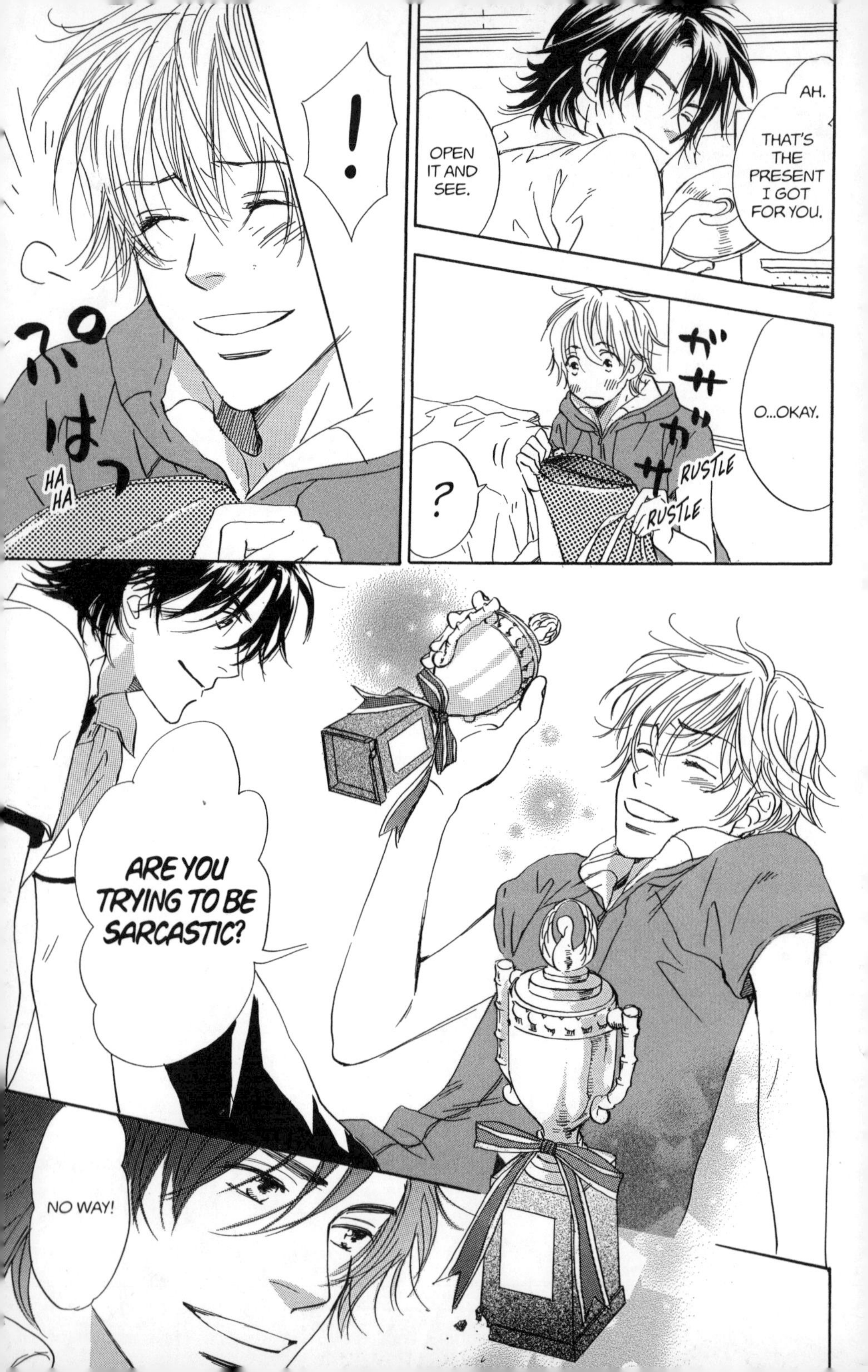
AH.
THAT'S THE PRESENT I GOT FOR YOU.
OPEN IT AND SEE.
O...OKAY.
ガサガサ
RUSTLE RUSTLE
?
!
ぷはっ
HA HA
ARE YOU TRYING TO BE SARCASTIC?
NO WAY!

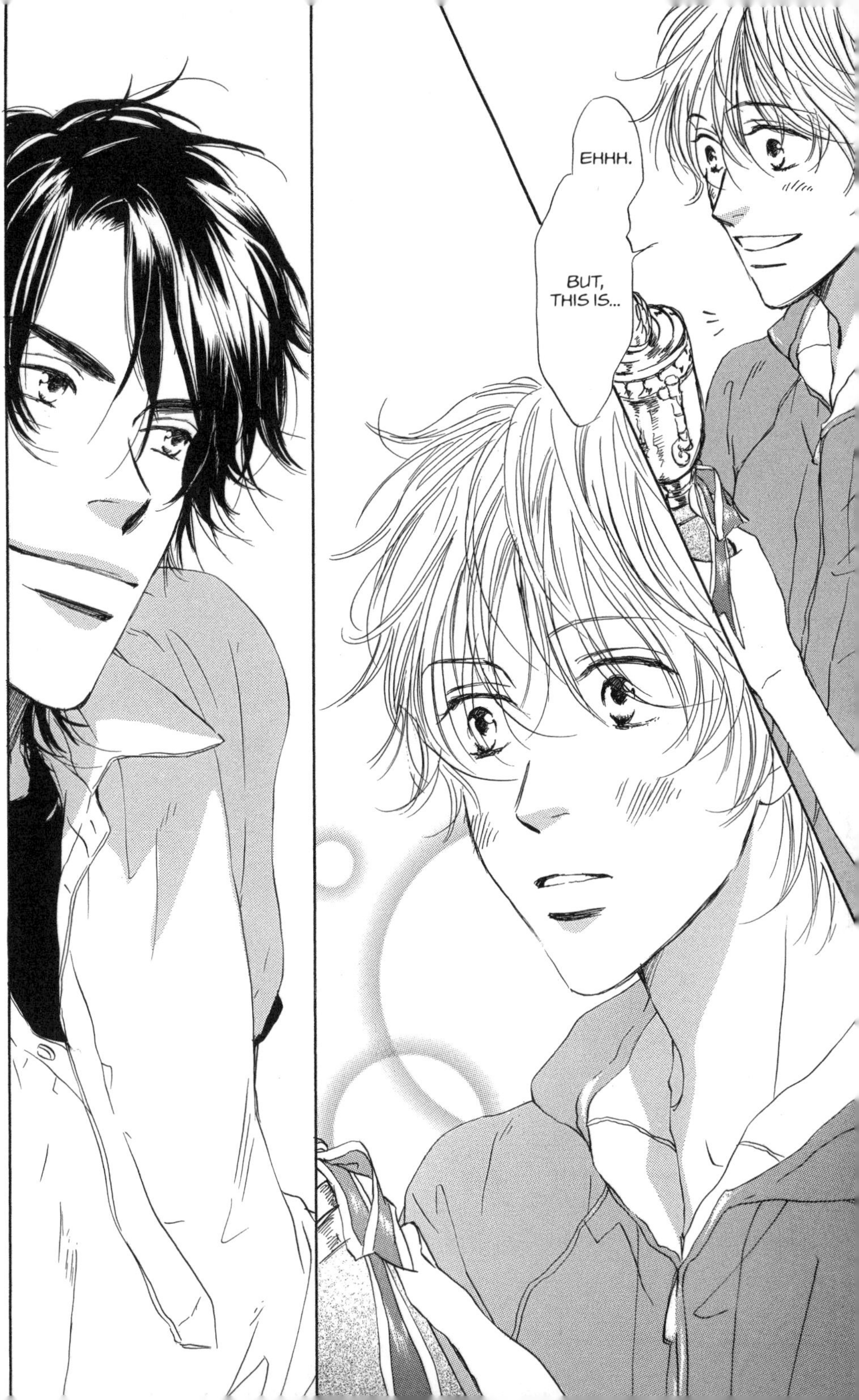
EHHH.
BUT, THIS IS...

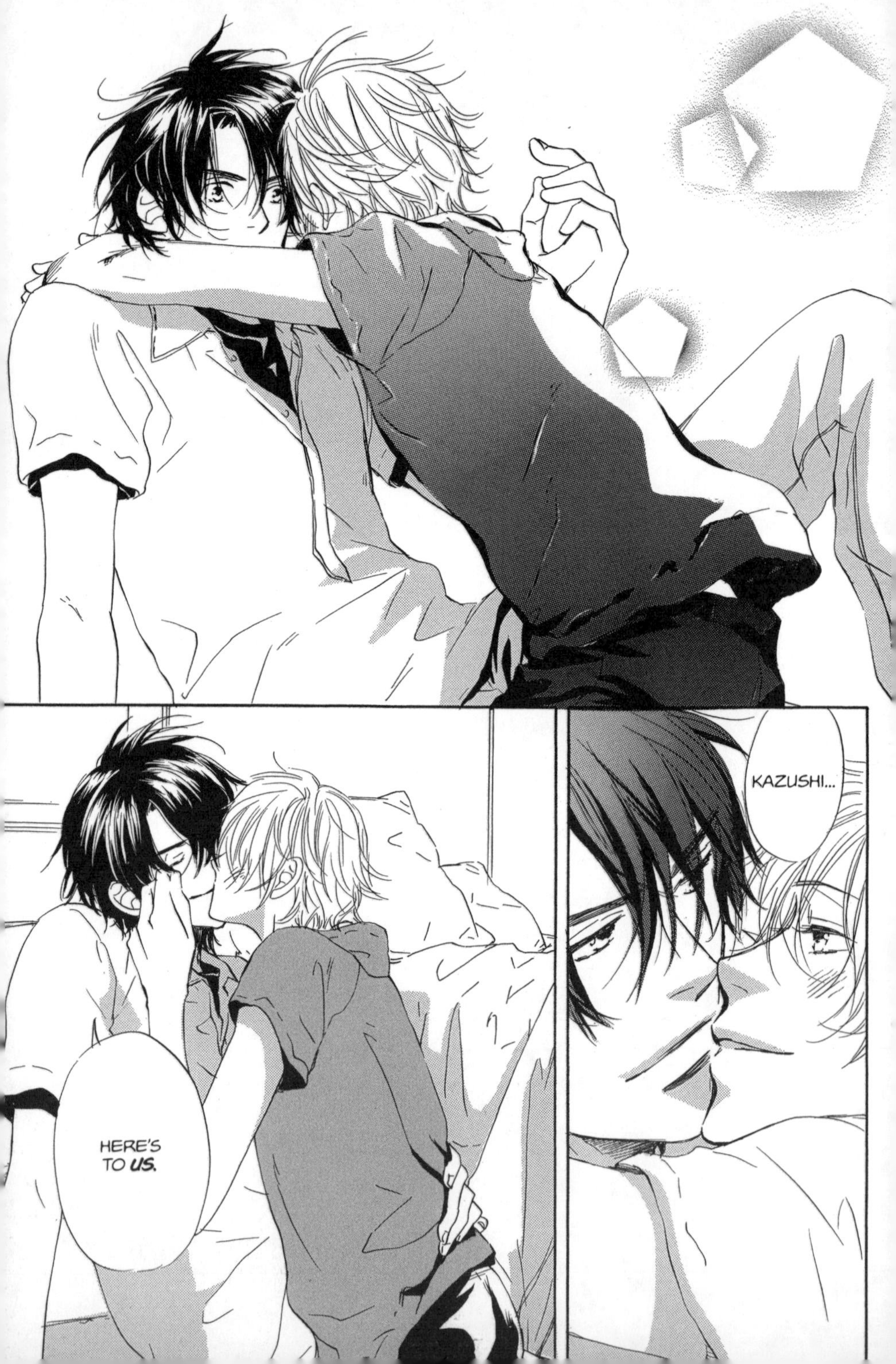
KAZUSHI...
HERE'S TO US.

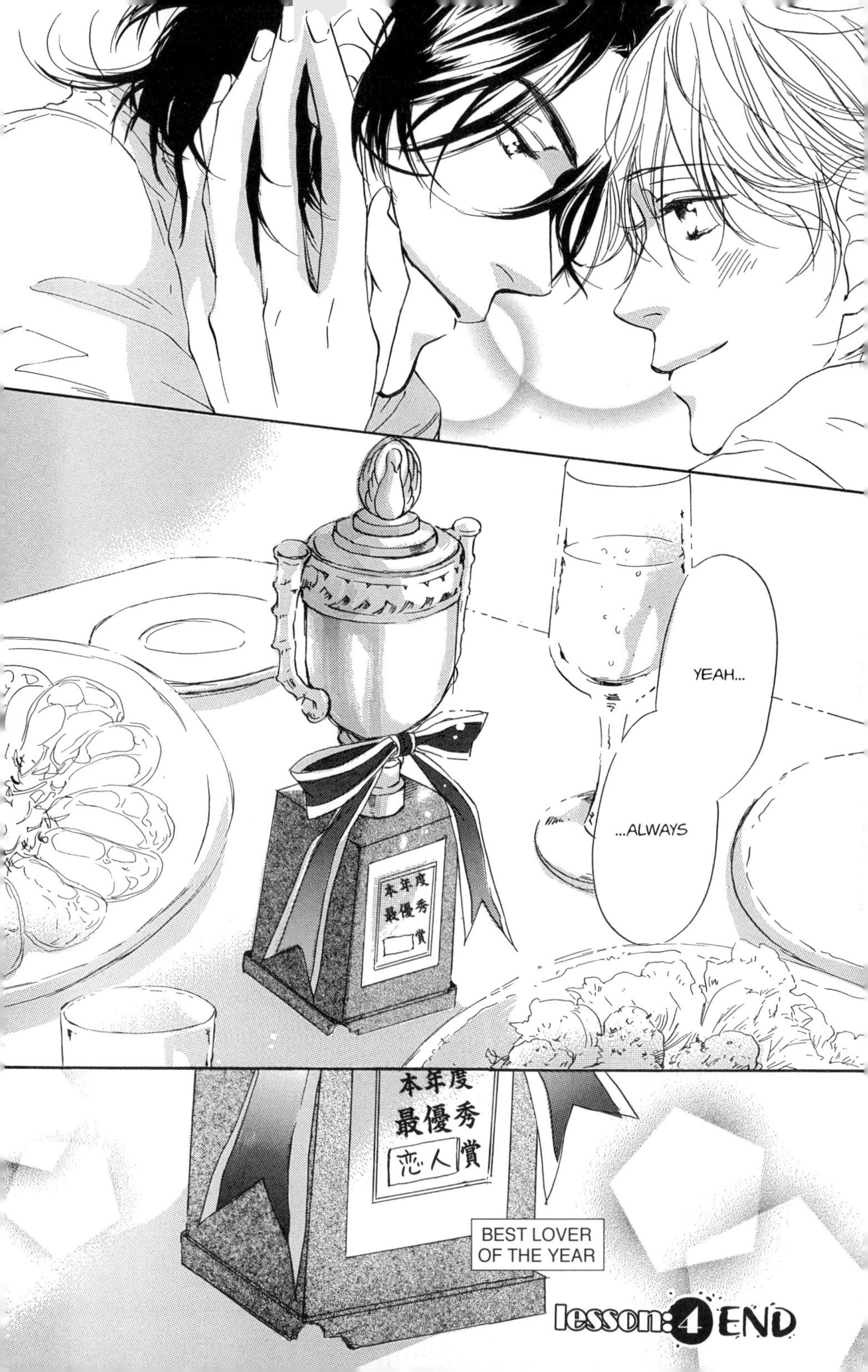
YEAH...
...ALWAYS
本年度
最優秀
賞
本年度
最優秀
恋人賞
BEST LOVER OF THE YEAR
lesson:4 END

Find a way

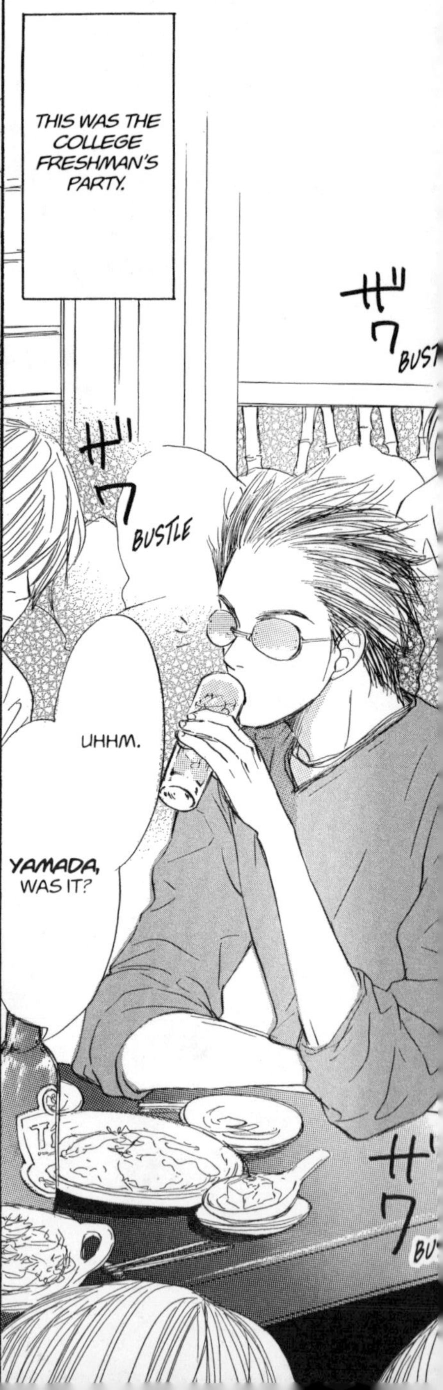
THIS WAS THE COLLEGE FRESHMAN'S PARTY.
ザワ BUST
ザワ BUSTLE
UHHM.
YAMADA, WAS IT?
ザワ BU

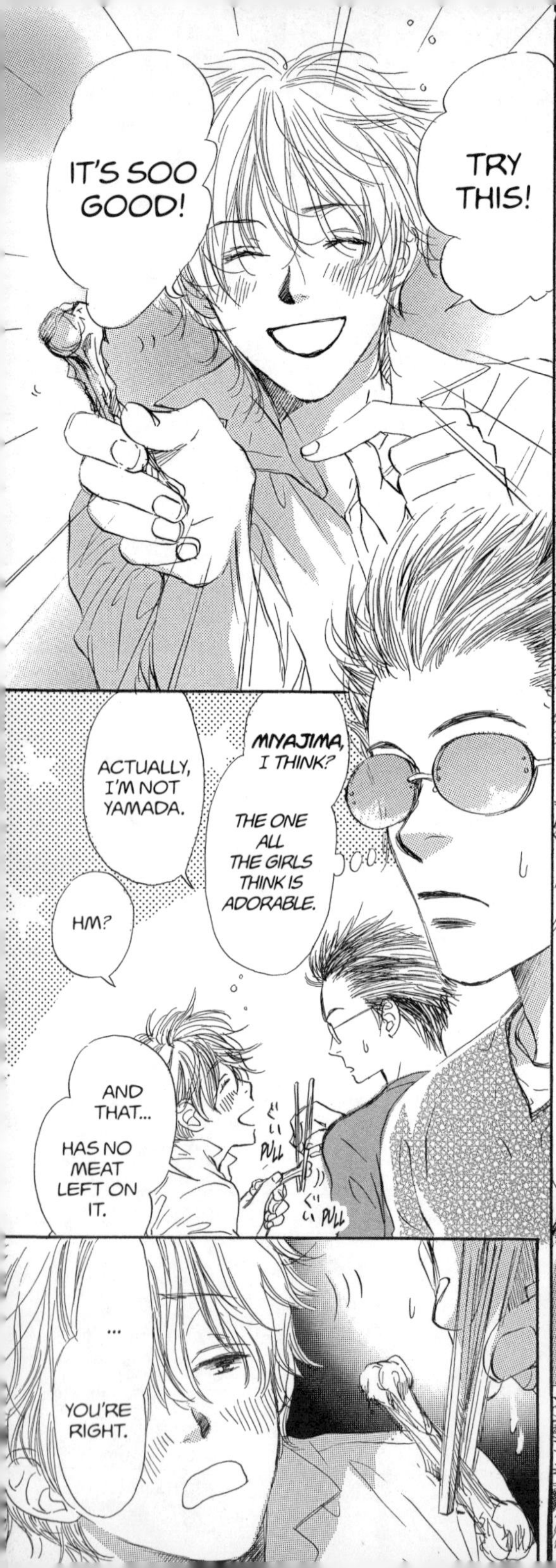
TRY THIS!
IT'S SOO GOOD!
MIYAJIMA, I THINK?
THE ONE ALL THE GIRLS THINK IS ADORABLE.
ACTUALLY, I'M NOT YAMADA.
HM?
ぐい PULL
ぐい PULL
AND THAT...
HAS NO MEAT LEFT ON IT.
...
YOU'RE RIGHT.

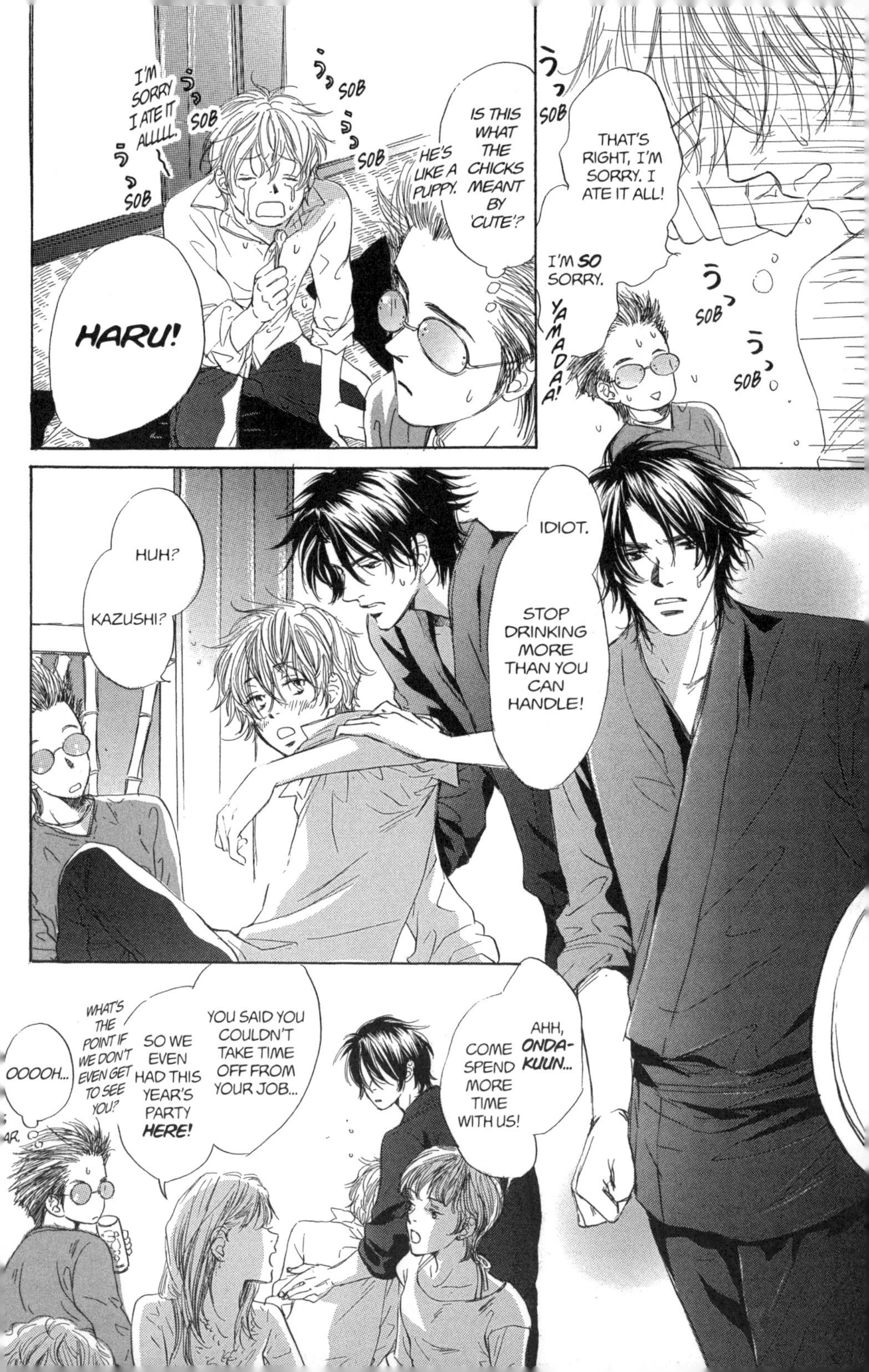
うっ SOB
THAT'S RIGHT, I'M SORRY. I ATE IT ALL!
I'M SO SORRY.
YAMADAA!
うっ SOB
うっ SOB
IS THIS WHAT THE CHICKS MEANT BY 'CUTE'?
HE'S LIKE A PUPPY.
うっ SOB
うっ SOB
うっ SOB
I'M SORRY I ATE IT ALLLLL.
うっ SOB
HARU!
IDIOT.
STOP DRINKING MORE THAN YOU CAN HANDLE!
HUH?
KAZUSHI?
AHH, ONDA-KUUN...
COME SPEND MORE TIME WITH US!
YOU SAID YOU COULDN'T TAKE TIME OFF FROM YOUR JOB...
SO WE EVEN HAD THIS YEAR'S PARTY HERE!
WHAT'S THE POINT IF WE DON'T EVEN GET TO SEE YOU?
OOOOH...

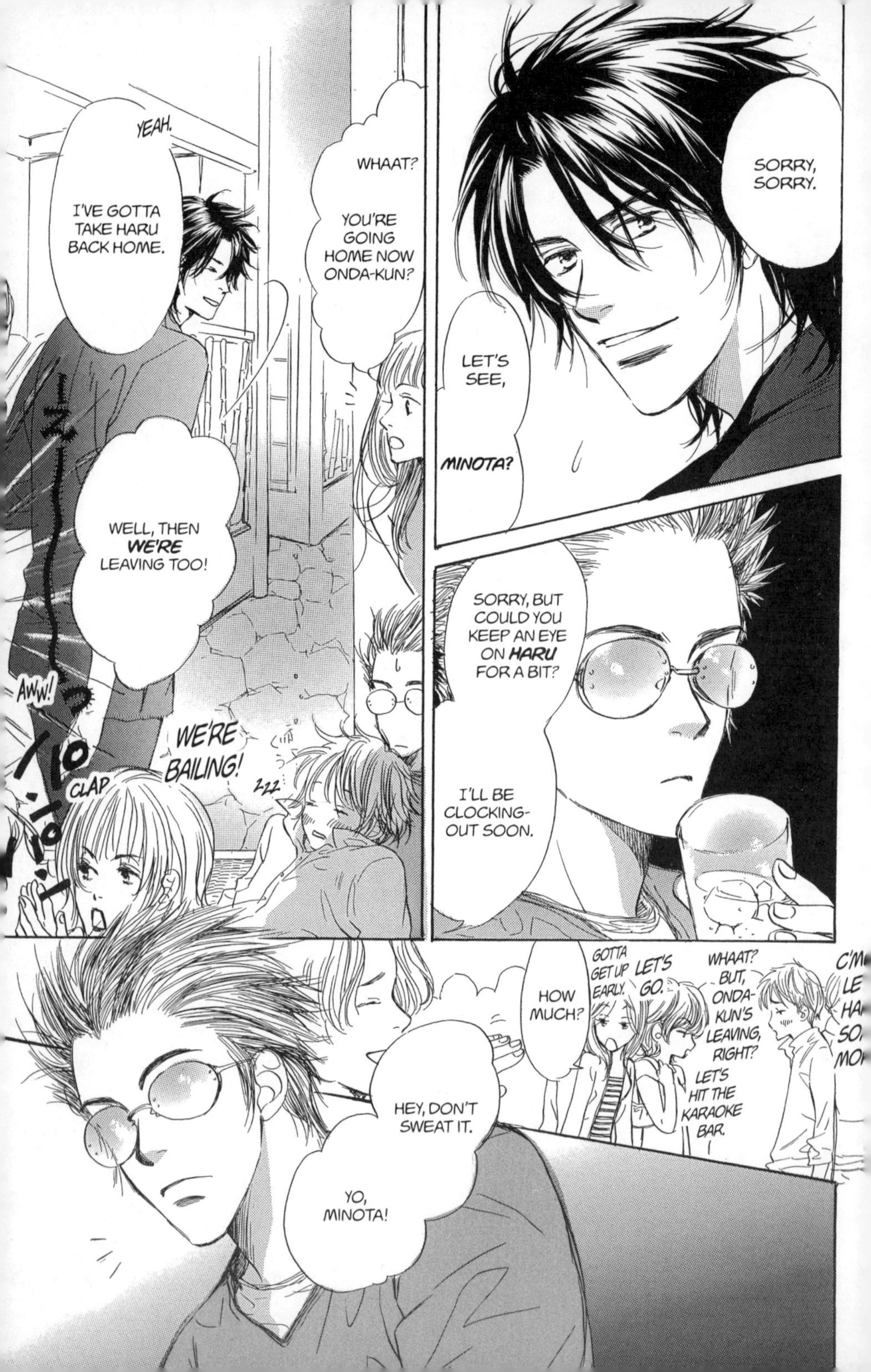
SORRY, SORRY.
LET'S SEE, MINOTA?
SORRY, BUT COULD YOU KEEP AN EYE ON HARU FOR A BIT?
I'LL BE CLOCKING-OUT SOON.
WHAAT?
YOU'RE GOING HOME NOW ONDA-KUN?
YEAH.
I'VE GOTTA TAKE HARU BACK HOME.
WELL, THEN WE'RE LEAVING TOO!
WE'RE BAILING!
ZZZ...
CLAP
AWW!
WHAAT? BUT, ONDA-KUN'S LEAVING, RIGHT?
LET'S HIT THE KARAOKE BAR.
LET'S GO.
GOTTA GET UP EARLY.
HOW MUCH?
HEY, DON'T SWEAT IT.
YO, MINOTA!

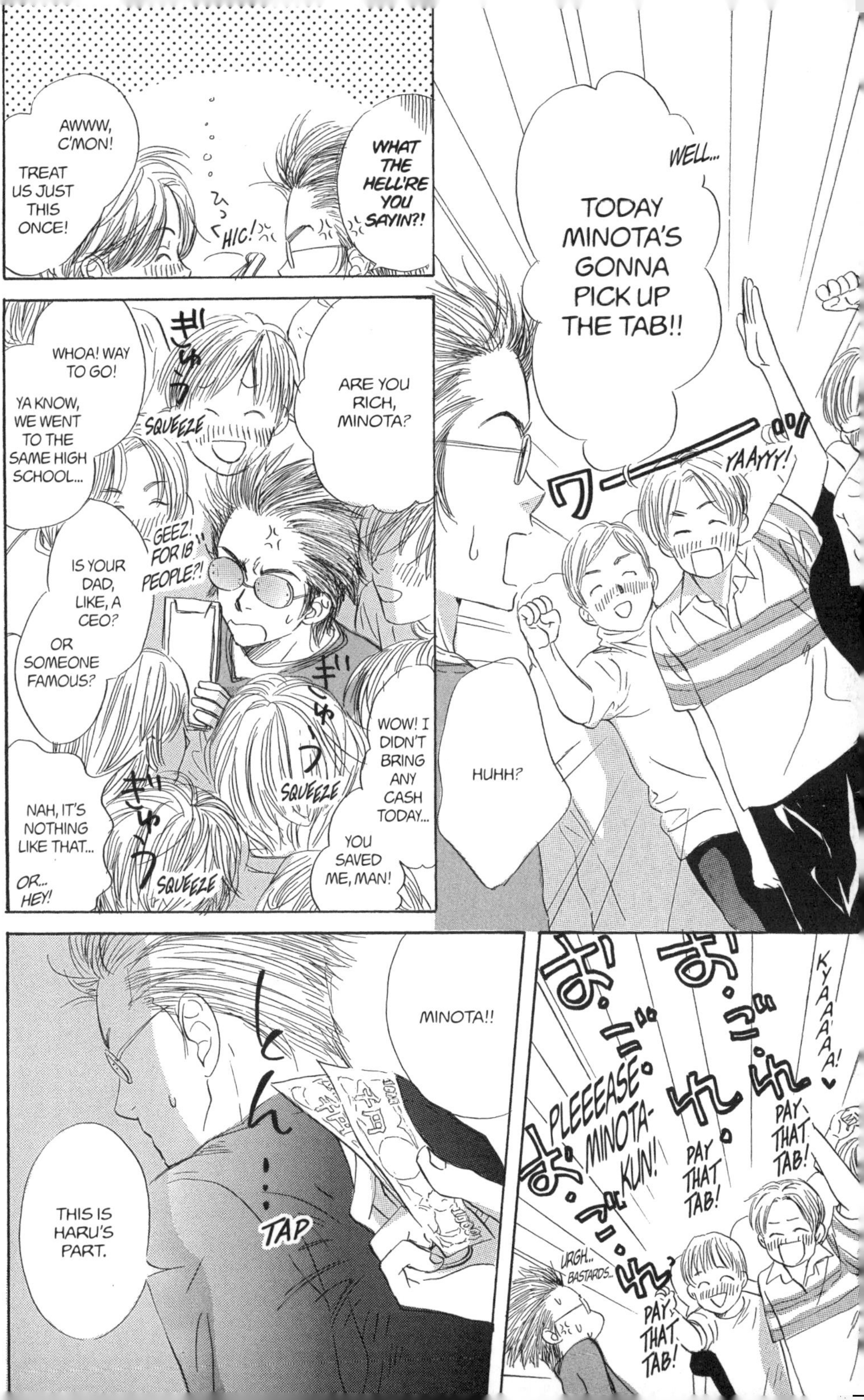
WELL...
TODAY MINOTA'S GONNA PICK UP THE TAB!!
YAAYYY!
HUHH?
AWWW, C'MON!
TREAT US JUST THIS ONCE!
HIC!
WHAT THE HELL'RE YOU SAYIN?!
ARE YOU RICH, MINOTA?
WHOA! WAY TO GO!
YA KNOW, WE WENT TO THE SAME HIGH SCHOOL...
SQUEEZE
GEEZ! FOR 18 PEOPLE?!
IS YOUR DAD, LIKE, A CEO?
OR SOMEONE FAMOUS?
WOW! I DIDN'T BRING ANY CASH TODAY...
YOU SAVED ME, MAN!
SQUEEZE
NAH, IT'S NOTHING LIKE THAT...
OR... HEY!
SQUEEZE
KYAAAAA!♥
PAY THAT TAB!
PAY THAT TAB!
PLEEEASE, MINOTA-KUN!
URGH... BASTARDS...
PAY THAT TAB!
MINOTA!!
THIS IS HARU'S PART.
TAP

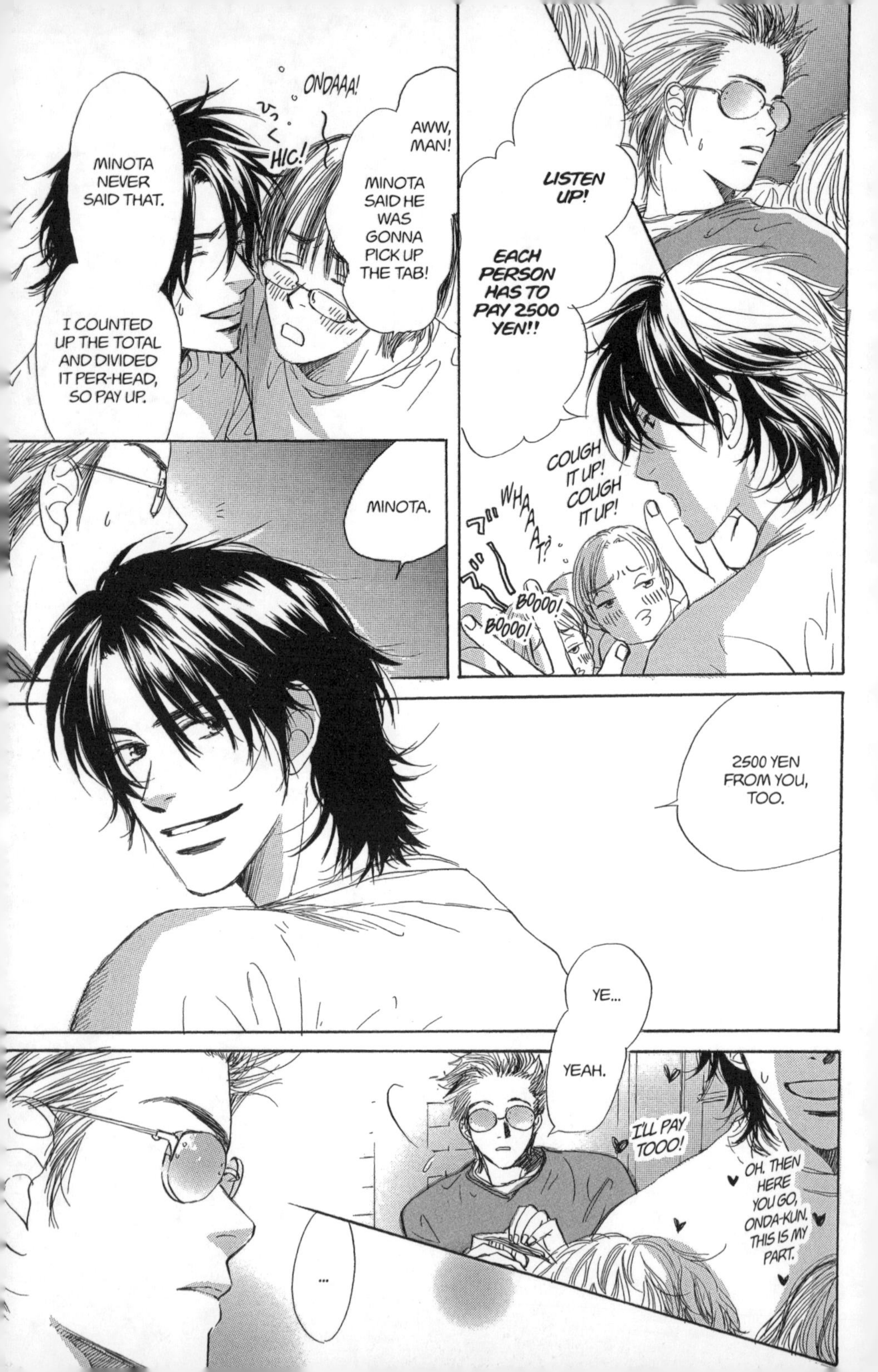
LISTEN UP!
EACH PERSON HAS TO PAY 2500 YEN!!
COUGH IT UP! COUGH IT UP!
WHAAAAT?
BOOOO!
BOOOO!
AWW, MAN!
MINOTA SAID HE WAS GONNA PICK UP THE TAB!
ONDAAA!
HIC!
MINOTA NEVER SAID THAT.
I COUNTED UP THE TOTAL AND DIVIDED IT PER-HEAD, SO PAY UP.
MINOTA.
2500 YEN FROM YOU, TOO.
YE...
YEAH.
OH. THEN HERE YOU GO, ONDA-KUN. THIS IS MY PART.
I'LL PAY TOOO!
...

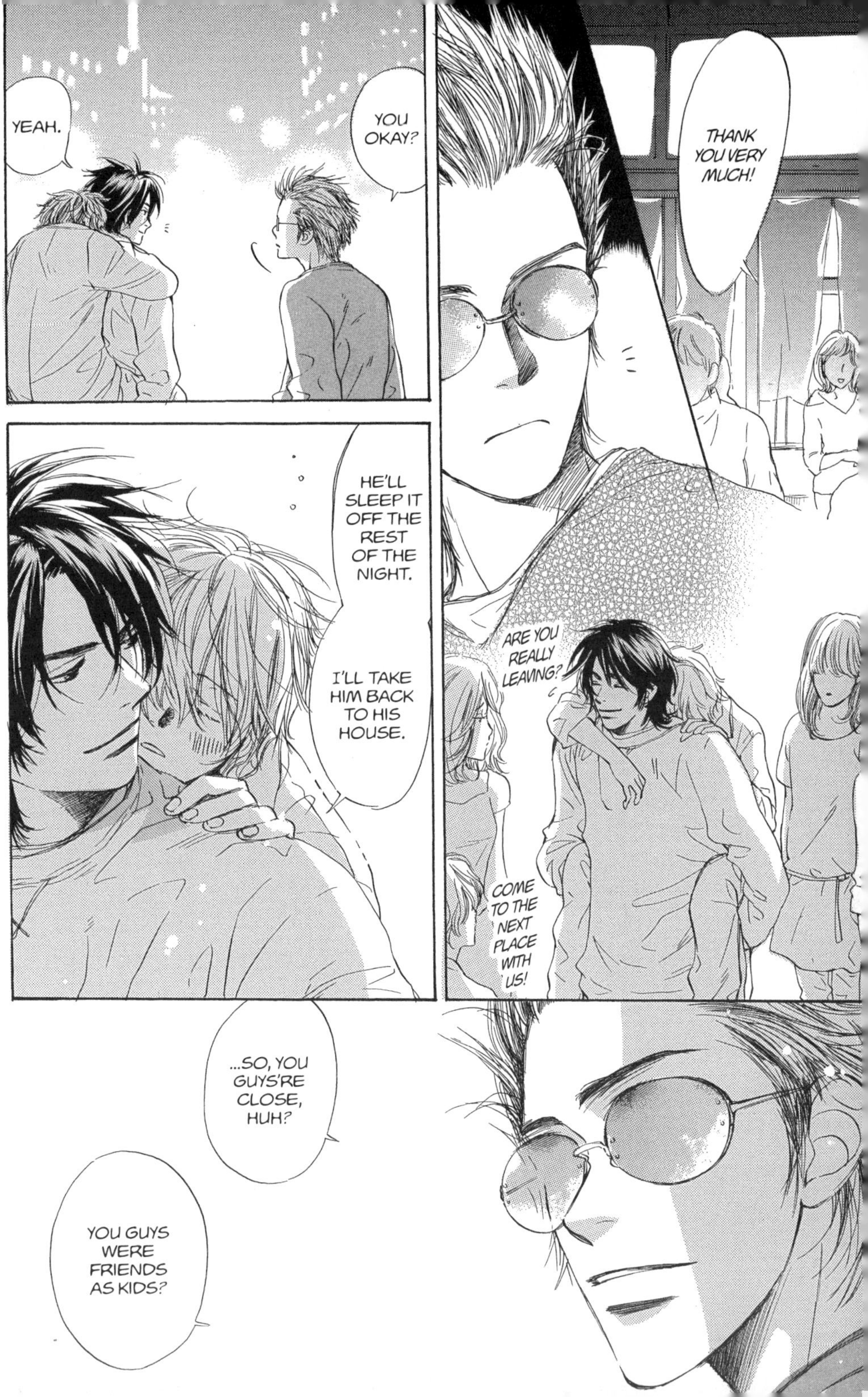
THANK YOU VERY MUCH!
ARE YOU REALLY LEAVING?
COME TO THE NEXT PLACE WITH US!
YOU OKAY?
YEAH.
HE'LL SLEEP IT OFF THE REST OF THE NIGHT.
I'LL TAKE HIM BACK TO HIS HOUSE.
...SO, YOU GUYS'RE CLOSE, HUH?
YOU GUYS WERE FRIENDS AS KIDS?

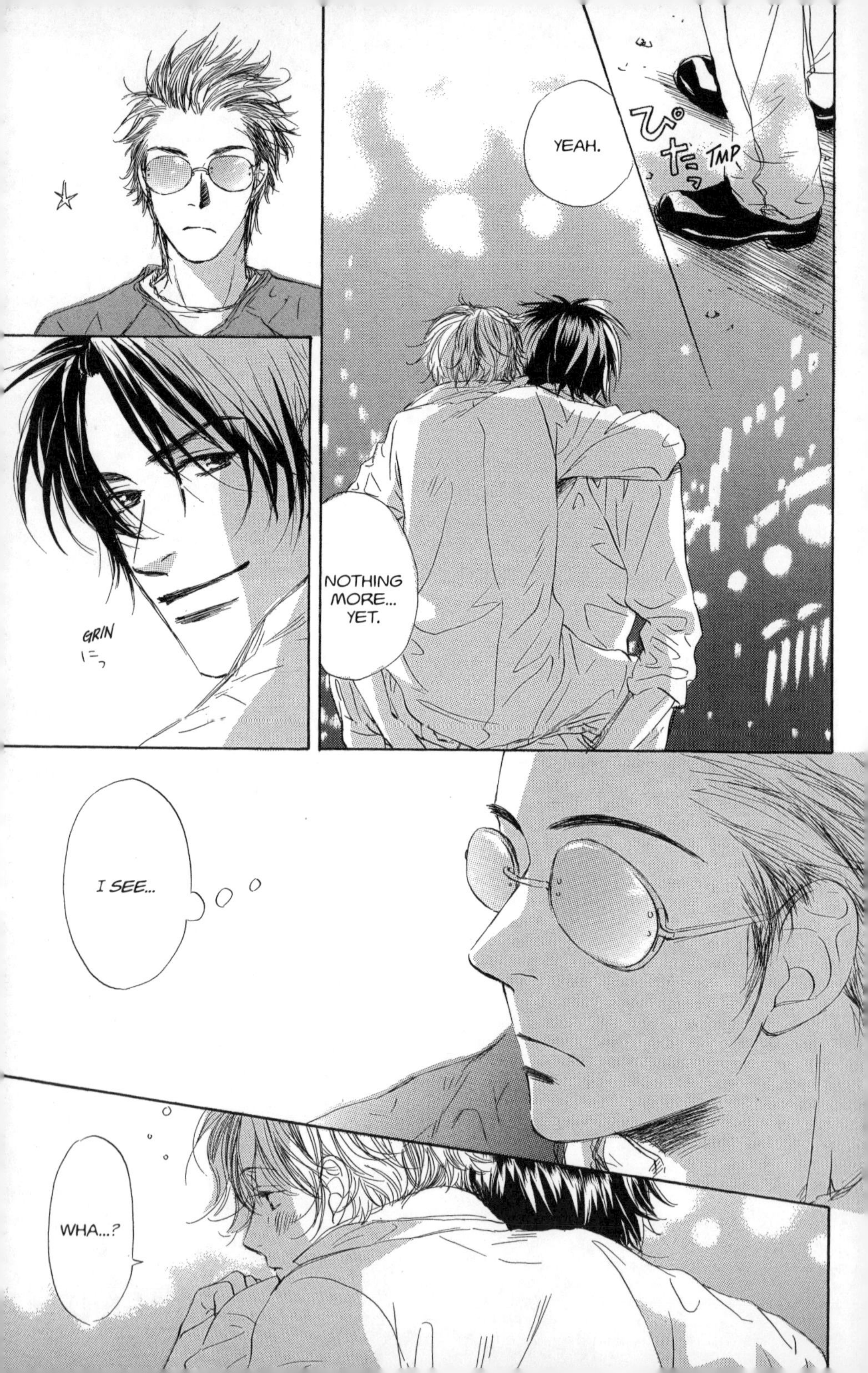

ぴたっ TMP
YEAH.
NOTHING MORE... YET.
GRIN
にっ
I SEE...
WHA...?

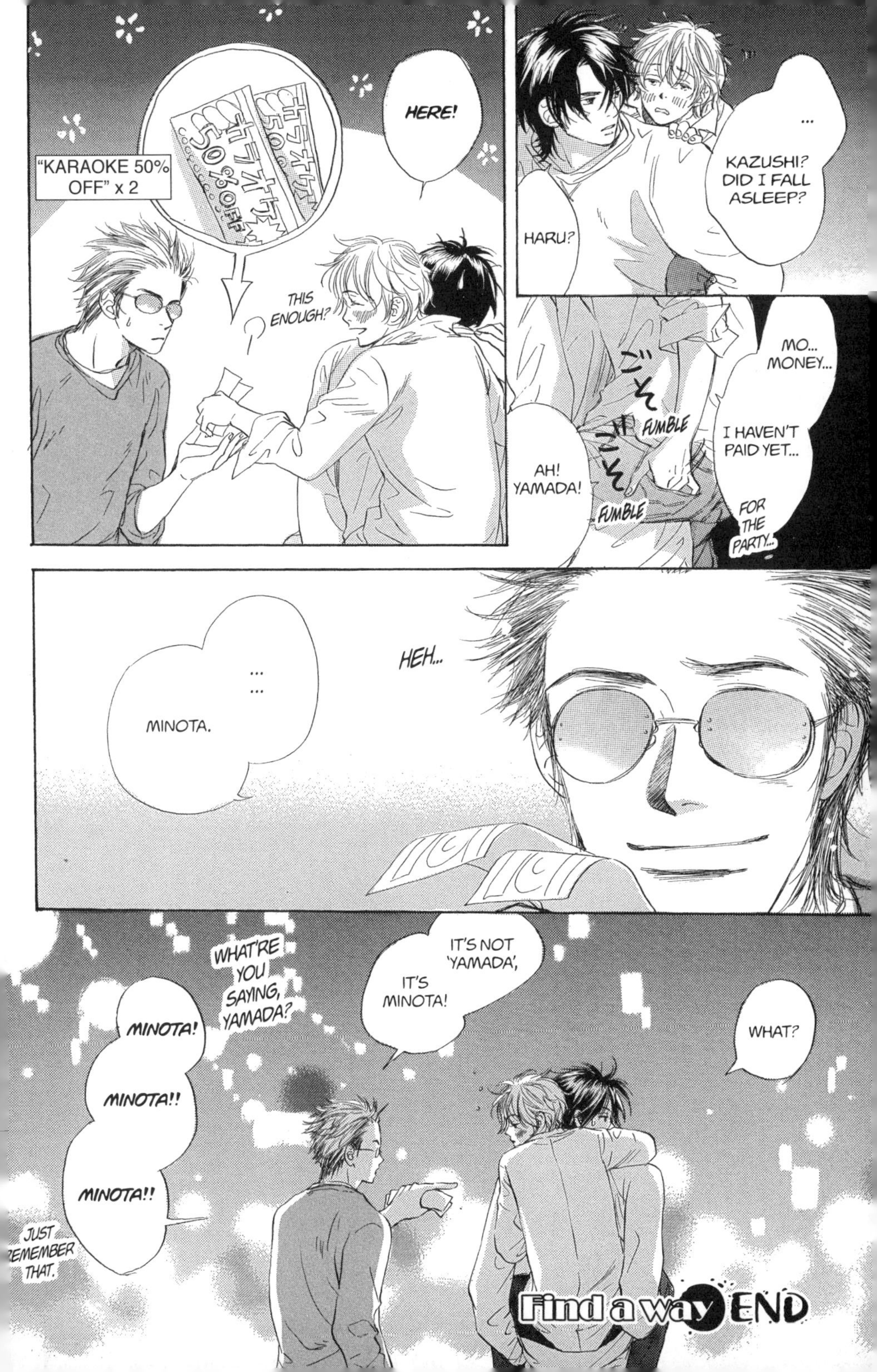
...
KAZUSHI? DID I FALL ASLEEP?
HARU?
MO... MONEY...
I HAVEN'T PAID YET...
FOR THE PARTY...
FUMBLE
FUMBLE
AH! YAMADA!
HERE!
THIS ENOUGH?
"KARAOKE 50% OFF" x 2
HEH...
... ... MINOTA.
WHAT?
IT'S NOT 'YAMADA', IT'S MINOTA!
WHAT'RE YOU SAYING, YAMADA?
MINOTA!
MINOTA!!
MINOTA!!
JUST REMEMBER THAT.
Find a way END

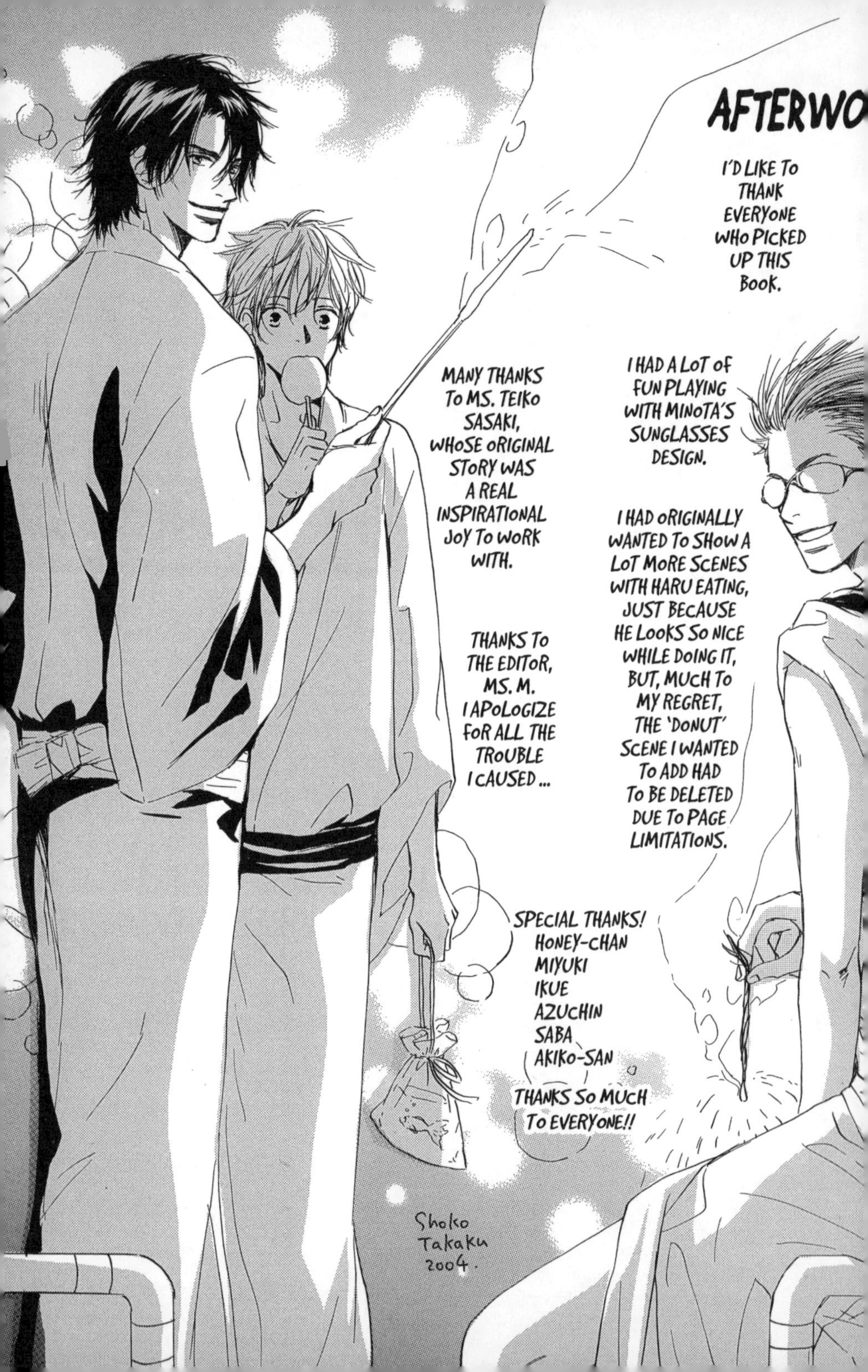
AFTERWO
I'D LIKE TO THANK EVERYONE WHO PICKED UP THIS BOOK.
I HAD A LOT OF FUN PLAYING WITH MINOTA'S SUNGLASSES DESIGN.
I HAD ORIGINALLY WANTED TO SHOW A LOT MORE SCENES WITH HARU EATING, JUST BECAUSE HE LOOKS SO NICE WHILE DOING IT, BUT, MUCH TO MY REGRET, THE 'DONUT' SCENE I WANTED TO ADD HAD TO BE DELETED DUE TO PAGE LIMITATIONS.
MANY THANKS TO MS. TEIKO SASAKI, WHOSE ORIGINAL STORY WAS A REAL INSPIRATIONAL JOY TO WORK WITH.
THANKS TO THE EDITOR, MS. M. I APOLOGIZE FOR ALL THE TROUBLE I CAUSED...
SPECIAL THANKS!
HONEY-CHAN
MIYUKI
IKUE
AZUCHIN
SABA
AKIKO-SAN
THANKS SO MUCH TO EVERYONE!!
Shoko Takaku 2004.

佐々木禎子
TEIKO·SASAKI
Afterword

Hello to everyone. I'm Teiko Sasaki. I took this job thinking what fun it would be to write for a manga, but once I started I realized it wasn't as easy as I'd thought. I think I was a little unprepared, but just knowing that Ms. Takaku would be doing the illustrations was encouragement in and of itself.

Kazushi is just plain cool, Haru is all about cute, and Minota knows just about anything. I got all excited just going over the character roughs, these were *my* characters!!

I think I should also confess that when I saw my characters interacting with each other, it started me thinking about the discrepancy between their actions and what's considered normal. If this had been a short novel, I probably wouldn't have paid as much attention to the characters' actions as I did. Like, 'Haru, do not jump out of the second floor window. You're not even drunk!' and the likes.

To Ms. Takaku, I apologize for loading you up with all those hyper characters that acted like drunkards 24/7. Thank you so much for doing such an excellent job illustrating them. Also, my heartfelt thanks goes out to all the readers out there!

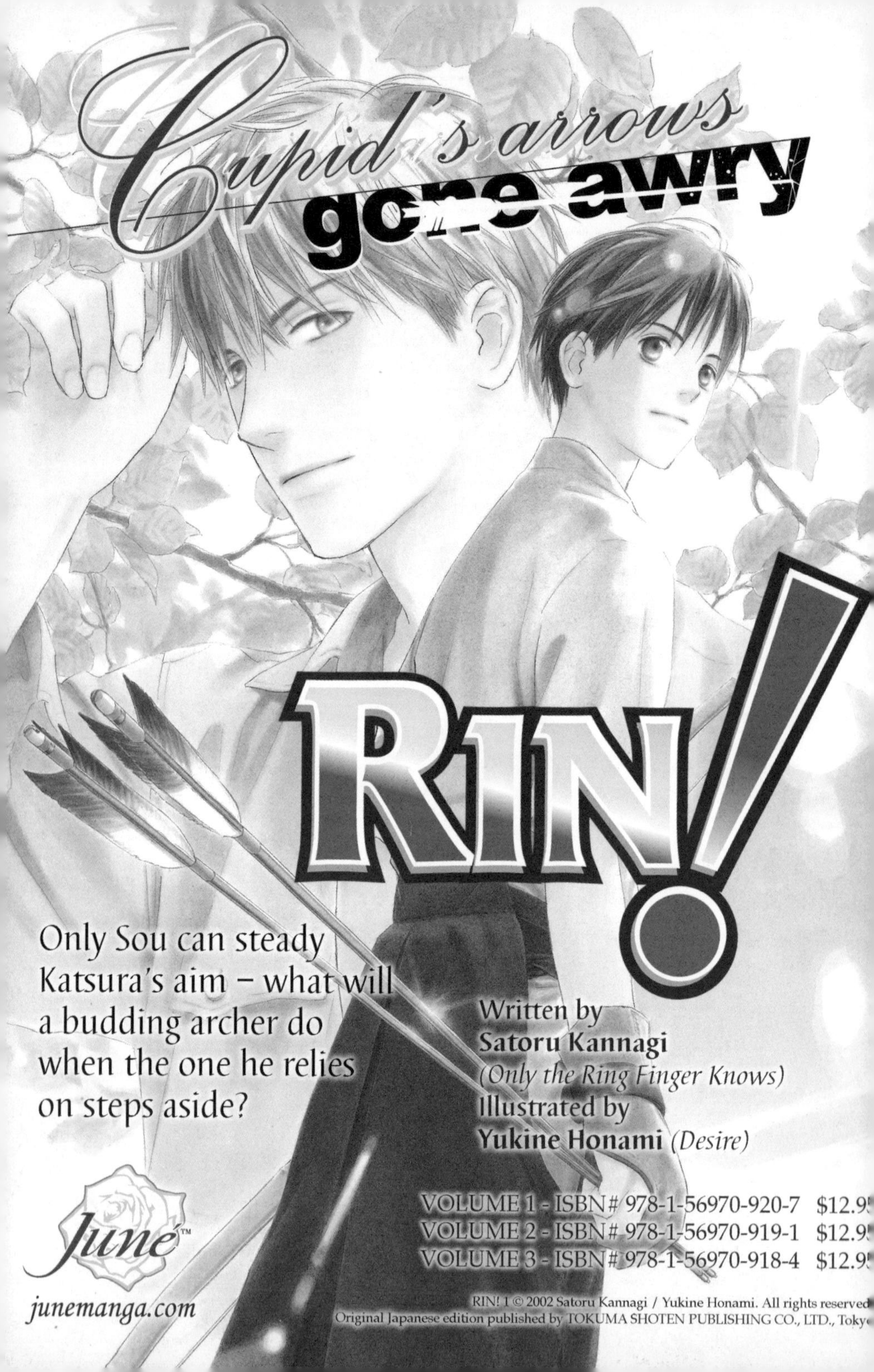
Cupid's arrows gone awry
RIN!
Only Sou can steady Katsura's aim – what will a budding archer do when the one he relies on steps aside?
Written by
Satoru Kannagi
(Only the Ring Finger Knows)
Illustrated by
Yukine Honami (Desire)
VOLUME 1 - ISBN# 978-1-56970-920-7 $12.9
VOLUME 2 - ISBN# 978-1-56970-919-1 $12.9
VOLUME 3 - ISBN# 978-1-56970-918-4 $12.9
June™
junemanga.com
RIN! 1 © 2002 Satoru Kannagi / Yukine Honami. All rights reserved
Original Japanese edition published by TOKUMA SHOTEN PUBLISHING CO., LTD., Toky